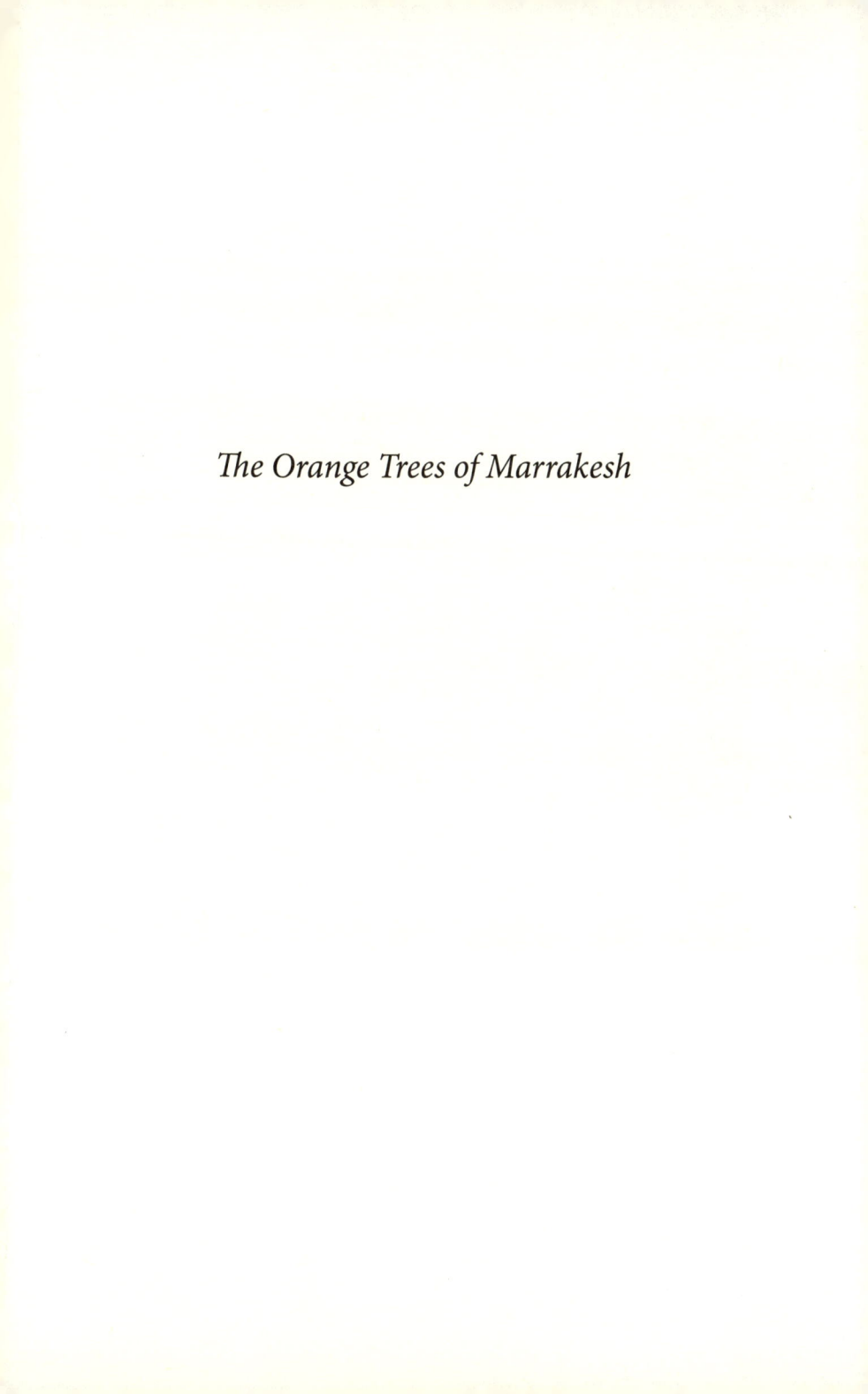

The Orange Trees of Marrakesh

Camel caravan at the Biskra Oasis

THE ORANGE TREES *of* MARRAKESH

Ibn Khaldun and the Science of Man

STEPHEN FREDERIC DALE

Harvard University Press

CAMBRIDGE, MASSACHUSETTS
LONDON, ENGLAND
2015

Copyright © 2015 by the President and Fellows of Harvard College
All rights reserved
Printed in the United States of America

First printing

Frontispiece: Vintage photogravure "Small caravan near Biskra' Oasis" by Rudolf Lehnert and Ernst Landrock, 1924. Reproduced by kind permission of Musée de l'Elysée via Fondation de l'Elysée.

Cataloging-in-Publication Data available from the Library of Congress
ISBN: 978-0-674-96765-6 (alk. paper)

For Gangadharan

CONTENTS

	Preface	ix
	Introduction ⊷ Principles and Purpose	1
1	Ibn Khaldun's World	33
2	The Two Paths to Knowledge	74
3	A Scholar-Official in a Dangerous World	118
4	The Method and the Model	151
5	The Rational State and the Laissez-Faire Economy	207
6	The Science of Man	254
	Conclusion ⊷ A Question of Knowledge	288
	Chronology	301
	Notes	305
	Glossary	339
	Bibliography	343
	Index	361

PREFACE

WHEN I FIRST VISITED Marrakesh beneath the foothills of the Atlas Mountains in Morocco, the scent of orange blossoms stirred thoughts of the paradisiacal Mughal gardens I had just left behind in India. Yet many years later I learned that Ibn Khaldun (1332–1406), North Africa's preeminent Muslim historical scholar, regarded the presence of decorative orange trees in the towns of his homeland as the floral equivalents of canaries in the coal mine of North African society, a sign of urban decadence and impending dynastic senility.[1] He considered these particular trees that produced inedible fruit to be just one more piece of evidence that documented the dialectical, historical model he devised to explain the cyclical nature of North African politics, a phenomenon in which vigorous tribes conquered cities and formed dynasties, only to descend into corrupt impotence four generations later. He explained his theories in the *Muqaddimah,* the single most intellectually formidable work of historical and sociological scholarship produced in any civilization up to that time.

In the twenty-first century, Ibn Khaldun is widely regarded as a seminal scholar and the *Muqaddimah,* his principal work, has generated a cottage industry of studies throughout the world. It is probably safe to say that more books and articles have been written about Ibn Khaldun than any other Muslim historian.

Much of this scholarship has been limited to précis of his model, which has an explanatory allure similar to Karl Marx's dialectical materialism. It appears to offer clear and relatively simple explanations for complex social and political histories; in this case, histories of the Middle East, Central Asia, and elsewhere, where rural tribes comprised a major segment of the population. Additionally, social scientists have highlighted specific elements of Ibn Khaldun's thought that anticipated aspects of modern social analysis. Most of this scholarship is descriptive, and in these cases it has produced only a limited understanding of the nature and scope of his achievement. Remarkably little attention has been paid to Ibn Khaldun's intellectual stature as an individual who used philosophy to revolutionize the historical discipline and, applying his new methodology, composed a comprehensive science of man and society in fourteenth-century North Africa.

The present study is written as an intellectual biography of a brilliant and complex individual. It is based on the premise that to understand Ibn Khaldun and his writings, it is necessary to return to the text of the *Muqaddimah* and ground a study of his ideas in his clearly stated original intent. He forcefully and repeatedly indicates he has adopted Greco-Islamic philosophical ideas and methodology to revolutionize historical research, which he then employs to produce a comprehensive study of North African Muslims in his era. The single greatest disappointment in the existing scholarship on Ibn Khaldun is its failure to explain how philosophy permeates and structures the *Muqaddimah*. In contrast with Ibn Khaldun's own thorough education in both the religious and also the philosophical sciences, most modern historians and social scientists are not familiar with the philosophical vocabulary, concepts, and methods he repeatedly invokes to explain his proposed new science. Lacking this knowledge, scholars cannot understand the text beyond a certain level. Nor, in consequence, can they adequately explain why later European political economists, historians, and sociologists produced studies of man whose assumptions and methodology so closely resembled Ibn Khaldun's *Muqaddimah*. The similarity is due to the fact that Ibn Khaldun and Europeans were inspired by the same Greek philosophic ideas. More than any other factor, modern scholars' lack of philosophical knowledge explains why, when so much has been written about the *Muqaddimah*, there is still much to be said.

The source of Ibn Khaldun's ideas constitutes the single greatest challenge for a student of his work. He repeatedly reminds readers that the work is grounded in Greco-Islamic philosophy, and in some cases he directly attributes his ideas to specific individuals, citing, for example, Aristotle, the Greco-Islamic philosopher Ibn Sina, the Iranian theologian al-Ghazali, and a galaxy of Muslim scholars. When it comes to identifying specific inspirations for his original theories, however, he is uniformly silent. Ultimately it requires an encyclopedic knowledge of Greek, Neoplatonic, and Greco-Islamic rationalists and a familiarity with an entire universe of Muslim scholars to identify the possible source of an idea. Franz Rosenthal, in his preeminent English translation of the *Muqaddimah*, appropriately remarks in his translator's introduction, "We should perhaps be justified in assuming that practically every matter of detail found in the *Muqaddimah* was probably not original with Ibn Khaldun, but had previously been expressed elsewhere."[2] In saying this, Rosenthal was not disputing Ibn Khaldun's creative genius any more than Shakespeare scholars question the playwright's brilliant originality because he borrowed plots from so many sources. Quite the opposite, for as Rosenthal also remarks, "The *Muqaddimah* re-evaluates, in an altogether unprecedented way, practically every single individual manifestation of a great and highly developed civilization."[3] In that respect the work is a monument to the achievements of Arab Muslim culture.

An account of the scholarship on Ibn Khaldun would require a separate volume, but among the vast accumulation of books and articles on the man and his theories I have found five modern studies to be particularly stimulating. These are, first, two books of the preeminent Moroccan Ibn Khaldun scholar Abdesselam Cheddadi. These are his impressive critical analysis, *Ibn Khaldūn L'homme et le théoricien de la civilization* (2006), and his edited translation of Ibn Khaldun's history of the Berbers titled *Ibn Khaldūn Le Livre des Exemples, Histoire des Arabes et des Berbères du Magreb* (2012). Second, Claude Horrut, a French political theorist and African scholar, has written an important study of Ibn Khaldun titled *Ibn Khaldūn, un islam des "Lumières"?* (2006), which includes a valuable set of notes and an extensive bibliography of articles and books on Ibn Khaldun, concentrating on the large number of French-language studies of the historian. Third, there is Muhsin Mahdi's pioneering intellectual history of Ibn Khaldun, *Ibn Khaldun's Philosophy of History* (1957). Finally, Syed Farid Alatas, a sociologist, has written a brief but insightful study of Ibn Khaldun, titled simply *Ibn Khaldun*. This book is intended as an introduction for a broad audience, but it contains a sophisticated analysis of Ibn Khaldun's argument. It also includes a valuable annotated bibliography.

It is important to emphasize that ultimately the two most important works for studying Ibn Khaldun's ideas are the Arab scholar's original Arabic text and Rosenthal's fine English translation. The earliest European edition of the Arabic text, M. Quatremère's 1858 edition, *Prolégomènes D'Ebn-Khaldoun,* is still the most useful. It is based on a reliable copy and the print is mercifully large and easy to read, compared with most recent Middle Eastern editions. More important than mere legibility is the fact that Franz Rosenthal keys his precise, carefully annotated translation of the *Muqaddimah* to Quatremère's text, thus making it easy for readers of this English translation to navigate back and forth from this work to the original Arabic text. Rosenthal's scholarly introduction and notes also represent a vital source of information about Ibn Khaldun and his work. The only caveat about Rosenthal's work has to do with its stature, for even distinguished Arabists writing in Western languages sometimes rely too uncritically on his translations, without examining the Arabic text.[4]

The present study opens with a survey of Ibn Khaldun's world: his geographic and social environment and a précis of North African history. It includes his own comments on the society and history of his homeland, which serve as an introduction to the later explanation of his dialectical model. An analysis of his religious and philosophical education follows in Chapter 2. It is designed both to explain certain aspects of his career and also to introduce the philosophical concepts he uses to structure the *Muqaddimah*. After Chapter 3, which narrates his peripatetic administrative and legal career, Chapter 4 is devoted to an explanation of the principles of Ibn Khaldun's new science and an analysis of his model. Chapter 5 discusses his political and economic theories, subjects second in importance only to the model itself. Chapter 6 reflects briefly on the limited legacy of the *Muqaddimah* before comparing Ibn Khaldun's ideas with those of eighteenth-, nineteenth-, and twentieth-century European scholars. This chapter demonstrates that as these Europeans formulated sciences of man, they studied human society with the same fundamental philosophical questions, concepts, and logic he used centuries earlier. The conclusion returns to earlier questions of knowledge and personal identity.

I have more often than not used Rosenthal's translation when quoting the *Muqaddimah*, but in many instances I have substituted my own renderings, especially where critical philosophical concepts are concerned. Rosenthal alerted readers to his lack of engagement with Greco-Islamic philosophy, and one of the few ways his superb work could be improved would be to carefully revise some of this crucial terminology. In the notes I have cited Rosenthal's translation of the *Muqaddimah* first, followed by the pagination of Quatremère's 1858 Arabic text. A citation M, I, 15/8–9, for example, refers to Rosenthal's translation of the *Muqaddimah*, volume I, page 15, and Quatremère's Arabic text pages 8–9. Ibn Khaldun's autobiography or memoir, in this instance Abdesselam Cheddadi's bilingual Arabic and French edition, is cited simply by the letter *A*, followed by the page number, as, for example, A, 76. Apart from the *Muqaddimah* and the memoir, references are cited in full. Regarding transliteration, to lessen confusion I have largely followed Rosenthal's transliterations. But I have not distinguished between *Dāl* and *Dād*, *Sīn* and *Sād*, the two *Hā*s and the two *Tā*s. Arabists will be familiar with the vocabulary and original spelling, which is not germane for non-Arabists, who will be concerned only with meaning. All dates are "Common Era" unless otherwise indicated.

I am deeply indebted, especially to Bruce Lawrence of Duke University, for his support of my interest in Ibn Khaldun over many years. I also thank Cornell Fleischer of the University of Chicago, and Bahram Tavakolian of Denison University for their encouragement of my Ibn Khaldun studies and particular help with this book. Their different disciplinary perspectives and linguistic expertise have been particularly helpful as I thought about the many dimensions of Ibn Khaldun's work. Anonymous readers' valuable comments on the manuscript also helped prepare the final draft for publication. My gracious wife, Lillian, has acted as a foster mother to this work over many years. Finally, I fondly recall ideas generated by a group of tolerant, insightful graduate students at the Ohio State University who participated in my seminars on Greco-Islamic philosophy and Ibn Khaldun's *Muqaddimah*.

I have dedicated this book to my longtime colleague and valued Malayali friend, Dr. M. Gangadharan, an inspiring literary scholar, historian, and sophisticated rationalist in Parappanangadi, Kerala.

Ibn Khaldun's World

INTRODUCTION

Principles and Purpose

IN 1377 THE Arab Muslim scholar, administrator, and religious judge Ibn Khaldun (1332–1406) justified writing the history he had just begun by announcing that at certain times in history the world altered so fundamentally that someone had to chronicle the changes and describe newly emerging conditions. He ascribed the fundamental changes his North African and wider Mediterranean world had recently undergone to the catastrophic effects of the plague, a pestilence that three decades earlier killed untold thousands, including his parents at their home in Tunis. The plague, he reported, ravaged the entire western Mediterranean, precipitating a calamitous loss of population and a devastating decline of cities and urban culture, deterioration of roads and buildings, and the enfeeblement of already senile dynasties. Ibn Khaldun lamented, "The entire inhabited world changed."[1] He announced his plan to write a history for his disease-ravaged homeland, just as the great Muslim historian al-Mas'udi (888–957) had comprehensively chronicled his own period in the tenth century.[2] Then in a comment that suggests the scope of his ambitions, Ibn Khaldun noted that Mas'udi's history was so thorough it became a reference work for later historians, "their principal source for verifying historical information."[3]

Yet while Ibn Khaldun placed himself within the tradition of classic Muslim historical writing, he devised a radically new approach to historical research and the study of human societies. A beneficiary of the same Greek intellectual bequest that subsequently influenced the social and political thought of Montesquieu, Hume, Smith, and Durkheim, he argued that history ought to be practiced as a science, a philosophical discipline. Most of the ideas and methods Ibn Khaldun advocated were directly or indirectly derived from Aristotle, whom Muslim rationalists universally revered as their "First Teacher."[4] Implicitly agreeing with Aristotle's refusal to designate traditional history a science because it dealt only with particulars, Ibn Khaldun urged historians to cease writing meaningless narratives of transient political and military events.[5] Instead, he argued, they should transform history in subject and method and add it to the corpus of Aristotelian sciences, which included logic, physics, mathematics, astronomy, music, rhetoric, and poetry but not, before Ibn Khaldun's time, history. He explained his ideas in the Arabic prose work titled the *Muqaddimah*, literally the "introduction" to his history of North Africa and the wider Islamic world.

Echoing Aristotle, Ibn Khaldun insisted that his *'ilm*, his science, constituted an entirely new field of study. It was "rooted" in philosophy, *hikmah*, but it did not belong to any of the recognized philosophical disciplines.[6] Certainly it could not be considered to represent a branch of rhetoric, the art of persuasion, or politics, the study of ethical and philosophical criteria for administering a city.[7] Its subject would be "human social organization." The philosophical historian was obligated to penetrate beneath the surface of events to identify the indelible traits or natures of social organizations and also analyze what Ibn Khaldun terms their "essential accidents." By the latter, Aristotelian phrase, he referred to secondary but necessary attributes of societies, including, for him, "states, rulers, gainful occupations, crafts, and sciences."[8] If philosophical historians not only devoted themselves to analyzing human social organizations and identifying their accidents but also mediated their analysis with an exhaustive knowledge of *haqa'iq al-ashya'*, objective reality, that is, an encyclopedic understanding of every aspect of these societies, they would be able to explain the underlying structures and circumstances that determined trajectories of historical change. Implicit in Ibn Khaldun's argument was the assumption that philosophical historians could use this new science to identify the characteristics and accurately interpret the history of any society, even though he was exclusively concerned with the validity of historical scholarship in the Islamic world.[9]

The medical science advanced by the Greek physician and philosopher Galen (129–216), constituted the nearest methodological parallel to Ibn Khaldun's philosophical historical science.[10] Galen proposed a system of medicine that would combine *logos* and *peira*, rationalism and empirical testing, to achieve a proper diagnosis of medical conditions. Rationalism, *logos,* meant a philosophical understanding and method that proceeded from a knowledge of the nature or essence of the body as the necessary first step in identifying the underlying or hidden causes of disease. Comprehending the essential nature of things, whether physical objects or human beings, was an Aristotelian principle, which Galen felt had been neglected by physicians, partly accounting for the poor state of medicine in his time. He embraced the Aristotelian program of inductive and deductive logic, which proceeded from axiomatic statements of accepted truths about the nature of an entity to demonstrably or deductively reach certain conclusions. It was part of an Aristotelian approach to knowledge, which also included perceiving "the distinction between essential and accidental attributes familiar from the Aristotelian *Categories.*"[11] Galen also believed, as did so many Greco-Islamic thinkers, in the persuasive example of geometric proofs to demonstrate the power of logical argument.[12] He insisted, though, that reason should be anchored in reality. Empiricism, *peira*, in medicine meant a reliance on proven treatments for known diseases or conditions and a study of human anatomy. "The method envisaged by Galen can roughly be characterized as comprising a stage of discovery steered by reason (i.e., rational methods), followed by one of confirmation or otherwise by means of experience."[13] As scholars or scientists, both Galen and Ibn Khaldun were essentially clinicians, one of medicine and the other of society and politics. They insisted that philosophical premises had to be grounded in practical or empirical knowledge in order for Galen correctly to diagnose illness or to enable Ibn Khaldun accurately to interpret the histories of Muslim societies.[14]

Ibn Khaldun's reimagining history as a philosophical discipline by itself constituted a major intellectual achievement, the creation of *a science of man*, a phrase chosen because it is associated with the philosophically informed studies of human society by European Enlightenment scholars and more particularly with the eighteenth-century Scottish philosopher David Hume. Yet the assumptions, principles, and methodology of this science, which, had they been widely accepted, would have revolutionized historical research, have been largely ignored over the centuries. He is instead mainly known for applying what he characterized as his "remarkable and original method," to analyze the society and explain the history of his North African homeland. As his new science required, he based his analysis on an identification of the region's social organizations or societies and their associated accidents or traits. In North Africa Ibn Khaldun identified two distinct and antithetical societies—rural tribes and populations of cities—and he constructed his account of the region's history around the relations of these two types of human social organization. The intellectual power of his new science of man in North Africa is partly due to his treatment of societies as natural facts, the fundamental unit of historical analysis for philosophical historians. The *Muqaddimah*'s enormous appeal is, however, directly attributable to the fact that he presented his comprehensive account of North African society and history within the framework of a cyclical, dialectical model that explained, he said, the chronic political instability and persistently anemic culture that had plagued his North African homeland for centuries and still persisted in his own day. His model resembled Marx's later dialectical materialism to the degree that the nature of societies inexorably generated fundamental changes that produced new social characteristics and political structures. Unlike Marx, however, Ibn Khaldun did not describe a process that culminated in an idyllic synthesis, but rather one that was characterized by an endless series of repetitive cycles.

Ibn Khaldun attributed this phenomenon to the fundamentally disparate natures that distinguished rural tribesmen from urbanites in North Africa—and elsewhere, where both types of societies coexisted. These contrasts, he said, generated repeated historical cycles of approximately four generations in which morally pure, socially cohesive, and militarily tested rural tribes conquered morally corrupt, socially atomized, and militarily inexperienced urbanites and founded new dynasties, only to suffer inevitable political senescence, social fragmentation, cultural decay, and eventual conquest by other tribes. By constructing this model, Ibn Khaldun created the world's first known example of historical sociology, a philosophically inspired discipline commonly thought to have originated in Western Europe. It is difficult to underestimate the intellectual significance of his achievement, which included innovative social analyses, a sophisticated, dynamic structuralism, pragmatic political theories, and an account of economic phenomenon as an interrelated system. Ibn Khaldun belongs to an intellectual lineage of philosophically inspired political and social theorists that began with Plato, Aristotle, and Galen; continued with Greco-Islamic rationalists; and was revived by Europeans in the eighteenth, nineteenth, and twentieth centuries.

He was justifiably proud of his achievement and repeatedly expressed his satisfaction that he had used his philosophical history successfully in the *Muqaddimah* to fashion a comprehensive analysis of North African Muslim society and politics and explain its history. Ibn Khaldun also applied his science to Muslim Iberia and to the classical history of the Arab Muslim community. Alluding perhaps to his desire to reprise Masʿudi's earlier monumental history, he wrote: "I omitted nothing concerning the origin of races and dynasties, concerning the synchronism of the earliest nations, concerning the reasons for change and variation in past periods and within religious groups, concerning dynasties and religious groups, towns and hamlets, strength and humiliation, large numbers and small numbers, sciences and crafts, gains and losses, changing general conditions, nomadic and sedentary life, actual events and future events, all things expected to occur in civilization. I treated everything," he continued, "comprehensively and exhaustively," and then, referring to the philosophical methodology that characterized his new historical science, Ibn Khaldun concluded he had "exhaustively... explained the arguments for and causes of it(s existence)."[15]

Ibn Khaldun's attempt to fashion a comprehensive science of North African and Islamic man within the framework of his dialectical model explains one trait of the *Muqaddimah* that has bemused some readers and frustrated others, his extended treatises on a vast number of subjects, many of which seem marginal to his social and political analysis. His informed treatment of conic sections in geometry is one such section. Most readers have been unaware why he tried to be so all-inclusive, despite his clearly stated intent of imitating Masʿudi's thoroughness by chronicling and explaining all aspects of his world following the cataclysm of the plague. The major puzzlement about Ibn Khaldun's work is not the nature of his ambition, but his failure to return to the issue of the plague, his declared reason for writing.[16] He firmly believed his world was in a state of flux, and, by the evidence of the *Muqaddimah*, he never wavered from his mission to describe comprehensively his newly changed world for future generations. Yet, throughout the *Muqaddimah*, Ibn Khaldun attributes the politically chaotic, culturally morbid state of western Islamic society solely to social forces he describes and analyzes in his dialectical model of historical interpretation. Perhaps as Ibn Khaldun suggests in the introduction, the plague administered the coup de grâce to senile dynasties, but if so, he does not allude to this catastrophe as a cause of the decline of North African or Iberian Muslim states he so carefully analyzes in the *Muqaddimah*.

Whatever his thinking on this matter and however much his ideas may have changed as he wrote, he seems to have decanted into the vessel of the *Muqaddimah* all of his religious and philosophical education, historical knowledge, and personal experience of

North African, Iberian, and Egyptian politics, economics, and society. Information pours onto the page, sometimes threatening to drown the readers in minutiae. It is as massive a work as Montesquieu's *Esprit des Lois* and complex as Adam Smith's *Wealth of Nations*. Franz Rosenthal, without alluding to Ibn Khaldun's plague explanation, observed in his translator's introduction: "The *Muqaddimah* was composed nearly at the end of the intellectual development of medieval Islam and the work covers practically all its aspects."[17] In saying this, Rosenthal was largely correct; the work is in many respects a comprehensive survey of Islamic and, more particularly, North African Arab Muslim society, politics, and culture in the fourteenth century.

The *Muqaddimah* Ibn Khaldun finished is an ambitious science of man, a massive, varied, complex, and endlessly stimulating work, although some readers might wish that editors had been thicker on the ground in fourteenth-century Cairo, where he revised the text over the course of many years. Nonetheless, readers who are willing to read the entire work, not the abridgment, but the entire three volumes of Rosenthal's superb edited English translation, will be repaid by finding themselves engaged with the mind of a man who offers a philosophically informed study of society and history, which is based in the first instance on explicit assumptions about human nature.

Thus he repeatedly reasserts his conviction that all humans were born with identical capabilities and only came to differ after they lived in distinct environments. In saying this, Ibn Khaldun meant that members of rural and urban populations overall were born with the same raw intelligence, although he qualifies this generalization in two important ways, depending on the context of his argument. Attentive readers of the *Muqaddimah* will notice he sometimes indicates rural inhabitants were more mentally acute than their urban brethren, while in other passages he asserts people could be said to have different levels of speculative intelligence. In making the latter point, he meant that some individuals possessed a mental capacity that could transcend simple observations to make generalizations or abstractions of varying degrees of sophistication, abstractions that Aristotle and Ibn Khaldun believed to be the basis of the sciences or philosophical disciplines. By implication, though, these intellectually adept persons lived in economically vibrant, highly cultured urban societies.

Beyond the question of individual capabilities and intellectual range, Ibn Khaldun's effort to be comprehensive is most visibly and valuably on display in the chapters that contain his analysis of the politics, cultures, and economics of complex urban societies, which in his model, evolved over time. Yet his analysis is so thorough these sections also constitute distinct essays whose value transcends his theoretical framework. In them he examines first the nature of the "rational state," the pragmatic, realpolitik sultanate, and its relationship with urban society and culture. He devotes special attention to explaining the causal relationship between population density and economic growth, and he studies the urban economy itself almost as another kind of entity or social fact, at least a distinct phenomenon that deserves rational analysis. His economic studies represent an especially important part of the text, so varied and insightful it vies with his methodology and dialectical historical model in importance as an original intellectual achievement. Not only was his analysis unique in the Islamic world; it was not equaled elsewhere until 1776. Then Adam Smith invoked the division of labor in *The Wealth of Nations* to explain increasing prosperity in language that resembles a paraphrase of Ibn Khaldun's similar explanation for the exponential growth of agrarian and urban wealth in the *Muqaddimah*.

IBN KHALDUN'S WORKS

Understanding how Ibn Khaldun came to write this work is a matter of examining the life and interpreting the thought of an individual, who, apart from writing the *Muqaddimah* otherwise lived the typical professional life of an elite member of the Arab Muslim urban society of his day. Few extant sources are available for scholars to study the gestation of his social, cultural, or economic ideas. Apart from the *Muqaddimah*, these include the narrative history, for which the *Muqaddimah* serves as an introduction, a memoir, a treatise on Sufi *shaikh*s, the *Shifa' al-sa'il li Tahdhib al-Masa'il*, and a few scattered recollections of his contemporaries. The Sufi treatise, it should be mentioned, represents a type of analysis. It is not an affirmation of mystical spiritualism or praise for a particular order, but appears to complement the *Muqaddimah*'s survey of fourteenth-century North African Muslim society.

The *Muqaddimah* remains the single most important source for discerning the strands of Ibn Khaldun's mentalité. Even though it is more often than not discussed solely in terms of his dialectical model, the work is not a dry, abstract theoretical treatise—quite the opposite. While it contains only a few of the self-referential or openly egotistical assertions associated with an autobiography, in terms of personal information it represents a particularly rich example of what the *Annales* historian Marc Bloch has termed an unintentional source. It is a text that contains meaningful information about Ibn Khaldun's theology, philosophical principles, social attitudes, and, more generally, his remarkable intellectual range. As has been indicated and the *Muqaddimah*'s table of contents reveals, Ibn Khaldun devoted most of the work to discussing the traits of the sedentary states formed by tribal conquerors, men who evolved from tribal chiefs to autocratic sultans, ruling over prosperous, socially complex towns and cities. His analysis of sultanate regimes and the urban society and economy that these independent rulers governed is openly, unmistakably, if often only implicitly, autobiographical. He is, after all, describing the Arab Muslim urban society, his society, which he valued and whose decay in his era he poignantly mourned. Often, however, it is difficult to know whether or not Ibn Khaldun has abstracted certain sections of the *Muqaddimah* directly from his own experience or from some other source, and in these cases conclusions about his life constitute a kind of inferential gleaning from the text.

Initially at least, Ibn Khaldun meant the *Muqaddimah* to serve as an introduction to his entire historical corpus, the *Kitab al-'ibar*, or "The Book of Lessons [or Examples]," the abbreviated title for the massive work, part of which he wrote simultaneously with the *Muqaddimah* between 1375 and 1378.[18] He wrote the first draft of the *Muqaddimah* during an intensely creative five-month period in 1377. "I completed the composition and draft of this first part [of the *Muqaddimah*], before revision and correction [in Tunis and Cairo], in a period of five months ending in the middle of the year 779 [November 1377]." Subsequently he finished the entire *'Ibar* between 1378 and 1382.[19]

Apart from the *Muqaddimah*, the remaining volumes of this work include a traditional narrative history of the Islamic community and an original account of politically influential Berber tribes. Except for residents of Tunis and other Mediterranean coastal towns, Berbers comprised the vast majority of the indigenous pre-Islamic inhabitants of North Africa. Sections in the history on the Berbers constitute a uniquely valuable Arabic-language source for studying the history of these poorly documented North African tribes, whose own languages and dialects had not yet generated a historical literature. Ibn Khaldun's account of individual tribes is principally of interest to readers of the *Muqaddimah* because his minutely detailed narrative of their histories contains the narrative account he evidently intended, considering the full wording of the title, to illustrate his dialectical model. His history of the Berbers also includes one minor but intriguing discordant element: in one passage he offers seemingly heartfelt, undiluted praise of Berber qualities, a sentiment seemingly at odds with his negative characterization of most Berber and Arab tribes in the *Muqaddimah*. The fact that he dedicated the work to a Berber ruler of Tunis might have something to do with this brief encomium.

The second major source for Ibn Khaldun's life is his memoir, *al-Ta'rif bi-Ibn Khaldun,* which he continued writing until just before his death in 1406.[20] As its full title indicates, it is, at least in some measure, a *rihlah,* or a type of travel account, a genre that originated in North Africa and was made famous by Ibn Battuta, a near contemporary of Ibn Khaldun.[21] The fourteenth-century Granadan *wazir* Ibn al-Khatib also composed elegant, literary *rihlah*s about his journeys in North Africa. Ibn Khaldun's *rihlah* is, however, a far more complex description of his entire career, in which geography plays a minor role. Still, it typifies premodern or precolonial Arab Muslim personal narratives in that it presents a chronological account of places, individuals, and experiences rather than an autobiography, as that genre has come to be understood since the publication of the first volume of Rousseau's *Confessions* in 1782.[22] This general characterization seems a particularly apt label for Ibn Khaldun's memoir, for he does not meditate on his emotions or speak of his wife and children, whom he scarcely mentions and does not name. If Muslim authors wished to express their personal feelings, they commonly did so in verse. In Ibn Khaldun's case, his feelings are most openly on display in affecting poems he exchanged with his friend, his most intimate literary companion, Ibn al-Khatib, the historian, writer, and sometime first minister of Granada. Ibn Khaldun devotes much of his attention to his juridical education and administrative career as a government secretary and religious judge. Beyond that typical professional concern, the memoir in most pages constitutes a mind-numbing chronology of his turbulent administrative and political life in unstable North African and Iberian courts. Nonetheless, these political and military data are invaluable, but not so much for their minute details of intrigues and campaigns, the kind of narrative he decries in traditional Muslim historical accounts. They are, rather, vitally important for the crucial insight they provide into his knowledge and experience of the instability of North African and also Iberian Muslim states.

Not only does the memoir contain few introspective passages and little emotive rhetoric; it includes no reflections on the plague that killed his parents, teachers, and thousands of others in North Africa and southern Europe. Nor does it explain or even allude to the mental growth that led Ibn Khaldun to develop a philosophical historical methodology and write the *Muqaddimah*. In the memoir, for example, he mentions the *Muqaddimah* but once, without citing a single political or intellectual experience that might have led him to produce such an ambitious work. Apart from his original but largely overlooked explanation for composing the work, the impact of the plague, it seems likely that his personal knowledge of and experience with North African tribal states stimulated his interest in explaining the seemingly inchoate political chaos that infected the region. It is also possible his knowledge of the classical era of Arab Muslim history contributed to his thinking. In the course of developing his dialectical model of North African politics, he frequently alludes to the parallels between North African tribal dynastic history and the historical trajectory of Arab Muslim Bedouins from 622 until the late tenth century C.E. Unlike his careful construction of a model to explain North African historical cycles, he does not separately consider the entirety of early Islamic history, but only uses it as a frame of reference. An educated Muslim might possibly have reflected that in North Africa Ibn Khaldun saw a pattern already familiar to him in Arab Muslim history.

Ibn Khaldun observes that after the death of the Prophet Muhammad in 632, Arab Muslims passed through three social and political phases. The general periodization was not unique with him, but was commonly accepted and often taken from the eleventh-century political theorist al-Mawardi (d. 1052).[23] What is original is his conceptualization of Arab Muslim history in these centuries, which conforms to the vocabulary and theory of his dialectical model. In the golden age of Muhammad's immediate successors, the era of the Four Rashidun or Rightly Guided Caliphs: Abu Bakr, ʿUmar, Uthman, and ʿAli (632–667), Arab Muslims exemplified, he said, the rural or tribal phase of their history. Members of these Bedouin tribes possessed social solidarity, military aptitude, and a simple but vital piety Muhammad bequeathed to them through his divinely inspired prophecy. Possessed of these qualities, Bedouin tribes arose out of their rural environment in the Hijaz to conquer sedentary states, just as Muslim Berber tribes were to do later on a smaller scale in North Africa. The second phase of Arab Muslim history represented a prolonged example of what Ibn Khaldun thought of as the inevitable evolutionary phase of tribal states, the gradual degeneration of vibrant tribal government and society in an urban setting. It encompassed the reigns of the Umayyad caliphs of Damascus (661–750) and the ʿAbbasid caliphs of Baghdad. (750–1258). During the reign of these caliphs, Arabs' social cohesion, military vigor, and original, uncomplicated religiosity gradually atrophied, Ibn Khaldun asserts, as they adopted habits of pre-Islamic imperial powers and enjoyed the enervating pleasures of sedentary life.[24]

As early as the Umayyad era, Ibn Khaldun argued, some caliphs began acting less like their Rightly Guided predecessors, who had seen to their fellow Muslims' spiritual lives, as well as protecting their worldly interests, and functioned more like Byzantine or Iranian emperors. Ibn Khaldun, in agreeing with al-Mawardi, dates the onset of the Arab break with theocratic Muslim politics and the growth of increasingly secular Muslim monarchical rule with the Umayyad caliph ʿAbd al-Mālik b. Marwan (646/7–705).[25] This trend accelerated during the ʿAbbasid era, which witnessed the abandonment of Islamic theocracy and a full-scale revival of pre-Islamic imperial rule, or *mulk*.[26] More than any other state, Sasanid Iran (224–651) exemplified for Ibn Khaldun, as for so many other Muslims, pre-Islamic kingship, and he often cites Iranian history to illustrate his political analysis of later Muslim states. This third or monarchical phase developed fully in later ʿAbbasid years, when caliphs ceded power to their non-Arab ministers or military commanders, Iranians or Turks, or to autonomous, autocratic military rulers known as sultans. At this point, he observed, Arab Muslim social cohesion evaporated and the Arab Muslim Empire, the Caliphate, ceased to exist.[27] Sultanates of various ethnicities, Arab, Iranian, and Turk, arose in its place, and Ibn Khaldun constructed his model to explain this latter phase of Islamic history in North Africa and Muslim Iberia, one no longer exclusively dominated by pious or pure-blooded Arabs.

PERSONALITY AND SOCIAL IDENTITY

Given the materials at hand, there seems to be no reasonable means of tracing the process of Ibn Khaldun's thought. Still, while Ibn Khaldun offers no meaningful intellectual reflection on the evolution of his ideas in his memoir or the *Muqaddimah*, both texts are replete with comments that implicitly illustrate both his apparently satisfied sense of self and a number of revelatory social, political, and racial biases. Ibn Khaldun's pride, observed by contemporaries and later commentators, who have sometimes cited it as a factor in his largely unsuccessful political career, is frequently on display. It can be seen in the first instance in his account of his birth into a family of Yemeni Arab Muslims. His *nisbah*, the final word in a Muslim's name that usually indicates descent or geographic origin, was al-Hadhrami, an indication his ancestors originated in the Yemen coastal region of southern Arabia. Large numbers of Yemeni Arabs served in the Muslim armies that crossed the straits of Gibraltar in 711 and afterward, on their way to conquer sections of the Iberian Peninsula. Many, including Ibn Khaldun's ancestors, settled and prospered there, as well.

Little is known of the Banu Khaldun, the larger Khaldun "House" during the succeeding three centuries, but by the eleventh century if not before, members of the lineage had become landed country gentry in the fertile plains of southern Iberia, as well as influential scholars, officials, and clergy in the region's important towns. Members of the Banu Khaldun family became scholar-officials, to borrow a term, if not its precise original significance, from the historiography of China. Muslim scholar-officials were men whose landed wealth, social status, and education virtually guaranteed them influential and lucrative appointments in the various sultanate governments that ruled Iberia for eight centuries. In Seville particularly Ibn Khaldun's immediate family enjoyed prosperity and prestige and exercised political influence for many centuries. Writing in the eleventh century, Ibn Hayyan (b. 997–998), the preeminent historian of medieval Iberia, reported that the renowned Banu Khaldun house, *bait Banu Khaldun*, occupied prominent governmental and scholarly positions in Seville.[28] The extended family's name was still so well known that in 1364, when the Muslim ruler of Granada dispatched Ibn Khaldun as an emissary to the now-Christian city, its ruler, Pedro the Cruel, offered to restore the family lands if Ibn Khaldun embraced Christianity. Members of the Banu Khaldun house also served as high officials in Granada until Christians captured the city in 1492.

Ibn Khaldun never dwells on his privileged status in Muslim society; he did not need to do so for his Arab Muslim readers. His family's prestige as members of the Iberian Muslim elite seems to have survived undiminished after they fled as refugees from Seville to Tunis in 1232, prior to the Christian reconquest of Seville in 1248. North African rulers habitually welcomed cultured, highly educated, and administratively experienced Iberian Muslims to a region, which was a thinly populated provincial backwater of the Muslim world. Arab and Berber monarchs alike commonly appointed Iberian immigrants to religious offices or influential administrative posts in the underdeveloped region. Ibn Khaldun himself repeatedly stresses the civilizing role of Iberian Muslims, who were often influential in developing political structures in administratively primitive tribal states and raising the cultural level of these states' towns.[29] His own family's history epitomized this relationship between the Muslims of Iberia and North Africa. Even before emigrating from Andalusia, they were well connected in North Africa.

His great-grandfather served as an official of the Hafsids, the Muslim Berber dynasty that ruled Tunis for many generations. In an all too common fate of many such men who served in these chronically unstable regimes, Ibn Khaldun was later to describe in the *Muqaddimah,* his great-grandfather was arrested, tortured, and murdered by the reigning Hafsid sultan. His son, Ibn Khaldun's grandfather, also served the Hafsids in several minor posts, but perhaps with a view to his own father's fate, he eschewed higher appointments and, following two pilgrimages to Mecca, retired to lead the pious life of a religious scholar, an altogether typical recourse of Muslim scholar-officials, whose careers in that respect resembled some of their Chinese literati counterparts during dynastic upheavals. He died peacefully four years after Ibn Khaldun's birth in 1332, and his son altogether avoided potentially fatal involvement in the shifting dynastic sands of Hafsid politics, which had become even more treacherously violent by the early fourteenth century than they had been earlier. He was known as an *adib,* a cultured man of belles lettres and he became a *faqih,* a scholar of *fiqh,* or Islamic jurisprudence.

Ibn Khaldun grew up and matured in this elite urban social environment of former Iberian Muslim scholar-officials and prestigious North African administrators and religious scholars. As his family's status warranted, he was married to the daughter of a socially influential and wealthy Hafsid general and official. He was also educated in Tunis by his father and a coterie of prominent Iberian and North African scholars in the religious and philosophical sciences. His status, education, and considerable self-regard enabled him to move easily and self-confidently among religious scholars, tribal chiefs, literati, and monarchs of his day. He exemplified the type of well-born, prestigious, urban Muslim intellectual who, while lacking an independent tribal power base, nonetheless enjoyed easy access to patronage of ambitious rulers. During his life he was his father's son in several respects. Like his father, he could be characterized as an *adib,* an urbane man of letters who possessed, as he approvingly defines the type, "some knowledge regarding every science."[30]

Ibn Khaldun, who throughout his writings conveys a confident self-image as an accomplished, privileged individual, was very likely thinking of himself when he praised *adib*s and also observed that *katibun,* government scribes and secretaries, "must be selected from the upper classes and be a refined gentleman of great knowledge and with a good deal of stylistic ability."[31] He was, after all, an upper-class, refined individual, who joined the Hafsid court as a calligrapher in Tunis at age twenty, an altogether typical first appointment for a promising young man of an elite family. Like his father, Ibn Khaldun studied Islamic law. Unlike like his father, though, he not only served in later life as a state-appointed *qadi* or judge of the Maliki branch of Islamic law but he also accepted or sought out other state appointments throughout his career in various North African and Iberian Muslim regimes. In doing so he had to navigate the treacherous factional shoals of North African and Iberian politics and on two occasions endured imprisonment or confinement after becoming too closely involved in the internecine political struggles of the day. Ibn Khaldun was most unlike his father, though, in his ability to embrace a socially conservative but intellectual strain of Sunni Muslim orthodoxy while simultaneously espousing the use of Greco-Islamic philosophy for historical analysis.

Ibn Khaldun's social and political views typified men of his class and education. They were traditional and hierarchical. God ordained a hierarchical society, he insisted, in which certain individuals enforced social stability that primordial human beings could not manage as individuals, an allusion to Greco-Islamic rationalist ideas about the primordial origins of states. This was necessary because humans possessed intelligence and free will, and as a result, he implies, their egotism drove them to antisocial behavior. To achieve God's plan of preserving human society, it was essential to make them cooperate. He said this was what was meant by the Quranic verse "And we placed some of you over others in various grades, so that they might use others for forced labor." God ordained rank, *tabaqah*, the power to force people to do what was good for them, as something essential, and each class within the society of a town or climate zone exercised power over classes below it. Rulers were at the top, and at the bottom were those with nothing. "This was," Ibn Khaldun wrote, "God's wise plan with regard to His creation. It regulates their [classes'] livelihood, facilitates their affairs, and guarantees their eminence."[32]

Ibn Khaldun's elitist bias was often on display, and it could lead him on occasion to suspend critical judgment of sources in favor of status, race, and religion, as when he dismisses a scandalous story about the sister of the well-known ʿAbbasid caliph Harun al-Rashid (766–809), saying the story was unbelievable because of the sister's position, piety, parentage, and exalted rank. Ibn Khaldun followed this comment with an entire paragraph, venting his seemingly deeply felt outrage at the suggestion the caliph's sister could conceivably stain her chastity, modesty, cleanliness, and purity by engaging in a dalliance with an Iranian, a *mawali*, a non-Arab client, of all people![33] In part he felt, that because al-ʿAbbasah, the sister, lived when Arab Muslims still breathed the desert ethos of *badawah al-Arabiyah,* Arab bedouinism, the story depicting such immorality could not be countenanced.[34] His comment also serves as an anecdotal introduction, both to his pronounced sense of regret at the loss of what he imagined to be a kind of ancient or original and vital Arab essence and also to his conviction, on display in other parts of the *Muqaddimah,* that the loss of Arab social purity contributed to the decline of later Arab Muslim society.

In describing various elements of North African and Iberian Muslim populations, Ibn Khaldun further revealed his own biases when he referred disdainfully to "unmanly" merchants and contemptuously dismissed uneducated, common people, whose emotional religious enthusiasms he feared might threaten social stability.[35] He reserved his greatest praise for urbane intellectuals of his own social class, whether they were theologians, legal scholars, literati, philosophers, or erudite administrators. While occasionally acknowledging individual rulers if they recognized, honored, and employed men of his status and education, he rarely glorifies particular monarchs in the *Muqaddimah* or in the memoir. In fact, he harshly criticizes obsequious Muslim historians who shamelessly eulogized their rulers or prominent political figures in Islamic history.

While Ibn Khaldun reveals much about himself in the *Muqaddimah* and memoir, his private emotional life and personal intellectual history will always remain hidden. In terms of his ambitious goals for a science of man and society, it is important to consider that a portrait of the man will always, like a painting, consist of a single image of a mature individual and not a series of sketches that document intellectual growth and change over his entire life. One other and very important thing to emphasize when studying Ibn Khaldun's social and political ideas is that even though he can rightfully claim to have created a new philosophical science and to have deployed it in creative ways, he was not a philosopher and did not write like one.

Unlike Greco-Islamic rationalists, such as the philosopher Ibn Sina (980–1037), the European Avicenna, he never defines his terms or explains allusions to philosophical concepts, so that modern readers of the Arabic text or translations, who are unfamiliar with his vocabulary or his sometimes novel use of Arabic terminology, may easily mistake his meaning. He may have felt he preemptively justified his failure to do so, for he ritually excuses himself at both the beginning and end of the *Muqaddimah* for faulty arguments or gaps in the text. His new historical science was, he said, a difficult subject, and founders of new sciences were not obliged to solve all problems connected with them.[36]

Whether or not he truly believed his philosophical methodology and science of North African man required additional thought, his caution to readers is worth noting. Not only does he routinely fail to define terms or concepts; he also frequently fails to explore, much less resolve, logical implications of his arguments. In some cases he has left fundamentally important contradictions unresolved. These include two especially important instances where he expresses irreconcilable religious and philosophical opinions. In one instance, he implicitly contradicts his philosophical assumptions about causation when he discusses Muslim theology. In another he negates fundamental aspects of his rationalist dialectical model by offering a religious explanation for social change. It is scarcely surprising to find issues with a massive, innovative, complex work of this kind, in which Ibn Khaldun's dialectical structure itself often becomes obscured or compromised by his comprehensive survey of contemporary Islamic culture. Indeed, the contradictions within the *Muqad-*

dimah can be primarily attributed to the nature of his survey, in which he describes and comments on various aspects of Muslim society in discrete sections. Anyone trying to explain Ibn Khaldun's ideas often has to find ways to interpret the implications of incompletely articulated or conflicting theories in a manner that would be consistent with his thought. In that spirit this introduction will conclude by defining some of the most important Greco-Islamic philosophical concepts and also Arabic social terms he uses throughout the text, beginning with the word *muqaddimah*.

THE LANGUAGE OF REASON AND SOCIETY

As is true of many significant terms in Ibn Khaldun's *Muqaddimah* vocabulary, the word *muqaddimah* has both a common and a philosophical meaning. Commonly it means *introduction*, and it is used throughout the Islamic world to introduce books of all kinds. Philosophically, the word means a premise, proposition, or axiom that is an inductively derived statement of a generally acknowledged truth. In Aristotelian and Greco-Islamic logic, the premise forms the first element of the syllogism, the form of reasoning that constitutes the core principle of deductive logic. The Aristotelian syllogism contains three elements: a major premise, followed by a minor premise, which produces the conclusion. Thus in the "classical" example of the syllogism: "All men are mortal" is the premise or major proposition; followed by the minor proposition "Socrates is a man"; and concluding with the irrefutable third statement, "Socrates is mortal." Greco-Islamic scholars recognized dozens of variant logical *muqaddimah*s, and Ibn Khaldun sometimes uses the term in its philosophical sense.[37] That is not to say, however, that he explicitly constructs the *Muqaddimah* as a series of tripartite syllogisms. He does not. Still not only does he base his dialectical model on specific axioms, which he sometimes explicitly identifies as *muqaddimah*s, but he also often insists that a particular argument or case he has made constitutes a *burhan*, a perfectly conceived logical proof.

Ibn Khaldun also uses another word derived from the same root to make an important point about the transition or evolution from rural tribal to urban sedentary states. *Aqdam* means prior, and Aristotle used it in a variety of combinations: "prior in knowledge," "prior in time," "prior in rank," and "prior in perfection," but also *al-taqaddum biltabʿ*, "prior by nature." The latter variant of the word and phrase prior by or in nature indicates that not only does one thing come after another but the existence of one thing is impossible without the other. In discussing how tribal societies evolve into sedentary states, Ibn Khaldun uses the term, but as usual without comment. Some of his rationalist colleagues might have gotten the point, but others, then and now, would not.[38]

Within the *Muqaddimah* Ibn Khaldun uses the term *tabiʿah*, or "nature," more frequently than any other philosophical concept; its meaning and implications are fundamentally important to his argument throughout the text.[39] Aristotle defined the term in a variety of ways, but most commonly as things that have within them "the principle of movement and rest," or, as he alternatively expresses it, "the primary underlying matter of things which have in themselves a principle of motion or change" or the "shape or form" of something. A popular book based on Aristotle's *Physics*, where Aristotle repeatedly discusses the idea, was widely available to Muslim scholars in an early Arabic translation.[40] It offered a variety of related explanations of the concept, including one that nature could also signify the *dhat* or the essence of something. Most Arabic definitions convey Aristotle's original idea of something, which has potentiality, *quwah*, and, when its form is realized, actuality, *fi'l*.[41]

Ibn Sina, the enormously influential Greco-Muslim philosopher, who was the most widely read Muslim rationalist in the North Africa and Iberia of Ibn Khaldun's day, discussed the concept of *tabi'ah* extensively in his work *The Physics of the Healing*.[42] He applied the term to human beings as well as inert physical objects, but he modified the concept, since humans possessed complex natures, which he described as "composite bodies." They had complex natures, he reasoned, because humans possessed souls as well as physical traits, a unique combination that constituted the "essence of humanness." This distinguished them from physical objects, but the argument does not imply Ibn Sina or any other Muslim philosopher considered all humans to be identical. They did not, and Ibn Khaldun certainly did not. He remarks, perhaps deriving his idea from Ibn Sina, that while humans comprise a single species, they differed from one another as individuals.[43]

Apart from simply identifying or categorizing some thing, the philosophical idea of some entity's nature was fundamental to Ibn Khaldun's thought, as it was to be later for European philosophers, historians, and sociologists, because different natures were thought to have distinct potentials, as Aristotle's original idea makes clear. Understanding the nature of a physical object or a human being enabled a scholar accurately to reconstruct its history or predict its trajectory, whether physical or historical. Ibn Khaldun applied the idea to societies, which is why he insisted a historian's first task was to identify the nature of whatever society or social group he was studying. Once scholars determined a nature, they could evaluate the relative veracity of historical evidence concerning a particular community by comparing its nature, its known qualities, with written reports of its history.

Then some of these reports could be dismissed as logical absurdities. Even more important in his case, the idea of nature formed the basis of Ibn Khaldun's historical sociology, in which rural tribes possessed certain traits or potentials that evolved and radically altered when and if they moved from impoverished rural environments to prosperous urban situations.

Ibn Khaldun's word for social organization was *ijtima'*, a word he often combined with *human* or *insan* or *humanity*. This was the term he and such earlier Greco-Islamic scholars as al-Farabi used to render the Aristotelian notion of *koinonia*, the cooperative society or community humans had to form in order to survive and prosper.[44] *Ijtima'* will be translated here as *social organization* when Ibn Khaldun uses it in the Greco-Islamic sense of this necessary primordial community. "Human social organization [*al-ijtima' al-insani*], is something necessary," Ibn Khaldun writes, an idea *hukama'* or "philosophers expressed . . . by saying, "mankind is civilized," *madani*, by nature."[45] Ibn Khaldun, who alludes to the idea of the city-state or polis later in this passage, seems, like the philosopher al-Farabi, to use it in the sense of a state, rather than a city.

In going beyond this primordial account of the origin of the human community, Ibn Khaldun accounted for a particular society's relative cohesion or integrity by measuring its degree of *'asabiyah,* an Arabic term he adapted from its earlier Arabic sense of clannishness or tribalism and elevated to his fundamental historical principle of social solidarity. *'Asabiyah* was, he says, "one of the natural powers," meaning it had a predictable effect determined and limited by its very nature.[46] In his dialectical model, *'asabiyah* connoted communal solidarity derived from individuals' knowledge of their kinship or blood relationship, and rural tribal members, he felt, possessed the strongest degree of ʿasabiyah. Ibn Khaldun did not, however, mean to suggest that consulting a genealogical chart could, by itself, produce this bond. It was, rather, generated when closely related individuals shared everyday experiences, as pastoral nomadic kinsmen did when they conducted tribal raids. Ibn Khaldun discusses two varieties of ʿasabiyah in the *Muqaddimah,* that of Arabs and another of Berbers, and also in his memoir, alluding to its existence among Central Asian Turks. He believed the presence or relative lack of ʿasabiyah constituted the single-most important trait that distinguished the nature of one society from another.

Ibn Khaldun also thought human beings equally shared fundamental qualities, Ibn Sina's "essence of humanness," but they differed radically from each other owing to the determining effects of their distinct environments. The rural and urban environments in North Africa produced two societies with fundamentally different natures he labeled as ʿumran badawi and ʿumran hadari. ʿUmran is derived from an Arabic verbal root meaning, variously, *to live, to prosper, to populate, to reconstruct, to preserve,* and, sometimes, *to civilize,* and Ibn Khaldun primarily uses it to mean either *society* or *culture* and *population.* Particular care must be taken with the context of the term, for when he uses it to mean *population,* he is often making a point about the relationship between the number of inhabitants and economic prosperity. As far as *badawi* or *bedouin* is concerned, Ibn Khaldun used the term as a generic label for all tribal people, both nomads and agriculturalists, living in rural areas, including the Arabic-speaking Bedouins from the Arabian Peninsula, as well as the Berbers, Berber-speaking natives of North Africa. His usage reflects the true meaning of the word *badawi* (pl. *badw*) as "desert dweller." By *hadari,* Ibn Khaldun means the society of sedentary inhabitants of towns and cities, the *mudun, amsar,* or *bilad* of the Arabic-speaking world.

When he pairs *'umran badawi* and *'umran hadari* as contrasting phrases, as he does throughout the *Muqaddimah, 'umran* means *society* or *culture* and not, as the word has been generally translated in English, *civilization.* Its meaning is the same when Ibn Khaldun uses the single phrase *'umran badawi, tribal society* or *tribal culture.* In a few *Muqaddimah* passages, *'umran* might safely be translated as *civilization,* but it never carries this meaning when Ibn Khaldun refers to Arab Bedouins, Berbers, or any pastoral nomadic tribal group, such as the Central Asian Mongols and Turks.

These meanings are unmistakable because based on his repeated characterizations of these two types of human society, Ibn Khaldun would have considered it an oxymoron, a contradictory expression, to translate *'umran badawi* in the *Muqaddimah* as *bedouin* or *tribal civilization.* He adamantly and repeatedly insisted bedouin or tribal life was in most instances antithetical to and destructive of urban society and its culture, a society and culture he sometimes identifies as representing *tamaddun, civilization,* a word derived from the Arabic root *to found* or *build cities* or simply *to civilize.*[47] He explicitly associated pastoral nomadic Arabs, or a particular Arab tribal confederation settled in North Africa, the Banu Hilal, with anarchy and chaos. Civilization for Ibn Khaldun connoted the culture of Arab Muslim individuals like himself, people who lived in cities, characterized physically by elaborate, permanent buildings; socially by a complex division of labor and professionalization of occupations; culturally by sophisticated intellectual and artistic achievement; and politically by stable, effective political leadership. Tribal society, by contrast, exhibited opposite traits, which in political terms sometimes meant a virtual state of anarchy, thereby hardly deserving the name of an Aristotelian social organization, *ijtimaʿ*, at all. He applied his derisive characterization to all tribes, except the very few that possessed sufficient social cohesion, military skills, and leadership to conquer cities, establish stable dynasties, and preside over prosperous, cultured societies.

If tribal and urban societies exhibited fundamentally different natures, these natures or essences also possessed distinct *ʿarad* (s. *aʿrad*) or "accidental" qualities, a critically important philosophical concept, which Ibn Khaldun repeatedly invokes in the *Muqaddimah* and that has been habitually mistranslated or misunderstood. He employs *ʿarad* to convey exactly the same sense as did Aristotle or Ibn Sina or the Spanish Muslim philosopher Ibn Rushd (1126–1198), known in Europe as Averroes, or the Paris-based European theologian Thomas Aquinas (1225–1274). *Accident* meant for all four men a secondary characteristic of some entity, whether of a geometric form, such as a triangle, a physical object, such as a chair, or, for Ibn Khaldun, a society. Ibn Sina, for example, includes *ʿarad* as one of the four traits of any particular entity, whether physical or mathematical, writing "Every body has a nature, form, matter and accidents." This idea appears in varying verbal guises in European sociological literature; including Marx's writings, where it is rendered as "superstructure."

Aristotle and his Greco-Islamic acolytes identified two types of accidents: essential and contingent. The first may be illustrated by a triangle, the example Aristotle uses and Ibn Rushd repeats. The fact that all the angles of a triangle equal two right angles or 180 degrees is an accidental or secondary characteristic of a three-sided figure, but it is unvarying and therefore an essential accident, an '*arad dhati*, of triangles. The color of a chair, in contrast, an example that both Aristotle and Ibn Sina cite, is a contingent or ancillary accident. A particular color is not an essential trait of a chair, one that makes a chair a chair. A chair might be black or white and still be a chair. Ibn Khaldun considered government itself and a society's crafts or professions to be essential accidents and such traits as monarchical prestige, nonessential or contingent accidents.

There are, finally, two other important terms in this basic list of Ibn Khaldun's philosophical and social vocabulary: *form* and *matter*. Originally Aristotle meant them to mean simply the "shape," *form*, and "stuff," *substance*, of physical objects.[48] To illustrate this idea, Ibn Sina offered the example of a physical object, a chair or a bed, saying of a bed, for example, the shape of the bed form is its form, while the bed's substance or matter is the wood from which it is made.[49] Later the words took on other meanings. Greco-Islamic rationalists and Ibn Khaldun adopted some of these to convey two related ideas. First, he uses them to illustrate the relationship between society and the state. Society is matter, *maddah*, and the state, which preserves society, is form, *surah*. In this usage society is a natural entity and the state its necessary "accident." Second, Ibn Khaldun also invokes these terms to distinguish an empty vessel, something with a form but possessing no matter or substance, from something that is whole, having both a shape or design and a core. In the case of Ibn Sina's chair, without the wood, there was form without matter, and for Greco-Islamic thinkers, form comes before matter.

In the *Muqaddimah* Ibn Khaldun repeatedly invokes these concepts in the second sense to distinguish meaningless narrative ephemera from the philosophical analysis he pioneered in Muslim historical writing. He does so initially in the foreword, where he characterizes Muslim historians of his day as being "dull of nature and intelligence," because they wrote narrative histories based mindlessly on earlier texts.[50] They offered, he writes, "historical information about dynasties and stories of events from the early period," as "mere forms [*suwar*] without substances [*mawadd*]," or, as he puts it more pointedly, what they presented as knowledge has to be considered ignorance.[51] These historians wrote texts that might appear to contain valuable knowledge but instead they offered only uncritical, crowd-pleasing narratives, which, since they failed to consider the "nature" of human societies, constituted forms without substance. That is, their superficial narrative texts represented empty vessels or chimeras. It was this deeply flawed tradition of historical writing Ibn Khaldun repudiated and tried to replace with one based on philosophic principles and methods and practical realities in the *Muqaddimah*.

1

IBN KHALDUN'S WORLD

IBN KHALDUN WAS BORN in 1332 in Tunis, where his ancestors had fled shortly before Seville fell to the Christian forces of Castile in 1248. Until 1382, when he was forty years old and settled in Cairo, Ibn Khaldun lived, studied, and worked mainly in Tunis, Fez, and other towns and villages of North Africa, the region that includes the modern states of Libya, Tunisia, Algeria, and Morocco. He and Arab geographers distinguished two sections within this region: "Ifriqiyah," or Roman Africa, comprising Tunis and eastern North Africa but not Egypt, and the Maghrib, the Arabic "West," encompassing Algeria and Morocco.[1] He also spent brief periods of his adult life at the Arab Muslim Nasrid court of Granada, then the last state in al-Andalus or Andalusia, the Arab name for the Muslim-ruled areas of Portugal and Spain within the Iberian Peninsula. In composing the *Muqaddimah*, Ibn Khaldun assumed readers would be familiar with these closely entwined regions of the western Islamic world, a world he knew, analyzed, and, in certain respects, mourned. His theories are rooted in these regions' geography, settlement patterns, histories, and societies, and if modern readers are to find their way through Ibn Khaldun's sprawling work and come away with an accurate understanding of his science of man, they too must familiarize themselves with Ibn Khaldun's world.

NORTH AFRICA

Ibn Khaldun based his model on the premise that environment, directly or indirectly, determined human nature. Environment was responsible, therefore, for the distinctive traits or natures of particular human social organizations. He attributed the dynamics of his dialectical model in the first instance to the contrasting rural and urban environments of the North African landscape.[2] North Africa consists of two major regions, a largely arid interior and a Mediterranean coastal plain. The interior comprises a broad swath of extremely dry territory, interrupted by two mountain ranges. These two ranges are the Rif, a continuation of a geologic formation from Gibraltar and southern Spain, which continues into the heart of central Morocco, and the Atlas, a range comprising a complex series of chains, extending from southwestern Morocco northeast to the Mediterranean coast and continuing eastward through both coastal and interior Algeria as far as northern Tunisia. South of these mountain chains lie steppe land and the vast Sahara, separating Ifriqiyah and the Maghrib from Africa proper.

Lacking major river systems, no area of North Africa contains terrain suitable for dense human settlement such as developed in Andalusia, Egypt, and Iraq. "Atlantic" Morocco, south-southwest of Tangier and the Rif, and west of the Middle and High Atlas chains, contains the most productive agricultural lands in the region. It benefits from an Atlantic climate, which produces rains and mild, humid weather, so plains in this area between the mountains and the sea support numerous agricultural villages and a few substantial towns. Fez in the north and Marrakesh in the southwest, oasis towns founded by different dynasties during the Islamic era, are located here along the western slopes of the mountains. The remainder of North Africa is far less hospitable. Eastern Morocco, Algeria, Tunisia, and Libya have sparse rainfall and a narrow Mediterranean coastal plain, hemmed in by rugged mountains, with steppe and desert immediately to the south.

Apart from a few areas such as Atlantic Morocco and some sections of the Mediterranean coast, the entire North African region has remained sparsely populated throughout its recorded history. Historically, urban settlements, even in Atlantic Morocco, were relatively small—relative, that is, to towns and cities throughout the eastern Mediterranean. As Ibn Khaldun remarks about North Africa in the *Muqaddimah*, "There are few cities and towns in Ifriqiya and the Maghrib. The reason for this is that these regions belonged to the Berbers for thousands of years before Islam."[3] Three principal types of towns, however modest, were nonetheless found in the two sections before and during his lifetime: Mediterranean coastal settlements, military or political centers, and interior commercial entrepôts.

Historically, the most populous North African towns and cities were scattered along the Mediterranean coast, a significant area of human habitation since Phoenician times during the second and first millennium B.C.E. Tunis, a major port in later Roman times, which regained its importance following the Muslim conquest of North Africa in the seventh century, was one of the most important of these settlements. Tunis possessed valuable agricultural lands that supported a substantial population, but it prospered because of its links with both Mediterranean and also trans-Saharan commercial networks. Ibn Khaldun's home, it represented the only North African urban center he thought to be comparable in certain limited respects with the great cities of Andalusia, Egypt, and Iraq. With its religious buildings, libraries, scholarly traditions, and vibrant economy, Tunis manifested the type of Arab Islamic urban culture he valued, and that he directly associated with densely populated human settlements elsewhere in the Islamic world.[4] In fact, as seen in the later analysis of his dialectical model, he equated the strength of an economy and the level of civilization or cultural sophistication of any town or city with the size of its population.

Apart from historic coastal sites, there were two other major types of urban settlements in North Africa: military and political towns and interior trading centers. Qayrawan, whose name was derived from the Persian *karvan* or caravansary, was founded about 670 by an army of the Umayyad Caliphate of Damascus (661–750). It was the earliest Arab Muslim settlement in the region. Located just south of Tunis on the site of a former Byzantine military camp, the city began life as a military encampment but evolved into a fortified city that became Ifriqiyah's most important Muslim religious center from the early ninth to the middle of the eleventh century. The city's legal scholars composed, among other works, fundamental texts of Maliki law, the conservative Sunni *madhhab* or legal school that took root throughout North Africa and Andalusia well before the fourteenth century, when Ibn Khaldun studied it and later became a Maliki judge in Cairo.

North Africa's two most important political centers from the eleventh century until Ibn Khaldun's day were the Moroccan oasis towns of Fez and Marrakesh. Fez, first founded in 789, was rebuilt in 1276, while Marrakesh, situated along the piedmont of the Atlas Mountains, was established in 1062. As capitals of different dynasties, these towns also developed into religious and cultural centers of the Maghrib at different times, which attracted scholars from throughout North Africa, including Ibn Khaldun. In the twelfth and thirteenth centuries, Marrakesh became the single-most important city in North Africa, but by Ibn Khaldun's day, following extended periods of political turmoil, it had become a shadow of its former self, although the magnificent walls of the city remained intact as they do to the present day. By the fourteenth century, when Ibn Khaldun traveled to Morocco, Fez had become the most important city in Morocco, owing to the dynastic shifts in the region.

Apart from these military and political centers, there were important commercial towns situated inland from the coast or farther south in the desert, owing their size and prosperity primarily to their strategic locations on trans-Saharan trade routes. These included, among several others, two particularly important settlements, Tilimsan, located in the highlands, southwest of Oran in western Algeria, which began life as a Roman garrison in the fourth century, and Sijilmasa, initially founded as a Berber tribal camp in the eighth century, which is situated south of the Atlas Mountains, at the northern edge of the Sahara. Both cities were thriving in Ibn Khaldun's day. After visiting Sijilmasa in 1351, his contemporary Ibn Battuta (1304–1368), praised the beauty and prosperity of the town, the principal northern terminus of African gold caravans.[5]

Outside its few towns and cities, the prevalent human settlement pattern throughout most of the North African interior before and during Ibn Khaldun's era featured tribal populations. They were composed of small, isolated hamlets of farmers, scattered throughout the mountains but found in greater concentrations in a few well-watered oases and plains, as well as substantial numbers of pastoral nomads living in the steppe areas and the slopes of the Atlas Mountains and farther south along the fringes of the Sahara.[6] According to Ibn Khaldun, during his lifetime agriculturalists living in the plains and in the mountains comprised the majority of indigenous tribes and non-Arabs in North

Africa, while nomadic pastoralists, camel herders, whose mounts were adapted for the dry, austere North African environment, accounted for the remainder of the rural population.[7] Within any particular locality, farmers and herders traditionally belonged to the same tribe, whose chiefs or religious leaders founded most of the dynasties Ibn Khaldun cited to illustrate his dialectical model.

At the time of the Muslim conquests in the seventh century and during Ibn Khaldun's lifetime, as well, the bulk of these rural tribes consisted of an indigenous, ethnically mixed population known to Greeks, Romans, and Muslims as Berbers, that is, "barbarians." These people called themselves *Imazighen*, "noble" or freeborn, a term emphasizing an individualized, heroic warrior image typical of the ideology of pastoral nomadic tribesmen, which Berber tribal poets conveyed in their verse and sometimes proclaimed in defiant song before battles, stirring tribal warriors to self-sacrifice.[8] It was a self-image verified in a purported tenth-century statement of one tribesman, who said: "Each man of us [in the Kutamah tribe] is his own master, although each tribe has its elders and advisers in matters of (religious) conduct to whom we take our disputes."[9]

In Ibn Khaldun's day, most Berbers were Muslims to varying degrees of sophistication, but they spoke their own language and most remained culturally distinct from Arabs in both North Africa and Andalusia. Nearly all Berbers were identified with one or another of the region's tribes living in the countryside, and, as Ibn Khaldun remarks in one of his innumerable expressions of regret about the lack of vibrant urban centers in his North African homeland, "No sedentary society existed among (the Berbers) long enough to reach any degree of perfection."[10] The greatest part of North African society was, therefore, in Ibn Khaldun's phrase, "a bedouin one," using the Arabic word *bedouin* here and throughout the *Muqaddimah* as a generic term for all pastoral nomadic and rural agrarian tribal populations. In his mind this environmentally determined social reality amid its few modest towns shaped the political and cultural history of the region.

In fact, centuries before Ibn Khaldun's time, many true Bedouins, members of Arabic-speaking tribes from the Arabian Peninsula, had also settled in parts of the Maghrib. Some were members of the original Arab Muslim armies, such as those who lived in Qayrawan, but there were others who came later and in greater numbers. He identified one particular Arab tribal confederation, whose members arrived in the eleventh century, the Banu Hilal, as bedouins, that is, tribesmen, who initially at least seem to have been made up entirely of pastoral nomads and to have epitomized nomadic society at its most anarchic and destructive.[11] Ibn Khaldun and other Arab scholars condemned the appalling havoc this tribal group wreaked on North African sedentary society over several centuries, expressing themselves with the same vehemence Chinese or Iranian observers spoke of Mongols after they tore through Eurasia in the twelfth and thirteenth centuries. Ibn Khaldun blamed the Banu Hilal especially for much of the decay of North African urbanism over a period of 350 years. He wrote, with some exaggeration, that while the entire region between the Sudan and the Mediterranean had historically been settled, as architectural ruins testified, the Banu Hilal had destroyed all traces of urban society.[12]

In his memoir Ibn Khaldun compared pastoral nomads generally, including both Arabs and Berbers, with Mongols. "Like the bedouins [Arab and Berber tribes], they [the Mongols] show an extraordinary disposition for raids and pillages and acts of violence against civilized populations."[13] Neither he nor any other commentator would have applied the phrase *'umran badawi* to the Mongols or the Banu Hilal in the sense of *tribal civilization*. Not when, as he said, the "nature" of Arabs, that is, the nature of Arab tribes, was "antithetical to and incompatible with [sedentary] society." Indeed, "the nature of Arab existence" was antithetical even to built structures, the physical basis of sedentary society.[14] Unstructured, fluid, chaotic, and destructive were only some of the derogatory adjectives Ibn Khaldun applied to tribes, that is, to bedouins of all ethnicities: Arab, Berber, Mongol, and Turk.

ANDALUSIA

Andalusia, Ibn Khaldun's ancestral home, contrasted favorably with the difficult environment and thinly populated North African landscape. Its relatively fertile agricultural lands supported far more dense settlement, which in turn gave rise to populous and culturally vibrant Muslim towns and cities. In some cases, such as Granada, these natural and human resources provided the basis of enduring kingdoms. The contrast between the few North African towns and their vast, lightly populated, arid hinterland and Andalusia's relatively well-watered agricultural lands and numerous cities comes into high relief on a map of Iberia, which plots the pattern of the largest cities on major river systems of the kind absent in the Maghrib. These included Lisbon and Toledo, both situated on the Tagus River in western Iberia; Zaragoza or Saragossa, located on the Ebro River in Aragon; Valencia, a coastal city at the mouth of the Guadalaviar or Turia River in the east and three major southern cities at the heart of Andalusia; Cordoba and Seville, situated along the Guadalquivir River; and nearby Granada, located at the confluence of the Beiro and two other rivers. Iberia contains extensive mountainous regions and areas of low agricultural productivity, but one needs only to fly into a North African oasis city such as Marrakesh and then into Seville over its lush surrounding fields to understand the starkly different levels of agrarian wealth and urban prosperity in North Africa and Andalusia.[15]

Ibn Khaldun served at the court of Granada between 1362 and 1365, and he accounted the rule of the kingdom between 1228 and 1492 as one of the two great periods of urban cultural florescence in Iberia. The other, he reported, occurred during the golden age of the western Umayyad Caliphate in the tenth century, architecturally commemorated by the great mosque at Cordoba, its capital city.[16] Ibn Khaldun indicates that no North African city or dynasty attained a similar level. The magnificent Alhambra fortress and palaces in Granada, partly constructed before he arrived in the city, represented the architectural emblems of the type of wealthy, populous, sophisticated urban culture he appreciated and preferred for himself. As Ibn Khaldun repeatedly observes, the monuments of a dynasty were proportionate to its power, and the Alhambra complex exhibited monumental structures and pleasure gardens, which were difficult to replicate on the same scale or in as many cities in North Africa.[17] The poetry he quotes, which extolls the pleasures of Seville and Granada, is only one sign of the attraction he and other Muslims felt for the Andalusian environment. A poet contemporary of Ibn Khaldun's, 'Abd al-'Azīm, wrote in colloquial *zajal* verse of Granada and the pleasures to be had in its well-watered countryside:

> Dissipation is permitted, you clever fellows,
> Since the sun has entered into Aries.
> Thus, commit a new immorality every day!

> . . . Let us go after them at the Genil [Granada's river]
> Upon the verdant meadows there!
> Let Baghdad alone and do not talk about the Nile!
> I like these regions better,
> A plain which is better than an expanse of forty miles.
> When the wind blows over it to and fro
> No trace of dust is found,
> Not even enough to apply as antimony to the eyes.[18]

In fact, it is difficult to exaggerate the nostalgia that individuals throughout the entire Islamic world still feel for the real or imagined pleasures of Andalusia, where, unlike Ifriqiyah and the Maghrib, "no trace of dust is found."[19]

Ibn Khaldun thought Andalusia's "towns and cities" constituted what he considered *tamaddun,* a civilization that produced the finest crafts, a term he uses for the products of such skills as silk weaving or the work of goldsmiths, but that he also applies to artistic or intellectual attainments, what he terms the "noble crafts," of writing, book production, and teaching.[20] Andalusians, he reported, developed a superior education system to that in North Africa, not just limited to studies of the Quran, which was the practice there. These Iberian Muslims also excelled at Arabic poetry, prose, and linguistics.[21] North African bedouins, in contrast, whether Berber or Arab tribesmen, developed crude, practical versions of crafts required by their "desert" life, such as carpentry and weaving, which were never polished or artful. To the extent that North Africans did improve their physical and intellectual crafts, it was often, Ibn Khaldun repeatedly says, the result of Iberian influence. Thinking perhaps of his own family's history, Ibn Khaldun remarks that following the Christian Reconquista, people from eastern Spain brought their sophisticated sedentary culture to Ifriqiyah and this was also true of Marrakesh and other towns in the North African region. Andalusians helped to develop Tunis in particular, his birthplace, a city where "crafts were developed to perfection ... Though less so than in Iberia."[22]

THE CONQUESTS

Understanding the political history of these closely connected but geographically distinct regions is as important as appreciating their geography, settlement patterns, and societies, for Ibn Khaldun derived the evidence to document his dialectical theory as much from his knowledge of North African and Andalusian history as from his own administrative and legal experience. He also, as will be seen, drew on the example of Muhammad's prophecy and the tribal composition of early Arab Muslim society to support his arguments. Nonetheless, his principal concern throughout the *Muqaddimah* was to explain the trajectory of North African and, secondarily, Andalusian history. He created his dialectical model for that purpose and not, it has repeatedly to be emphasized, as a universally valid philosophy of human history.

Muslim rule in North Africa and Andalusia went through several distinct phases prior to Ibn Khaldun's birth. In the first, or conquest phase, Arab Muslims, many of them Yemenis, including, evidently, Ibn Khaldun's ancestors, the Banu Khaldun, the greater Khaldun lineage or "house," occupied North Africa and parts of the Iberian Peninsula, where some formed distinctive Yemeni military units.[23] Arab Muslim armies from Egypt initially subjugated major Berber tribes in a series of difficult campaigns lasting more than half a century before they reached the Atlantic coast. After occupying Alexandria in 642, they were able to establish their first military camp in North Africa proper at

Qayrawan.[24] Ibn Khaldun thought Qayrawan was badly sited and believed the decision to locate it on the steppe reflected Arab Bedouin inexperience with urban life and consequent incompetence at town planning.[25] His comment is one of many such observations about the early history of Muslim North Africa in which he identifies traits that illustrate what he considers to be the identical nature of tribal and/or pastoral nomadic societies, whether Arab Bedouin, Berber, Mongol, or Turk. In this case it is one of many comments revealing, he believed, that early Arab Muslim history had evolved in an identical fashion and for the same environmental and social reasons as later North African tribal dynasties did.

As Arab Muslim armies slowly fought their way across North Africa, they began to convert Berber tribes to Islam, and some of these early converts subsequently constituted the majority of the Arab-led Muslim army that crossed the Gibraltar Strait in 711 on its way to profitable *jihads* in Iberia. These *jihads,* religiously sanctioned conquests, led one Andalusian poet later to write that "God created the Christians to be raided," in a *zajal* verse depicting lovers raiding the hearts of their beloveds.[26] Following the Muslims' rapid defeat of the Visigoths, the Germanic Christian rulers of the peninsula, Muslims occupied the principal Iberian river valleys in the south and east and then gradually moved north, until they were finally halted by Charles Martel, who was able to defeat a Muslim army at Poitiers in France in 732.

Despite the numerical predominance of Berber converts in these early Arab Muslim–led armies, Arabs remained the dominant social and political class in Andalusia throughout its history. Arabs attracted to Iberia's fertile agricultural lands gradually evolved into prosperous agrarian communities, closely linked with the principal Muslim fortress cities in each region. Well before the twelfth century, Ibn Khaldun's Yemeni ancestors had become, as rewards for their military service, part of the Andalusian Arab Muslim gentry, whose landed wealth, education, and social status gave them, in his family's case at least, social and political influence in various Andalusian cities. Members of the Banu Khaldun lineage are known to have served as prominent scholars and officials in both Seville and also Granada for centuries before the final Christian Reconquista of Andalusia.

Arab Muslims also dominated North Africa for several centuries after the initial conquest, but controlling the region was far more difficult and contentious for Arabs than governing Andalusia, given the overwhelming Berber majority. The Umayyad caliphs initially ruled North Africa as part of an Egyptian province, and Arab conquerors and occupiers treated Berber converts contemptuously as a subject class. Technically these new Muslims may have been *mawali*s, Arab tribal clients, but they were dealt with far worse than were the Arab Muslims' sophisticated Iranian converts. Arabs also brutally exploited unconverted Berbers as a source of booty, tribute, concubines, or slaves. In North Africa, ruthless Arab treatment of Berbers triggered an uprising in 739–740, as some tribesmen united around the same Khariji ideology that had inspired the well-known revolts in Iraq against the Umayyad Caliphate during the late seventh century.[27] This revolt fundamentally altered both Muslim North Africa and Andalusia.

THE KHARIJI REBELLION

Kharijis, who emerged as a distinct, dissenting faction during the Muslims' first *fitnah* or civil war in the mid-seventh century, rejected Arabs' claim to be the natural leaders of the Muslim community, and, more particularly, they objected to the Umayyad practice of hereditary succession to the Caliphate. They also preached an extreme doctrine in which a merely sinning Muslim could be labeled a heretic. Inspired, evidently, by Iraqi Arab Muslim Khariji propagandists, who traveled to North Africa, a group of Berbers united around the Kharijis' inclusive political ideals. This was the first documented North African instance in which Islamic sectarian ideology was used to unify a group of otherwise disparate and habitually antagonistic Berber tribesmen into a cohesive military force, in this case, challenging Arab Muslim rule from within the faith. While it did not lead to the establishment of a Berber tribal state at this time, it established a pattern for the catalytic role of religion in the emergence of the two major Berber tribal sultanates in the eleventh and twelfth centuries: the Almoravids and the Almohads. Ibn Khaldun later came to see religious ideology as a critical unifying force in the rise of many tribal dynasties and incorporated it into his model, although typically he does not explain what led him to develop this idea. Apart from demonstrating the importance of religious legitimacy as a kind of ideological glue that, in Ibn Khaldun's theory, magnified the strength of tribal social cohesion or 'asabiyah, the revolt had two serious consequences for both North Africa and Andalusia.

First of all, the Berber Khariji revolt decisively established the autonomy of North Africa within the Islamic world, for in 741 this Berber coalition defeated an Arab army dispatched by the Umayyad caliph in Damascus to reassert central Arab Muslim control of the region. In the following years neither the Damascene Umayyads nor their successors, the 'Abbasid caliphs of Baghdad (750–1258) succeeded in reestablishing direct control over the Maghrib. Second, as a consequence of the Berber victory, a new Arab element entered Andalusia, for remnants of the defeated Syrian forces subsequently fled across the straits to Iberia.

In Iberia these troops succeeded in allying themselves with Arab members of the original invading force, at least to the extent of suppressing Andalusian Berbers, who had joined in the anti-Arab revolt of their North African brethren.

ARABS AND BERBERS IN ANDALUSIA

The arrival of this new group of Arab Muslims in Andalusia also affected the nature of Andalusian society in two distinct ways. It diluted the influence of the original Yemeni Arab military contingent in Iberia. Far more important, the settlement of Umayyad-led Arab Muslim forces in Andalusia created an Umayyad bridgehead in Iberia, as some of these men were personally connected with the Umayyad caliphal family in Damascus. Following the ʿAbbasid Revolution in 750, when many Umayyad family members were massacred, some survivors of the family took refuge with their friends in Andalusia, and in a century-long series of bitterly contested campaigns between 756 and 852, Umayyads and their Syrian Arab allies founded an Iberian Umayyad Caliphate. The Umayyad victory further reinforced the military, social, and political dominance of Arab Muslims in the western Mediterranean, and it introduced Muslim imperial political and administrative traditions and the court culture of the Umayyad Caliphate of Damascus to the western frontiers of the Muslim world. Later, Andalusian refugees brought these traditions to North Africa.

Drawing on their own family's heritage as well as the influential example of the imposing Iranian-inspired imperial edifice constructed by the ʿAbbasid caliphs in Baghdad after 750, Iberian Umayyads ruling from Cordoba exploited their agricultural wealth and Mediterranean commercial connections to preside over a militarily powerful, administratively sophisticated, and culturally vibrant state, whose individual rulers proffered dazzling displays of their prosperity and piety through royal patronage. Until 1031 the Umayyads of Cordoba contrasted brilliantly both with Christian states to the north and also with the small, relatively impoverished North African Muslim regimes across the Mediterranean. The Arab Muslim Nasrids of Granada, Ibn Khaldun's sometime patrons, were the most prominent and successful of the regimes that rose out of the chaos following the Umayyad collapse—and the subsequent disintegration of the Berber Almohad regime in the thirteenth century. These Nasrids maintained their Arab predecessors' political and cultural traditions and became closely linked with Arab Muslim society and Muslim states throughout the Mediterranean.

The Umayyads represented a forceful continuance of Arab dominance in Andalusia, even as they employed Berber forces throughout the period of their rule. The Andalusian Umayyad caliph al-Hakam II (961–976), for example, recruited more than seven hundred Berber troops during his reign to replace Arabs, who by this time had settled on their estates and become an entrenched agrarian class. Umayyads, however, brought Berbers to Andalusia in tribal units, and these tribesmen evidently retained what Arabic sources termed their own Berber ʿasabiyah or social cohesion. Most Berbers also seem to have maintained their distinct cultural identity, and from the Arab point of view, they represented a foreign presence within the Iberian Muslim population. This remained true even when the Almoravid and Almohad Berber dynasties from the Maghrib successively occupied Andalusia in the eleventh and twelfth centuries. Both dynasties remained foreign North African regimes. Over the centuries only a few Berbers are known to have become socially prominent, politically influential members of the elite, Arab-dominated

Andalusian society. In some cases Berbers long settled in Andalusia found it advantageous to return to their native North Africa.

TRIBES AND DYNASTIES IN NORTH AFRICA

In composing the *Muqaddimah*, Ibn Khaldun offered a model to explain the signature political features of North African society and its history: the plethora of tribes and the tenuous fragility of tribal states. To understand the perennially unstable nature and limited duration of North African regimes, it is useful to reiterate that in the physical conditions of Ifriqiyah and the Maghrib, the lack of major rivers and scarcity of arable land dictated a small, scattered tribal settlement pattern outside the coastal towns that virtually eliminated the possibility of establishing large-scale, economically vibrant political structures. In describing this persisting socioeconomic and political reality of North Africa throughout most of the Islamic period to his day, Ibn Khaldun wrote that the innumerable number of Berber tribes in Ifriqiyah and the Maghrib made the region ungovernable. "Whenever one tribe is destroyed," he wrote, "another takes its place and is as refractory and rebellious as the former one had been."[28] Whether in this passage he meant the word *qabilah* to refer to tribes, tribal confederations, *buyutat,* houses, or family lineages is not clear, but the distinction is important.

As is true of his failure to define philosophical terminology, Ibn Khaldun does not pause to explain the terms he employs when he discusses pastoral nomads or farmers belonging to the same tribe.[29] He sometimes identifies Berber or Arab tribes as *ummah,* communities, or as *tawa'if,* peoples or groups, but he more commonly uses the word *qabilah* for large number of tribesmen. Yet he also sometimes employs *qabilah* to mean both a tribe and a tribal confederation, as when he says one particular *qabilah* belongs to another *qabilah*. He consistently says, however, that *qabilah*s consisted of varying numbers of *buyutat*, by which he meant small segments of tribes led by powerful families, designated *Banu*, literally "sons" of a particular family lineage. Occasionally he also uses the term *hayy*, which he distinguishes from *qabilah*, and *hayy* may mean something like the modern term *clan*. Distinguishing among various tribal segments is a crucial issue for his dialectical model, which is grounded in the idea that tribes, or parts of tribes, possessed *'asabiyah*, the crucial social sense or common identity that empowered them to vanquish sedentary states.[30]

Based on Ibn Khaldun's testimony and other evidence, historically and during his lifetime politics in North Africa was characterized by fluid, shifting alliances of innumerable families, clans, and tribes, which continually yielded new patterns of evanescent political formations. The persistent conflicts, which characterized personal and social relations within and among tribes, were bewilderingly complex. When asked if his tribe was united, the same tenth-century Kutamah tribesman who stressed the autonomy of individual male tribesmen, stated, "We fight each other and then make peace, and make peace with one group while we fight another."[31] Occasionally, as Ibn Khaldun tried to explain, out of this political maelstrom, important members of a particular *buyutat* or house emerged as tribal leaders to conquer towns and form a state. Apart from possessing *'asabiyah*, a sense of shared identity, and other vital traits of rural societies, houses or tribes who made this transition were often energized, he repeatedly says, by religion, which could double or triple their cohesion and ultimately their power of conquest.

North African political history can be divided into three relatively distinct periods between the time of the Berber revolt of

739–740 and Ibn Khaldun's birth in 1332. First, there was a period of more than two hundred years that featured the rule of three small, ephemeral, and localized states ruled by non-Berber dynasties over predominantly Berber inhabitants that climaxed with the rise of a Shi'i sect that founded the Fatimid dynasty of Egypt in 969. Second, this was followed by a period when two Berber lineages, the Almoravids and Almohads, conquered and ruled most of North Africa and also Andalusia between 1031 and 1269. Third, these two Berber empires were succeeded by a group of small Berber dynasties, whose seemingly endless struggles initiated an especially unstable, tumultuous period, which lasted throughout Ibn Khaldun's lifetime. The history and nature of these various states provided the data for Ibn Khaldun's dialectical model, as well as essential information for analyzing and also critiquing his ideas.

EARLY ISLAMIC NORTH AFRICA, 772–1054

An Iranian family ruled one of the earliest of these states, although in terms of ethnic composition, it was largely a Berber entity. Known as the Rustamids, its founder, 'Abd al-Rahman b. Rustam b. Bahram, named apparently after Rustam, the hero of the Iranian epic *the Shah Namah*, was an Iranian born in Tunisia, where he was converted to radical and, in Ibn Khaldun's mind, heretical Khariji ideology in Qayrawan.[32] After studying in Basra, the fountainhead of Khariji teachings, he returned to the Maghrib as a missionary, and, having formed a coalition of Berber tribes, he was elected as *Imam* in 772 and made his capital at Tahert in Algeria. There he presided over a small anti-'Abbasid Berber theocracy, really a city-state defined principally by its inhabitants' piety and spiritual exercises. It was a theocracy, nonetheless, noted for its tolerance of prosperous Christian merchants. The Rustamids represented the second major instance in Muslim North Africa of a state, formed by a tribal coalition united by a common allegiance to a religious leader, as well as the first of several subsequent occasions when a North African Muslim led a religious reform movement following a journey or pilgrimage to the Arab heartland. While unique in North African history as a government of an Iranian family lineage, one supported financially by a number of wealthy Iranian merchants, the Rustamid state nonetheless typified religiously inspired but politically fragile tribal states, more charismatically inspired tribal coalition than a structured bureaucratic polity. The political authority of the ruling family of hereditary Imams quickly atrophied as their original religious inspiration faded. By 909, the militant Ismaʿilis, the Fatimids, the movement of radical or revolutionary Shiʿahs, easily pushed the Rustamids aside into the desert.

Arabs ruled three other significant if ephemeral states during the eighth and ninth centuries C.E. The Idrisids first established a small state in Morocco and western Algeria. The founder, Idris b. ʿAbdallah (r. 789–791) was a Zaydi Shiʿah, a branch of the Shiʿi faith that most resembled Sunni Islam. Idris had fled from the Meccan region after suffering defeat in battle. Arriving as a refugee in Tilimsan, he relied for protection of the powerful, long-established Awrabah Berber tribe, whose chief proclaimed Idris as *Imam* six months after his arrival in the Tangier region, evidently exploiting Idris's quasi-Shiʿi charisma to solidify his tribal leadership. Idris's spiritual claim rested on his supposed descent from the Prophet Muhammad's Hashimi clan, a lineage that gave descendants known as *sharif*s, noble or highborn Muslims, a special sanctity and religious authority. Yet, typically for these tribal-based dynasties, which did not practice primogeniture, instead recognizing the right of any competent male family member to be a legitimate ruler, the Idrisids fragmented into multiple family units by the third generation.³³ It was less a dynasty than a contentious family enterprise. By the early ninth century the Idrisid state was divided into nine provinces ruled by nine brothers. Members of the family continued to rule parts of their original state until 985 C.E., when their rulers were besieged both by the Isma'ilis, then ruling in Egypt as the Fatimids, and also by the Umayyads of Andalusia.

Apart from exemplifying the fragile nature of Berber tribal lineages, or nearly any tribal dynasty for that matter, the Idrisids were important in the history of the Maghrib principally because they founded Fez, in southwestern Morocco, and this city later developed an increasingly Arab Muslim character as Arabs migrated there from Tunisia and Andalusia.³⁴ The association of Arabs with Fez, Mediterranean coastal towns, and religious centers is significant, because these towns became the islands of Arab urban Middle Eastern Islamic culture in a largely Berber sea, where heterodox religious sects continued to flourish. In the ninth century many Berbers were still Christians, Jews, or animists.³⁵ Even if they were Muslims, the majority of rural Berber-speaking tribesmen remained linguistically, culturally, and socially distinct in North Africa as they did in Andalusia, and few actively participated in the Arab Muslim culture of the towns, the cultural milieu of Ibn Khaldun and other sophisticated Muslim intellectuals.

The third of these non-Berber dynasties, the Aghlabids, was, nonetheless, culturally more important in these centuries than the Rustamids, Idrisids, or the bewildering miscellany of minor tribal chiefdoms that so swiftly rose to power and quickly fell into obscurity in North Africa throughout these centuries.³⁶ Ibrahim b. al-Aghlab, the founder of this lineage, which endured from 800 to 909, was an Arab official appointed by the 'Abbasid caliph, Harun al-Rashid (r. 786–809). The son of an important Arab family, he was educated in Cairo, and thus, unlike the Rustamids and Idrisids, personified high Arab urban culture of the time. While technically a caliphal agent, he and his successors remained largely autonomous, ruling a territory in eastern Algeria and Tunisia from a fortress just outside Qayrawan. Establishing an aristocratic Arab autocracy notable for its tyrannical brutality and self-indulgence, the Aghlabids were even more contemptuous of Berbers in the countryside than other Arabs had been, but they also showed little respect even for Arab commercial and artisan classes in their cities. Nonetheless, despite their social attitudes and brutal politics, the Aghlabids presided over a brief urban cultural golden age for Tunisia in the second half of the ninth century. They were great builders of mosques and other public buildings in Qayrawan and Tunis and transformed Qayrawan, already an important religious city in the late seventh century, into a major educational center for Islamic theology and law. During this period the town attracted scholars from throughout the Mediterranean Muslim world.

The dynasty's embrace of the 'Abbasid's Hanafi law was only one of many actions that alienated many of the indigenous *'ulama'*, the loosely knit class of Muslim religious scholars, mosque personnel, and government religious officials, whose members by this time had already embraced the conservative Maliki *madhhab*. The Maliki branch of religious law was an exceptionally conservative legal school derived from the teachings developed in Medina by Malik b. Anas. Maliki law remained the dominant and nearly exclusive branch of Islamic law in North Africa and Andalusia from this time forward.[37] As for the Aghlabids' political fate, their contempt for the Berber majority and even for their own Arab kin, whom they routinely massacred, combined with an ostentatiously self-indulgent life to destroy any legitimacy they might once have enjoyed. Their calamitous loss of prestige and influence left the dynasty incapable of resisting the Isma'ilis as they moved on Ifriqiyah, as well as overrunning the Rustamids and Idrisids.

It was the Fatimid Isma'ilis who dominated the last phase of this turbulent early Islamic period in North Africa between the Arab Muslim conquests and the later rise of the Berber Almoravid dynasty (ca. 1054–1137), which succeeded for the first time in unifying North Africa and Andalusia. As part of a systematic missionary program of *da'iyah*s or spiritual emissaries, Isma'ilis had initiated their quest for sovereignty by dispatching agents from Syria to various parts of the Muslim world. One such man, a Yemeni, contacted and converted a group of Kutamah Berbers in 892, while they were performing the *hajj* in Mecca. Like other religious leaders, who entered North Africa before or after him, this man, Husayn b. al-Zakariya', began his religious mission as a guest under the protection of a particular Berber tribe. Like later Almoravid leaders, he enforced strict military discipline among his followers, and as his victories increased, other North African tribes joined his cause, a common demonstration among tribal confederations throughout the Middle East and Central Asia of how a powerful charisma could be generated by military success and the distribution of plunder.

Al-Zakariya' founded a nascent state, legitimizing his rule through the Shi'i doctrine of the *Imam,* a hereditary spiritual lineage descended from the family of the Prophet Muhammad. Nonetheless, he converted most of the Maliki Sunni Muslims in the region to the Isma'ili Shi'i cause by force. After first failing to conquer Egypt in the early tenth century, the Fatimids sought to extend their authority over both Ifriqiyah and the Maghrib, and they spent more than four decades unsuccessfully trying to subjugate all of Morocco. Failing to accomplish this owing to the military opposition of the Umayyads of Andalusia and the hostility of local Maliki scholars, the Fatimids' religious intolerance and oppressive taxation policies triggered a major Sunni Muslim rebellion in North Africa in 945. Nonetheless, by 969 the Fatimids finally conquered Egypt and emerged as a major force in Ifriqiyah, as well as in the broader Islamic world.

For Ibn Khaldun and many North African historians, the most notable consequence of the clash between the Fatimids and North African Muslims who resisted their rule was the Fatimid decision to punish the Zirids, a group of Sinhajah Berbers who had acted as vassals of the Fatimids in late tenth-century Algeria and Tunisia. In the mid-eleventh century the Zirids, who, Ibn Khaldun reports, had raised the sedentary culture and consequently the crafts of Tunis to a high level, revolted against the Fatimids, perhaps because of pressure from the overwhelmingly Sunni population of North Africa, including influential Maliki jurists in Qayrawan.[38] The Zirids proclaimed themselves Sunnis, and in an explicitly insurrectionary act, recognized the authority of the ʿAbbasid caliphs, the Sunni enemies of the Fatimids. In retaliation Fatimids unleashed on Ifriqiyah two exceptionally primitive Arab Bedouin tribal groups from the Hijaz, the Banu Hilal and Banu Sulaym, whose rustic members had long been a disruptive, destructive presence in Egypt.

These two loosely knit tribes or tribal confederations mobilized an estimated force of fifty thousand warriors, like most such estimates, probably exaggerated, but perhaps at least a reliable indicator of their substantial numbers. Their eruption into North Africa increased the Arab element in the countryside but at a terrible cost to its sedentary society.[39] The tribesmen tore much of sedentary Ifriqiyah and the Maghrib to pieces, destroying small towns and agricultural settlements. Their depredation gave Ibn Khaldun his most persuasive evidence of the destructive nature of all primitive bedouins, all primitive tribesmen, in this case actual Arab Bedouins, who he knew wreaked havoc on any settled society they encountered, as Arab Muslims had earlier done, he writes, in Yemen. His comments on these tribes' depredations help illumine his sense of self, which he reveals in various contexts throughout the *Muqaddimah*. In this instance Ibn Khaldun's denunciation of the Banu Hilal and Banu Sulaym demonstrates his lack of racial consciousness when it came to the destruction of sedentary society and advanced urban culture, his underlying personal concern about North African civilization. In these cases he did not, it is important to emphasize, prefer Arabs to Berbers but favored towns over the rural hinterland and literate, cultured urbanites over primitive, uncultured bedouins, whatever their ethnicity.

THE BERBER MONARCHIES, 1054-1269

Nearly contemporaneous with this Arab Bedouin onslaught, North Africa experienced the first of two successive Berber tribal dynasties, the Almoravids (1054-1137), later succeeded by the Almohads (1120-1269).[40] These dynasties represent the next or Berber imperial phase of the region's history, which Ibn Khaldun's narrates in the *Kitāb al-'ibar*. By contrast, in the *Muqaddimah* he does not chronicle their history but cites the evidence of their culture, social structure, and history to illustrate different aspects of his dialectical model. Most of all, he argues, the dynasties exemplified two fundamental aspects of his ideas: the primitive simplicity of what he terms Berber bedouins, that is, Berber tribes, and the doubling effect religious ideology had on the social cohesion and ultimately the military power of pastoral nomads. He might also have added that Almohad rulers also patronized the most important philosophers in the western Islamic world. One of these men, Ibn Rushd, was probably responsible for Ibn Khaldun's accurate understanding of Aristotelian thought.

The history of the first of these Berber dynasties, the Almoravids, provided Ibn Khaldun with what he considered to be one of his earliest well-documented examples of the rise and fall of a tribal coalition, united by the reformist religious ideology of its leaders. Citing evidence from the dynasty repeatedly in the *Muqaddimah,* he thought Almoravid history illustrated how a coalition of primitive nomadic and seminomadic tribesmen gradually coalesced around religious doctrine and developed into a cohesive military force, which subjugated urban centers and established a new dynasty—which then deteriorated and collapsed within a century of its initial conquests. His generalizations about the rise to power of this tribal coalition and others have to be viewed, however, with the same rationalist analysis he used to critique other Muslim historians. The early histories of these tribal dynasties are poorly documented, and Ibn Khaldun's accounts, while often persuasive, do not always fully substantiate his theories.

The name *Almoravid,* the Spanish rendition of the Arabic *al-mulaththamun,* "the muffled," was a name given to these tribesmen because of their distinctive face-muffle protection against the windblown Sahara sand. They retained their distinctive physical identity throughout their brief political history. The Almoravid tribal homeland was located deep in the Western Sahara between the Maghrib and the African region of Mali. The dynasty originated when the chief of the Gudalah, one of the tribes of the larger Sinhajah Berber group Ibn Khaldun variously labels as *ummah*, communities, or *tā'ifah*, a people, returned from *hajj* in 1035. Inspired by his religious experience in the Hijaz, this man stopped in Qayrawan and enlisted an ʿ*alim,* a Muslim cleric, a member of another Sinhajah tribe, to accompany him to the tribe's distant and desolate homeland far to the southwest. There he introduced basic Islamic doctrine to his superficially Islamized Sinhajah tribesmen. Initially this missionary, ʿAbdullah b. Yasin (d. 1059), enforced a brutal, puritanical regime, so offending tribal customs that infuriated tribesmen drove him away. He fled and found tribal supporters in yet another Sinhajah tribe or clan, the Lamtunah, who embraced his religious mission, perhaps with a view to increasing their own power within the larger tribal confederation. Members of the Lamtunah became the elite of the Almoravid movement, sharing, in Ibn Khaldun's assessment, a strong sense of social solidarity, or in his terms, a strong ʿ*asabiyah* or group feeling.[41]

The history of the Almoravids closely approximates certain aspects of Ibn Khaldun's dialectical model of North African history, for not only did the Lamtunah, initially led by an elite family of camel-herding nomads, possess ʿ*asabiyah,* but, Ibn Khaldun argued, the lineage doubled the strength of that social cohesion and consequently their own power, because they, like the later Almohads, professed a Muslim reformist ideology.[42] Yet, there is no real evidence that tribal ʿ*asabiyah* initially affected more than a small fraction of tribal members. In its early history, Ibn Yasin, as he is generally known, cooperated with the chief of another branch of the Sinhajah group forcefully to subjugate his fellow tribesmen, including his own clan. This was a brutal, nasty business, typical, as has been suggested, of the early history of these tribal regimes. Modeling himself on Muhammad, Ibn Yasin sought to replicate Muhammad's initial campaigns from Medina against Mecca to defeat and unite tribes around a religious ideal.

After Ibn Yasin's death in 1059 his brother, Abu Bakr, and a cousin, Ibn Tashfin, neither of whom laid claim to Ibn Yasin's religious authority, commanded Almoravid armies and established what amounted to a Lamtunah tribal oligarchy with members of this particular Sinhajah tribe, constituting its privileged warrior and aristocratic class. These men turned their backs on the relatively sophisticated and socially liberal ethos of Idrisid Fez and built a new city, Marrakesh, perhaps because Fez offended their puritan sensibilities and also as a consideration that the new city was situated closer to their tribal homelands in the south. Ibn Tashfin, who became the dominant Almoravid leader in the later years of the century, was an ascetic tribal chief of simple habits who exemplified the social and religious purity Ibn Khaldun respected as vital characteristics of tribesmen, uncorrupted by sedentary society.

In religious or ideological terms, the Almoravids advocated a simple reformist Muslim faith, articulated by *fuqaha'* or religious scholars, who relied, however, not on the Quran and *hadith*, for most Muslims, Islam's original and sacred spiritual sources, but on Maliki legal texts. Scholars who adhered to this *madhhab* or legal school became and remained partisans for and partners of this regime. Ibn Khaldun reports, dismissively, that the Almoravids professed a "simple religion," one he characterized as having anthropomorphic characteristics of a primitive faith,[43] which he believed to be a symptomatic product of their isolated, rural nomadic environment. His comment also typifies how a highly cultured, urban, upper-class Arab Muslim regarded the religious attitudes of Berber coreligionists in the countryside: vital perhaps but intellectually primitive.

Maliki clerics did preach an exceptionally restrictive legalistic faith and condemned *kalam* or rationalist theology, by then a technique of religious argument widely accepted by many Muslim theologians, who used Aristotelian logic to prove the tenets of the faith. The Almoravid rulers and their clerical allies became so intolerant of this logically infused theology that in 1109 Ibn Tashfin's son ordered a book of the great Iranian-born theologian and his near contemporary al-Ghazali (1058–1111), titled *The Revival of the Religious Sciences*, burned. He threatened death to anyone who possessed the scholar's texts. Later their antagonists and successors, the Almohads reversed Almoravid religious policy and al-Ghazali's works became accepted throughout North Africa, as in most other Sunni lands, as the standard orthodox doctrine of Ibn Khaldun's sophisticated class of urban Muslim scholars.

Al-Ghazali's book was burned in the courtyard of the great mosque of Cordoba, which Almoravids had made their Iberian capital after their victories in Andalusia. The western Umayyad Caliphate had collapsed in 1031, giving rise to a congeries of minor rulers of small states, known in Arabic as the *muluk al-tawa'if*, and in its Spanish translation, as the *reyes de taifa*s, literally and accurately rendered as the "kings of factions." In 1086 Ibn Tashfin crossed the straits with a reported twelve thousand men, nearly all Berbers, and most Iberian Muslim inhabitants, Arabs included, appear to have welcomed the new dynasty, since Almoravids restored order in the chaotic politics of post-Umayyad Muslim Iberia, fended off newly aggressive Christian monarchs who threatened Andalusia, and abolished all but canonical taxes sanctioned by the Quran. Members of the Iberian *'ulama'*, many of whom were members of prosperous mercantile families, seem to have been especially enthusiastic, for the Almoravids restored social order and also patronized clerics who were adherents of Maliki law as their natural ideological allies. Otherwise in Spain they imposed a narrow Lamtunah family regime allied with Andalusian Maliki clerics and kept themselves separate from the bulk of the Iberian Muslim population, while excluding most Andalusians from military leadership. They ruled, in essence, as an ideologically charged Berber colonial regime, Muslim but not really an integral part of Andalusian urban culture, a society and culture that they must have felt represented a foreign homeland.

The Almoravids constituted a brittle, socially isolated dynasty, which began to fragment just as soon as it ceased to conduct profitable anti-Christian *jihad*s in Iberia. Yet, for all its dynastic isolation and oppressive legalism, Almoravid rule bequeathed two important legacies to North Africa. First, it laid the foundation for the dominance of Maliki *fiqh* throughout Ifriqiyah, the Maghrib, and West Africa. As rulers of both North Africa and Andalusia, it also raised the administrative, cultural, and scientific quality of North African society and states by encouraging, as Ibn Khaldun repeatedly notes, Andalusian bureaucrats and scholars from Iberia's sophisticated states to take positions in the relatively less-developed North African courts. North Africa became and long remained something of an employment agency for the émigré Andalusian literati class. In Spain itself Almoravid rule disappeared within a single generation, compromised by its oppressive, legalistic religious policies, the corruption of elite Berber families, and, most of all, by the eventual failure of its anti-Christian *jihad* and the taxes it then began imposing to pay for its increasingly futile campaigns. Its rise and precipitous collapse provided Ibn Khaldun with one critical set of data for his dialectical model of tribal dynastic cycles.

It was, appropriately enough for North African politics and Ibn Khaldun's model, in the Berber tribal homelands, not Iberia, where the most serious challenge to the dynasty arose, the threat of yet another religiously fueled Berber tribal confederation. These were the Almohads, led by Muhammad b. Tumart, a Harghah Berber tribesman from the Anti-Atlas mountains who returned from studies in Cordoba and Baghdad to preach a purified Muslim faith. Almohad, like Almoravid, is a Spanish rendition of an Arabic word, in this case *al-Muwahiddun,* the "Unitarians." Like the Almoravid Ibn Tashfin, Ibn Tumart personified the archetypal tribal leader, also a religious reformer, in that he was a man of simple tastes who never married and did not seek or attain great wealth. In his case, though, he condemned the primitive, anthropomorphic legalism of the Almoravids, preaching instead a return to the fundamental faith of early Islam.

Ibn Tumart, preaching and writing in Berber, emphasized *tauhid,* the unity of God, a knowledge acquired from studying the two original sources for the faith, the Quran and the *hadith,* which had been relegated to secondary importance by their legalistic predecessors. Ibn Khaldun characterized the essence of Ibn Tumart's religious message to be an adoption of the faith of conservative Ash'ari speculative theologians, a tradition, as will be seen, he belonged to himself. The swing of the sectarian pendulum between the Almoravid and Almohad eras was illustrated by the order of one Almohad leader to publicly incinerate Maliki legal texts, just as an Almoravid had burned al-Ghazali's work in Cordoba.

Ibn Tumart exemplified the repeated North African phenomena of religious teachers who either came from the eastern cultural centers of Islam or North Africa or were inspired by their education there or during their experience in the *hajj.* More than any earlier ideologues, except possibly the Isma'ilis, Ibn Tumart claimed to possess a powerful religious charisma as the *Mahdi,* the "Expected One," of the Islamic millennium. His claim was, as

Ibn Khaldun points out, essentially a Shiʻi message.[44] He first took the title of the *Imam al-maʻsum,* the "Infallible *Imam*," having previously constructed a spurious genealogy, demonstrating he was a *saiyid,* a descendant of the Prophet Muhammad.

Ibn Khaldun also characterizes Ibn Tumart and his early followers, as he does Ibn Tashfin, as the personification of simple "bedouins," who initially exemplified the typical "desert" mentality he often praised or at least respected. He was a man who taught his followers "the ways of religion and simplicity," forswearing garments of silk and gold, sleeping in simple tents, and only later assuming the political trappings of sedentary culture by embracing luxury and the culture of the palace."[45] Ibn Khaldun also reports that they, like the Almoravids, were typical of tribal insurgents in that they took nearly thirty years of struggle before gaining power.[46] In doing so he provides another glimpse into reality of the rise to power of tribal dynasties.

Nonetheless, like Ibn Yasin before him, Ibn Tumart could only realize his religious vision with Berber tribal support and like his Almoravid predecessor and the Prophet Muhammad he initially achieved his goal of establishing a new reformist regime by force of arms. After initially failing to win support in the Almoravid capital, Marrakesh, he fled to his homeland in the Atlas Mountains and, secure within his own Harghah tribe, gained support of the Masmudah confederation to which his tribe belonged. Then from 1124 to 1125 he began transforming his religious reform movement into a military force capable of overthrowing the Almoravid regime. Employing draconian tactics, including a purge and the reported slaughter of thousands of his own insufficiently pious or obsequious community of believers, he founded a nascent state based on tribal social structures, with his relatives, his *buyutat* or household, and early converts constituting the inner circle of the new regime. His early murderous brutality should give pause to anyone who may be inclined to believe that tribesmen in the thousands spontaneously flocked to the banners and doctrines of such men. It was brute force rather than faith, power rather than ʿasabiyah, that initially brought most tribesmen to the Almohad side. Belief or at least affirmation of the religious message followed only later; whether ʿasabiyah did also is impossible to say. The degree to which the influence or the reality of ʿasabiyah shaped this or other tribal dynasties remains a largely unresolved issue in Ibn Khaldun's model, which will be discussed in Chapter 4.

Despite the fervent religious commitment of Ibn Tumart, following his death in 1159 the Almohad regime assumed more of the character of a tribal monarchy dedicated to conquest and plunder, rather than one concerned with systematic religious or social reform. Under his immediate successor, ʿAbd al-Muʾmin (r. 1130–1163), the Almohad Berber army conquered the entire coastal zone of the Maghrib by the 1150s, but it did so with appalling brutality, massacring and persecuting thousands of civilians, including a reported thirty thousand Berbers suspected of disloyalty, following a revolt in 1148. In the 1150s ʿAbd al-Muʾmin also brought a number of Arab tribesmen to settle in Morocco, diluting the Berber population there and introducing another highly disruptive tribal element in the region. A year earlier Almohad Berbers had occupied Fez and the Almohad capital of Marrakesh, and in 1148 defectors from the Iberian Almoravids took Seville for the new Berber regime. With its conquests in Andalusia, climaxed a half century later with a victory over Castile in 1195, the Almohad state, with the help of sophisticated Andalusian personnel, gradually evolved into a third phase of a bureaucratic state, controlled by ʿAbd al-Muʾmin's descendants. It was the kind of progression from primitive tribe to monarchical regime Ibn Khaldun depicts when he describes the evolution of tribal states.

Remarkably, later Almohad rulers neither sustained a claim to be descended from or to represent the *Mahdi,* nor did they codify, much less institutionalize, Ibn Tumart's theology—either by disseminating texts or establishing *madrasahs.* ʿAbd al-Muʾmin's grandson at least had Maliki texts burned but at the same time publicly rejected the idea Ibn Tumart had been the Mahdi. These later Almohad rulers are principally memorable and important for their intellectual interests and patronage of Andalusia's three most notable *falasifah* or philosophers: Ibn Bajjah (d. 1138–1139), the Latin Avempace; Ibn Tufayl (1105–1185); and, most significant, the great Aristotelian scholar Ibn Rushd (Averroes) (1126–1198). All three men were born in Andalusia, but they also spent considerable time at Marrakesh, the Almohad capital.[47] They constituted a significant but ephemeral philosophical moment in the western Islamic world.

Ibn Bajjah introduced Greco-Islamic rationalism to Andalusia. Ibn Tufayl, who enjoyed cordial relations with the Almohad caliph Abu Yaʿqub Yusuf and acted as a court physician, is known for his belief in unaided reason in determining truth and his conviction that there was harmony not conflict between reason and revelation. This idea was a theme of Muslim Neoplatonism, the confusing pastiche of Platonic and Aristotelian ideas popular among philosophically inclined Almohad rulers. Ibn Tufayl is also justly famous as the individual who introduced Ibn Rushd to Abu Yaʿqub Yusuf in 1169.

Ibn Rushd's works, especially his commentaries on Aristotle's texts, are important for understanding Ibn Khaldun's *Muqaddimah.* More than any other individual, this enormously productive scholar bequeathed a fundamental philosophical legacy to the Islamic and European worlds in his insistence on reclaiming Aristotle's original meaning and his disentangling of Aristotle's and Plato's thought from the bewildering philosophical thickets of Neoplatonism. Ibn Khaldun, as well as some of his scholarly contemporaries in Iberia and North Africa, studied Ibn Rushd's careful recapitulation of Aristotle's principal works. It is possible to suggest, although not to demonstrate, this philosopher's greatest influence on Islamic thought was Ibn Khaldun's *Muqaddimah,* as his Aristotelian commentaries and other philosophical works otherwise had little discernable influence on other Muslims, even while they became the first textual sources for Aristotelian thought in France and medieval Europe. They continued to influence European intellectuals during the Italian Renaissance. At that time in Italy "Averroism" became a contentious ideological issue, as it had been to a degree earlier in Thomas Aquinas's Paris.

Apart from providing historical grist for Ibn Khaldun's dialectical mill, Almoravid and Almohad dynasties together exerted profound combined effects on the subsequent history and culture of North Africa. First, Almoravid commitment to Maliki law ensured that *madhhab* would continue as the predominant Muslim legal tradition in the Maghrib, and its hold on the ʿulamaʾ of the region continued after the Almohad period, even down to the present day. Second, the Almohad embrace of al-Ghazali's rationalist theology enshrined an Aristotelian logical strain among Muslim religious scholars, hitherto largely untouched by the philosophical developments in the Muslim heartland of Iraq, Iran, and Egypt. In his religious thought, Ibn Khaldun belonged, as he showed by his comments in the *Muqaddimah,* to the sophisticated, moderate, and philosophically informed Islamic faith of al-Ghazali, himself a student of speculative theology. Third, both the Almoravid and Almohad conquests and simultaneous rule of Andalusia and North Africa stimulated the further migration of Spanish Muslims to North African courts, where, as Ibn Khaldun noted when discussing the Almohads in particular, they served as administrators and architects, as well as enriching the local *'ulama'* class with literati and intellectuals from the relatively more sophisticated urban centers of Andalusia. The Almohads also unified the Maghrib under a single government for the first and last time before being defeated by a tribal uprising against their rule in the mid-thirteenth century C.E.

LATER BERBER STATES, 1169–1373

It was yet another North African tribal group, the Marinids, Zanatah Berbers, who overthrew their former overlords in a long series of campaigns against the principal Almohad towns in Morocco, capturing Fez in 1248 and the Almohad capital of Marrakesh in 1269.[48] The collapse of the Almohads began a new phase in the history of the Maghrib. The Marinids and two other Berber dynasties, the Hafsids of Tunis and the 'Abd al-Wadids of Tilimsan, dominated most of North Africa in the decades immediately prior to Ibn Khaldun's birth and during his lifetime. All three Berber lineages, but especially the Marinids, exemplified Ibn Khaldun's model of an evolution of a tribe or tribal house from rural tribesmen to sedentary rulers. The Marinids, 'Abd al-Wadids, and Hafsids all had been at one time or another, willingly or unwillingly, associated with the Almohads, and they initially retained many of the social and administrative traits of their former overlords. The Hafsids in particular publicly conducted themselves as the political heirs of the former regime. Struggles among these lineages, directly or indirectly also involving many small tribal "houses," became the norm in the region for many decades.

Regarding the Marinids of Fez, Ibn Khaldun reported that nomadic tribesmen within the Zanatah Berber group of *umam* or communities were in his words, like the Arabs, Kurds, Turkomans, and the Turks, "the most savage human beings who exist."[49] Originally, like their predecessors, an exceptionally rustic group of pastoral nomads, they migrated in territory near the present border of Morocco and Algeria, along the southern edge of the Atlas Mountains. Zanatahs were, Ibn Khaldun added, "among human beings what beasts of prey are among dumb animals."[50] Thus, he said, they had the power to defeat other communities. The tribe provided rulers for the Marinids based in Morocco and the Abd al-Wadids, the latter, a minor lineage, which fitfully controlled the region in and around Tilimsan. The two dynasties fielded an estimated three thousand and one thousand troops, respectively, at the beginning of their rule, a valid measure of the modest size of these states.[51]

The Marinids, who used Fez not Marrakesh as their capital, developed into the most prosperous and powerful of the three successor regimes. Little is known about the founder of the Marinid lineage, but its rulers conducted successful campaigns in Iberia against Castile and in the mid-fourteenth century briefly subjugated nearly all North Africa, twice successfully invading territories of the Hafsids and ʿAbd al-Wadids. Led by their most formidable ruler, Abu l-Hasan (r. 1331–1348), they occupied Tilimsan in 1337 and used their base there to seize Ibn Khaldun's Tunis in 1347, when he still resided in the city. After suffering a defeat at the hands of local tribes in 1348, they retreated back to the Maghrib but returned to Ifriqiyah under Abu ʿInan (r. 1348–1358) between 1352 and 1358, occupying Tunis once again in 1357. After the sultan, who led these later campaigns, died in 1358, the Marinids declined into internecine dynastic conflicts under short-lived sultans, which Ibn Khaldun participated in after he moved to Fez in 1352.

The ʿAbd al-Wadids of Tilimsan were also Zanatah Berbers, whose power originated as partisans of the Almohad campaigns in Ifriqiyah. The founder of the city-state of Tilimsan was one Yaghmurasan, the *shaikh* or chief of a section of the Zanatah tribe. A man who spoke only a Berber dialect, he ruled in Tilimsan from 1236 to 1283, first as an Almohad feudatory and subsequently as a rival of the more powerful Marinids of Fez, as well as with the Hafsids of Tunis. His rule involved a remarkably successful balancing act, which involved mediating among his own Zanatah relatives, cooperating with the rapacious Banu Hilal bedouins in the countryside, defending his small city-state by forming alliances with Muslim Granada and Christian Castile, and expanding his power by exploiting Hafsid weaknesses whenever possible. Between 1337 and 1359 his successors in Tilimsan were twice overrun by the Marinids, who occupied the city for a total of seventeen years, but the ʿAbd al-Wadids regained control of the principality in 1359, led by a particularly effective and enlightened chief, Abu Hammu II, who ruled until 1389, well after the time Ibn Khaldun emigrated to Egypt.

The Hafsids were also Berbers, who traced their own history to a companion of Ibn Tumart, and regarded themselves as descendants of the Almohad regime, as did Ibn Khaldun, who, when thinking of their reign, spoke of living in "Almohad times."[84] They became an independent dynasty in Tunis in 1259. The founder of the state gradually expanded his authority and by the end of his life established paramount authority over northern Morocco and parts of Andalusia. This man, Abu Zakariya Yahya (r. 1228–1249), decorated Tunis with the physical trappings of sovereignty, the beginning of an imposing sedentary culture, which Ibn Khaldun grew up in and admired, including a market and the oldest public *madrasah* or seminary in North Africa. Later rulers added to the imposing religious architecture of the city. Perhaps more than any other North African lineage, the Hafsids benefited from the flow of experienced émigré Muslims fleeing the Christian Reconquista in Iberia, who brought administrative talents to help develop the Hafsid state. Hafsid rulers, for example, appointed experienced Andalusians who hailed from the Granada region to collect their taxes.[53]

In the early decades of the fourteenth century, however, Hafsids became increasingly threatened by internecine disputes, persistent conflicts with Arab tribes, and battles with the ʿAbd al-Wadids. By the middle of the century, three Hafsids ruled different cities in Ifriqiyah, with various Arab families in control of lesser towns and parts of the immediate countryside. The rulers of what were little more than city-states lost any semblance of control in their desert hinterlands and constantly fought with one another for supremacy. The political situation became so atomized and chaotic as to defy easy summary. Only in 1370 did a single Hafsid ruler regain control over nearly all the dynasty's historic lands, after which the dynasty enjoyed something of a renaissance.

Ibn Khaldun was born into and educated up to his twentieth year in this exceptionally unstable, impossibly complex Berber- and Arab-dominated tribal political environment. It was characterized by persistent conflict, within and among these three lineages, which also involved unnamed other families, clans, or tribes within their presumptive territories and throughout the adjacent countryside. In political terms the Marinids, Abd al-Wadids, and Hafsids constituted decentralized tribal confederations, which ruled during a period Ibn Khaldun repeatedly decries for its bedouin depredations and consequent decay of urban life. Speaking of the Maghrib, Ibn Khaldun wrote: "today all or most of it is a waste, empty, and desert area, except for the coastal regions of the hills near it."[54] Ifriqiyah, he thought, had fared somewhat better, and it still retained "traces" of sedentary culture, principally in Tunis, partly because of its proximity to Egypt and Cairo's flourishing urban society.[55] Political fragmentation was reflected in the minuscule armies fielded by various combatants, reflected in Ibn Khaldun's observation that "we live in a time when dynasties possess small armies, which cannot mistake each other on the field of battle. Most of the soldiers of both parties together," he continues, "could nowadays be assembled in a hamlet or a town."[56] Arabs constituted a larger percentage of the population than they had done four hundred years earlier, but in Ibn Khaldun's eyes the intellectual integrity and vitality of Arab Muslim urban culture, including even the scribal skills of clerks and administrators in Fez, had declined everywhere as towns and cities decayed amid the internecine struggles of tribal lineages.

Even in Andalusia, Ibn Khaldun's idealized ancestral homeland, where the Nasrids still maintained themselves amid political revolutions and encroaching Christian powers, Ibn Khaldun believed the social cohesion and therefore the power of Arab Muslims had largely evaporated, leaving behind a fragile, vulnerable Granadan state. He was adamant that 'asabiyah had long since disappeared among Andalusians, and he criticizes the philosopher Ibn Rushd to make his point. Ibn Rushd, Ibn Khaldun reports, wrote in an abridgement of Aristotle's *Rhetoric* that townsmen possessed prestige if they were descended from older residents in a particular town. Ibn Khaldun writes that the philosopher failed to realize that descent did not produce prestige, and that if such men tried to use rhetoric to influence others, they would fail because they had no power. "I should like to know," he writes dismissively of Ibn Rushd's notion, "how long residence in a town can help (anyone to gain prestige) if he does not belong to a group that makes him feared." He notes that Ibn Rushd could not be expected to understand that individuals derived power from their membership in a cohesive social group that possessed ʿasabiyah, since he lived at a time when people no longer possessed this sense of social cohesion.[57]

To have Ibn Khaldun regard even fourteenth-century Andalusia as a failed society suggests something of the despair he felt about the depressed cultural state of the western Islamic world. His repeated allusion to the deterioration of urban life in both North Africa and Andalusia seems like a deeply felt cri de coeur. It also highlights a dilemma of an individual like Ibn Khaldun, who was a creature of urban society, for, as will be seen in the analysis of his dialectical historical model, he believed that in North Africa fully developed urban society contained the seeds of its own inevitable destruction. He was never able to discover in the urban settings of his homeland the social coherence and vitality that explained, he felt, not only the rise of North African tribal dynasties but also the triumph of Muhammad and the Rightly Guided Caliphs. Yet he decried the undeveloped simplicity and cultural ignorance he observed in the early phases of tribal dynasties. Ibn Khaldun was not the first and certainly not the last highly educated intellectual to regard his own society as stagnant and corrupt while admiring its earlier simpler and supposedly purer form as vital and dynamic. Nor was he the first individual to feel this way without noting the irony of his own situation. What is remarkable is that he particularly, a man from a traditional, upper-class Arab Muslim urban household, should use philosophy to offer a sophisticated explanation for North Africa's depressing political circumstance as well as his homeland's tortured earlier history.

2

THE TWO PATHS
TO KNOWLEDGE

IBN KHALDUN WAS EDUCATED amid the fractious political environment and cultural decay of his North African homeland, but he nonetheless benefited from his family's privileged status in Tunis and received the best possible training for a potential scholar-official, education both in the religious and also the philosophic sciences. His education left him with a commitment to two forms of knowledge, revelation and reason. By the evidence of the *Muqaddimah* and his memoir, he did not experience any difficulty in simultaneously affirming the truth of Muhammad's prophetic message, while vigorously asserting the validity of reason when it came to examining the external world, including the arenas of society and politics. Islam, submission to God, demanded the uncritical faith of Abrahamic revealed religions, but faith in reason required the logical, analytical study of the material world. In embracing both forms of knowledge, Ibn Khaldun was hardly an original or unique figure in the Mediterranean world. Both Greeks and Greco-Islamic thinkers had done so earlier.[1]

Ibn Rushd wrote an essay titled the *Decisive Treatise on the Relation of Philosophy and Religion*, in which he asserted the parity of the two forms of knowledge in an attempt to negate theologians' sustained assault on Greco-Islamic philosophy. In it he stressed the truth and supremacy of Islam and the necessity of faith for salvation, since reason could not penetrate the spiritual realm. At the same time Ibn Rushd revealed his rationalist bias and maintained that philosophical reasoning through logical demonstration produced the highest form of truth, whereas theologians and the public relied on dialectic and rhetoric, less rigorous methods of reasoning.[2] In saying this he comes very close to rejecting faith as a valid means of acquiring knowledge, and earlier al-Farabi had unambiguously asserted philosophy's precedence over religion when it came to the certainty of proof.[3] Unlike Ibn Rushd and al-Farabi, Ibn Khaldun was not a philosopher and evidently felt no need to debate this issue at length, but he implicitly agreed with Ibn Rushd's stated position on the comparable validity of faith and reason. That is, he rejected the idea that reason trumped faith when it came to acquiring knowledge of the divine. He merely asserted, almost in passing, that philosophy prevailed over faith when it came to explaining the dynamics of North African, Iberian, and even Arab Muslim political history.

Nonetheless Ibn Khaldun's comments can leave readers uncertain as to what he ultimately thought about the relative values of religion and philosophy. In the *Muqaddimah* he cites, without comment, the hostile attitude of Byzantine emperors and early Arab Muslim leaders toward what he calls the "intellectual sciences": logic, physics, metaphysics, and mathematics. Probably alluding to Justinian I's closure of the Platonic Academy in 529, Ibn Khaldun observes that after the Byzantine emperors adopted Christianity, they "shunned" the philosophic sciences "as religious groups and their laws require," and in the case of the second Muslim caliph, ʿUmar b. al-Khattab (r. 634–644), he reports that following the Muslim conquest of the Iranian Sasanid Empire (224–651), the caliph ordered his men to destroy the huge cache of books and scientific papers they had captured, saying: "Throw them into the water. If what they contain is right guidance, God has given us better guidance. If it is error, God has protected us against it."[4] Yet not only does he suggest by his wording that he did not approve of clerical-mandated destruction of books, rather than praising Christian and Muslim assaults on secular learning, he expresses regret over the loss of Iranian sciences and subsequently lauds the scientific achievements of Muslim urban culture. Some Muslim scholars, he notes with evident pride, even "contradicted the First Teacher (Aristotle) on many points" and generally "surpassed their predecessors in the intellectual sciences."[5] He also repeats his lament, a requiem really by the end of the *Muqaddimah,* for the decline of scientific scholarship in North Africa and Andalusia in his day, remarking that only a few isolated individuals and orthodox religious scholars maintained these scholarly traditions.

Still Ibn Khaldun does criticize the subversive influence of philosophy on Islam, saying that these intellectual sciences and their "representatives succeeded in some degree in penetrating Islam. They seduced many people who were eager to study those sciences and accept the opinions expressed in them. In this respect, the sin falls upon the person who commits it."[6] It is not, however, so difficult to reconcile such seemingly contradictory comments, as Ibn Khaldun in subsequent sections of the *Muqaddimah* reserves his criticism of philosophy almost entirely for metaphysics—and the misuse of logic in the service of metaphysics—the one philosophical discipline that questions the assumptions of revealed religion.

A PROFESSIONAL EDUCATION

As a student and a privileged young man in Tunis, Ibn Khaldun benefited from an introduction to both the revealed and also the rational paths to knowledge, and, as an individual with a ravenous and seemingly unquenchable intellectual thirst, he continued studying these sciences throughout his career. As far as one can conclude from pronouncements in the *Muqaddimah* and his memoir, Ibn Khaldun's Islamic education, initially the product of schooling during his Tunisian years, left him with the restrained, sophisticated faith of many elite urban Muslims of his time and place: an unquestioned faith in the unique and final prophetic role of Muhammad, a conservative but logically rigorous theology probably derived from the teachings of the theologian Abu Hamid Muhammad ibn Muhammad al-Ghazali and his speculative theological predecessors, an appreciation of Sufi teachings without noticeable commitment to the mystical practices of a particular order, and a zealous professional attachment to the conservative Maliki juridical tradition.

The rational intellect could not, Ibn Khaldun vigorously asserted, comprehend God; nor could reason be trusted to offer an alternative explanation of the creation or provide a valid moral guide for human behavior. It was nonetheless able to explain all facets of human existence. As was the case also with many contemporary Christians who were familiar with Greek philosophical thought, Ibn Khaldun valued rational sciences that dealt with the visible world, such as poetry, rhetoric, physics, and mathematics. Ibn Khaldun's training in the philosophical sciences, which also began in Tunis, revealed an extensive knowledge of Greek and Greco-Islamic thinkers, especially Aristotle, Galen, Ibn Sina, and the Muslim Aristotelian, Ibn Rushd.

Based on his testimony, Ibn Khaldun began his education studying both the Islamic and the rational sciences under his father's tutelage, a formative period lasting until both his parents, along with many thousands of North Africans and Andalusians, died of the plague in 1348–1349. As would have been typical for a son of an erudite and socially prominent family, he studied a standard curriculum that would qualify him for either scholarly or administrative professions, such as the secretarial and governmental posts he describes in the *Muqaddimah* and held at various periods in his career. In addition to his father, his teachers included a number of locally prominent Tunisian and Moroccan scholars, as well as Andalusian émigrés, so many of whom, like Ibn Khaldun's family, had taken refuge in Tunis or other North African towns as Christians reduced the boundaries of Andalusia to the sliver of territory held by the Nasrid rulers of Granada in southeastern Iberia.

With his father and other scholars in Tunis, he initially mastered a traditional curriculum in the religious sciences. He studied Arabic with his father and several Tunisian grammarians and literary scholars and the Quran and didactic religious poems with a number of individuals, including another émigré or refugee from Andalusia, Abu 'Abdallah Muhammad al-Ansari. During these years Ibn Khaldun also read commentaries on Maliki law, as well as the founding text of that legal school, the *Kitab al-Muwatta'* by the Medinian scholar Imam Malik (c. 711–795). This training laid the basis for his lifelong engagement with religious law, which led to his appointments as Maliki *qadi* or judge of religious law in Tunis and Cairo. Throughout his memoir he alludes to his studies of Maliki law and repeatedly expresses admiration for accomplished legal scholars of that school, proudly reporting that when he arrived in Cairo in 1382 the Turkic Mamluk, sultan of Egypt, acknowledged his reputation by identifying him as "al-Maliki" in a formal pronouncement of welcome. Nonetheless, however accomplished a student of Maliki law, Ibn Khaldun is not known to have composed original legal commentaries or to have become a noted legal scholar, although he appears to have succeeded as a dynamic teacher of law. The modesty of his legal credentials may have been one of several reasons why established Maliki jurists in Tunis and Cairo resented him when rulers passed them over to appoint Ibn Khaldun to lucrative and prestigious judicial posts in their cities.

During his youth Ibn Khaldun also benefited from the arrival in Tunis of scholars from nearby towns. Many came to the city in 1347 in the train of the Marinid Sultan Abu l-Hasan, who occupied the city during his successful military campaign in Ifriqiyah.[7] Some of these learned men had previously resided in Tilimsan, the caravan and commercial center, which since the thirteenth century had attracted settlers fleeing the Christian Reconquista of Iberia. These included scholars of Maliki law, experts in *hadith*, authorities in Quranic studies, and a man he particularly identifies as a friend, Abu Qasim 'Abu Allah b. Yusuf b. Ridwan, a native of Malaga in Andalusia and a literate official, calligrapher, poet, and intellectual—a model *adib*. As he mentions in his memoir, Ibn Khaldun knew Ibn Ridwan to be not merely an intellectual or a member of the literati class but also a practiced official, whose skills he admired and may have tried to emulate when later he accepted his first position at court in Tunis. Another man who accompanied the Marinid sultan to Tunis at this time was Muhammad b. Sulayman al-Sati, a North African native of the Fez, in Ibn Khaldun's words, an "incomparable scholar of Maliki law," whose critical legal scholarship Ibn Khaldun reports knowing well.[8]

In terms of Ibn Khaldun's historical thought, the most influential man who accompanied the Marinid sultan to Tunis was Abu ʿAbdallah Muhammad b. Ibrahim al-Abili, the "great master of the rational sciences."[9] Al-Abili had formed a friendship with Ibn Khaldun's father, which offered Ibn Khaldun the opportunity to work with this eminent scholar, who evidently exerted a transformative influence on his young student. With al-Abili Ibn Khaldun began the study of the rational sciences with mathematics and logic, the two fundamental sciences, he notes, within philosophy.[10] It is impossible to know the titles of most of the philosophical texts Ibn Khaldun studied at this early period. He probably read many of these works later in life, including at least some of the voluminous writings of Ibn Rushd, the Andalusian Aristotelian. Nonetheless, it was his study of Greek and Greco-Islamic philosophical thought that provided him with the materialist assumptions, logical methodology, social ideas, and terminology he later employed to formulate his innovative methodology and dialectical model. In the medieval Muslim and Christian worlds, philosophical study comprised logic and metaphysics, as well as such subjects as physics and mathematics that in Europe, until relatively recently, were categorized in Aristotelian terms as natural philosophy.

Al-Abili, who became Ibn Khaldun's principal teacher of the rational sciences, was a member of an Andalusian Muslim family from Avila in northern Spain that had settled in Tilimsan in the thirteenth century. Born of a prestigious union between his father and the daughter of the *qadi* of Tilimsan, al-Abili demonstrated a penchant for the sciences as a youth and in particular developed a passion for mathematics, in which he excelled. In the early years of the fourteenth century, he fled from a recently besieged Tilimsan to go on *hajj,* and he arrived in Egypt at a time when its inhabitants included many scholars of the rational and traditional or religious sciences. Returning to Tilimsan sometime before 1310, he later moved to Fez and then Marrakesh, where he studied with the eminent Moroccan mathematician, astronomer, and mystic devotee of astrology and the occult, Ibn al-Banna' al-Marrakushi (d. 1331). Al-Abili, who later returned to his home in Tilimsan, was a man profoundly influenced by some of the giants of Greco-Islamic thought, in particular the philosopher and logician al-Farabi (872–951), the Neoplatonist philosopher, Ibn Sina (980–1037), the Andalusian Aristotelian Ibn Rushd, and the Sunni Muslim theologian and philosopher Fakhr al-Din al-Razi (1149–1209). These men were four of the most important Greco-Islamic scholars, whose thought was informed by Greek philosophical treatises that had been translated into Arabic during the reigns of the 'Abbasid caliphs of Baghdad.

In 1348–1349 Ibn Khaldun's initial period of schooling abruptly and tragically ended when both his parents died of the plague. During the next three years he nonetheless continued his formal education. In particular he continued working with al-Abili, and in 1351, at age nineteen, he completed an abridgement of a work of al-Razi's titled *Lubab al-Muhassal fi usul al-din*.[11] Al-Razi was a disciple of al-Ghazali, whose influential theological works had been burned by the Almoravids but respected and resurrected by the Almohads. Al-Razi subscribed to the conservative school of speculative theology, which Ibn Khaldun describes appreciatively in the *Muqaddimah*. A polymath but essentially, as Ibn Khaldun notes, a theologian, al-Razi wrote on a dazzlingly broad variety of religious and philosophical issues, including his criticism of the Neoplatonic doctrines of Ibn Sina.[12] In abridging this complex work, Ibn Khaldun demonstrated a sophisticated comprehension of al-Razi's critique of Ibn Sina's thought, as well as an appreciation for the philosophical response to these arguments by Nasir al-Din al-Tusi (1201–1274), the Iranian Shi'i theologian and natural philosopher.

Al-Tusi, in contrast to al-Razi, while a pious Shi'ah who wrote ambitious theological and ethical treatises, became one of the Muslim world's foremost natural philosophers. He produced esoteric studies of mathematics, geometry, physics, and, perhaps most notably, astronomy, which he pursued for two decades while he worked near Tabriz as the court astrologer/astronomer of the Il-Khanid Mongol rulers of Iran. Ibn Khaldun's précis of this complex text hints at the intellectual level of his studies during this period. He does not, however, suggest anywhere in the *Muqaddimah* that he was inspired by al-Razi's logically informed theology or al-Tusi's critique and defense of Ibn Sina's ideas, to pursue a particular line of study. In retrospect, Ibn Khaldun's completion of this précis represents something of a graduation exercise. It marks the end of his student days, for the following year, at age twenty, he accepted a minor post as a calligrapher at the Hafsid Tunisian court, then thoroughly subordinated to the Marinid dynasty at Fez.

THE RELIGIOUS SCIENCES

Ibn Khaldun may be intellectually situated between these two scholars. Both al-Razi and his critic al-Tusi were men who occupied a middle ground on the spectrum of Muslim intellectuals, neither mindlessly conservative nor radically secular. Like al-Razi and al-Tusi, Ibn Khaldun was a Muslim who believed, as he remarks when discussing the importance of religious law, in the legitimacy and fundamental purpose of faith. "The entire world," he warned, "is trifling and futile. It ends in death and annihilation... The purpose (of human beings) is their religion, which leads them to happiness in the other world."[13] In contrast to rational or philosophical speculation, the Islamic religious sciences, the Quran, and associated disciplines such as religious law rested on unquestioning belief in divine authority. "There is no place for the intellect in them," Ibn Khaldun wrote, although he, like many other scholars who were heirs of al-Ghazali, utilized Aristotelian logic to ratify particular aspects of Islamic doctrine.[14] Furthermore, Ibn Khaldun categorically asserted, revealing his uncompromising faith in terms that must be taken seriously, that whereas other religions possessed somewhat similar kinds of spiritual sciences, "Islam is different from all other religious groups, because it abrogates them."[15] In consequence, "The religious law has forbidden the study of all revealed scriptures except the Qur'ān."[16] Ibn Khaldun, for all his research into the history of non-Muslim peoples, evidently took this prohibition to heart. He never exhibited a sustained interest in other faiths, although he was familiar with the histories of Abrahamic faiths and, evidently, some aspects of Zoroastrianism.[17]

The Islamic sciences were based on Muhammad's divinely inspired revelation, the Quran, as well as on the Prophet's practices and observations known as the *Sunnah,* or "tradition," which was preserved in *hadith,* the reports of Muhammad's actions or conversations. Muslim sciences were expressed in and studied through Arabic, the language of God's revelation. Many distinct subjects, Ibn Khaldun continued, comprised the body of Muslim sciences, including in order of importance, he continued, Quran reading, Arabic grammar, *tafsir* or Quranic interpretation, *hadith* studies, and jurisprudence or *fiqh,* which, he asserted, was "one of the greatest and most important and most useful disciplines of the religious law." This latter juridical science or *fiqh* was devoted, he writes, to "the knowledge of the classification of the laws of God, which concern the actions of all responsible Muslims."[18]

Ibn Khaldun's religious life and occupation as a religious judge and teacher of Maliki jurisprudence represented a distinct aspect of his mental world, and his piety and juridical profession were as typical of his class and era as his historical ideas were revolutionary. Raised as a Sunni Muslim educated in traditional Islamic subjects, Ibn Khaldun remained an unquestioning, and, in terms of his attitude to Christians, an uncompromising believer throughout his life. His faith comprised the following: belief in the unity or oneness of God, "the real core of the articles of the faith"; the divinity of Muhammad's revelation; Muhammad's unique status as a prophet in the Mosaic tradition; the existence of the soul as a spiritual entity, distinct and hidden from the corporeal world; and the power of the simple profession of faith "There is no God but God" to guarantee entry into heaven.[19] The spectrum of Ibn Khaldun's faith ranged from a common religiosity he shared with the general public to a sophisticated knowledge of the speculative or Ash'ari theology articulated by al-Ghazali and his disciple al-Razi.

PIETY

He shared the common Muslim belief, first of all, that certain individuals manifested exceptional spiritual qualities in their daily life. Such persons included prophets, soothsayers, augurs, and Sufis, but all possessed the same recognizable traits. They were innocent, morally blameless individuals, who enjoyed prestige in their own society, individuals who were also outwardly pious and, above all else, had the ability to work wonders or miracles, acts that other human beings could not perform. The immediate physical sign of their special spiritual status was signaled by occasions on which they became abstracted from their surroundings and suffered a kind of fit or relapsed into an unconscious state that indicated a degree of connection with the spiritual world. Prophets were the most important individuals who experienced supernatural perceptions, for their souls were the most complex and sophisticated, allowing them simultaneously to have contact with both the angelic sphere and the mundane human worlds.[20] God created them in order that they could know him and communicate his divine will for rightly guided human life that would culminate in salvation. Muhammad, as Ibn Khaldun describes him, resembled other prophets only to the extent he, like them, was a unique individual of his time, one whose soul simultaneously coexisted with the spiritual and the material world.

Yet, the Prophet Muhammad, Ibn Khaldun argues, not only possessed all the qualities of earlier individuals, who had supernatural perceptions, but he exhibited the greatest miracle of all when God spoke through him and revealed the Quran, "the greatest, noblest and clearest miracle."[21] The Quran was, in the philosophical vocabulary, which in this argument Ibn Khaldun may have borrowed from the idiom of speculative theology, "its own proof," uniting "in itself both the proof and what is to be proved."[22] Not only was the Quran a wondrous miracle, Ibn Khaldun argues, it was a unique book in the prophetic tradition since it represented a direct revelation in which Muhammad recorded God's own Arabic words. This revelation thus differed from that of biblical prophets, who used their own human vocabulary, after God had transmitted his ideas to them.[23] The Quran was, therefore, "inimitable" as was every *surah* or verse in it. Thus as Ibn Khaldun demonstrates but does not explicitly say, when

Muslims referred to Muhammad as the "Seal of the Prophets" they did not mean simply that he was the final prophet in the Mosaic tradition, who "abrogated" earlier revelations; they also meant he was superior to all others, since his revelation preserved God's words, and, as God said to Muhammad, he gave him an Arabic Quran, thus sanctifying the language.

Prophets, however, constituted only the most superior type of individual who had contact with the supernatural. Reasoning again like a speculative theologian by using logic to prove a religious point, Ibn Khaldun insists logic "requires" that other, spiritually less perfect individuals must also exist. If, he says, there are souls capable of moving between angelic and human perception, that necessarily means other less perfect types must also be found, "as inferior to the first kind as anything that has something perfect for its opposite must be inferior to that (perfect) opposite."[24] Soothsaying, as Ibn Khaldun presents it, represented the perception of individuals whose souls were inferior by nature, a comment that raises questions, one of several such statements in the *Muqaddimah* that appears to complicate his insistence on a common human nature. Such persons had the power of imagination he says, which allowed them, again invoking idioms of Aristotelian thought, to see only particulars rather than universals, either of the senses or the imagination. In Aristotelian terms, individuals who could perceive only particulars and could not generalize from what they sensed or imagined belonged to the intellectual hoi polloi, a conceptually deficient class. Soothsayers had some limited and imperfect ability to attain supernatural perception, but alluding to the *kuhhan*, the soothsayers of Muhammad's day, Ibn Khaldun, says that they received knowledge from their own souls as well as from the devils and thus, unlike prophets, often spoke both truth and falsehoods. Superior soothsayers were distinguished, according to Ibn Khaldun, by their ability to speak in rhymed prose. Ibn Khaldun himself was able to write rhymed Arabic prose, but this talent did not prompt him to claim to be a soothsayer, something that would probably have seemed very déclassé for someone of his birth, education, and social status.

Other individuals, such as augurs, Ibn Khaldun writes, might have limited contact with the divine, as they were blessed with imaginative powers, similar to those who experienced dream visions, to interpret certain events. Far more important than augurs, however, were Sufis, individuals within the Muslim population who in their mystical states were capable of having valid supernatural experiences. Ibn Khaldun's appointment in 1389 in Cairo as the *shaikh*, the head of the Sufi Baybarsiyyah *khanagah*, a Sufi center of worship in the city, suggests that he at least sympathized with Sufi piety, although the comparatively lavish income from this *waqf*, or religious endowment, must also have attracted him. Whatever his immediate motives in accepting this position, he gives a sympathetic account of early Sufi doctrine in the *Muqaddimah*.[25]

As Ibn Khaldun notes, the earliest Sufis did not follow complex rituals or articulate elaborate religious doctrines; they merely withdrew from the world, practiced asceticism, and constantly performed divine worship. Later they developed certain spiritual exercises, such as rhythmic chanting or *dhikr*, which allowed them to pierce the opaque veil of sense perception and to perceive the spiritual world. In fact, Ibn Khaldun asserts, only by practicing *dhikr* exercises could ordinary men achieve this knowledge of the divine.[26] While many Muslim jurists criticized Sufis and sometimes entirely repudiated Sufi faith and practice, Ibn Khaldun rejected the idea that arguments and proofs could rationally analyze the Sufi path, as it belonged to "intuitive experience."[27] He accepted the validity of Sufi mystical or ecstatic experiences as constituting a special kind of human perception—not rational but emotional—and wrote that Sufis' reports of receiving divine grace were sound. It appears his appreciation of Sufism and its relation to orthodox worship was rooted in the thought of al-Ghazali, whose integration of moderate Sufism within broadly accepted principles of Islamic belief legitimized mysticism as a valid aspect of the faith. After citing al-Ghazali's writings on Sufism, Ibn Khaldun concludes: "Thus the science of Sufism became a systematically treated discipline in Islam."[28]

Beyond these specific instances of divine perception, all men, Ibn Khaldun implies, possessed the ability to have a kind of temporary access to the otherwise inaccessible spiritual world in their dream visions. Some of these individuals were prophets like Muhammad, who, he says, experienced such visions for a six-month period at the beginning of his prophetic mission. He implies, however, that all men, whether or not they exhibited special moral or physical qualities associated with prophecy, soothsaying, or augury, could perceive the spiritual realm while asleep. Dream visions were valid, Ibn Khaldun writes, because sleep freed people from the physical world and the limited perceptions of that sphere of existence. This was possible because the rational soul was composed of a physical animal spirit, an entity, which had, he points out, been described by the Greek philosopher and physician Galen, for Muslims, the third most influential Greek or classical rationalist thinker after Plato and Aristotle.[29]

As Ibn Khaldun represented Galen's ideas, "The spirit is a fine vapor which is concentrated in the left cavity of the heart, as stated in the anatomical works of Galen and others. It spreads with the blood in the veins and arteries and makes sensual perception, motion and all other corporeal actions possible. Its finest part goes to the brain."[30] Sleep allowed the soul, preoccupied in daytime with the corporeal world, to turn inward toward its spiritual essence, giving it the ability to have supernatural or spiritual sensations, and briefly, at least, enabled it to acquire insight into future events. Souls did not give humans the same power or status as prophets, but nonetheless allowed them to enjoy a fleeting glimpse of the divine world—at least if the visions were God given. On the other hand, some disturbed or opaque dreams, Ibn Khaldun reports, originated with the devil. His argument represents an implicit reminder that only prophets were capable of offering pure or uncorrupted visions of the divine.

THEOLOGY

Ibn Khaldun's piety and seemingly uncritical belief that humans other than prophets could perceive or have contact with the spiritual world reveal an aspect of his religion he shared with many individuals in the wider Muslim population. The intellectual sophistication that distinguished him from less-well-educated Muslims is not only suggested by the logical vocabulary he frequently used when discussing the most mundane religious topics. It was also demonstrated by his knowledge of and value he attributed to the discipline known as speculative theology, which revealed him to be a Muslim intellectual in the well-established conservative theological tradition of al-Ash'ari, al-Ghazali, and al-Razi.

Speculative theology is a "science," Ibn Khaldun reports, "that involves arguing with logical proofs in defense of the articles of the faith and refuting innovators who deviate in their dogmas from the early Muslims and Muslim orthodoxly."[31] Abu'l-Hasan al-Ash'ari (d. 936) was the most influential founder of this theological school, whose doctrines Ibn Tumart, the founder of the Berber Almohad dynasty, may have studied during his brief tenure as a student in Baghdad. Al-Ash'ari affirmed many of the doctrines of "ancient Muslims" by employing logic to defend tenets of the faith. "He refuted the innovators," Ibn Khaldun reported, so that, in Ibn Khaldun's words, "innovations may be repulsed and doubts and misgivings concerning the articles of the faith be removed."[32] One of the four texts of speculative theology dealing with Islamic law, which Ibn Khaldun approvingly cites, is one that suggests the prevalent use of logic among theologians of this school. Written by al-Ghazali's Ash'ari teacher, Abu l-Ma'ali al-Juwayni (1085–1128), otherwise and more popularly known as Imam al-Haramayn, the treatise is suggestively titled *Kitab al-burhan fi usul al-fiqh* or *The Book of Categorical Proofs in Jurisprudence*.[33] The author probably chose the first part of the title intentionally to echo Aristotle's fourth book of logic, in Arabic the *Kitab al-burhan*. *Burhan* is, not so incidentally, the term Ibn Khaldun uses when he claims to have demonstratively and irrefutably, that is, logically, proven an argument. In philosophical terms *burhan* was an apodictic proof, exemplified in mathematics by the simple equation $2+2=4$.[34]

Speculative theology differed from the philosophical procedure by which Ibn Khaldun identified fundamental truths of human society in the *Muqaddimah* through inductive reasoning, that is, by first identifying essences or natures of things or people in the external or corporeal world, which became his premises or axioms. The speculative theologian's fundamental truths or, in logical terms, his basic premises, were the divinity of the Quran and the sanctity of the Sunnah. These were premises based on faith rather than being intuited through reason, and originally speculative theology used reason only to ratify faith. Beyond that modest goal, the Quran taught that men who used logic in an original effort to try to understand the creation became lost, confused, and ultimately unable to reach God.[35] Men, Muslims were taught, must necessarily abstain from using their intellect for spiritual purposes. "The intellect should not be used to weigh such matters as the oneness of God, the other world, the truth of prophecy, the real character of the divine attributes, or anything else that lies beyond the level of the intellect... When the lawmaker (Muhammad) guides us toward some perception, we must prefer that (perception) to our own perception."[36]

Given this command, logic had, Ibn Khaldun notes, "only a single fruit" when it came to religion; "it sharpens the mind in the orderly presentation of proofs and arguments."[37] It could not be used to understand the resurrection, which only religious law was able to explain, and, in fact, logic contained ideas contrary to religious law and students ought never to study logic until the religious sciences were mastered.[38] The phrase *speculative theology* was therefore mistranslated. It was never speculative in the philosophical sense, and Ibn Khaldun, in fact, remarks that originally the word meant no more than the "science of speech or talk."[39] Its theologians, he added, "do not use the (rational) arguments they talk about as do the philosophers, in order to investigate the truth of the (articles of faith), to prove the truth of what had previously not been known," but "to bolster the articles of faith and the opinions of early Muslims concerning them and to refute the doubts of innovators who believe that their perceptions... are rational ones."[40] "The intellect," Ibn Khaldun continues, rephrasing previous arguments, "has nothing to do with religious law," which is known to be true because it is derived from the

Quran and *hadith*.[41] Eventually Ibn Khaldun played a kind of classical trump card by concluding: "The great philosopher Plato said that no certainty could be achieved with regard to the Divine."[42]

Al-Ash'ari, for example, refuted the "innovations" of the school of philosophically inclined Muslim theologians known as the Mu'tazilah. These scholars, who were active between the eighth and tenth centuries, valued reason as a means of interpreting faith. In comments that revealed how strongly he felt that rationalist thought was antithetical to revealed religion, Ibn Khaldun applauded al-Ash'ari and his followers for repudiating the Mu'tazilah assumption that humans' intellectual power gave them the ability to understand God and his creation. It was absurd to think, Ibn Khaldun argued, that people could perceive spiritual essence, which existed outside of or above the corporeal world. He cites as an example of disreputable Mu'tazilah reasoning the idea that the Quran was created, instead of eternally existing, denouncing this and other Mu'tazili "innovations" such as their belief that man was "the creator of his own actions and that ... [they] have nothing to do with the divine power ... Originally they had denied predestination."[43] He also recalls how some of the 'Abbasid caliphs, who accepted Mu'tazili ideas, persecuted leaders of the *'ulama'*, who, he approvingly notes, opposed such innovations and, as good speculative theologians, used logic to ratify the fundamental tenets of the faith.

Eventually, Ibn Khaldun notes, as Muslims became more familiar with logic, they did begin to use it not merely as al-Ash'ari had done, to support traditional tenets of the faith, but aggressively to refute philosophers, reasoning that arguments derived from studies of physics and metaphysics were irrelevant to theology. Al-Ghazali, was, Ibn Khaldun remarks, the first scholar in this so-called school of recent scholars. Indeed, in his famous treatise, *Tahafut al-falasifah (The Incoherence of the Philosophers)*, al-Ghazali indirectly criticized Aristotle, or at least Aristotelian metaphysics, using Aristotelian logic, and directly attacked the Muslim rationalists al-Farabi and Ibn Sina. His principal goal was to demonstrate that their arguments did not fulfill the standard of *burhan*, irrefutable demonstrative proof.[44] Yet Ibn Khaldun also observes in an enigmatic aside, which suggests his own conflicted view of these questions, that these "recent theologians" sometimes contradicted some articles of the faith. He then concludes that these later thinkers proved "many premises of the premises of speculative theologians were wrong."[45] In making this point, he seems implicitly to be agreeing with al-Farabi and Ibn Rushd in their insistence that philosophy offered a standard of proof that surpassed theological reasoning, but he does not explicitly discuss the issue.

Ultimately Ibn Khaldun even cautions students to be careful about following the speculative theologians in using logic to defend theological positions. Asserting that students of the faith need not study this school, he says the "School of Later Scholars," al-Ghazali and others, became so enamored of the use of logic that theology and philosophy became inextricably intertwined and students could not distinguish one field from another. "Recent speculative theologians," he writes, "confused the problems of theology with those of philosophy." Theology "deals with articles of faith derived from religious law as transmitted by the early Muslims ... The intellect has nothing to do with the religious law and its views."[46] Expressing the conservatism many Muslim scholars felt about the dangers of ordinary individuals assimilating poorly understood philosophical ideas, Ibn Khaldun says that since orthodox *'ulama'* had already destroyed "heretics and innovators" the majority of Muslims need not concern themselves with speculative theology.[47] Still, Ibn Khaldun wrote that a few scholars, educated men such as himself, ought to study this discipline. If they did, then they should consult the works of al-Ghazali and al-Razi rather than later (unnamed) non-Arab scholars, Iranians most probably, who universally embraced this dangerous philosophical discipline.[48]

In his defense of Islam, Ibn Khaldun reserved his strongest criticism of philosophy for metaphysics. In the course of explaining the two sciences, Ibn Khaldun devotes a special section to "A Refutation of Philosophy." Like his warning about the limited applicability of logic in speculative theology, Ibn Khaldun evidently wrote the "Refutation" to throw a mental cordon sanitaire around Islamic doctrine, protecting it from rational speculation. In the essay he specifies thinkers whose philosophical thought included metaphysics, beginning with Aristotle and including the Muslim thinkers al-Farabi and Ibn Sina, al-Ghazali's principal targets, whom he criticizes because they "restrict themselves to affirming the intellect and neglect everything beyond it."[49] "They also think," Ibn Khaldun writes, "that the articles of the faith are established as correct through (intellectual) speculation and not through tradition ... Such people are called "philosophers"—*falasifah*."[50] Metaphysics was a threat to revealed religion, he argued, because its Greek and Muslim practitioners assumed they could analyze and explain "beyond," *meta,* the physical world. He even criticizes Aristotle, the Muslims' First Teacher, because the logic he systematized contributed to metaphysical speculation. "He [Aristotle] would, in fact, have done very well with his norm of logic if (only) it had absolved him of responsibility for the philosophical tendencies that concern metaphysics."[51] After all, it is well known, he reminds readers, that humans cannot, unless they are prophets, perceive the whole of existence, the spiritual as well as the physical.

CONSERVATISM

Ibn Khaldun articulated, therefore, a nearly immaculate Sunni orthodoxy, characteristic of many educated Muslim scholars of his time; it was a precise, emotionally restrained faith in the tradition of al-Ghazali. Typically for someone of his class and faith, he strongly criticized what he considered the irresponsible religious propaganda of Shi'ahs and some Sufis. Many Sufis, Ibn Khaldun reported, were influenced by Shi'i predictions of the appearance of the *Mahdi*, an idea, as he makes clear, mixed up with that of the Second Coming of Christ. Acknowledging the prevalence of the belief that a descendant of the Prophet Muhammad would appear on earth in order to purify Islam and reestablish justice, Ibn Khaldun systematically critiqued the *hadith* literature testifying to its validity. His exhaustive and exhausting critical analysis of these traditions exemplified this mode of personality criticism, which '*ulama*' employed to verify the Prophet's *Sunnah*. He found most individuals who transmitted this idea were unreliable; "few," he reported, could be accepted. In addition, most of those who believed such an individual would appear were ignorant common people, who blindly accepted popular traditions, "not guided by any intelligence or helped by any knowledge."[52]

Ibn Khaldun's ultimate proof that *hadith* proclaiming the coming of the *Mahdi* were unreliable was, he points out, the undeniable fact that despite the predicted appearance of such a figure, he had never materialized.[53] He ultimately suggests that the *Mahdi* stories should be seen as examples of propaganda designed to influence political causes that do not usually succeed, because those who claimed to represent the *Mahdi* did not usually share in or possess the ʿ*asabiyah,* the social cohesion, needed to force people to accept such notions. His dismissal of these millenarian appeals seems partly rooted in practical politics, his fear of social chaos, and his deep attachment to the political stability and stratified society that typified most Muslim political theorists.

Ibn Khaldun's religious and social conservatism can be more fully understood from his discussions of two pursuits explicitly or implicitly associated with religion: astrology and alchemy. In addition to philosophy, both astrology and alchemy were capable, he says, of doing great harm to religion. Astrology he refutes with logical proofs, pointing out that astrologers, who believe they can predict events through heavenly studies, may easily be disproved. Arguments for astrology are worthless, he asserts, both when examined rationally and when measured against religious doctrine. Citing Ptolemy's guarded conclusions about the validity of astrology, Ibn Khaldun observes it has never been proven that every star has a particular power and that even Ptolemy's method proving that the five observable planets exert influence is weak. More to the point, Ibn Khaldun argues, he has proven previously with deductive arguments about causation "that there is no agent but God."[54] Prophecy too, he adds, citing a *hadith* quoting Muhammad, rejects the notion that the stars influence humans' fates. Religious law, Ibn Khaldun adds, forbids Muslims from studying astrology.[55] In addition, Ibn Khaldun, an upper-class individual who speaks contemptuously of popular enthusiasm and quotes verse condemning rebellion reports that astrological predictions of crises, with which he was familiar, damaged society by encouraging revolt and threatening peoples' faith and the stability of governments. "We have," he concludes, "observed much of the sort."[56]

Alchemy, too, he denounces. Rejecting the idea it could be considered a science, Ibn Khaldun suggests that if alchemy were possible, as some philosophers suggest, it would have to be considered a miracle, an act of divine grace, or an act of sorcery. "It may be sorcery, because the sorcerer . . . may change the identity of matter by his magic power."[57] "No intelligent person," he says, "doubts the existence of sorcery," but religious laws forbid it because, like astrology, it focuses on other beings rather than God.[58] In social terms it is contemptible and dangerous, as it is prompted by ignorance and greed. Many alchemists, he argued, were charlatans who preyed on the stupid masses, deceiving especially ignorant Berber tribesmen in the countryside. Apart from despicably defrauding rich but naive bedouins who, like all people, desired gold and silver, alchemists posed a danger to the economy, for their activities threatened the value of the currency. Rulers, therefore, were obligated to act against alchemists who threatened everyone's wealth. Then, after citing arguments supporting the validity of alchemy, Ibn Khaldun systematically sets about to refute the idea. His arguments are philosophical, religious, and socioeconomic.

First he agrees with Ibn Sina, who, as a philosopher, dismissed the possibility of transmutation of elements, since each element constituted a different species and belonged to a different genus, rendering transmutation impossible. Each element, in fact, possessed a different nature, the fundamental Aristotelian idea, composed of different proportions of the four elements—earth, air, fire, and water—comprising each thing. Second, each created thing, including human beings, went through a series of stages, and gold, he reports, evolved over a period of 1,080 years. It would be impossible, therefore, to transmute elements instantaneously. Third, it was God's plan that gold and silver would be rare, so people could have a standard measure of profit. It would be counter to divine will and damaging to the economy if precious metals could be produced at will. Finally, Ibn Khaldun observed from his privileged social height, only the poor, who are incapable of making a living, practiced or believed in alchemy, whereas Ibn Sina, who was a *wazir* and a wealthy man, said alchemy was impossible.[59]

Ibn Khaldun's presentation of his religious beliefs and critique of the threats to faith and society were not examples of original theology but erudite recapitulations of Sunni orthodoxy, tinged with his conservative social and political views. He was no more a theologian than he was a philosopher. In discussing his faith in light of what is known about his career, what stands out is his devotion to the practice of Islamic law and impassioned assertion that jurisprudence represented one of the most important religious sciences. Jurisprudence was, after all, where orthodox theology was given practical application. In religious terms, Ibn Khaldun was a legalist, and the nature of his orthodoxy can be more clearly seen in his discussion of Islamic law and more substantially in his repeated allusions to Maliki scholars, his own studies, and his précis of the history and characteristics of the four traditional Sunni legal schools, or *madhhabs*, as a subsection of his discussion of the "traditional" or Islamic sciences. He points out that the four extant legal schools evolved from two original schools, the Iraqi, whose scholars emphasized the use of opinion, *qiyas*, and analogy, and the Hijazis, who based their rulings on tradition. Of the four, he says that his own specialty, the conservative, tradition-bound Maliki school, predominated among Maghribis and Spanish Muslims.

Ibn Khaldun provides a standard description of Muslim legal history and then concentrates on the Maliki school, which emphasized, he reports, tradition rather than the use of *qiyas* or analogy, the principal trait of the Iraqi school. His explanation for the principal characteristic of the Maliki legal school, its simplicity, is consistent with his social model, for he derived it from his analysis of the two types of human social organizations, rural tribes and city dwellers. Bedouins, that is, members of rural tribes of various ethnicities, were mentally characterized by a naturally unrefined or uneducated mentality, in contrast with the complex intellects of the residents of densely populated cities. Most of the Maliki scholars did not speculate but relied on tradition, for "most of them are Magribis who are bedouins, who cared only a little for the crafts."[60] Maliki legal thinking consequently lacked complexity or sophistication. Ibn Khaldun notes that students of Malik b. Anas, the founder of the Maliki school, had previously spread his legal ideas to Egypt and Iraq, but that in his day this school was largely, if not entirely, confined to North Africans and Iberian Muslims, although his Cairo appointment as a Maliki *qadi* suggests that substantial numbers of Maliki devotees still lived in that city in the late fourteenth century.

Ibn Khaldun then repeats his conviction that jurisprudence, his own profession, was "one of the greatest, most important, and most useful [scientific] disciplines of the religious law."[61] He distinguishes two categories of religious law: one the purview of jurists and *mufti*s, the other a special subject of Sufis, reflecting again his acceptance of moderate Sufi practice and mystical religious insight. Many jurists studied or wrote on the subjects Ibn Khaldun dealt with as a judge in Egypt, such as Quran interpretation and speculative theology. Sufi scholars described and analyzed the Sufi path of asceticism, self-scrutiny, leading through stages to ecstatic or mystical states, which enabled them to perceive God's oneness and obtain the gnosis, the knowledge of divine mysteries. Ibn Khaldun discusses both categories, but in Egypt he practiced what most jurists considered orthodox jurisprudence, concerned with such practical, everyday matters of the faith as ritual and inheritance. He mentions that the arithmetical craft of inheritance laws, a subdivision of the philosophical science of mathematics, constituted an especially important aspect of legal scholarship. Otherwise he simply reiterates the standard sources of the law: first the Quran and *hadith*, followed by *ijma'* or consensus, the majority opinion of the community, which Ibn Khaldun, like other Muslim scholars, held to be "infallible," and, finally, reasoning by analogy or *qiyas*, based on the assumption that if cases were similar, divine law covered both.

Judges, he asserted, speaking of his own experience and knowledge, had to know the degree of authority of each source of law, beginning with the miraculous quality of the Quran, and secondarily they had to understand Arabic grammar, syntax, and style in order to perceive meaning of the text. Therefore, Ibn Khaldun remarks, explaining the centrality of Arabic grammatical studies as a category of Islamic law, "(linguistic matters) thus became sciences that jurists had to know, in order to know the divine laws." Of these laws, he further notes, perhaps one-third to one-half of judicial scholarship was devoted to a broad category known as *fara'id*, which concerned religious worship, customs, and inheritance; the latter, inheritance laws, was "a noble discipline" for judicial scholars. Finally, Ibn Khaldun concludes, Muslim jurists developed a special discipline of "Dialectics," which established rules for debates among the religious schools, a discipline that, as he notes, was an aspect of logic that could, however, degenerate into sophistry, one of the charges Athenians levied against Socrates, who was condemned for impiety. However, he notes, dialectic was no longer studied in North Africa because of the overall decline in scholarship in cities of the region.[63] He lamented the pathetic state of all North African intellectual life in his era, highlighted by the ossification of Maliki law and the absence of philosophical speculation.

CAUSALITY IN RELIGION AND PHILOSOPHY

It does not seem remarkable that Ibn Khaldun could passionately defend conservative Sunni Muslim orthodoxy while recreating history as a philosophical discipline. Isaac Newton, a pious Christian, did not experience mental anguish when he revolutionized natural philosophy in the seventeenth century; quite the contrary. "No gulf divided Newton's theological reasoning from his physics and geometry."[64] Neither man questioned the fundamental tenets of his faith. What is noticeable in Ibn Khaldun's case is that in his defense of revealed religion he supported a doctrine that rejected the fundamental Aristotelian and Greco-Islamic idea of causation, which underlay his dialectical model of social evolution from rural tribal to sedentary monarchical societies. This contradiction represents one of the most serious unresolved issues in the *Muqaddimah*, which makes Ibn Khaldun's final escape clause all the more meaningful. This clause is his ritual final statement that persons who create new sciences

... ... issues associated with it. It is, on the other hand, possible to argue that theology was irrelevant to his dialectical model.

The problem of causality, which distinguishes his theological beliefs from his historical methodology, is briefly this. Ibn Khaldun's program for philosophical history and his dialectical model are rooted in Greek and Greco-Islamic notions of cause and effect. "Causality is at the heart of every Aristotelian approach to physics and metaphysics... For Aristotelians every effect is necessary in relation to its efficient cause."[65] Al-Ghazali, however, denied the necessity of this causal relationship and expressed an opinion about the material world that resembled the later skepticism of the eighteenth-century Scottish philosopher David Hume.[66] In bringing his faith to bear on critiques of Ibn Sina and al-Farabi, al-Ghazali argued that an observation of one thing consistently following another does not mean that the first is the efficient cause of the second. "Causal connections are, for al-Ghazālī, merely the repeated conjunction of two events."[67] Unlike Hume, whose skepticism extended to revealed religion, Al-Ghazali argued that "God both creates the event in the outside world and creates our knowledge independently to accord with the event."[68] Thus if fire is brought into contact with cotton and the cotton catches fire, that does not mean that fire causes the combustion. God is the cause—and God could alter the effect if he chose to do so.

Ibn Khaldun not only respected al-Ghazali as one of the outstanding speculative theologians, who, he advised, should be read in order to properly appreciate that discipline; he also approvingly paraphrased the argument al-Ghazali made about causation in his work the *Tahafut al-falasifah (The Incoherence of the Philosophers)*. "It has been proven deductively [*istidlal*], in the chapter on the Oneness of God," Ibn Khaldun writes, "that there is no agent but God." He further suggests, in an almost Humean manner, that humans' assumption about causation derived from empirical evidence is unreliable. "The way in which the causes exercise their influence upon the majority of things caused is unknown. They are only known through customary (experience) and through conclusions which attest to (the existence of an) apparent (causal) relationship. What the influence really is and how it takes place is not known... Therefore we have been commanded completely to abandon and suppress any speculation about them and to direct ourselves to the Causer of all causes who made them and brought them into existence... A man who stops at causes is frustrated. He is rightly (said to be) an Unbeliever... Therefore, we were forbidden by the Lawgiver (Muhammad) to study causes."[69] "The inability to perceive," Ibn Khaldun quotes from a Sufi source, "is a perception."[70]

If Ibn Khaldun were to have accepted al-Ghazali's notions of causation, one would have to conclude that nothing in the world follows its given nature. Everything can be changed if willed by God. It is, however, as Ibn Rushd pointed out in his refutation of the great theologian's ideas, "inimical to any rational view of the universe."[71] Ibn Khaldun's dialectical model is based on just this originally Aristotelian principle that everybody, that is, everything, possesses a nature or essence that determines its development or evolution. Just as seeds embody a certain potential to become specific plants, human societies possessed traits that determined their futures. God in this latter Greco-Islamic context is the prime mover and not al-Ghazali's God of small things.

While Ibn Khaldun's agreement with al-Ghazali's argument about causation would seem to compromise the certainty of cause and effect in the material world, he never openly collides with this issue in his discussion of what he calls the two "intellectual sciences": religion, *al-'ulum al-naqliyat*, and philosophy, *'ulum al-falsafah w-al hukama'*. There is no reason to believe that he was even aware of the contradiction, since he summarizes aspects of religious and philosophical knowledge separately. They remain two discrete subjects in the *Muqaddimah*, another reminder of the complex nature of the *Muqaddimah*, a text that contained innovative social theorizing within an encyclopedia of fourteenth-century Muslim culture and society. It is important to reiterate he wrote as a politically oriented scholar and not as a philosopher who, like Ibn Rushd and others, explicitly sought to reconcile the claims of the two sciences. Nonetheless, without specifically commenting on the question of causation, Ibn Khaldun argued pointedly that the purpose of Muslim theological argument rendered it unsuited for probing the nature of external reality.

Thus he insists *'ulama'* ought to refrain from making judgments about nondoctrinal matters because unlike philosophers, who expect their concepts to correspond to the physical world, *'ulama'* believed the outside world should conform to their religious laws, which are derived from the Quran and the Traditions, the *Sunnah*.[72] He included speculative theologians in this mental dichotomy, remarking that logicians assume that a "mental universal," which is divided into five universals, namely, genus, species, difference, property, and general accident, must correspond to a "natural universal" in the external world.[73] "This is wrong," he writes, "in the opinion of speculative theologians. The universal and essential is to them merely a mental concept having no correspondence outside (the mind)."[74] Speculative theologians, he adamantly insists, reject all the standard rules of logic. The arguments of these theologians imply "that the essential and necessary propositions on which argumentation is predicated are wrong and that the rational cause is a wrong (concept and thus not exist)."[75]

Ibn Khaldun draws this distinction between *'ulama'* and *falasifah* or *hukama'* for a very good reason, and that is he considers *'ulama'* so ignorant of the world beyond their faith and its texts, they are incapable of accurately describing how political systems work. In a section titled "*'Ulama'* Are... Those Least

Familiar with the Ways of Politics," Ibn Khaldun writes: "Thus, in all their intellectual activity ... [they] are accustomed to dealing with matters of the mind and with thoughts. They do not know anything else ... *'ulama'* are accustomed to generalizations and analogical conclusions. When they look at politics they press (their observations) into the mold of their views and their way of making deductions."[76] Politicians, on the other hand, have to deal with the difficult and unpredictable realities of the real world, sometimes negating some abstract ideal "to which one would like them to conform."[77] Therefore, when *'ulama'* observe political situations, they "cannot be trusted" to make valid conclusions.

THE PRINCIPLES OF REASON

Ibn Khaldun introduces the intellectual or rational sciences by emphasizing their universality. "The intellectual sciences are natural to man, in as much as he is a thinking being. They are not restricted to any particular religious group. They are studied by the people of all religious groups who are equally qualified to learn them and to do I research in them. They have existed and (and been known) to the human species since society had its beginning in the world. They are called the sciences of philosophy and wisdom."[78] By thus introducing philosophy, Ibn Khaldun

[...] places his socioeconomic model building within the larger Greco-Islamic philosophical tradition, where, in fact, it belongs.

The philosophical sciences, he states elsewhere, are guided by man's "ability to think" in contrast to the "traditional kind [religion] that he learns from those who invented it."[79] The ability to think involved three levels of intellect. These were, first, at the most primitive level of the average person the "discerning intellect," a limited, practical, everyman, unreflective sort of mediocre intelligence, which allowed for "simplistic observations" of external phenomena but not analytical thought. The second level, characteristic, perhaps, of the educated populace, was the "experimental intellect," an intelligence that allowed individuals to compare perceptions and formulate abstractions, called apperceptions. Finally superior minds, which may have included well-educated people and certainly scholars like Ibn Khaldun himself, possessed the "speculative intellect," *al-ʿaql al-nazari*, the highest form of intelligence, which enabled humans to use both perceptions and apperceptions to analyze and generalize about their experiences, allowing them to perceive "existence as it is" or to understand "the realities of things."[80]

Ibn Khaldun was hardly alone or original in specifying an intellectual hierarchy. Al-Farabi, a far more uncompromising rationalist, who largely ignored Islamic doctrine in his many writings, regarded philosophers as the elect followed, in descending order of their intellectual capacities, by "dialecticians, sophists, law-givers, theologians and doctors of the law [*fuqaha'*]."[81] As will be seen later, Ibn Khaldun, using the dual criteria of moral integrity and economic utility, also ranked *ʿulama'* very low, but in a system of social rather than intellectual stratification.

Ibn Khaldun believed, therefore, that experienced, philosophically trained scholar-officials could utilize the intellectual tools at their command to identify the nature of political systems, which would allow them to accurately understand their histories. It is not possible precisely to identify the sources of his philosophical concepts and methods. While he credits al-ʿAbili, his Andalusian mentor in the rational sciences, with a transformative influence on his education, he does not suggest that al-ʿAbili's guidance sparked an interest in a particular scholar or text. Another unknown factor is whether or not the example of his educated Andalusian ancestors may have inspired his thinking. Ibn Khaldun is known to have written abridged versions of a number of Ibn Rushd's works, and it is likely these included some of the great Andalusian philosopher's own recapitulations of Aristotle's logical and scientific texts.[82] Ibn Rushd had taken on himself the enormous task of wrenching Aristotle's original sense from the renderings of Neoplatonists, and Ibn Khaldun alludes to these works, adding that unlike Ibn Sina, Ibn Rushd did not criticize Aristotle but "followed him."[83] In fact, Ibn Rushd wrote thirty-six short, middle-length, and long commentaries on Aristotle's works, including a *Paraphrase* and a shorter *Epitome of the Physics,* as well as original medical, legal, and philosophical studies, such as his essay on the equivalence of Islam and philosophy.[84] He also commented on Plato's *Republic,* comparing it, misleadingly, with Aristotle's *Politics,* which he knew only secondhand.[85]

Still, it is impossible to say which of Aristotle's ideas Ibn Khaldun took directly from Ibn Rushd's works and which he may have derived from al-Farabi or Ibn Sina, both of whom he cites repeatedly in the *Muqaddimah.*[86] Al-Farabi (d. 950) wrote in the first half of the tenth century, at the height of the cosmopolitan cultural florescence of the 'Abbasid Caliphate. He founded sys-

... philosophy, intending to revive the philosophical tradition of Alexandria after it had declined as a result of the antiphilosophical policies of Christian monarchs. He was more Greek, more rigorously philosophical, and less pious than any subsequent Muslim scholar, and Muslim rationalists regarded him as the "Second Teacher" after Aristotle.

In cosmological terms al-Farabi fused Aristotelian with Neoplatonic notions of the emanating intellect. An accomplished musician, he also wrote several musical treatises. More to the point he commented on Aristotle's *Physics* in terms that are echoed in Ibn Khaldun's dialectical model, defining the study of physics as "the study of natural bodies and the accidents which adhere in them as well as the things from which, by which and for which those bodies and accidents inhering in them arise."[87] His most influential contributions, however, were his writings on Aristotle's *Organon*, which promoted logic as the principal tool of scientific analysis. Using the term *tasawwur, conceptualization*, and *tasdiq, assent*, al-Farabi developed a logical hierarchy of syllogisms with only the *qiyas burhani* qualifying as the sole example of logic that yielded complete certainty. These terms found their way into Ibn Khaldun's précis of philosophical knowledge, as did knowledge of al-Farabi's major restatement of the Greek philosophical concept of the perfect state.[88] Ibn Khaldun cites this latter text, the *Mabadi' ara' ahl al-madinat al-fadilah* ("The Views of Citizens of the Virtuous State"), as an example of the unrealistic strain of political theory he did not intend to discuss in the *Muqaddimah*.

Ibn Sina, the third of four scholars Ibn Khaldun accounts as the greatest Muslim philosophers, was the Muslim rationalist most commonly read in Ibn Khaldun's world of fourteenth-century North Africa and Andalusia. A student of al-Farabi's work, especially his analysis of Aristotle's metaphysics, and an author of the first philosophical treatise in Persian, he, like Ibn Rushd, was an extraordinarily prolific scholar. He is principally known for his massive, encyclopedic work the *Kitab al-Shifa' (The Physics of the Healing)*. Borrowing heavily from al-Farabi for his Neoplatonic cosmology, logic, and political ideas, he derived his metaphysical and physical concepts directly from Aristotle. In particular, his extensive treatment of causes and motion corresponds closely to Aristotle's *Physics*. Ibn Sina's opening chapter in *The Physics of the Healing*, titled "On the Cases and Principles of Natural Things," may very likely be the source of Ibn Khaldun's knowledge of the concepts and vocabulary of nature and accident, ideas that were fundamental to his dialectical model. Thus, while Ibn Khaldun mentions Aristotle's works on physics and says they were available to Muslim scholars, he reports that Ibn Sina's *Kitab al-Shifa'* was the most comprehensive commentary on the subject.[89]

Whatever the source of his philosophical ideas, and he could have encountered many of them in different texts, Ibn Khaldun offers an extensive survey of the philosophical sciences that existed prior to his own creation of the new science of philosophical history. As is the case with his elaborate discussion of Islamic piety and speculative theology, he goes to extraordinary lengths to summarize his knowledge of this field. In doing so he reminds readers once again that the *Muqaddimah*, far from being limited to social science model building, represents what seems to be a complete 360-degree tour of his vast intellectual horizon of fourteenth-century Arab Muslim culture in his effort to realize his intended goal of being comprehensive. In fact, Ibn Khaldun makes no effort to tell his readers which ideas and methods he has borrowed from Greco-Islamic philosophy to create his his-

Nonetheless, by displaying his knowledge of the "intellectual sciences," he enables readers both to appreciate the depth of his philosophical knowledge and to understand the original sense and implications of the concepts he employs in the *Muqaddimah* to analyze societies.

Ibn Khaldun reports that before he wrote the *Muqaddimah* there were four intellectual or philosophical sciences and their subdivisions. The four were logic, physics, metaphysics, *al-ʿilm al-ilahi,* and mathematics. Physics included medicine while mathematics or "quantities" comprised arithmetic, geometry, music, and astronomy. His discussion of mathematics offers an example of his ambition to comprehensively survey knowledge. Thus in his discussion of arithmetic he describes both arithmetic and also geometrical progression and the "remarkable numerical properties" that are revealed when numerical triangles, squares, pentagons, and hexagons are constructed. After simply describing calculation—addition, multiplication, subtraction, and division— he defines roots and rational and irrational numbers. To understand these phenomena he recommends a book by Ibn al-Bannaʾ al-Marrakushi, with whom Ibn Khaldun's teacher al-Abili studied in Marrakesh earlier in the century. Following arithmetic he takes up algebra and business arithmetic, the latter a specialty of Andalusian scholars, including a member of his own family, Abu Muslim Ibn Khaldun (d. 1057 1058), who had also once designed astrolabes. Next he explains the mathematics of inheritance laws, one of his own special interests, and then describes the geometrical sciences, a section in which he devotes most of his attention to Euclid's book, the first Greek text translated, as he notes, during the reign of the ʿAbbasid caliph al-Mansur (714–775) and later summarized by Ibn Sina and many other scholars. Geometry, he concludes, echoing the importance Greeks, including Galen, placed on the discipline "Enlightens the intellect and sets one's mind right." "All its proofs are very clear and orderly. It is hardly possible for errors to enter into geometrical reasoning, because it is well arranged and orderly ... Our teachers used to say that one's application to geometry does to the mind what soap does to a garment. It washes off stains and cleanses it of grease and dirt."[90]

Echoing Aristotle and three of the most prominent Muslim philosophers he mentioned earlier, al-Farabi, Ibn Sina, and Ibn Rushd, any one of whom might have been the source of his account, Ibn Khaldun emphasized that logic was the first science, not merely first in his list but in order of significance in the acquisition of knowledge. Logic, he reports, gave people the ability to think in the correct way so they could acquire knowledge, which he defines as "information about the essence [*tasawwur*] of things."[91] Knowledge of the essence of societies was Ibn Khaldun's fundamental goal in historical studies. Aristotle, Ibn Khaldun notes, had systematized earlier "unconnected" Greek logical writings and, in his corpus of works, known collectively in the West as the *Organon*, established logic as the fundamental intellectual discipline, the first program for analytical thought, on which all other disciplines were based. That is why, Ibn Khaldun reports, Aristotle was called the First Teacher.

The *Organon* comprised several distinct categories of texts, of which the first four are especially significant for understanding the logic Ibn Khaldun employed when he developed his historical methodology. These are texts on generalizations and a second group dealing with the use of syllogisms in formal logical reasoning. The first book, the *Kitab al-maqulat*, dealt with generalizations or abstractions, which humans, as thinking animals, could f

sense experience. These abstractions were termed universals. "Man," Ibn Khaldun wrote, "is distinguished from the animals by his ability to perceive universals, which are things abstracted from the *sensibilia*."[92] It was this process of forming generalizations or universals from similar individual objects that led Aristotle to distinguish sciences, such as geometry, from nonsciences, such as history, that dealt only with particulars. The second, third, and fourth books in Aristotle's *Organon* dealt with propositions and syllogisms. Of these, the fourth, the *Kitab al-Burhan*, was especially significant as it explained the kind of analogical reasoning that produced certainty or necessity, proofs of the kind Ibn Khaldun claimed to produce at various times in the *Muqaddimah*.

He insisted that critical, logical reasoning was necessary in order to identify the essence of some object or entity. *Essence* was a synonym for *nature*, a concept and term that was fundamental to the Greco-Islamic sciences. The phrase *certain by nature*, knowledge the superior or speculative intellect could attain, constitutes Ibn Khaldun's restatement of this fundamental idiom and first principle of the Greco-Islamic philosophical sciences. Aristotle discusses the idea at length in his *Physics*, as does Ibn Sina in his recapitulation of Aristotle's work. Galen wrote that the first step in scientific discovery was the "methodical determination of the essential natures of things."[93] Galen and other Greco-Islamic thinkers also used the term *universals* or the phrase *objective first principles* as synonyms for *tabi'ah*, the nature or essence of something. These universals, first principles, natures, or essences were, in Aristotle's words, self-evident truths, which represented the primary features of the world. Plants or animals were paradigmatic examples of things known by nature, but they also included for Aristotle the polis or city-state and the social nature of human beings.[94]

Ibn Khaldun might have taken his idea of nature or essence, which he repeatedly invokes, directly from Aristotle—or Ibn Rushd's précis of Aristotelian works—or perhaps he may have found it expressed more comprehensively by Ibn Sina. In his discussion of "nature's relation to matter, form and motion," Ibn Sina wrote: "Every body has a nature, form, matter and accidents. Its nature, again, is the power that gives rise to its producing motion and change, which are from [the body] itself, as well as its being at rest and stable. Its form is its essence, by which it is what it is, while its matter is the thing bearing its essence. Accidents are those things that, when [the body's] form shapes its matter and completes its specific nature, either necessarily belonging to it as concomitants or accidentally belong to it as concomitants or accidentally belong to it from some external agent."[95]

As Ibn Sina implies, but only makes clear in following commentary, *nature* and *form* or *essence* are his terms for discussing different aspects of the same thing. In the case of the elements—earth, air, fire, and water—*nature* and *form* usually refer to the same thing, the essence of something, but sometimes philosophers distinguish the two, with *nature* meaning the motions or consequences that come from some thing and *form* carrying the common sense of some thing's essence or identity. Ibn Khaldun also uses these three terms, *nature*, *form*, and *essence*, in similar ways, sometimes to mean the same thing, sometimes to indicate distinct aspects of a certain entity.

The Greco-Islamic concept of some thing's nature is so fundamentally important because of the philosophers' conviction that all things had a certain definable predisposition due to their natures. "Natural objects," Aristotle said, "contain within them-

rest."[96] Each entity, that is, developed according to the dictates of its unique nature. Some thing's nature represented a formal cause, one of four causes in the Aristotelian and Greco-Islamic canon, which also included final, efficient, and material causes. Aristotle dwelled at length on these causes in his *Physics*, which Ibn Khaldun summarizes as the "science that investigates bodies from the point of view of motion ... [including] heavenly and elementary substances, as well as human beings."[97] Ibn Rushd reiterated Aristotle's argument that a thing's nature shaped events associated with it, and, as will be seen later, Ibn Khaldun adapted this idea to his study of bedouin and sedentary societies as an explanatory concept and a predictive device.[98] If, he indicated, one knew the nature of a certain type of society, it would be possible to judge the veracity of historical evidence about it through critical analysis. In the case of tribal or sedentary societies, understanding their nature would enable scholars, such as Ibn Khaldun, to construct a model that explained their particular movement or trajectory, their history, that is, how it had evolved according to a definite, demonstrable pattern characteristic of its type.

The logical process of induction, the Arabic *istiqra'*, yielded this fundamental understanding. Aristotle employed the idea of induction for the type of perception or understanding derived from observation and an instantaneous, almost intuitive sense of some thing's essence or nature. In his *Physics* Aristotle introduced the fundamental steps in philosophical thought that began with induction, by saying: "Now induction is of first principles and of the universal and deduction proceeds *from* universals."[99] Inductively identifying the nature of something meant articulating what in more technical or mathematic terms was called an axiom or premise, which would constitute the first logical step in acquiring additional knowledge. In the *Nicomachean Ethics,* one of the texts of the *Organon,* Aristotle described deduction as the second step in the logical process of scientific investigation. The syllogism exemplified deductive logic in which one reasoned from a universally known or inductively observed truth to a conclusion about a specific case. In geometry, the Aristotelian and Greco-Islamic model par excellence of logical certainty the entire edifice was based on knowledge derived from axioms, which yielded certain theorems. According to Aristotelian logical theory, all sciences ought to take the form of a series of syllogistic deductions.[100] Yet Aristotle did not structure his scientific treatises as logical systems, explicitly identifying premises or axioms through induction and deriving conclusions through deductive reasoning. "Indeed, one can trawl the whole of Aristotle's considerable scientific oeuvre without netting a single instance of a fully worked-out syllogism."[101] Exactly the same point can be made about Ibn Khaldun's *Muqaddimah*, justified perhaps, by the example of the First Teacher, Ibn Khaldun's primary if distant intellectual mentor. The text includes his frequent assertions of logically demonstrated proofs but not single syllogism.

Apart from these fundamental inductive and deductive aspects of Greco-Islamic logical thought, it is important to understand one further aspect of Aristotle's ideas found in both his *Organon* and *Physics*, which is also included in Ibn Sina's introduction to chapter 6 of his work *The Physics of the Healing*. Ibn Sina's chapter is titled "On Nature's Relation to Matter, Form, and Motion." This is the notion that apart from something's nature or essence, an entity of whatever kind also possessed associated traits, which Aristotle and his Greco-Islamic disciples labeled "accidents," *aʿrad*.[102] Accidents constituted secondary characteristics of different branches of philosophical knowledge, whether of an

ʿUmar Khayyam (1048–1131), the Iranian mathematician and sometime poet, famous in English literature for translations of his quatrains or *rubaʿiyat*, cited Aristotle as his authority when he discussed this notion of philosophical accidents. "And it is known," he wrote, "from the work *On Demonstration* [Aristotle's *Posterior Analytics*] belonging to the science of logic that every demonstrative art has a subject of which the essential accidents and so on are studied."[103] As mentioned earlier, Ibn Rushd, Ibn Khaldun's probable Aristotelian source, illustrated this idea of accidents with the example of a triangle, whose "essential or proximate accident" was that fact all its angles added up to two right angles or 180 degrees. Aristotle and his Greco-Islamic disciples distinguished between such essential accidents, necessary secondary traits, and nonessential accidents, fortuitous or ephemeral characteristics. Ibn Khaldun was concerned primarily with essential accidents, necessary associations such as institutions or occupations, the subject of his later chapters on political and economic systems.

Ibn Khaldun believed Greco-Islamic philosophy provided the intellectual tools for acquiring knowledge about the visible world, but he was also profoundly pessimistic about the state of "scientific activity" in North Africa and Andalusia. This decline of scholarship represents a subtheme of the *Muqaddimah*, which was directly attributable to the erosion of sedentary life in both regions. Due to the bedouin ethos of North Africa, both among Arabs and Berbers, material and intellectual crafts or occupations had deteriorated to the point of irrelevance. Some states, he observed, alluding to the Almohads and, very probably, their Marinid, Hafsid, and Abd al-Wadid successors, "by their very nature [their bedouin nature] have no regard for scholarship on account of... [their] simplicity."[104] Simplicity, it should be recalled, Ibn Khaldun also identified as a prominent characteristic of Maliki law, which prevailed in North Africa and Andalusia.

Qayrawan, in the ninth century the center of Maliki scholarship, and Cordoba, once Andalusia's capital, had, Ibn Khaldun reports, previously become highly developed cultural centers in North Africa and Andalusia, respectively, but science, by which he meant both religious and philosophical thought, had deteriorated under Berber dynasties and the ravages of Arab tribes. This was especially evident in the Almohad capital of Marrakesh, the desert oasis city in western Morocco. The city's sedentary culture was retarded owing both to the original and persisting bedouin traits of the dynasty and the fact that its rulers controlled the city for such a short period and never had the opportunity to develop into a highly populated major urban center. In contrast, the sciences flourished in both Europe and eastern urban centers of the Islamic world, including Cairo and many cities in northeastern Iran, the region known as Khurasan, as well as Mawarannahr, that is, Transoxiana or western Central Asia. Ibn Khaldun adamantly insists that throughout Islamic history most scholars had been and continued to be Iranians.[105] Not even in Cairo, a city he extolled for its vibrant religious culture, could a vital philosophical tradition be found during the more than two decades he lived in the city at the end of the fourteenth century.

Ibn Khaldun was, as usual, well informed. Ibn Rushd's Aristotelian works had already been taken up in France, and their influence lingered for many centuries in Italy.[106] It was in Iran more than two centuries after Ibn Khaldun's death that the Islamic world experienced what is generally regarded as the last great moment in Islamic philosophy, in the work of Sadr al-Din al-Shirazi, known as Mulla Sadra (ca. 1571–1640), who decried the decline of philosophy in the seventeenth century. An intellectual descendant of Ibn Sina, Mulla Sadra believed in the fusion of Greco-Islamic thought with revealed religion and he sought to apply philosophical insights and Sufi mysticism to Shi'i theology. This Iranian Shi'ah went far beyond the speculative theologian's restricted use of logic in his willingness to glean truth from the Greco-Islamic philosophical tradition and use it to invigorate Iranian Shi'i thought.[107]

3

A SCHOLAR-OFFICIAL IN A DANGEROUS WORLD

FAITH AND PHILOSOPHY are prominent themes in the *Muqaddimah*, but not in Ibn Khaldun's memoir. After narrating the history of the Banu Khaldun house, a largely Andalusian history until the thirteenth century, and the flight of his family and other Muslims to North Africa, Ibn Khaldun chronicles his life and scholarly interests from the time he left Tunis in 1352 until his death in Cairo in 1406. Spiritual and intellectual introspection are largely absent in these pages, which have little resemblance to the modern autobiography. If it were not for the *Muqaddimah*, Ibn Khaldun's peripatetic professional career would not elicit much interest, but given the commanding achievement of that work, his narrative enables readers to gain a more complete picture of the man, if not, unfortunately, the genesis of the text itself. Two aspects of his halfcentury career pervade the memoir. First, it graphically illumines the difficulties and dangers faced by socially elite, politically ambitious scholar-officials as they maneuvered to advance their careers in the doubly treacherous worlds of court politics and unstable tribal dynasties. The whims of ministers and the unpredictable longevity of tribal regimes drove men like Ibn Khaldun on professional and geographic odysseys, which they often did not survive. Second, the memoir testifies to his deep and abiding commitment to scholarship. Ibn Khaldun's intellectual interests may be inferred from the praise he lavishes on individual religious, literary, and historical scholars, especially the attention he devotes to scholars of Islamic law, his own professional interest. Like Ibn Khaldun, some of these men were also well read in philosophy—note particularly Aristotle's *Organon* and the works of Ibn Sina—but apart from his teacher al-Abili, he does not mention any contemporary North African, Andalusian, or Egyptian who was primarily a philosopher.

ADAB IN FEZ AND GRANADA

In 1351, three years after his parents' death in the plague, Ibn Khaldun began what eventually became a checkered career as a government servant in various North African and Andalusian states. He took a post in Marinid-controlled Tunis as a calligrapher for royal edicts, a modest but typical appointment for a socially prominent, well-educated young man, which he knew himself to be. His position involved writing a phrase in praise of God on the messages and orders of the Sultan between the *basmalah*—the ritual phrase "In the Name of the One God"—and the main body of the text. Nonetheless, about a year later in 1352, suffering, as he writes in his memoir, from feelings of *istihash*, deep melancholy, owing to the loss of his teachers in the plague, which made it impossible for him to continue his scientific studies, Ibn Khaldun decided, against his older brother's advice, to leave Tunis for Fez, the Moroccan capital of Marinid territories.[1] Typically for the fractious politics of the times, he began his journey by having to thread his way between two warring tribal factions. During this trip he met Abu 'Inan, the reigning

Marinid sultan, for the first time in Tilimsan in 1353. In the winter of 1353–1354 he wintered in Bijayah (Bougie), a historic coastal city west of Tunis. Hafsids had earlier held the town, but a Marinid then ruled this important port. Ibn Khaldun finally arrived safely in Fez in 1354, after receiving a formal invitation from Abu ʿInan to join other scholars at his court. His subsequent eight-year residence in Marinid Fez exemplifies the life of an ambitious, socially elite scholar-official. Ibn Khaldun later incorporated his knowledge of such North African tribal regimes in the *Muqaddimah*'s dialectical model.

The ruler of Fez, Abu ʿInan, whose predecessor Abu l-Hasan had earlier brought so many scholars to Tunis from Tilimsan and elsewhere in North Africa, had assembled many such men in his capital, making it, for a brief moment in time, the cultural center of the Maghrib. Ibn Khaldun marks his arrival in the city by cataloguing important scholars he encountered, his habit at each point in his memoir, as he lets readers understand the diverse intellectual interests he continued pursuing during his administrative career in North Africa, Granada, and Egypt.[2] "Among the learned men" Ibn Khaldun met, he counted two in particular as his friends. One was a *qadi*, another former resident of Tilimsan, Abu ʿAbdallah Muhammad al-Maqqari, a Quranic and Maliki legal scholar who had studied with Ibn Khaldun's teacher, al-Abili, during the latter man's residence in Tilimsan.[3] Ibn Khaldun may have been critical of Maliki law in many respects but he continued to study this *madhhab* or legal school throughout his adult life. A second Maliki scholar, whom Ibn Khaldun identifies as his friend during this period, was a man of seemingly unparalleled religious prestige in the Maghrib of his day. He was also someone whose education ranged at least as widely throughout the Islamic and philosophical sciences as Ibn Khaldun's or any other intellectual's in North Africa. This man, Abu 'Abdallah Muhammad b. Ahmad al-Sharif al-'Alawi (1310-1370), known generally as Sharif al-Tilimsani or simply al-Tilimsani, had come to Fez in 1353 just prior to Ibn Khaldun's arrival, following the Marinid sultan's capture of the Tilimsan in 1352. Another former Tilimsan resident, Sharif al-Tilimsani a far more influential scholar of the traditional Islamic sciences and Maliki law in his day than Ibn Khaldun, left a considerable legacy of scholars whom he trained, beginning with his two sons.

Sharif al-Tilimsani's education and that of his sons exemplified the diversity of subjects Ibn Khaldun also studied at various periods in his life.[4] In addition to the standard religious curriculum, it included law and the sources of law, which in North Africa nearly always meant Maliki *fiqh*, the speculative theology of the Ash'ari school, and studies, probably of philosophy, with Ibn Khaldun's teacher Abu 'Abd Allah al-Abili. After studying with other teachers of law, mathematics, and astronomy, Sharif al-Tilimsani, who moved to nearby Tunis in 1339, also read about Sufism in Ibn Sina's work *Kitab al-isharat* and acquainted himself with the philosopher's greatest work, the *Kitab al-shifa*'. In Tunis he also had read some of the Andalusian philosopher Ibn Rushd's summaries and commentaries of Aristotle's logical and scientific texts, as well as doing additional work in mathematics and philosophy and the complexity of inheritance law.[5]

As typified the careers of accomplished and notable scholars, al-Tilimsani, like Ibn Khaldun after him, was sought out by rulers for his erudition and prestige. He worked first at the Marinid court in Fez, following the Abu 'Inan's capture of his hometown in 1352. He tutored aristocratic children there and advised the sultan on matters of Maliki law, his principal scholarly subject. In fact, he was the most prestigious Maliki legal scholar of his day in the Maghrib. In 1359 he returned to Tilimsan at the invitation of its most accomplished and now independent ruler, Abu Hammu II (1359–1389), who sought Sharif al-Tilimsani's daughter in marriage and subsequently appointed him as director of a *madrasah*, which the sultan founded and built specifically for the scholar. Al-Tilimsani's subsequent reputation derives principally from his lectures on Maliki law, the legal tradition that had flourished under the Almoravids and enjoyed a revival in North African courts after its haphazard suppression in the Almohad period. His approach to the law was not, however, characterized by the conservative legalism espoused by many North African and Andalusian ʿulamaʾ during the Almoravid period. That was the time when these legalists gave precedence to Maliki legal commentaries over the Quran and *hadith* and condemned both al-Ghazali's rationalism and Sufi mysticism. Instead al-Tilimsani appeared to follow Ashʿari theology in its emphasis on logical argument, not for philosophical purposes but as a means of demonstrating the truth of fundamental theological principles. In this he may have been an exception among well-educated Maliki ʿulamaʾ, at least if Ibn Khaldun's own characterization of Maliki law in his day as a rigidly conservative and antirationalist legal school is to be accepted.

Sharif al-Tilimsani's two sons became important scholars in their own right, an intellectual tradition that continued for several generations. His eldest son, Abu Muhammad ʿAbdallah b. Muhammad (ca. 1347–1390), taught at the Tilimsan Friday mosque, and, following his father's death, he inherited his position at the *madrasah* established for him. He studied the traditional religious sciences, as well as the theology and philosophy of al-Ghazali, whose work, despite earlier Almoravid persecution, had long since been absorbed into the North African curriculum in the post-Almohad Maliki revival. In addition he read the texts of Maliki law, the works of Ibn Sina, Aristotle's rhetoric, and the geometry of Euclid. He is generally regarded as a superior scholar to his father and also to his brother, Abu Yahya ʿAbd al-Rahman b. Muhammad (1356–1423), a reputed textual scholar who was much more narrowly a judicial specialist than his father and older brother were. One of ʿAbd al-Rahman's sons became the chief *qadi* of Granada, and he died in 1490, two years before the Christian capture of the city.

Ibn Khaldun describes the father, Sharif al-Tilimsani, as his friend, and his intimate connection with the family is indicated by his presence at the birth of the younger son, ʿAbd al-Rahman, in 1356 in Sharif al-Tilimsani's house. The evidence of this connection is instructive for providing a scholarly context for Ibn Khaldun's life at this stage, as well as indicating that for all its undeveloped primitiveness—as Ibn Khaldun and others depict North Africa in this period—the region was nonetheless home to well-educated scholars, even if they were not as thick on the ground as they had been previously in Iberia or were, perennially, in Cairo. It is not that Ibn Khaldun is known to have derived any of his interests from conversations with members of this family. He gives no indication that any one particular individual stimulated him to think of utilizing philosophy in the service of history before he sat down to write the *Muqaddimah*. It is just that nearly all the religious and philosophical strains present in Ibn Khaldun's mentalité are evident to varying degrees in the education and teaching of the al-Sharif al-Tilimsani family.

Sharif al-Tilimsani and his sons appear to have been profoundly learned individuals. Yet, unlike Ibn Khaldun, they functioned exclusively as *madrasah ʿulama*' in Tilimsan itself and had limited political experience, despite their connections with the Marinids in Fez or more intimately with the rulers of Tilimsan. They remained ʿ*ulama*', primarily *faqih*s or legal scholars, writing within the confines of what had become by that time a far more expansive theological and legal atmosphere than had previously existed in the Maghrib, combining conservative Maliki law with the theological sophistication of al-Ghazali. If Ibn Khaldun had followed more closely in the footsteps of his own grandfather and father, perhaps he too would have worked within similar intellectual confines rather than utilizing his education in a brilliantly original way, applying his philosophical knowledge not to study technical aspects of Maliki theology or the mathematics of Muslim inheritance law but employing it instead to analyze social structures and explain historical cycles. Sharif al-Tilimsani's broad education and career make Ibn Khaldun's creative rationalist outburst of activity in 1377 all the more remarkable and difficult to explain in any simple way.

If contact with the al-Tilimsani family of scholars and other individuals in Fez offered Ibn Khaldun at least a measure of the intellectual stimulus he had craved and found wanting in Tunis after plague ravaged the town, it also advanced his political education there. Initially he became a royal companion at the Marinid court, a recognized position in Islamic regimes for well-born or well-read *adib*s, and subsequently he accepted a minor bureaucratic post with the same regime. While serving in these positions he seems to have willingly entered into the perennial family factional disputes that marked nearly all these tribal dynasties and also plagued the Marinids in these years. Such lineages, like tribal governments throughout the Middle East and Central Asia, did not observe strict rules of inheritance or political succession by primogeniture, thus encouraging more internecine political struggles, fratricide and patricide common among them, than even contemporary European courts witnessed at this time. Ibn Khaldun's own sense of aristocratic worth as a Banu Khaldun and self-confidence in his intelligence seem, from the very first, to have led him to expect that during his life he would exert political influence in important government posts, including participation in these perennial intra-tribal conflicts.

Ibn Khaldun's familiar relations with Abu 'Inan and the security of his post in the sultan's government waned in 1356 and 1357 when, according to his account, he became careless and aroused the ruler's political suspicions. Given his family's previous association with the now-defeated Hafsid dynasty in Tunis, Ibn Khaldun writes with unexpected candor that he should have been more careful in forming a close friendship with the Hafsid *amir* Muhammad, the former ruler of Bijayah, the town where he wintered in 1353–1354, before traveling on to Fez. Abu 'Inan suspected this man intended to reoccupy his former city and arrested Ibn Khaldun for complicity in this supposed, and not altogether improbable, plot. After suffering badly, perhaps from torture, he was imprisoned. During his incarceration he wrote a supplicating poem to Abu 'Inan lamenting, in the opening verses, the "vicissitudes of fate," a typical literary trope in such situations, however much the vicissitudes might have been at least partly the political consequences of self-inflicted wounds.[6] Ibn Khaldun was finally released in November 1358, following Abu 'Inan's death.

After receiving a robe of honor for his suffering, the newly freed Ibn Khaldun appealed to the *wazir*, the chief minister, who released him and other prisoners, to be allowed to return to his own country, Ifriqiyah. The minister demurred, but continued to treat him well. While remaining in Fez, he successfully schemed against Abu 'Inan's successor to support an exiled family member, Abu Salim (r. 1359–1361), in the succession struggle for the Marinid throne. As a reward "for his services" he was appointed in 1359 by the new sultan, to the important position of secretary of the chancellery. In this position he handled correspondence and edited ordinances, writing, he reports, in simple rather than rhymed prose, since most people could not understand polished literary Arabic.[7] At the same time he performed typical *adib* duties by composing poems, in various meters, for such ritual events as *mawlids,* celebrations of the Prophet Muhammad's birthday. He does not say whether or not another verse he wrote to commemorate the Sudanese ambassador's gift of a giraffe to the Marinid court was widely appreciated.[8]

Two years later he received a second important appointment, a judgeship in the *mazalim* or administrative court, an institution distinct from and often in opposition to the *shari'ah* or religious legal system. The *mazalim* court was an important institution in sultanate regimes. It was an executive administrative office, which had become the norm in the Islamic world well before his time. Muslims adopted the idea of this court from Sasanid Iran, and it operated throughout the era of the 'Abbasid Caliphate. Its untrammeled administrative reach reflected the imperial nature of that caliphate as well as the autocratic/pragmatic character of regional sultanates. Ibn Khaldun reports he fulfilled his duties in the *mazalim* court conscientiously, rendering justice to a large number of people.[9]

While in this position he reports suffering from the envious intrigue of one Ibn Marzuq, but says the *wazir* confirmed him in his position and even increased his pay. Still, out of "youthful pride" he asked for a better position, managing to alienate the sultan in the process, who began treating him coldly.[10] Failing in his attempt to gain a more important post, Ibn Khaldun asked again to be allowed to return east, not to Tunis but to Tilimsan, where his friend Sharif al-Tilimsani was now securely established with his own mosque. The *wazir*, now exercising more power than the two men who pretended to rule between 1361 and 1362, refused his request, because the ʿAbd al-Wadids had retaken the city from the Marinids. Someone like Ibn Khaldun represented an individual who could lend prestige to this hostile but still fragile regime, as well as provide intelligence about the Marinid state.[11] He was finally allowed to leave Fez in 1362, not for the east, where he might cause difficulties for the Marinids, but for Andalusia.

From the time he left Tunis in 1352 Ibn Khaldun's life in Fez typified the career of a scholar-official in dangerous North African times. Did Ibn Khaldun reflect on his own role in these events or on the significance of his experience? Regarding his personal life he said little, apart from conceding that dangerous political friendships and youthful ambition brought down trouble on his head. Still, to that extent these pages of his memoir begin to resemble an autobiography, more frank in its admission of missteps and emotional immaturity than any other document from the period. Politically, did Ibn Khaldun's experiences provide historical grist for his later dialectical mill? Almost certainly yes, for it gave him, first of all, an intimate knowledge of the Marinid regime, a typically insecure tribal state, whose *mazalim* court testified to the essentially secular or pragmatic character of sultanate regimes, which unlike the great Arab Muslim caliphates, made no claim to religious legitimacy. Whatever knowledge Ibn Khaldun had earlier possessed of the nature of these post-Almohad tribal states, his experience with this court very likely left him with an understanding of the nature of sultanate governments. It is not always possible to demonstrate how his political experiences influenced the political theories he later advances in the *Muqaddimah*. Nonetheless, it is sometimes obvious that personal experiences he reported in his memoir later emerged as political theories in the *Muqaddimah,* and that is probably the case also when he explains discusses the rational or realpolitik sultanate.

This was certainly true, for example, of Ibn Khaldun's experience when the *Marinid wazir* refused to allow him to leave Fez and return east, for he learned, he reports in the *Muqaddimah,* that rulers were reluctant to allow prominent individuals, even young ones, to leave their courts to join other rulers. Some would not even allow their servants to go on *hajj* for fear they might never return. The tribal regimes of Ibn Khaldun's day were fragile, brittle institutions that were constantly under threat from within and without. In the *Muqaddimah* Ibn Khaldun cites this reluctance to allow administrators leave as one general rule of sultanate court politics. "It is difficult to escape from the servitude of royal authority, especially when the dynasty has reached its peak and its authority is shrinking."[12] Beyond such insights, his brief tenure allowed him to study the urban economies of these states, which he examines at length in the *Muqaddimah*'s chapters on sedentary societies. He frequently cites the example of Fez in particular when illustrating his arguments in the *Muqaddimah.*

IN THE GARDENS OF SPAIN

Ibn Khaldun's began his second brief chapter as a scholar-official when he reached Granada in December 1362. After dispatching his wife and children to live with relatives in Constantine, a city just west of Tunis, he traveled to Ceuta, the costal enclave opposite Jabal al-Fath or Gibraltar. Following a gracious reception by the cultured governor of Ceuta, who housed him for a time in a residence across from the Friday mosque, he crossed to Andalusia, sending messages ahead announcing his arrival to the sultan and his *wazir,* Ibn al-Khatib, one of the most important scholarly personalities in the western Islamic world at this time. The latter replied with a message, enclosing a verse of welcome. Ibn Khaldun reached the city on December 26, little more than a week before elaborate festivities were held at the Alhambra Palace commemorating the *mawlid al-nabi,* the Prophet Muhammad's birthday.[13] The celebration of the Prophet's birthday must also have been staged as a joyous occasion to mark the restitution of the Nasrid sultan Muhammad V, who had reclaimed his throne earlier in the year following a brief interregnum. It was a "splendid" affair attended by courtiers, "distinguished Mamluks," *Ashraf,* revered descendants of the Prophet, *'ulama',* Sufis, Italians, merchants from Tunisia, and other notables.[14] This was likely to have been Ibn Khaldun's first opportunity to meet Mamluks, members of Egypt's Turkic ruling oligarchy who later welcomed him to Cairo and patronized his scholarly and legal career there. Whether or not he made any personal friendships with these Turks at this time, he does not say.

Ibn Khaldun had earlier met both the Nasrid sultan of Granada, Muhammad V, and his *wazir,* Ibn al-Khatib, when he was in Fez, where both men had taken refuge in 1359 following a briefly sustained coup d'état by the sultan's cousin. Ibn Khaldun's friendship with these two men undoubtedly contributed to the enthusiastic welcome he received when he reached the city, but his reception was probably due also to his status as a descendant of the prestigious Banu Khaldun house. The sultan, "excited," Ibn Khaldun happily remarks, by his arrival, housed him in one of his palaces—unfortunately not identifying his residence among the imposing structures of the Alhambra on Granada's stunning promontory. Expressing his delight at Ibn Khaldun's visit, the sultan bestowed a traditional robe of honor on him.[15]

Subsequently Ibn Khaldun seems to have reprised part of his life as an *adib* in Fez, as when he assisted in another *mawlid* celebration two years later by reciting a verse "in the [unspecified] manner of the kings of the Maghrib." He typically composed other verses for public audiences, including one to commemorate the circumcision of Muhammad V's son.

Ibn Khaldun's account of his reception in Granada conveys a thrill of affirmation, which he did not experience at any other time during his political or judicial career. While he was later graciously received when he later reached Cairo in 1372, his welcome was more the kind of formal, official recognition that rulers routinely offered prestigious individuals. In Granada, Ibn al-Khatib admitted Ibn Khaldun into the inner court circle, where he participated in the entertainments and witty, festive gatherings of old friends. Enormously gratified by his reception, he writes with infectious enthusiasm of his delight at the social intimacy he enjoyed at *majlis soirees*, the social gatherings of the court elite.

It is impossible to know how much the sultan's and Ibn al-Khatib's warm embrace of Ibn Khaldun stemmed from his identity as a socially prestigious member of the old Andalusian aristocracy. Both men must also have considered they could exploit Ibn Khaldun's stature for their own purposes, which involved their desire to fend off increasing Christian threats by concluding a peace treaty with the Christian ruler of Seville. In 1363–1364 Muhammad V sent Ibn Khaldun on an embassy to Pedro the Cruel, the ruler of Seville, where he was also able to see with his own eyes evidence of his family's former presence in the city.[16] Whether or not Pedro knew much about the Banu Khaldun before Ibn Khaldun's arrival is not clear, but he soon "learned" of the family's historic and local prominence, evidently informed of the details provided by a semiprofessional Jewish diplomat

Ibrahim Ibn Zarzar, who had previously served the Marinids in Fez and the Nasrids in Granada.[17] Evidently impressed with his guest's prestigious lineage, Pedro the Cruel offered to restore the Banu Khaldun estates to Ibn Khaldun if he agreed to convert to Christianity.

In the event, Ibn Khaldun declined the offer, but it may have been during this period he became aware of the intellectual florescence of the Christian world to the north, whose philosophical dynamism he remarked on in the *Muqaddimah*. Paris, after all was not far away geographically, however distant culturally, and earlier translations of Ibn Rushd's précis of Aristotle's works had already introduced Europeans to Greek philosophy and helped stimulate the intellectual revitalization of Christian thought. Ibn Khaldun might have learned something of the translation movement from Ibn Zarzar, considering the Hispanic Jews' pivotal role in translating these texts. In any event, Christian theologians, most notably Saint Thomas Aquinas (1225–1274), had become Christian equivalents of Ashʿari speculative theologians and, like their Muslim counterparts, they began using Aristotelian logic to demonstrate the truth of their doctrines. Aquinas's works particularly are suffused with the philosophical vocabulary and mode of argument found in Muslim speculative theological texts.

Ibn Khaldun's visit to the Banu Khaldun former home of Seville ought to have ratified his own considerable sense of worth as a descendant of such a historically influential family. His experience in Granada also must have reinforced his conviction of Andalusia's cultural precedence in the western Islamic world, which numerous expatriate Andalusian scholars had earlier conveyed or personally exhibited to him as a youthful student in Tunis. It is important to remember he wrote in the *Muqaddimah* that Nasrid Granada presided over Andalusia's second golden age. His friendship with the accomplished Ibn al-Khatib may alone have persuaded him of the accuracy of his oft-repeated view that the thriving, populous cities of Andalusia, Seville, Cordoba, and Granada, represented an example of Arab Muslim urban culture that could not be found in North Africa, except for a brief moment in Fez and to a limited degree in Tunis. If anyone personified the cultural florescence and political influence that Ibn Khaldun seemed to crave, it was Ibn al Khatib working in Nasrid Granada.

IBN AL-KHATIB

Ibn al-Khatib was a far more accomplished individual than was Sharif al-Tilimsani, and if al-Tilimsani represented a religious scholarly ideal for Ibn Khaldun, Ibn al-Khatib personified the kind of scholar-official, or *adib*, Ibn Khaldun admired and, evidently, sought to become. No other individual occupies such a large amount of space in his memoir, including the many verses he exchanged with the Granadan *wazir*. A superbly educated and cultured individual, Ibn al-Khatib was an Arab whose ancestors, like those of Ibn Khaldun, originated in Yemen, although his more immediate family had emigrated from Syria to Andalusia in the eighth century, where he was born in 1313. He might, therefore, in certain respects be seen to personify the transmission of Umayyad Arab Muslim culture from Syria to Andalusia. Shortly after the family's arrival the amir of Granada invited his father to take an important post in the government, and in Granada Ibn al-Khatib received an elite education in religion, including Sufism, philosophy, and Arabic literature. Like Ibn Khaldun, he was trained for a career as a scholar-official, and he became secretary to the *wazir*, his former teacher, in 1340. Following his patron's death of plague in 1349, he was appointed as head of the royal chancellery. Steadily accumulating more titles, responsibility, land, and money in the following years, he became the senior state official after he aided one of the Nasrid dynasty's family members to succeed to the Granada throne as Muhammad V in 1354.[18]

Most of all a writer, an Arabic stylist, a major literary figure, and a historian but also a remarkably prolific polymath with encyclopedic interests, Ibn al-Khatib wrote dozens of works and excelled in diverse intellectual pursuits, including poetry, medicine, agriculture, *adab*, or belles lettres, music, Sufism, and history. His analytical study of the plague, which he attributed to contagion rather than to God, exhibited the kind of empirical rationalism that Ibn Khaldun came to admire but that conservative clerics must have deeply resented.[19] Ibn al-Khatib also became, tragically, an example of the treacherous political minefields in which such men operated, always subject to shifting courtly factions and unpredictable rulers. Partly, almost certainly, a victim of his own imperious manner and ruthless protection of his political eminence, Ibn al-Khatib became a victim of Granadan court intrigues of a later *wazir*, his former protégée and poet, Ibn Zamrak, as well as suffering from the hostility of the principal *qadi* of Granada.[20] Under threat, Ibn al-Khatib fled across the Mediterranean to Marinid-controlled Tilimsan in 1372–1373. He eventually fell into the hands of the Marinid sultan in 1374 or 1375, one of whose own officials instigated Star Chamber–like proceedings against him on the charge of heresy initiated in Granada. Despite Ibn Khaldun's efforts to save his friend and former patron, Ibn al-Khatib was strangled in his prison cell in May–June 1374–1375, but not before decrying in a moving poem the vicissitudes he suffered in his great fall from aristocratic eminence and political power. An elegant Arabic prose stylist widely regarded as the greatest writer in Andalusia, he also published an anthology of *muwashshah* poetry, including some of his own verse in this form, a complex but widely popular Andalusian genre Ibn Khaldun discusses in the *Muqaddimah*. Additionally he wrote several *rihlah*s, literate, artful travelogues embellished with verse, describing his journeys and sojourns in North Africa and Andalusia; medical works; and Sufi commentaries. Renowned primarily in his own time and later as literary figure, he is also known as a historian of Granada. In this work he chronicled the florescence of the Nasrid court of this late Andalusian city-state, including precise descriptions of the capital city as well as biographical sketches of its most famous inhabitants. It is in one of his last works, the *Aʿmal al-aʿlam (Acts of Fame)*, written just before his death, that he presented his most complete view of human history.

Ibn al-Khatib's historical writing, while focusing on the political centrality of the sultan and his *wazir*, that is, officials like himself, nonetheless produced vivid, egocentric, colorful images, emphasizing individual motivation but perceiving cycles in the history of dynasties as analogous to organisms, driven by human ambition, a Machiavellian view of politics and human history. Like Ibn Khaldun, he projected a pessimistic view of human history, one that was caused, however, not by tribal dynamics, but by cycles of petty jealousies, court intrigue, violence, and political revolution. Like Ibn Khaldun, too, Ibn al-Khatib largely ignored God's will as a determining force in Islamic history. Unlike Ibn Khaldun, and like most other Muslim writers, he focused on the human role in history, offering a complement to the work of his younger contemporary in vivid, pulsating prose. Enlivened by the vitality of his writing and the compelling accounts of human ambition, treachery, and loss, Ibn al-Khatib offered Shakespearean tableaux, the very kind of narrative that Ibn Khaldun criticized as a meaningless crowd-pleasing entertainment. It is not known if Ibn Khaldun read Ibn al-Khatib's last historical work, although he was familiar with many of the great *wazir*'s other writings. Still Ibn al-Khatib not only offered Ibn Khaldun a compelling personification of Andalusian Muslim high culture; he also provided him with additional insight into the Andalusian and North African political systems, if *system* adequately describes the vicious dynastic politics Ibn Khaldun later struggled to comprehend and analyze. Ibn al-Khatib offered his colleague and friend a compelling example of literate, vibrant, if altogether traditional, historical scholarship. Ibn al-Khatib's ideas of states as organic entities subject to cycles of growth and decay, and the essentially secular character of his narrative, unleavened by divine guidance, finds parallels in Ibn Khaldun's work. Otherwise the two men's histories are a study in contrast, vivid personalities enlivening the one, and sober philosophical analysis, entirely lacking individual portraits, driving the other. In fact, in characterizing his friend's work, Ibn Khaldun does not even allude to his histories, much less criticize them, as he denounces works of some great Muslim historians. He describes Ibn al-Khatib as a superb Arabic linguist and "leading poet [of Spain and the Maghrib] and a prose writer without peer in Islam."[21]

Little is known of Ibn Khaldun's other activities during his Andalusian interlude. Later comments in his memoir from his Cairene years indicate he studied Maliki law with the *qadi* of Granada, who certified Ibn Khaldun was authorized to teach the subject. Whether or not this *qadi* was the same man who later condemned Ibn al-Khatib is not clear. Otherwise he seems to have enjoyed a brief, restful, and stable two-year interlude in his otherwise tumultuous life, enjoying Muhammad V's patronage and feeling secure enough to bring his family to Granada. Yet unnamed "enemies and intriguers" schemed against him, he writes, because of his close relations with Muhammad V, leading to an unexplained deterioration of his relations with Ibn al-Khatib.[22] If Ibn al-Khatib was at fault, this perceived coolness in Ibn Khaldun's relations with the *wazir* may well have stemmed from his friend's well-known ruthlessness when it came to protecting his position at the Nasrid court. Ibn Khaldun's own assertiveness and sense of self-worth might equally have contributed to this tension. In 1365, therefore, even while still enjoying Muhammad V's favor, he decided to leave Granada and accept the position of chief minister of the small coastal city-state of Bijayah, the town where he had wintered on his trip from Tunis to Fez in 1353–1354. Thus for the second time since he left Tunis, Ibn Khaldun both entered into and lost out in the egotistical and political machinations of court politics, which is the small sum of what can be concluded about his poorly documented relations with other individuals at court.

NORTH AFRICA: THE ʿUMRAN BADAWI

At a distance of more than six centuries, it seems remarkable Ibn Khaldun decided to abandon cosmopolitan Granada for the tiny North African city-state of Bijayah, even if personal rivalries threatened his position at the Nasrid court. In doing so he reentered the fractious North African political scene during one of its most unstable eras and briefly took up a position in one of its most insignificant courts, a "frontier town," he writes, which was constantly exposed to the political ambitions and varying fortunes of Marinids, Abd al-Wadids, and warring members of the extended Hafsid house.[23] Thus began for him a tumultuous, decadelong participation in court intrigues and tribal conflicts, a difficult, unstable, and dangerous period in which he gained nothing except, probably, a heightened understanding of tribal life and intertribal politics. At least, it was during these years he went into the countryside at various times to tax or recruit or sometimes to live with tribesmen. This decade was the first period in his life he worked or lived in rural tribal society for any length of time, and it is likely that he acquired a greater understanding of the *tabi'ah*, the nature of generic bedouin society, as a result. Unfortunately, as is the case with his education and earlier political experiences, Ibn Khaldun never links any element of his dialectical model to his experiences during these years.

Bijayah, where he arrived from Granada in 1365 was then governed by the Hafsid Abu ʿAbdallah, with whom Ibn Khaldun had been friendly during his earlier Fez years. In 1364 Abu ʿAbdallah, who had just gained control of this coastal town, had written to Ibn Khaldun, inviting him to accept the position of *hajabah*, chamberlain or principal minister, a position that Ibn Khaldun may have found attractive because, as he writes, the chamberlain exercised "absolute power" in the government and acted as the intermediary between the sultan and the people of the state. Perhaps Ibn Khaldun preferred, or felt safer, exercising that kind of authority, even in a marginal North African city-state, to the uncertain life of a privileged courtier in Granada.[24] He was, in any case, given an effusive welcome by the population and by the sultan, who awarded him a robe of honor and a horse, typical presents for an honored new servant. In response Ibn Khaldun took on himself, as he says, all the burdens of the state and made every effort to administer its affairs and policy, including collecting taxes from nearby Berber tribes.[25] In his spare time, which must have been considerable in the modest Bijayah city-state, he taught at the mosque, probably offering commentaries on the Quran as well as Maliki law.

Yet his patron died within a year of his arrival, having lost a struggle for Hafsid supremacy with his cousin, the ruler of nearby Constantine. Ibn Khaldun's situation then drastically changed. As in Fez and Granada, he suffered, as he reports once again, from "intrigues" against him. Yet it is impossible to determine his degree of responsibility for these court conflicts in a memoir, which typifies this genre of rhetorical self-promotion. Whatever the exact circumstances he was uncomfortable with his position under the cousin's new regime and sought permission to leave. He was able to escape an uncertain situation and fled to the nearby Biskrah oasis, located south of Bijayah, where he knew the Arab chief and his son, whom he had met in 1352 after he left Tunis. His brother Yahya, who had also accepted a position with the Bijayah regime, was not so fortunate. The new Hafsid ruler of Bijayah imprisoned him and confiscated his property.

From 1366 until 1375, when he took refuge with another tribe deep in the interior, where he wrote the first draft of the *Muqaddimah*, Ibn Khaldun lived an unstable and dangerous existence in North Africa and briefly, once more, in Granada. Almost as soon as he settled in Biskrah, the Abd al-Wadid ruler of Tilimsan, who was married to the daughter of his recent patron, the ruler of Bijayah, wrote to offer him a ministerial post in his regime. By this time, however, Ibn Khaldun seemed to have become far more cautious about such seemingly prestigious appointments, whatever their title, for it was difficult for him to see a future in a regime that, like other small states, was constantly under threat.

"Unwilling," as he says, to expose himself to the unknown dangers of this position, he politely declined, "renouncing the delusion of rank" and preferring to resume his long-neglected scholarship.[26] Nonetheless, Ibn Khaldun still had to find a secure scholarly position somewhere, and he was a valuable human commodity in the endless conflicts among and within these different Berber tribal lineages.

While trying to negotiate the Scylla and Charybdis of unpredictable petty rulers and perennial tribal wars, he decided to return to Granada. Before he was able to do so, however, a new Marinid sultan invaded Ifriqiyah, overran Tilimsan, and captured Ibn Khaldun as he was trying to find a boat for Iberia. The sultan was evidently mistrustful of Ibn Khaldun because of his earlier involvement in the Marinid succession struggle and possibly fearful that his return to Granada presaged a Nasrid campaign against the Marinids in the Maghrib. He briefly imprisoned him and eventually pressed him into his service as an emissary to local Arab tribesmen, whom Ibn Khaldun knew well.

Two years later, in September 1372, after trying to recruit these tribes in and around Biskrah, the new Marinid sultan called him to Fez. Ibn Khaldun dutifully set out with his family and decided to continue the journey, even though news reached him of the death of the ruler. Escaping capture by Arab tribesmen en route, Ibn Khaldun finally reached Fez in the late fall, in the midst of another succession crises, which made it impossible to secure a stable position. Reprising his earlier difficulties in trying to leave Fez for his homeland, it took him two years before he could leave Fez for Granada, leaving his family behind more or less as hostages in the Marinid capital.

This time, however, he encountered a hostile environment in the Nasrid capital. His friend and patron Ibn al-Khatib was himself a refugee in Fez, having fled Granada in 1371–1372 after factional disputes at court and his condemnation for heresy. Now occupying his position as *wazir* in Granada was Ibn Zamrak, the former protégée now bitter enemy of the great scholar. The Nasrid sultan Muhammad V had also turned on his former favorite and ordered his arrest for heresy after Ibn al-Khatib had fled to North Africa. Given this situation Ibn Khaldun's return to Spain ought probably to be seen as an act of desperation. It was unsuccessful. He was quickly forced back to North Africa and took refuge with the Abd al-Wadid ruler of Tilimsan, whose invitation he had earlier refused. Pressed into service for this ruler, he agreed to lead a mission to a nearby Arab tribe, but instead he seized the opportunity in 1377 to take refuge, along with his family, with the Awlad ʿArif Arab family at the tribe's *Qalʿat Ibn Salamah*, a small fortress deep in the interior of Oran Province of modern Algeria.

Even a small fragment of Ibn Khaldun's account of his experience among the Hafsids, Abd al-Wadids, Marinids, and Arab and Berber tribes in the countryside at this period provides information that is almost impossible to summarize. His account conveys an image of a kind of political Brownian motion, the unpredictable movement of hundreds of different individual actors, families, clans, and tribes competing in a fluid social environment. It was just this atomized tradition Ibn Khaldun tried to explain as he wrote the first draft of the *Muqaddimah* in the isolated fortress of the Awlad ʿArif *qabilah*. What is remarkable, astonishing even, about his memoir for this period is that he devotes less than one hundred words to this entire period and only a single sentence to the *Muqaddimah*. The sentence, though, at least suggests something of his intellectual excitement for what he recalled as a supremely creative "moment" in the late summer and autumn of 1377. In those few months, he reports, words and ideas came pouring from his mind, flowing like cream from a pitcher into a churn, to produce an *al-nahw al-gharib*, "an extraordinary method," the first draft of his philosophical history and science of man. He also mentions he completed the first draft of his greater history, the *Kitab al-'ibar*, which contains a narrative of the Arabs, Berbers, and the Zanatahs, the latter one of three large Berber tribal confederations Ibn Khaldun describes.[27]

He adds, in the spirit of a true scholar, that living in the desert he was limited in what he could write, as he needed access to books and records that could only be found in cities to verify the references he had made from memory. Therefore, after writing to the Hafsid ruler of Tunis for permission to reenter his birthplace, he crossed the desert between October and November of 1378 with the aid of a group of Bedouins from the Arab al-Akhdar tribe, arriving back in his natal Tunis, "the country of his fathers, which preserved their traces and tombs," sometime in late November or December of that year.[28]

Ibn Khaldun spent nearly four years in Tunis finishing his history of the Berbers and adding information about pre-Islamic history and "two principal dynasties of Arabs," the Umayyads and 'Abbasids. He ceremonially gave one complete copy to the sultan's library. Ibn Khaldun also taught Maliki law to students, who clamored, he proudly remarks, to study with him. Otherwise he reports once again running afoul of local personalities, in this case sparking the resentment of the man who was both *Imam* of the Friday mosque and the *Shaikh al-futya*, the cleric who issued *fatwa*s or Islamic legal opinions. One of the charges laid against him, he further notes, was that he had failed to write eulogies. Ibn Khaldun responded to this charge by noting he had given up poetry to concentrate exclusively on science, presumably referring to the *Muqaddimah* and his historical work.[29] Just to refute his critics, he composed an epic verse celebrating the military glory and religious service of sultan and the Hafsids in enthusiastically baroque verse.[30]

Still, he writes, intrigues against him continued, and in 1382 he abandoned his native city, whose cultural dynamism he repeatedly praises in the *Muqaddimah,* intending to make the *hajj,* the excuse Muslims commonly used to escape difficult or dangerous court situations. Seen off, as he pointedly mentions, by a crowd of well-wishers of students and notables at the Tunis port, he traveled to Cairo, postponing the *hajj* until later. Egypt was then ruled by Mamluks, the dynasty established in 1250 by the Turkic slave commanders of the descendants of Salah al-Din or Saladin, the foe of the Crusaders, who had proclaimed himself sultan in 1174. With this move from bedouin North Africa to cosmopolitan Cairo, Ibn Khaldun's life symbolically mirrored the evolutionary trajectory of his dialectic model from *'umran badawi* to *'umran hadari,* from rural tribal to urban sedentary society.

CAIRO: THE *'UMRAN HADARI*

Arriving in Cairo, Ibn Khaldun described it as "city of the world," the "garden of the universe," "the assemblage of multitudes of mankind," "the palace of Islam," and "the capital of the empire." Here was a city where he hoped to experience the dynamic cultural milieu he found so wanting in North Africa. He knew from past report, he says, the city had attained a high degree of culture.[31] He must have been confirmed in his high opinion of the city when the Egyptian Sultan Barquq, typifying his predilection for men of science, immediately granted him a stipend and later wrote a fulsome letter in 1384 to Tunis, asking that Ibn Khaldun's family be allowed to join him.[32] Tragically, the family drowned in a shipwreck off Alexandria as they were en route to join him. In a rare recorded memory of emotional trauma, Ibn Khaldun wrote: "My pain was so great it devastated me."[33]

Even allowing for the typical hyperbole of royal correspondence, the Mamluk sultan's characterization of Ibn Khaldun in this letter was fulsome, speaking of him in grandiose terms as "the noble, the incomparable, the glorious, the friend of religion, the excellence of Islam and Muslims, outstanding among scholars in the world, the confidante of kings and sultans, Ibn Khaldun the Maliki, blessed by God."[34] Whoever supplied the information for the sultan's praise seems to have more or less accurately identified Ibn Khaldun's social status, orthodox Sunni piety, and knowledge of Maliki law. Even if the Mamluk ruler wildly exaggerated his essentially mediocre career in North Africa and Iberia, his praise at least suggests Ibn Khaldun had acquired an enviable Islamic scholarly reputation in the Arabic-speaking world. Based on his testimony and the sultan's letter, he was also known to the citizens of Cairo, but more probably for his personal dynamism, as a teacher of Maliki law. At this time few people outside Tunis could have known much if anything about the *Muqaddimah* and the *Kitab al-ʿibar*. These unnamed Cairenes "welcomed and honored" him, and students clamored, he reports, for his instruction.[35]

Ibn Khaldun's prestige was sufficient to be invited to lecture at the great al-Azhar mosque, where he impressed students with his erudition and especially, writes the historian and eminent *hadith* scholar Ibn Hajar al-ʿAsqalani (1332–1449), with his discussion of the "affairs of state," probably an allusion to Ibn Khaldun's lectures on sultanate government from the *Muqaddimah*.[36] Ibn Khaldun never discusses the subject of his political lectures in Cairo. Shortly afterward the sultan appointed him to teach at a *madrasah* devoted to Maliki law, which the sultan had endowed as a *waqf*, a religious or charitable endowment.[37] Ibn Khaldun delivered his inaugural lecture for this post, which he quotes in its entirety, in the presence of an assembly of Cairo's grand amirs. He praised the 'ulama' and delivered a hyperbolic panegyric to the Mamluk sultans for bringing the culture of Egypt to the greatest heights by patronizing religious institutions and increasing the power of Islam.[38]

His next appointment as the chief Maliki *qadi* in August 1384 demonstrated the scholarly renown he enjoyed in Cairo as a student of Maliki law and his privileged status at court, perhaps also it seems likely, based on his family's prestige. Taking charge of one of the four highest religious offices in the kingdom, Ibn Khaldun set about to administer justice to his Maliki coreligionists, as he describes his administration, with an exceptional degree of rigor, honesty, and contempt for political connections.[39] He had no experience with a legal position of such importance, and, from his own testimony, he seems to have brought to the post an intellectual's theoretical sense of justice and an unwillingness to administer law according to the social status or wealth of claimants. "I made the utmost efforts to enforce God's law, as I had been charged to do. I tried to conduct things fairly and in an exemplary manner. I considered the plaintiff and the accused equally, without any concern for their status or power in society; I gave assistance to any weaker party, to level out power inequalities. I refused mediation or petitions on either party's behalf. I focused on finding the truth only by attending to the evidence."[40]

Ibn Khaldun's assertion that he sought to decide cases based solely on an examination of the evidence seems to echo the *Muqaddimah*'s appeal to reason in historical research and his denunciation of traditional hagiographic narratives. He scornfully denounced the corrupted testimony of most traditional court witnesses, usually *'ulama'*, who were creatures of wealthy amirs and, he said, the willing recipients of bribes. Ibn Khaldun expressed himself in an especially caustic tone when he described how official witnesses conspired with influential individuals in the usurpation of valuable *waqf* property. He was also acerbic when denouncing the poor quality of Maliki *muftis*, legal scholars who could issue *fatwas* but who were, more often than not, fraudulent individuals who had no qualifications. He had some of these men, including smooth-talking Maghribis, imprisoned. "I set about reforming this [habit]," he writes, by arresting the muftis who were quacks or who lacked learning.[41]

Given his self-described probity and contemptuous assault on corrupt individuals in Maliki legal proceedings, it is scarcely surprising Ibn Khaldun quickly began to sense calumnies being leveled against him. Some charged him with an ignorance of law and procedure, but that was very likely a legitimizing smokescreen for the resentment this brash North African newcomer had provoked. In July 1385 he was removed from his prestigious post, and its former holder was reinstated. This was the first of four appointments and dismissals from the Maliki judgeship, a reflection most likely of both his own censorious, uncompromising manner and intrigue against him by members of the Egyptian *'ulama'* and probably also pressure from influential amirs with property interests in the capital. Cairenes also may have resented his sudden elevation to high office because he publically displayed his North African identity by ostentatiously continuing to wear typical North African dress after he settled in the city, another suggestive reminder of his confident sense of self.

Yet the sultan continued Ibn Khaldun's appointment as a lecturer in the Qamhiyah *madrasah* and shortly afterward made him a professor of Maliki law at another college. In 1388, after returning from his *hajj*, Ibn Khaldun was given two other appointments, first as a professor of *hadith* at the Salghatmish *madrasah* and second, a lucrative post, a sinecure probably, as the director of a Sufi *khanagah* or hospice named for Sultan Baibars (1260–1277), the most prestigious Mamluk sultan of Egypt. For his inaugural lecture at the *madrasah* school he gave an extended talk on the foundational text of Maliki law, the *Kitab al-muwatta'*, a lecture he cites in its entirety.

In his talk Ibn Khaldun recounted a history of the Maliki legal school from its origins to the present. He included a list of the principal Maliki scholars from the days of the founder, Malik b Anas (ca. 711–795), in Medina to scholars in both North Africa and Andalusia during Ibn Khaldun's lifetime. He completed his account of Maliki authorities by citing his own training and naming those teachers, including one at the Grand or Friday mosque of Granada, who gave him *ijazah*s or licenses to teach certain texts of this legal school. He had also received other licenses to teach the Quran, one of which was granted by Abu 'Abd Allah Muhammad b al-Saffar al-Marrakushi, who, he noted, was the "great" Quranic authority in the Maghrib.[42] If his readers needed reminding, in this lecture, Ibn Khaldun let them know the extent of his commitment to and expertise in Maliki law, a continual subject of his studies, beginning with his youthful days in Tunis. Following this appointment, as he briefly reports, he then spent the next fourteen years teaching and editing his writings, except for a pilgrimage to Mecca in 1387–1388, before being reappointed as Maliki *qadi* in 1399. Otherwise he says absolutely nothing of his life during these years, an illustration of the limited personal value of his memoir, in which these many years are glossed over in a single sentence.

A SCHOLAR-OFFICIAL IN A DANGEROUS WORLD 147

Within months of these appointments, Ibn Khaldun's life was turned upside down by a coup within the habitually unstable Turkic oligarchy ruling Egypt. Ibn Khaldun's patron, Sultan Barquq, was overthrown and briefly imprisoned, and Ibn Khaldun, who had benefited from his patronage, lost his positions. Such conflicts were endemic to military oligarchies in which no clear dynastic legitimacy existed, and Barquq regained his throne within a few months. The episode itself was not remarkable, but Ibn Khaldun's discussion of it is, because he included a detailed narrative of the coup in his memoir, which, without explanation, he prefaces with a brief summary of his dialectical historical model.

It has often been observed Ibn Khaldun wrote his *Kitab al-'ibar* as a traditional narrative history, without employing the ideas he introduced in the *Muqaddimah*. Yet this is not surprising, for, as will be seen, he wrote the *Muqaddimah* and the two narrative volumes of the history as a single work: the first as a conceptual program to introduce the second, his narrative historical examples. Here in his memoir, though, he offers an abridged précis of his ideas, but without explaining his reason for doing so and, even more surprising, without linking it with the political narrative of the rebellion he was about to relate.

Thus he prefaces his account of the Cairo coup, the "Fitnah of al-Nasiri," the Revolt of al-Nasiri, with a generalized account of how dynasties evolved from conditions of "grandeur and domination" to subsequent states of "decay and decline."[43] Alluding to "universal empires," evidently meaning Rome, Byzantium, and Iran, he says these states had a long series of monarchs succeed one another owing to their *'asabiyah al-nasab*, "kinship solidarity," or *wala'*, "kindred feeling," which was the basis of these rulers' authority and domination.[44] Their military dynamism, he continues, was due to their harsh life and "bedouin" habits. Yet as they acquired possessions and embraced luxuries of all kinds, provoking fiscal crises, they could no longer pay their troops and maintain them. As they became more enamored of luxurious living, the dynasty not only suffered monetary shortages but also compromised its military spirit, thus eventually triggering a cycle of decline and the rise of leadership based on a new kinship of kindred feeling. In his subsequent account of al-Nasiri's revolt, Ibn Khaldun does not, however, even refer to this précis, concluding it instead with a poem, which pleaded with his generous patron to excuse his vacillating behavior during this episode.

Ibn Khaldun's last seven years in Egypt, from his second appointment as Maliki *qadi* in 1399 until his death in 1406, were marked by a rapidly changing environment. Shortly after his reappointment his patron, Barquq, died and was succeeded by his son, whom Ibn Khaldun accompanied to Damascus, following the revolt of the Ayyubid governor of the city. On this journey he was able to visit Jerusalem, Bethlehem, and Gaza, and while in Jerusalem, he visited a mosque but felt disgusted at the thought of entering a nearby Christian church, which he identifies as "al-Qumamah," and refused "to set foot in it."[45] It is worth noting this episode if only to have it serve as a reminder that for all his philosophical sophistication and scholarly understanding of the faith, Ibn Khaldun possessed a deep emotional attachment to Islam and revulsion for the artifacts of other religions.

Following his account of this journey, Ibn Khaldun then devotes much of the remainder of his memoir to recounting the threat of invasion of the Central Asian Turk Taimür or Timur-i leng, Timur the Lame, or, in English, Tamerlane (1336–1405). His discussion of Timur is as intriguing as is his earlier narration of al-Nasiri's revolt—both for what he includes and what he omits.

Thus he begins by reprising his summary of Ptolemaic or Greco-Islamic geography, which prefaces the first section of the *Muqaddimah*, followed by material from his history—and other Islamic narratives—a standard genealogy of the human race from Adam and Noah through the early pre-Islamic empires, Muhammad, the Umayyad and ʿAbbasid caliphates, and a fairly detailed account of Middle Eastern history. The latter section includes accounts of North African dynasties and the Mongol invasions, down to the late fourteenth century, and the campaigns of Timur, who sacked Delhi in 1398 and appeared before Damascus in 1400, before returning to the north and defeating and capturing the Ottoman sultan Bayezid I (r. 1389–1402) near Ankara in 1402.

The intriguing aspect of this geographical and political summary is that apart from identifying the Turks of Mawarannahr or western Central Asia as nomads, he never attempts to discuss Mongol or Turkic history within the conceptual framework of the *Muqaddimah*, despite the fact his model fit the case of the Mongol tribes, the Mongol dynasties of Iran and China, and to a degree Timur himself. His historical knowledge of Mawarannahr was understandably sketchy, so he may have felt unable to discuss the region intelligently. He did have an excellent opportunity to get to know Timur during a monthlong series of meetings with the Turkic conqueror at his Damascus encampment. Timur, evidently considering a western campaign to Egypt and North Africa, quizzed him on the political environment of his North African homeland, including questions about its geography and many aspects of Islamic society and history. Timur demanded he prepare a description of the Maghrib, which he did, but after returning to Cairo, Ibn Khaldun sent a report to the Marinids in Fez, summarizing what had passed between Timur and himself during their meetings. In his memoir he summarized the history of the Mongols in Central Asia, Iran, and eastern Anatolia in some detail, and he attributed the strength of the Turks to their ʿasabiyah, which only they and Arabs possessed in such strength.[46] Then, finally and briefly, he compares the incredibly destructive campaigns of the "Tatars" with ravages of North African bedouins—Arabs and Berbers. But beyond that suggestive insight, he does not invoke his dialectical model to interpret Timur's career. He concludes with an evaluation of the Turkic conqueror's character—a simple but extremely intelligent man.[47] In that respect as well as in his ruthless campaigns, Timur was indeed an embodiment of Ibn Khaldun's vigorous bedouin type.

4

THE METHOD AND THE MODEL

CELEBRATING HIS SCHOLARLY achievement in 1377 at the isolated Ibn Salamah fortress, Ibn Khaldun alluded in his memoir to his *al-nahw al-gharib*, his "extraordinary method." In the *Muqaddimah* he reprises what might otherwise remain an enigmatic comment by explicitly asserting he has created *al-ʿulum al-gharibah*, an extraordinary science, and explaining at length that this science was a new philosophically informed historical discipline. In saying this, Ibn Khaldun refers to the methodology he developed and then applied to construct an explanatory model of a historical process peculiar to the predominantly tribal societies of North Africa. Both the methodology and the dialectical model represent major intellectual achievements, and they are inextricably linked. The model can be understood only in light of the method. Beyond seeing it as just a preface to the model, the method itself, with its novel devotion to social analysis, consists of a comprehensive program for social historical research, which did not become commonplace in the West until the French Annales School historians began reshaping European historiography in the twentieth century. It is not surprising that French historians, with their powerful rationalist traditions, first internalized the philosophical concepts and methods and rediscovered the wheel, intellectually speaking, that Ibn Khaldun had first imagined and designed in the fourteenth century.

METHODOLOGY

"On the surface," Ibn Khaldun observes, history "consists of reports of eras and dynasties and past events," but in contrast, the real, or what he terms the inner or esoteric meaning of history, involves "a search below the surface of events, a profound knowledge of underlying causes, a determination of the subtle origins and causes of existing things."[1] The search requires *nazar*, philosophical speculation, a product of the speculative intelligence, *al-ʿaql al-nazari*, the third and highest level of reasoning Ibn Khaldun describes in his section on human thought, a recapitulation of certain Greco-Islamic mental categories.[2] It enabled humans to make generalizations, true knowledge, and ultimately to attain a perception of existence as it is, *tasawwur al-wujud*, "with its various genera, differences, reasons, and causes."[3] Aristotle in his *Physics* and his Greco-Islamic acolytes used the latter four terms, the first two and second two as kinds of intellectual conceptual pairs, to discuss and analyze reality. Therefore, the mental discipline Ibn Khaldun demanded of historians was not simply a matter of careful observation and reflective thought. It was a philosophically informed critical sense, leading Ibn Khaldun to conclude that history, when practiced this way, deserved to be classified as one of the Greco-Islamic roster of philosophical subjects. "It deserves to be numbered," he asserts, "among the sciences."[4]

Just as Galen insisted the first step in any scientific research was the determination of the nature of its particular subject, Ibn

Khaldun was similarly adamant that historians had to begin their work by identifying the nature or characteristic traits of a society. Adapting an argument from Aristotle's *Physics*, he said: "Only knowledge of the nature of society" allowed an historian properly to investigate historical evidence and distinguish truth from falsehood. "This is more effective in critical investigation," he wrote, "than any other aspect of historical analysis."[5] Humans with speculative intelligence could understand the nature of their subject through inductive logic, an almost intuitive process by which they could immediately perceive the essence of some thing, or in this case, the essence of a particular society. Like Aristotle, Ibn Sina, and Ibn Rushd—and later Émile Durkheim—Ibn Khaldun believed a thing's nature, in his case a society's nature, shaped or caused events associated with it, and therefore once a scholar identified an entity's nature, he could understand "the possibility inherent in the matter that belongs to a given thing."[6] Such understanding meant that a historian would not suggest historical interpretations that were intellectually possible but realistically ridiculous when they were examining information about a particular society. Each type of society would generate institutions or occupations typical of its type and would follow certain predictable historical trajectories. Thus if historians were trying to understand an event, they could trace its origin or determine its cause from their knowledge of its society's nature, since every occurrence, he argues, "must inevitably produce an event peculiar to its essence [or nature] as well as to the accidental conditions that may attach themselves to it."[7]

Consideration of these accidents represented Ibn Khaldun's next rule for historians. In addition to identifying the nature of social organizations, he advised scholars to be certain to distinguish between traits, which constituted the essence of a society and secondary or ancillary characteristics known as "accidents," *aʿrad*. He invoked this standard Aristotelian and Greco-Islamic distinction to insist that historians should not mistake "the essence" of a society from these accidents or secondary characteristics, which might or might not be associated with the society's fundamental nature. He was especially careful to warn scholars against considering adventitious or ephemeral traits as an integral or essential part of something's nature. Prestige of monarchs in sedentary societies constituted one such example of a nonessential or ephemeral accident, which a ruler might or might not possess or lose over the course of time. Understanding this distinction was crucial, since it determined whether or not historians founded their analyses on accurate perceptions of a society's fundamental qualities.

As Ibn Khaldun explains at great length, and Galen would have been quick to point out, identifying the nature of a scientific subject and distinguishing its substance from associated accidents only constituted the philosophical historian's first steps in the extremely complex and demanding scientific process. As Ibn Khaldun wrote, historians not only needed to use speculative intelligence; they also must be thorough.[8] In logical terms they had to use deductive logic to verify the validity of a whole range of subjects, which they needed to consider to accurately judge evidence. First of all, in order to distinguish truth, *haqq*, from fiction, *batil*, to verify so-called factual historical information, historical scholars had to compare reports of events with what they knew about the nature or essence of a particular society, the specific human social organization they were examining. This constituted a "logical method," *wajh burhani*, for ascertaining the truth. Marc Bloch, a cofounder of the Annales School, reiterated this point in the twentieth century when he described comparison as the "dialectic of the historian."⁹ In related contexts Ibn Khaldun speaks of the need for scholars to formulate what he terms "natural proofs," *al-barahin al-tabʿi*, to verify the reliability of recorded information. While Ibn Khaldun does not construct his own arguments or critique of sources in syllogistic terms, he frequently claims to have demonstrated the absolute proof, *burhan*, of a particular statement.

Apart from appreciating the nature and accidents of a particular societies and comparing these with evidence, historians had to take into account a number of different factors that affected the nature of the societies they studied. These included his almost encyclopedic list that reveals a fourteenth-century scholar's acute awareness of the reasons why historical analysis was and is so difficult to do well and so easy to do poorly—and he thought most contemporary Muslim historians produced vacuous work. In summarizing everything the philosophical or scientific historian must know and how they ought to proceed in making judgments, Ibn Khaldun writes that these scholars must:

> Know the principles of politics, the ... nature of existent things, and the differences among nations, places, and periods, with regards to ways of life, character qualities, customs, sects, schools and everything else. He further needs a comprehensive knowledge of present conditions in all these respects. He must compare similarities or differences between the present and the past ... conditions. He must know the causes of similarities in certain cases and the differences in others. He must be aware of the differing origins and beginnings of ... dynasties and religious groups, as well as the reasons and incentives that brought them into being and the circumstances and history of the

persons who supported them. *His goal must be to have complete knowledge of the reasons for every happening and to be acquainted with the origin of every event. Then, he must check transmitted information with the basic principles [of nature and accident] he knows.*[10]

Ibn Khaldun's final sentence requiring that historians must combine rationalist knowledge of nature and accident with empirical research almost perfectly recapitulates Galen's method of combining *logos,* rationalism, with *peira,* empiricism, for medical diagnosis. Then finally, in the midst of all these considerations, Ibn Khaldun warned historians to practice textual criticism. They had not only to be aware of "the intentions of former authors" but also to understand how reports of "conditions are affected by ambiguities and artificial distortions. The informant," he said, "reports the conditions as he saw them, but on account of artificial distortions he himself has no true picture of them."[11]

Ibn Khaldun also stressed that history concerned events peculiar to a particular era and people and that conditions within communities and populations changed from day to day, from one condition to another.[12] "History," he writes, "relates events intrinsic to an era or people," and "the condition of the world and of nations, their customs and sects, does not persist in the same form or in a constant manner."[13] He specifically praised the great tenth-century historian al-Mas'udi for identifying the different conditions and customs of nations and peoples.[14] In this regard it was particularly dangerous, he thought, if scholars made analogies between the present, whose conditions they understood, and the past, with which they were personally unfamiliar, without being aware of such differences.[15] His denunciation of this kind of presentism and awareness of the constantly evolving conditions of societies and states is one reason why Ibn Khaldun ought to be seen as a historical sociologist. His model explains social change over time and space.

Ibn Khaldun took an almost obscene delight in criticizing, sometimes ridiculing, and occasionally eviscerating former Muslim historians for their faulty, absurd, or even contemptible works. He thought they were intellectually impoverished and socially corrupt. His comments may be—may partly be—one reflection of a well-known feature of his personality: his imperious self-regard. In any event there is no mistaking the substance of Ibn Khaldun's critique, and his slashing and burning his way through the historical profession offers readers a guilty pleasure. He writes that most historians even lacked qualifications for studying history. They were reporters not scientists. "Dull of nature and intelligence," they put an uncritical faith in tradition, "the pasture of stupidity." They were in essence reporters who uncritically passed on material.[16] Contemporary Muslim historians were not philosophers or scientists.

The basis of his critique was, as one might expect from reading his own proposal for a philosophical history, that earlier Muslim historians wrote superficial and largely worthless historical narratives because of their "ignorance, [*jahl*], of the nature, [*tabīʿah*], of conditions, [*ahwal*], in society, [*ʿumran*]."[17] Most Muslim historians, he thus implies, lived in a condition of intellectual *jahiliyah*, a state of ignorance, the philosophical equivalent of pre-Islamic paganism. In Ibn Khaldun's eyes, nothing was more important than this failure to identify the nature of things, because without comprehending the fundamental essence, the structures and values of a particular society, historians could not possibly explain its legal and political systems or its historical trajectory. Nor could they, without such fundamental knowledge, adequately judge the likely truth or falsity of historical information. In consequence, contemporary historians produced worthless, superficial narratives "elegantly presented and spiced with proverbs."[18]

Muslim historians produced works, which did not really constitute knowledge, as "mere forms without substance," and concerning "species, the genera of which are not taken into consideration," he says, using Greco-Islamic philosophical vocabulary.[19] By his first phrase, "forms without substance," Ibn Khaldun alluded to what he felt was the superficial narrative character of these historians' works, while his comment that they discuss species but not genera or genus reflected his conviction they did not generalize but dealt only with particulars, rather than trying to compare similarities in phenomena and classify them, moving from an identification of a species to the perception that the species composed part of a genus. It was just this failure of Greek historians to generalize that had prompted Aristotle to dismiss the notion that history was a science, although Ibn Khaldun does not cite Aristotle's opinion.

Beyond these fundamental issues, Ibn Khaldun criticized Muslim historians for several failings, most of which reflected their lack of intellectual and personal integrity. Thus, he accused them of mistakenly interpreting verses in the Quran—and falsifying history because of their desire for sensationalism. This latter instinct, he felt, led these scholars to heighten the entertainment value of their narratives, by inventing ridiculous, titillating stories about the supposed luxurious, dissolute lives of others. A host of other deficiencies vitiated their work, most notably their failure to be impartial, writing instead as partisans of "opinions and schools" and acting like sycophants when discussing powerful individuals. "Prejudice and partisanship," he said, "obscure the critical faculty and preclude critical investigation."[20]

He was particularly troubled, outraged even, by this latter tendency, historians' eagerness to ingratiate themselves with the rich and powerful through unjustified praise. Without considering premodern writers' or historians' need for patronage, he denounced the unjustified fame and renown of so many individuals who did not deserve glorious reputations in the first place. Yet, more often than not, he says, historians falsely praised individuals who did not deserve it, whether rulers, 'ulama', or pious men. Historians erred through uncritical acceptance of historical information, partly owing to their failure to compare stories with what was known about conditions, partly through bias and partisanship, but most of all because of the human desire for praise. People sought fame rather than virtue, the Greco-Islamic norm. Given this reality, and historians' willingness to pander to their subjects' thirst for fame, how could anyone expect that glowing reports of influential men could have any resemblance to truth?[21]

Ibn Khaldun respected a few earlier Muslim historians, although he says the important ones "can almost be counted on the fingers of one hand."[22] He included in this list two of the most prestigious classical scholars, al-Tabari and al-Mas'udi, who, he says, produced "exhaustive collections of historical events" and accurate, systematic accounts of the history of nations and dynasties. Ibn Khaldun implies that these men and a few others made valuable contributions because they wrote critically and were familiar with the time and place of the events they described and because some of them, at least, produced broad, sweeping accounts of human societies. He particularly associated this latter trait with al-Mas'udi, the tenth-century scholar whose work he cites more often than any other Muslim historian. Al-Mas'udi (d. 956) was the most cosmopolitan and broadly learned historical scholar among the early or classical Arab Muslim historians. A widely traveled and unusually cosmopolitan-minded individual who wrote on a variety of scientific and cultural subjects, he conceived his histories broadly to include both Islamic and non-Islamic peoples, as well as discussions of geography, culture, and sectarian beliefs. His works were, in Ibn Khaldun's view, "exhaustive." Yet even men such as al-Masʿudi, he notes, often made ridiculous mistakes and reported absurd stories because, he implies, they did not conceive of history as a branch of philosophy and failed to use even elementary logic. One pertinent example, Ibn Khaldun argued, was al-Masʿudi's strange belief, derived from unnamed philosophers, that God first created humans with perfect bodies and uniformly long lives, an idea, he says, using two of his favorite philosophical terms, that had no "natural or logical" basis.[23]

Ibn Khaldun based his historical methodology on the conviction that only rational or philosophical analysis combined with practical knowledge and/or experience could reveal the truth about historical processes. The priority of reason led him to contrast the different goals and standards of proof that distinguished philosophical historians from ʿulamaʾ, who wrote about historical aspects of the Muslim community. Reprising the general arguments he made about the distinction between philosophical and theological reasoning, he said clerics made for poor historians when they discussed any aspect of the historical record beyond the principles of their own faith. Not only did their ideological or theological assumptions and lack of practical knowledge make them incapable of accurately analyzing politics; it also meant they were unable to correctly interpret historical evidence.

Religious scholars' ignorance of the material world was the basis for Ibn Khaldun's critique of their "science" of personality criticism, which attempted to validate the reliability of individuals whose testimony forms the isnad, the chain or lineage of transmitters who attested to the validity of the *hadith*, the reports of the saying or practices of the Prophet Muhammad. Ibn Khaldun himself often used *hadith* to substantiate his arguments, most extensively in his critique of the Shi'i idea of the Mahdi, and he does not always apply the same rigorous standards to these reports.[24] Nonetheless, he felt that if *'ulama'* accepted the evidence of *hadith*-based evidence solely on personality criticism, which relied on stories about individuals, their conclusions would be unreliable since they relied entirely on the "soundness... of Muslim religious information."[25] If they were to produce valid conclusions, they had to act like philosophical historians and familiarize themselves with the "nature of society" so they could develop a general basis for evaluating the likelihood that a particular story about a transmitter was valid or not. Just as legal scholars had to be familiar with contemporary politics if they were to make proper judgments, *'ulama'* had to acquire reliable historical knowledge about "human social organization," *al-ijtima' al-bashari*, if they were to establish a rigorous, error-free logical method, a *qanun*, as logical criteria, for evaluating *hadith*. Most, he implied, did not.

MUQADDIMAH AND THE *KITAB AL-'IBAR*

Ibn Khaldun's explanation of the basic principles of historical methodology occupies a relatively small portion of the *Muqaddimah*. The text is largely given over to explanations of his dialectical model and elaborate accounts of sedentary life, which together constitute his science of man in North Africa. As the work is presently constituted, he explains his purpose in writing twice, in the introduction and the foreword. In both parts he offers slightly different versions of his philosophical commitment to the study of history. In the far longer introduction, probably written in 1377, during the five-month period when he completed the first draft of the work, and certainly before leaving Tunis for Egypt in 1382, Ibn Khaldun primarily discusses the *Muqaddimah*, only alluding to the *Kitab al-'ibar*. He emphasizes his original intention to relate only the history of the Maghrib, as he was not familiar with the East when he wrote it in his isolated tribal refuge south of Tunis. He wrote the foreword in Egypt, sometime after he returned from the *hajj* in 1388. The foreword, which immediately follows the religious invocation praising God and the Prophet Muhammad, implicitly discusses the *Muqaddimah* as part of the *Kitab al-'ibar*, whose second and third volumes comprised his larger narrative history of North Africa, the Islamic world, and brief accounts of non-Muslims, including Copts, Greeks, Byzantines, and Iranians, as well as Turks and Mongols of Central Asia. The foreword thus represents Ibn Khaldun's mature reflection on the nature of his entire historical corpus, which he continued to revise while living in Cairo.

In the foreword he announced his novel historical methodology constituted analyses of conditions, *ahwal*, society, *'umran*, and civilization, *tamaddun*, and the essential accidents, *al-a'rad al-dhatiyah*, of human social organization, *al-ijtima' al-insani*, a philosophical method that would compel readers to repudiate the stranglehold of *taqlid*, uncritically rendered tradition.[26] Ibn Khaldun leaves no doubt he considers the *Muqaddimah* and the narrative sections of the *Kitab al-'ibar* to comprise a unitary work, saying he divided it into an introduction, a *muqaddimah*, and three parts. In the *muqaddimah* he discusses the science of history, while book I, now known as the *Muqaddimah*, concerns society and its essential accidents, including monarchy, power, occupations, crafts, and sciences. Books II and III deal first with the history of the Arabs from the earliest time to the present, as well as non-Arab dynasties such as the Persians, the Israelis, the Copts, the Greeks, the Byzantines, and the Turks, and then relates the history of the Berbers, particularly the Zanatah, and Berber dynasties and monarchies in the Maghrib.

Ibn Khaldun summarized these discursive sections when he titled the entire work *The Book of Precepts/Lessons and the Account of Beginnings and Information Regarding the Times of the Arabs, Non-Arabs, Berbers, and Great Sultans Contemporary with Them*.[27] In this title, Ibn Khaldun evidently refers first to the methodology and dialectical model of the *Muqaddimah*, what he terms its "precepts," that is, the premises or axioms of the *Muqaddimah*, and in the second phrase, "Account of Beginnings and Information," he alludes to his work's narrative volumes, which, as many scholars have observed, lack philosophical commentary or structure. He follows the title with a brief peroration in which he exalts his achievement in a passage that reiterates much of what he has said earlier, but emphasizes both the comprehensive scope of his achievement and its explanatory power. His work concerned, he writes, the origins of races and dynasties, the causes of change in the past, descriptions of towns and villages, sciences and crafts, tribal (bedouin) life, and sedentary life. Finally, he reports he offered *barahin*, logical proofs, for these things.[28]

THE AXIOMS OF SOCIETY

In the *Muqaddimah*, book I of the three-volume *Kitab al-'ibar*, Ibn Khaldun organizes his vast reservoir of social, political, and economic data, his science of North African man, into six parts. As he initially titles them in his preliminary remarks, they are:

1. Human Population in Brief, Its Type, and Range of Settlement
2. Bedouin Society and an Account of Tribes and Barbarous Communities
3. Dynasties, the Caliphate, Kingship, and Government Offices
4. Sedentary Society, Countries, and Cities
5. Crafts, Occupations, Professions, and Their Aspects
6. The Sciences and Their Acquisition and Study[29]

The first three parts discuss stages of human development, logically sequential phases of what he describes as the evolutionary progression from primordial man to rural tribe and then to sedentary dynasties. These sections constitute the core of Ibn Khaldun's dialectical model. He analyzed the government, society, and economy of the urban monarchical state in chapters 4, 5, and 6 as it evolved through four generations from vital, cohesive tribal conquest dynasty to corrupt, impotent, doomed sedentary regime.

Ibn Khaldun begins this historical sociology of North African tribal and sedentary societies by retitling part I as the heading for chapter 1. It is now more precisely rendered as "On Human Society in Brief and Premises Concerning It." As the word *premises* suggests, he constructs this chapter to provide an intellectual foundation of premises or axioms, which he identifies as *muqaddimat*, the plural of *muqaddimah*, that is, inductively derived truths. He follows a similar plan in chapters 2 and 3. Yet, while he begins constructing his dialectical model by identifying a group of axioms or *muqaddimat* about human society in general, it is important to recognize he does not systematically identify all his assumptions or premises that logically belong in chapter 1.

His most startling omission is his failure to include one of his principal axioms, the universal constant of human nature, a premise he reiterates throughout the *Muqaddimah* text. Ibn Khaldun never explicitly identifies a common human nature as an axiom, even though he repeatedly invokes the idea as a truism to substantiate his argument. He was not, it is worth repeating, a systematizing philosopher.

His oft-repeated axiom about human nature is easily summarized. Ordinary people suppose, he writes, individuals of different societies are inherently different. After all, urbanites appear more clever than bedouins, and one might conclude they are endowed with higher intelligence. He concedes that it is natural for simple tribesmen to make this mistake, because city dwellers practiced all manner of crafts, including scholarly pursuits, and these have left an imprint on their brain, the intellectual part of their souls, giving them a certain polish. Bedouins, though, err in believing themselves inferior because they actually possess the highest degree of intelligence and innate moral character. People make a similar error, he concludes, when they assume that Maghribis are less intelligent and thus less perfectly human than Cairenes and members of the great urban societies of the East.[30] As he so frequently observed, Maghribis just lived in a culturally deprived environment. At birth they possessed the same capacities as their urban Egyptian brethren. Therefore, it was nurture, not nature, that yielded distinct human social organizations.

Chapter 1 itself is devoted to six *muqaddimat*, six axioms that serve as principles for understanding human social organization and religious belief. He begins by restating another fundamental premise of the *Muqaddimah*, which Aristotle and his Greco-Muslim acolytes declared to be the first axiomatic truth about human society: "human social organization is necessary," *al-*

ijtima' lilinsan daruri.[31] Human beings could not, that is, survive as individuals but needed the cooperation of others both to mediate conflict and obtain sufficient food. He also mentions, inter alia, that humans do not require prophecy in order to generate human social organization. Early Muslims, Ibn Khaldun writes, believed that, but to substantiate his position he points out only a few human beings possessed sacred texts—the Old Testament, New Testament, or Quran. Yet Zoroastrians and others, the majority of the world's inhabitants, still formed societies, established dynasties, and built monuments, the outward manifestations, as he notes elsewhere, of powerful monarchies.[32] Ibn Khaldun then pointed out to his readers that even though he was not required to do so, in these initial remarks he was defining the object, the *mawdu'*, of his new science, which in mathematics was numbers; in physics, substances; and in history, human social organization. His comment alluded to Aristotle's caveat—or perhaps to Ibn Sina's restatement of Aristotle—that "'the craft of logic' did not require scholars to establish the existence of an object in a particular science, although it was not forbidden to do so."[33]

Ibn Khaldun devotes the remainder of chapter 1 to a description of five other major *muqaddimat*, five other premises or axioms. Four of these include geographic and environmental factors that determined patterns of human settlement throughout the globe and that also, to a degree, shaped human personalities. The fifth concerns individuals who have supernatural powers. Derived in large part from al-Idrisi's (1099–1165 or 1166) famous twelfth-century geographical work, *Kitāb nuzhat al-mushtāq fī 'khtirāk al-āfāk*, otherwise known as the *Book of Roger*, the geographic sections constitute certain premises of Ibn Khaldun's dialectical model.[34] Ibn Khaldun's presentation of these *muqaddimat* should also alert readers once more to his often-conflicting goals of comprehensively cataloging fourteenth-century Arab Muslim knowledge while advancing a philosophical science of man and then applying it to North Africa. Thus, in his second geographical *muqaddimat,* he explains what regions of the earth support human society, and to do so he summarizes nearly the entire body of Muslim geographical literature, most of which was ultimately derived from Ptolemy's *Geography.* This is interesting information for those readers unfamiliar with Muslims' extensive geographical knowledge, but it is difficult to integrate information about such topics as the earth's declination, its spherical shape, geographies of lands extending from the Maghrib to China, the monuments of Rome, the breadth of the English Channel, or the variant pronunciations of the Central Asian Turkic tribal designation Ghuzz with his purpose of distinguishing the societies that develop in the temperate zones from the marginal populations in other areas.

Ibn Khaldun demonstrates a scholar's erudite knowledge of geography, but he uses only a fraction of this information to make his principal point, which is that of the seven Greco-Islamic climatic zones, the third, fourth, and fifth were the most temperate regions and the ones that supported extensive human settlement. Berbers inhabited parts of the second and third zones, which also included the North African coast, the Mediterranean, most of Egypt, and the Fertile Crescent, and farther to the northeast the desert plains of Central Asia, the home of Turkic peoples, a roaming population of nomads, who had camels, sheep, cattle, and horses. The third, fourth, and fifth zones contained the most temperate and broadly cultivated regions, which included the Maghrib, Syria, Iraq, Iran, western India, China, Spain, and nearby Christian lands. Iraq and Syria, he notes, were the most temperate of all these countries.

Ibn Khaldun applies the word *i'tidal, temperate, moderate,* or *symmetrical,* not merely to climates but also to people, animals, buildings, food, and even architecture. He seems to intend it to convey an ideal of the golden mean for physical, social, and cultural life. More particularly he writes that people of the middle climate zones have moderate physiques and dispositions and enjoy the "natural conditions" for supporting a vibrant sedentary or urban economy, society, and political structure, including the development of religions, sciences, crafts, agriculture, monetary systems using gold and silver, stone buildings, and dynasties.[35] The fortunate peoples who resided in these climates and societies included, he said, residents of the Maghrib, Syria, Iraq, Iran, western India, China, Spain, and Europe. People outside these zones lived in what Ibn Khaldun describes as a state of semi-barbarism, living in fragile, temporary buildings, eating strange foods, ignorant of precious metals for commerce, untouched by prophecy, and generally resembling dumb animals. He assigns Slavs and Negroes to this category.

In general terms, then, climate determined where civilization, that is, populous, prosperous, vibrant urban culture, could develop. Ibn Khaldun's environmental determinism was, however, far more complex than a simple assumption about settlement in these zones. First of all he believed that climate shaped personality but only to a limited degree. Apart from his assertion that Slavs and Negroes lived in a semi-barbarous state because of their residence in uncongenial zones, he also believed identifying traits of Negroes, their levity and emotionalism, was due to weather. He ascribed their effusive spirits to the fact, previously known to unnamed philosophers, that Negroes lived in a hot climate. Heat caused expansion of their animal spirits of joy, and therefore people in hot climates would often burst into song.[36]

Humans living in coastal zones, Ibn Khaldun writes, somewhat resembled inhabitants of southern regions, due to the fact that the reflection of the sun off the sea heated the air. Egypt, he observed, was a case in point, as its inhabitants were joyful, playful, and careless of the future. The residents of Fez, in contrast, lived in a cooler climate, surrounded by mountains, and became in consequence dour folks who always planned for future contingencies. In Ibn Khaldun's formulation it is difficult to resist the temptation to regard these Fez residents as the Scots of North Africa.

In Ibn Khaldun's characterization of Egyptians, he appears to offer another minor example of the compartmentalization of knowledge that can be seen in his contradictory assumptions about causation: al-Ghazali versus Aristotle, al-Farabi and Ibn Sina. That is, he never reconciled this highly theoretical information about Egyptians, derived ultimately from a philosophical source, with his later experience of living in Egypt for more than two decades. Based on his memoir, it is difficult to imagine Ibn Khaldun found Egyptians to be so lighthearted and careless as he suggests here. Given his experience in Cairo, one would think he would characterize Egyptians as ambitious, conniving, rapacious, and corrupt. At least he leaves that impression when discussing members of the legal profession. At no time does he reflect that his theoretical knowledge of Egyptians was contradicted by experience, although he urged similar critical cautions on historians. Nor does he ever imply that Egypt's Turkic rulers were especially prone to levity, a trait that historians rarely if ever have attributed to Mamluks, if indeed any scholars ever drew psychological characterizations of these Turks or any other pre-modern Muslim rulers.[37]

While climate determined overall settlement patterns and some general traits that distinguished people from one zone to the next, it did not explain the differentiation of personality types within each zone. It did not account for the fundamental differences between rural tribes and urban inhabitants in North Africa, human social organizations that were located in the same temperate region. Given his unstated premise about the essential similarity of human beings at birth, Ibn Khaldun attributes the contrast between tribes and city dwellers to the distinguishing effects of their immediate physical environments, a phenomenon he includes among his geographical *muqaddimat*. He asserts that certain human physical, mental, and spiritual traits resulted from diets, which in turn were determined by distinct environments within temperate zones.

Ibn Khaldun observed that the physical environments of populations in these temperate regions differed markedly from one area to the next. Some people lived in fertile agrarian areas and enjoyed abundant food and comfortable lives. Others, such as natives of desiccated parts of the Hijaz, Yemen, or the Maghrib, existed in austere circumstances, where agriculture was limited or impossible and food was sharply limited. The latter environment, Ibn Khaldun repeatedly insisted, created a society whose members lacked grain, fruit, and seasonings. In consequence, while they were often hungry, they were healthier, longer lived, better looking, morally superior, more intelligent—if not more cultured—and even more pious than both "hill people" and town dwellers. Even desert animals such as the gazelle had superior physiques, health, and, yes, sharper intellects than domesticated animals, such as goats, which lived on the plains where pasturage was abundant.[38] His assertion that rural tribesmen were more intelligent, while seemingly contradicting his thesis about a common human nature, can be interpreted to mean that both rural tribesmen and urbanites are born with identical mental capacities but that the intellect of tribesmen remained relatively uncorrupted in their austere environment while the minds of townspeople were afflicted by luxurious indulgence common to urban populations.

Despite his caustic opinion of bedouins such as the Arab tribes of the Banu Hilal and Banu Sulaym tribes, at one level Ibn Khaldun believed in their *kheir,* a quality of religious purity or even nobility. This seems to have been true for him even though he wrote: "Places that succumb to Arabs are quickly ruined."[39] Given Muhammad's assertion that the soul of a child was a tabula rasa, a blank slate at birth, Ibn Khaldun concludes that bedouins were morally as well as physically superior to sedentary inhabitants. Tribesmen, that is, were by force of circumstance closer to the original "natural state" of mankind.[40] They were North African noble savages. "They were," he writes, "closer to being good than sedentary people."[41] What Ibn Khaldun describes is a kind of Rousseau-like state of nature, an existence of relative moral purity, not completely angelic, but nonetheless a life lived closer to nature than city dwellers managed. Bedouins were largely untouched by the debilitating, sirenlike appeal of dissolute urban society, where luxurious life and personal ambition had a corrosive effect on the personality. If naturalness was a moral trait of bedouinism, *fasad,* depravity, immorality, or corruption, a term that still resonates in debates within the contemporary Islamic world, characterized the urban population, at least in the latter stages of a tribe's urban and monarchical phase of existence.

Thus the association between sparse diets and superior traits was primarily due, Ibn Khaldun writes, to the fact that moisture in food produced corrupting superfluous matter in the body, which ultimately would rise to the brain, the rational part of the soul.[42] His assumptions about diet, disease, health, intelligence, and piety are based, first of all, on Galen's tripartite soul, an entity intrinsically part of the physical body, an idea ultimately derived from Plato. Rural tribesmen who had to struggle for basic necessities and ate relatively little, were not affected by the negative consequence of lavish diets. "Hunger," so prevalent in the steppe and desert, kept the body "free from corrupt superfluities and mixed fluids that destroy body and intellect."[43] In contrast, the indulgence of urbanites led to corpulence, poor complexions, and ugly bodies. It also dulled the brain and consequently the ability to think. Inhabitants of fertile regions were known to be stupid and coarse. He added that one additional factor of diet also contributed to the stark differences between rural tribesmen and urbanities. Tribesmen who consumed the meat and milk of strong animals such as camels, absorbed these animals' traits. They became tough, patient, and persevering, without physical weaknesses. City dwellers, with their elaborate cooked dishes, lacked these qualities, absorbed no vigorous animal qualities, and became as delicate as their diets.

Ibn Khaldun detected subtle variants of typical rural traits among Berbers, and some, who lived in more fertile zones where food was plentiful, physically and mentally resembled indulgent townspeople. Within towns the inhabitants also differed according to their levels of prosperity and relative indulgence. One might think he would classify the relatively prosperous Andalusians in the same category as ugly, slow-witted, prosperous, sedentary North Africans, but anyone imagining this would be wrong. Andalusians, he says, lacked butter; their principal foods, he claimed, were sorghum and olive oil. Consequently they possessed penetrating intellects, *zaka' al-'aql*, agile bodies, *khiffah al-ajsam*, and a predilection for learning, *qabul al-ta'lim*. Can we imagine fourteenth-century Andalusians were all so abstemious?

Were poets' depictions of parties on the Genil near Granada just tropes or literary license? Perhaps, but Ibn Khaldun was, after all, an expatriate Andalusian with a sharp mind, a demonstrable penchant for study, and an enthusiastic participant in the *majlis*es, the court soirees of Granada. It is difficult to imagine he and his aristocratic friends limited themselves to olives and sorghum at these gatherings. As Ibn al-Khatib reported, those individuals fortunate to be guests at Granadan *mawlid* celebrations were hardly so restrained.

Finally, a special note is required about bedouin piety, one of the signal traits of rural inhabitants. Ibn Khaldun also attributed religiosity to diet, and the religious or spiritual instincts of tribesmen were, he repeatedly asserted, a catalytic factor of his dialectical model. Thinking possibly of the leaders of both the Almoravid and Almohad movements, he reported that members of austere rural communities, who, by necessity, could not indulge themselves, were more inclined to be religious than residents of towns. The pious ascetic, he reported, could be found only in the desert. Few such abstemious individuals were known to reside in urban areas, where people were generally known to be hard-hearted and indolent.[44] Their spiritual weakness was directly linked to their excessive consumption of meat, seasoning, and fine wheat with its production of superfluous vapors that affected the tripartite soul. Typically, Ibn Khaldun does not link his observation about diet and ascetic piety with his final *muqaddimah*, a premise devoted to the truth that God has chosen certain individuals to mediate between God himself and mankind.[45]

In this *muqaddimah* he continues to compartmentalize his religious and philosophical discussions visible in other sections, however closely related these subjects would seem to be, even in this particular instance where his discussion of spirituality and prophecy follows on the explanation of the relation of diet to piety.

Muhammad, after all, was not a desert ascetic until he retired to the hills, despite later European orientalist assumptions, including Fernand Braudel's early assertion that Islam arose as a desert religion. Ibn Khaldun, in discussing prophecy, Muhammad's unique status among the Prophets, and other manifestations of divine inspiration or perception, never considers the possible environmental, socioeconomic, or the culinary context of the Prophet's spiritual inspiration. He confines his discussion of Muhammad's prophecy entirely to theological questions, including the nature of souls and the ability of the superior type of soul to undergo a metamorphosis from a human to an angelic state of prophecy.

'UMRAN BADAWI

Having laid out basic premises that were relevant to all human social organizations, rural or urban, tribal or sedentary, in chapter 2 Ibn Khaldun turns to an analysis of bedouin society. He uses the term as a generic label for all tribal groups, including pastoral nomads and farmers, and specifically includes in this category Berbers, Arabs, Kurds, Turkomans, and Turks. First, he states several premises about bedouins in particular, as he suggests by titling the chapter "Bedouin Society, Barbaric Communities, and Their Conditions and the Premises and Preliminaries Concerning Them." In this title he uses the term *usul* instead of *muqaddimat* for premises.[46] *Usul* (s. *asl*) is another Arabic word that has multiple meanings, including those with both common and philosophical definitions. It can mean root, basis, principle, and even ancestor, but also axiom, and Ibn Khaldun begins the chapter by stating that bedouins and sedentary people are "natural." Natural means, as he subsequently indicates, that both social groups follow ways of making a living that are dictated by their environments: agriculture and nomadism for people living in the plains and deserts and highly developed crafts, commerce, or business for residents of cities.

Next Ibn Khaldun cites a second premise that bedouins are not only "natural" but historically primary, thereby offering the first clue to the initial evolutionary phase of his dialectical model. "Bedouins," he says "are the basis of, and prior to/more ancient than, cities and sedentary people."[47] This notion of *priority* is yet another Greco-Islamic philosophical term. Aristotle, in his work *The Categories*, discusses several possible meanings of this kind of idea of precedent or priority, which were well known to Greco-Islamic rationalists. These seem to explain what Ibn Khaldun means here. Something may precede or be prior to something else in respect of time or as a part of a necessary sequence, as the number one must come before two, or prior in nature, in the sense one thing is a necessary cause of something else.[48]

All these senses of priority seem to apply to the ideas Ibn Khaldun expresses here, for he sketches out how a generic bedouin society gradually evolves from a subsistence agrarian and/or herding life in the desert to a sedentary existence as its people became enamored of luxuries, constructed towns and cities, and became craftsmen or merchants. It is, for Ibn Khaldun, a given, an axiom, that bedouin society and the chiefdom naturally evolved into sedentary society and a monarchical institution, and he expresses the idea in many different contexts, including the fundamental premise of the entire *Muqaddimah* and his science of man mentioned above, the notion of primordial society.[49] In this instance, however, he attributes this evolution to bedouin psychology. "The toughness of the desert life," he remarks, precedes the softness of sedentary life. The evolution of bedouin or tribal society from one stage to the next results from the fact that "urbanization is found to be the goal of the bedouin." Ibn Khaldun then concludes, "This is the case with all bedouin tribes."[50] Later he adds that the allure of wealth and luxury represented the only conceivable reason Berbers were willing to exchange their social integrity and independence for the dependent status of urban inhabitants and that it only happened on rare occasions.[51] He documents his point about this social evolutionary process by citing the evidence of populations in North African towns. The majority of urban residents, he says, were well-to-do bedouins who had previously lived on the fringes of these towns. This confirms, he argues, that desert societies are prior to and the basis of sedentary communities.[52] Later he qualifies this observation by noting that most bedouins were, nonetheless, incapable of settling in large cities, as they did not have the skills or the wealth to survive in large, prosperous urban economies.[53]

Not only is it necessary to reconcile sections of the *Muqaddimah* in an effort to more clearly grasp Ibn Khaldun's arguments; it is also important to recognize that the premises or generalizations he cites in his model of social change often render opaque the reality of what these processes involved. Even his phrase *barbarous communities* only hints at what he considers to be the actual nature of these tribes. His vocabulary of natural states, priority, and social evolution may explain a process in generalizations that constitute knowledge, but these philosophical concepts do not illuminate the immediate cause of tribal conquest. Unless they are very attentive, readers of the *Muqaddimah* may assume that a tribe's natural social evolution to sedentary life, wealth, and kingship was a seamless process. Students of pastoral nomads generally, and the Mongols in particular, know what happens and understand what Ibn Khaldun means when he says that a tribe's "rapacious habits," taʿawwud al-iftaras, constituted a crucial factor in its acquisitive instincts or sedentary ambitions.[54] These "habits" represented the proximate cause of tribal conquest, otherwise masked by the neutral phrase *natural evolution*. Sociological abstractions then and now tend to obscure the gritty realities of everyday life.[55] In this case Ibn Khaldun's account of a natural process involved and masked, as he knew better than most closeted historians, destructive tribal raids. He repeatedly asserts that Arab Bedouins exemplified the rapacity that preceded tribal conquests of sedentary states and the establishment of new dynasties, but that in many other cases continued unabated and produced nothing more than the ruin of sedentary societies.

Ibn Khaldun spends far more effort describing the rapacious habits of Arabs than the plundering instincts of Berbers. He lacerates Arabs for their savage nature and predatory instincts, which were antithetical to and destructive of the sedentary society he valued. Expressing what seems to be a deeply felt moral outrage, he says that Arabs ruined any regions they conquered because their anarchic, individualistic nature, hostility to laws, and contempt for social responsibility were antithetical or contrary to society. Under Arabs people lived in a state of anarchy, *fauda*, without law. It was their nature, their *nature*, he asserts, to plunder whatever they could, and, perhaps most damning of all, Ibn Khaldun says that even when they acquired sovereignty and kingship they plundered as they pleased—an observation he fails to integrate into his dialectical model.[56]

Ibn Khaldun cites as examples what Arab Muslims had done to Yemen and North Africa as two cases in which tribal raids produced only destruction. Yemen, his family's historic homeland, was, he said, depopulated and largely lay in ruins because of the Arab Muslim conquests. Still, he reserved his harshest denunciation for the two Arab tribes, the Banu Hilal and the Banu Sulaym, who were unleashed on Ifriqiyah and the Maghrib in the eleventh century and who in his estimation destroyed much of urban life and settled society in the Maghrib particularly over a period of more than 350 years.[57] He writes dismissively of reform movements in which individuals tried to end these tribes' raids by persuading tribesmen to embrace Islamic values. Insisting that religion for these tribes meant no more to them than ending destructive depredations, Ibn Khaldun insists that no measure of religious affirmation could dissuade these tribes from their rapacious habits. Some self-proclaimed reformers he considers to have been charlatans who embraced Islam but failed to live by its precepts.[58]

Only in the case of the original Arab Muslims does Ibn Khaldun see that Arab predatory tribal instincts were ultimately channeled into positive goals, and that happened, he says, only because Muhammad's prophecy transformed these Bedouins' original nature.[59] Even so, he implies that in the initial phase of Arab Muslim conquests, when the Arabs were still "simple," traditional tribal instincts still prevailed, for he reports that Arab conquest of both Iran and Syria left these countries depopulated and in ruins.[60] His claim, when later discussing philosophy, that Muslims developed the greatest sedentary society the world had ever seen must refer to the eras of the Umayyad and ʿAbbasid caliphates.[61] Ibn Khaldun extols many aspects of ʿAbbasid culture in particular, although attentive readers will also reflect that he regards both caliphates as having exemplified varying degrees of sedentary social and political decadence.

After discussing the concept of priority and social evolution, Ibn Khaldun devotes most of chapter 2 to an explanation of a series of axioms about bedouin society, which accounted for their ability to overwhelm senescent urban-based states. Five of these are central to the dynamics of his dialectical model of rural urban conflict. These are the following: (1) "Group feeling ['asabiyah] results only from (blood) relationship or something corresponding to it"; (2) "purity of lineage is found only among the savage Arabs of the desert and other such people"; (3) "Bedouins are more disposed to courage than sedentary people"; (4) "savage peoples [umam] are better able to achieve superiority than others"; and (5) "leadership over people who share in a given group feeling cannot be vested in those not of the same descent."[62] These five premises and others of related significance reveal the principal qualities or traits he thought enabled tribesmen to move beyond their simple lust for urban luxuries and rapacious habits to conquer weakened sedentary states. The most important of these traits were tribes' social cohesion, military abilities, and tribal leadership.

'ASABIYAH AND TRIBAL WARFARE

Ibn Khaldun never fully explains which tribal segments possessed 'asabiyah in sufficient strength to overcome enemies, although given his experience in recruiting tribes, he presumably recognized 'asabiyah when he saw it! He is clear, though, as to what he meant by the term, writing "'asabiyah was generated by common descent [nasab] or something similar," because blood ties stimulated "affection for one's relations," a "natural" human emotion.[63] Kinship by itself, however, did not produce deeply felt emotion that generated social bonds within tribes. Copies or memoires of genealogies did not generate spontaneous acclamation among otherwise fractious individuals who possessed a common tribal identity. Shared genealogies constituted merely an abstraction, which represented no more than an imaginary relationship. "A pedigree," Ibn Khaldun writes, "is something imaginary and devoid of reality. Its usefulness consists only in the resulting connection and close contact."[64]

The critical importance of close contact in generating ʿasabiyah is highlighted by Ibn Khaldun's insistence that tribal clients, *mawalis*, and followers/allies, *istinaʿ*, could share in the ʿasabiyah of their masters or leaders even if they were not related. While only tribesmen of common descent could belong to a particular house and share its nobility, clients, followers, and individuals born into slavery, *ʿibbida*, might assume the social identities of their masters.[65] Such individuals, now cut off from their own families or communities and bereft of their original communal consciousness, could approximate this new ʿasabiyah, particularly if they were descendants of men who had earlier been absorbed into service of a different tribe. Even so, while these clients, followers, or slaves may have acquired a certain degree of nobility, *sharaf*, of their masters, they always remained inferior to them. Turkic troops and members of the important Iranian family the Barmakids, formerly prominent Buddhists from northeastern Iran, who were employed as ministers for the ʿAbbasids were, Ibn Khaldun reports, men who actually achieved a degree of identity with the ʿAbbasid house and shared in its nobility.[66] Nonetheless, as Ibn Khaldun himself indicated when he expressed outrage that the sister of the ʿAbbasid caliph could have had an affair with an Iranian Muslim client, such men could never be considered true Arabs. Nor could they completely absorb their identity and prestige or, consequently, their ʿasabiyah.[67]

ʿAsabiyah gained considerably more force if tribes were motivated by religious ideas rather than being moved solely by envy or rapacity. Nothing could withstand a tribe, Ibn Khaldun argued, whose members shared a religious ideal, and his analysis of rural life and the natural piety of tribesmen implies they were more susceptible to religious appeals than townspeople would have been. Shared belief had the effect of dampening factional feeling within tribes, and made them willing to die for their cause. In North Africa both the Almoravids and their successors, the Almohads, fought and defeated tribes that possessed superior numbers and enjoyed even more intensely felt ʿasabiyah. Leaders of both Berber movements preached religious reform of different qualities, which had, Ibn Khaldun asserts, the effect of doubling the strength of their own ʿasabiyah.[68] Ibn Khaldun was particularly adamant about the catalytic power of religion in early Arab Muslim campaigns. He pictured the Arab Bedouins of the Hijaz in the days before Muhammad's prophecy as living, like many North African tribes of his day, in a virtual state of anarchy, incapable of uniting because of the rampant individualism of tribesmen. Each tribe or clan or camping group may have possessed ʿasabiyah, but they never united for a common purpose. The transformative effect of religious ideology was demonstrated, he said, by Arab Muslim victories over vastly superior Iranian and Byzantine armies.[69]

Ibn Khaldun regarded the social cohesion of ʿasabiyah as the sine qua non of tribal conquest and successful state building. Still, he attributed the historic success of tribal warfare to another trait of tribes' demanding rural existence: military prowess. Bedouins were courageous or warlike because they lived unprotected in the countryside, the steppe, or the desert. They hunted, always went armed, and relied on themselves for their safety rather than assuming, as urban residents did, that a state would protect them. Accustomed to traveling alone in these environments, each man developed survival habits or instincts. "Fortitude," Ibn Khaldun remarked, undoubtedly on the basis of his own experience with tribal groups, "has become a character quality of theirs, and courage their nature."[70] Such traits were most easily appreciated when reading tribal verse, celebrating thrilling tales of heroic warriors, tribal raids, plunder—the successful product of rapacity—and the lure of captive women.[71] In stressing the many ways a steppe or desert environment gave rise to natural bedouin military skills, Ibn Khaldun concluded by reiterating his belief that it was nurture not inherited nature that determined human character. "It is a fact," he says, "that man is a child of ... customs ... He is not the product of his natural [inherited] disposition and temperament."[72] The desert created hardy, warlike bedouins; towns generated a population of impotent, dependent citizens.

Tribes' *ʿasabiyah* and military qualities gave them a formidable potential for expansion and conquests, but it was leadership that enabled a particular tribe to emerge from the desert to overrun established states and found new dynasties. Ibn Khaldun explains the emergence of a tribal leader as part of the natural process of social evolution, analogous to the original birth of human society posited by Aristotle. Tribes, like the earliest human beings, required leaders to act as restraining influences.[73] Therefore, he concludes, *ʿasabiyah* inevitably produced leaders from within the tribe due to the "necessity of existence," *zarurah al-wujud*. Persons who emerged as leaders possessed definitive traits. They needed, first of all, an absolutely pure descent or lineage within their own community. Beyond that they had to be distinguished by their prestige, which they enjoyed because they were members of a traditionally powerful and influential house or lineage, a *bait al-sharif*. Such individuals were therefore said to embody superior ʿ*asabiyah,* a particularly intensely felt sense of identity or pride in a particular tribe. Within each tribe or *qabilah,* Ibn Khaldun adds, there might be a number of different houses or *buyutat,* each with its own individual leader, one of whom would be capable of subordinating the other houses to his will. These dominant individuals, tribal *shaikhs,* could attain *mulk,* or sovereignty, which consisted of political dominance, the ability to collect taxes, conduct military campaigns, defend frontiers, and, psychologically, a satisfied feeling of complete independence.[74] *Mulk,* he is careful to add, alluding again to primordial humans, is something natural to human beings, as they have a need for restraining authority, the stage that followed human social organization.[75] As such it was a "noble institution" that ensured a society would not collapse into a state of anarchy.[76]

Ibn Khaldun is careful to say that not all tribes evolved to produce a leader with superior ʿ*asabiyah,* thereby allowing for the fact that only a few Berber tribes ever made the transition from rural tribe to sedentary monarchy. Not every tribe with ʿ*asabiyah,* he writes, could generate *mulk* or kingship. Sometimes ʿ*asabiyah* was insufficiently strong; in other cases a tribe might lack dynamic leadership.[77] Ibn Khaldun also indicates that tribesmen who lived on the fringes of cities rarely exhibited the three qualities required for state formation: social cohesion, military strength, and effective leadership. He notes that in most instances urbanites dominated tribes on their periphery economically and militarily. Bedouins, he writes, depended on cities for necessities, while supplying only useful but marginally valuable raw materials to city dwellers. Monarchs otherwise controlled tribes either through bribery or naked force.[78] Many tribes in these situations remained weak and impotent and consequently had only a diluted level of ʿ*asabiyah.* A case in point Ibn Khaldun observes were the Israelites under Egyptian domination. Only after they fled into the desert and lived in its environment for forty years did they respond to new demanding conditions and acquire both social cohesion and aggressive habits.[79]

ʿUMRAN BADAWI TO ʿUMRAN HADARĪ

Ibn Khaldun conceptualized his analysis of the rise and eventual decline of the monarchical government stage of social evolution with the Greco-Islamic concepts of form and matter. It is a "fact" he writes, "that the state, *daulah,* and monarchy, *mulk,* have the same relationship to society, *ʿumran,* as does form, *surah,* to matter, *maddah.* The form preserves the existence of matter . . . It is established in philosophy," he remarks, echoing Aristotle, "that one cannot be separated from the other. One cannot imagine a state without society, while a society without a state and monarchy is impossible because human beings must by nature cooperate and that calls for a restraining influence."[80] The tribal monarchy and the state it developed constituted "the form of society" while people, cities, and everything else constituted its matter.[81] When matter, that is, society, decayed, so did its form, the state and monarchy.

The rise of tribal dynasties constitutes the first stage of Ibn Khaldun's four-stage or four-generation dialectical model. To explain the inevitability of this progression from vigorous tribal conquerors to decadent tribal states, as well as the notion that this process was cyclical and continuous, Ibn Khaldun introduced an additional axiom, another Aristotelian concept, which had long since become a hoary truth that Ibn al-Khatib also used in his histories. It also had to be understood, Ibn Khaldun insisted, that everything comes into being and then decays. This affected both substances and conditions. Substances included the elements, animals and man, while conditions referred to the environment or surroundings that influenced all created things. These ranged from the sciences and crafts to such intangibles as prestige and nobility. Therefore, just as humanity persisted through endless cycles of birth, maturity, senility, and death, political life in North Africa grew and declined. Dynasties, like individuals, experienced a life cycle mirroring the human condition, but in four generations, which Ibn Khaldun now set out to describe and explain.[82]

Ibn Khaldun's conviction that a generational dialectic of tribal dynasties drove North African historical change, or at least the trajectory of its major Berber dynasties, constitutes the theoretical core of the *Muqaddimah*. His explanation consists of three major elements: a social analysis of the alterations tribes underwent over several generations, a political explanation of the special role of the monarch in this process, and a distinct but crucial account of psychological change affecting successive members of the dynasty. Economic traits of urban societies, which also evolved over time in concert with social and political developments, will be considered separately below. He presents the social thesis and descriptions of the monarch in chapter 3, titled "Dynasties, Kingship, Sultanate Offices, and Everything Associated with These Conditions and Concerning Them, Premises and Complements." Here the terminology *premises* and *complements* seems to be mathematical, for *premise, qawaʿid* (pl. *qaʿidah*), which has a general meaning of foundation or rule, is also used in geometry in the sense of a base, while *complements, mutamammat,* is sometimes used in mathematics, as well. These words appear to convey the same meaning as earlier terms for premises and ancillary arguments, since at the end of the section on dynastic generations Ibn Khaldun claims he has demonstrated his thesis with *argument, burhan,* derived from previously established *premises, muqaddimat.*[83]

THE FOUR GENERATIONS OF SEDENTARY LIFE

Ibn Khaldun begins his account of the evolution or, more accurately, the ascent and decline of tribal dynasties, by citing the axiom that these dynasties had a natural life span of four generations. His principal or social explanation for the process that then played out over time rests on the dual assumptions, the previously stated premises, that humans are naturally everywhere born with identical traits and physical and social environments are the sole determinants of human personality and customs. Given those assumptions, it followed that the qualities tribes possessed in their natural rural environment fundamentally altered after they defeated established states and settled in towns and cities. These included all the traits that defined their natures as rural tribesmen: piety, moral purity, health, intelligence, ferocity, and, most of all ʿasabiyah and military prowess. Not only did their bedouin traits begin to atrophy as soon as they experienced sedentary life but also their nature altered continuously as newly founded sedentary society and its monarchy evolved over time. Traits of character, he reminded his readers, are the result of the peculiar situations in which they are found.[84]

In the first generation after conquest, tribal conquerors retained their desert traits, highlighted by cohesive ʿasabiyah, as well as the bravery or toughness and savagery they developed in harsh desert environments. Embodying all the traits of his fellow tribesmen in addition to his critical leadership qualities, the chief in this stage acted as a primus inter pares, a first among equals, who neither claimed special privileges nor differentiated himself from his fellows, but governed moderately, collecting taxes, protecting property, and defending the community. In this earliest phase of the dynasty, Ibn Khaldun says that these leaders also endeavored to perfect themselves by exhibiting admirable qualities demonstrating, among other things, their capacity for administering God's laws, the latter point a moral imperative and seemingly dissonant idea considering his later secular characterization of sultanate rule.

An individual ruler's qualities ought to include, he suggests, generosity, forgiveness for error, tolerance toward the weak, hospitality for guests, support of dependents and the poor, honoring of obligations, liberality with money, respect for religious law and its scholars, veneration for men of religion, and respect for old men and teachers. In summary: "It should be known that a quality belonging to perfection, that tribes possessing 'asabiyah are eager to cultivate and which attests to their (right to) royal authority, is respect for 'ulama', pious men, nobles, well-born persons, and the different kinds of merchants and foreigners, as well as the ability to assign everybody to his proper station. The respect shown by tribes and persons of group feelings and families, for men of comparable nobility, tribal position, and rank, is something natural ... the first thing to disappear in a tribe that exercises royal authority, when God wants to deprive the members of that tribe of their royal and governmental authority, is respect for these kinds of people."[85] Nowhere, it should be noted, does Ibn Khaldun list philosophers among the members of a particular society and state whom rulers ought to respect. Nor does he, in fact, cite the example of any Muslim ruler whose actions exemplified this ideal, a suggestive omission, considering his habit of citing examples from Islamic history to prove other aspects of his treatise. Nevertheless, the comment is valuable as a kind of reflection of his idealized hope for a moral and stable social hierarchy in North African Muslim states. It is a conservative view he shared with many eighteenth- and nineteenth-century European social theorists. While some new monarchs, formerly bedouin chiefs, may have exhibited such exemplary qualities with their fellow tribesmen, they nonetheless took brutal, realistic steps to neutralize the followers of the previous dynasty. Ibn Khaldun contrasts the tribal chieftain, who naturally exhibits leadership, with the chieftain as monarch, who has the power to rule by force.[86] After all, as Ibn Khaldun noted in one of his many comments on kingship, the institution rested on two foundations: power, composed of "might and group feeling," and "money."[87] As is the case with his comments about tribal rapacity, this is a rare instance in which Ibn Khaldun describes the violent reality of tribal conquest.[88] As he explains, changes occurred in the period immediately following a victory; most of the social and political elite of conquered capital cities comprised partisans of the previous regime, so they had to be forcibly removed and settled in the new monarch's native territories, where they could be effectively controlled. I have "seen it and know it," Ibn Khaldun reports, adding that eventually only common people and criminals remained from the earlier population, to be replaced by the troops and partisans of the new regime. "This is the meaning," he says, of "discontinuities in society," with one sedentary population replaced by another.[89] Social shifts were in turn matched by physical changes as new rulers destroyed existing buildings and constructed new ones designed according to their own tastes and ambitions.

While the first or conquest generation of tribesmen broke with the past in several respects Ibn Khaldun does not suggest that in terms of knowledge or cultural traditions each dynasty created a new society and urban culture ex nihilo. Quite the contrary, for while he predicts a dark future for tribal societies suffering perennially recurring political cycles, in explaining North African and Iberian history Ibn Khaldun still offers a prospect of continued intellectual or cultural progress, even as dynamic new tribes displaced senescent sedentary kingdoms. He cites historical evidence showing that conquerors absorbed or adopted the sedentary culture of their defeated enemies. Examples of this cultural transmission occurred, he says, when Persian culture was transferred to Umayyads and ʿAbbasids, or when ʿAbbasid culture was absorbed by successive dynasties, such as the Saljuq Turks, who overran Iran in the eleventh century, or when the highly developed culture of the Iberian Umayyads was transferred to the Berber Almohads.[90]

In the new tribal dynasty's second generation, the qualities that originally empowered the tribe began to atrophy, an indeterminate process that continues throughout the remaining life of the regime.[91] First and always foremost in Ibn Khaldun's mind, ʿasabiyah, the tribe's single most important quality, slowly weakened, as tribesmen abandoned social restraint, particularly as it concerned their relations with women. They indulged in adultery and homosexuality and intermarriage with unrelated individuals in the city. Intermarriage severely compromised and eventually destroyed tribesmens' ʿasabiyah, for in these interracial or intertribal marriages they formed new small lineage groups or extended families, each with its own modest degree of social cohesion. These now-prosperous socially or racially mixed families did not as a group, however, possess the powerful, broadly shared experience or sense of connection with a large community that typified members of the original tribe.[92] Atomized urban social isolation replaced communal cohesion. Ibn Khaldun adamantly insists that while long-settled urbanites might claim their ancestors' good qualities and publically assert that they themselves were decent people, they could not have a house, a socially cohesive community with ʿasabiyah.[93] Citing, as he so often did, an early Arab Muslim example to prove his argument, Ibn Khaldun says when Arab Muslim conquerors intermarried with Iranians and other non-Arabs, they diluted their lineages, which ultimately led to their diminution of social cohesion and political strength.[94]

The tribesmen's second most important trait, military skills, which included endurance, individual initiative, and experience with arms, also began to deteriorate in the second generation of sedentary life. By settling in cities, tribesmen inevitably lost their physical toughness. "They forget the customs of desert life that enabled them to achieve royal authority, such as great energy, the habit of rapacity, and the ability to travel in the wilderness."[95] They no longer lived the demanding, dangerous life of desert warriors. Additionally, they began to indulge in the luxuries of urban life that attracted them to cities in the first place. Their new sedentary, lavishly endowed urban life not only further drained their physical prowess but also exerted a pernicious effect on their bodies and mental capacities and damaged their religious instincts. Thus lack of exercise caused physical decline, and indulgence in excessive amounts of new types of food known to spread poisonous fluids throughout the body, including the brain, meant they sickened more easily, deteriorated mentally, and lost the spiritual purity fostered by asceticism.[96]

Parallel to and partly the cause of tribesmen's deterioration as a socially cohesive, militarily robust community was the evolution of the leader of a tribal house into a monarch, as he mortgaged his superior ʿasabiyah, his chiefly legitimacy, for royal wealth and power. This was the evolution of an individual who originally embodied the ʿasabiyah of his house, clan, or tribe but

THE METHOD AND THE MODEL

who, sometime after the conquest, began to disassociate himself from his kinsmen as he assumed the trappings and prerogatives of traditional kingship.[97] While the chieftain had originally functioned as a natural leader, legitimized by descent in a noble house, but claiming no special privileges beyond his traditional lineage status, he now began to reserve all the glory of conquest for himself and gradually adopted the authoritarian traits of pre-Islamic empires. As time passed he began hiring mercenary troops, as indeed ʿAbbasid rulers had originally done when they formed Turkic slave regiments to resolve the troublesome unreliability of their *muqatilah* Arab tribes. The former chief now monarch came to spend as much time trying to keep his kinsmen at bay as he had previously devoted to conquest. To consolidate his power, the ruler first humiliated and then killed his relatives and close supporters.[98] Exactly this kind of process occurred, Ibn Khaldun observes, when Arab Muslims conquered Byzantine territories and Iran and when Berber Almohads adopted the sedentary habits of Iberian Umayyads.

By the third generation the previously noble, savage bedouins ceased to be either noble or savage. The transition from ascetic, moral, robust, egalitarian, socially cohesive tribal life to self-indulgent, luxurious, morally corrupt, physically inert, politically subordinate, socially fragmented sedentary life was nearly complete. Tribesmen had become "devoted to lying, gambling, cheating, fraud, theft, perjury and usury" in their pursuit of luxuries.[99] Having lost their ʿasabiyah and forgotten desert life, they no longer possessed autonomous power but had become supine subjects of their former chiefs, now autocratic monarchs, and lost even the ability to defend themselves. By now their monarch had gained complete authority and established an authoritarian, bureaucratic state and for a period ruled successfully, enjoying,

Ibn Khaldun emphasizes, a period of tranquil domination and luxuriating in the enjoyment of the things that "human nature" desired: property, imposing monuments, and fame.[100] Monarchs now found it increasingly necessary to increase taxes to support their extravagant lives and were initially able to do so because their cowed subjects did not resist. Some monarchs even confiscated property, and this injustice hastened the fall of the dynasty, as it had a negative ripple effect throughout the economy.

With the original tribesmen sunk in luxury and bereft of their former ascetic habits, moral purity, aggressive instincts, and ʿasabiyah, and separated from their former chiefs, physically, socially, and politically, the dynasty descended into a kind of political senile dementia, *haram*, a corrupt or decadent condition in the fourth and last generation. In these last two generations secular legal codes regulating behavior also enabled monarchs to destroy the initiative of previously aggressive, individualistic tribesmen. Ibn Khaldun notes the one exception to this pattern occurred in the seventh century, as the religious laws of the Prophet Muhammad did not, Ibn Khaldun insists, have this effect, as they merely inculcated moral restraint within each person, rather than enforcing some kind of pervasive, debilitating state administrative code. Rulers also became isolated in their palaces, indulged in dissolute behavior, diverted funds intended for troops' salaries, and failed to supervise the military. They appointed unqualified low-class individuals as administrators and tried to destroy the great families, the crucial supporters of their predecessors. The nobility, superior ʿasabiyah, and other personal traits that characterized chiefs three generations earlier had, by the fourth generation, entirely dissipated.

In addition to explaining how social, military, and political traits of bedouin conquerors altered after they entered a sedentary environment, Ibn Khaldun added another psychological dimension to his dialectical model. In doing so, he indicated that for rulers their generational position in the dynastic lineage exerted a telling effect on the mentality of monarchs, quite apart from how they, as former chiefs now monarchs, may have responded to urban environments. In this he once again anticipated a theory widely associated with modern social thought and given compelling literary expression in Thomas Mann's twentieth-century novel *Buddenbrooks*. In the novel, Mann chronicled three generations in the life of a north German commercial family, as it evolved from business success through social prominence and artistic preoccupations to nullity, a process known to modern sociologists as the Buddenbrooks' dynamic, otherwise expressed in the phrase "from shirtsleeves to shirtsleeves in three generations." The American economist W. W. Rostow also adapted the idea to frame his model of economic development.[101]

In his dynastic variant of this argument, Ibn Khaldun only briefly alludes to his sociopolitical discussion when he shifts his analysis from the underlying structural factors that determined the fate of tribal dynasties to an explanation of the generational shifts in the mentality of rulers. He attributes the later generations' diminished abilities to psychological changes that accompanied altered circumstances of a royal lineage, spanning the entire period of the dynasty from its foundation to its senility and collapse. Thus, the founder of the dynasty, knowing the effort he required to establish the state, understands what has to be done to sustain it, while his son, who has learned from his father, but not, in Ibn Khaldun's telling, participated in the conquest, possessed an inferior understanding of statecraft, "in as much as a person who learns things through study is inferior to a person who knows them from practical application."[102] In the third generation, Ibn Khaldun writes, the grandson of the founder knows things only by report. Rather than being taught, he relies on tradition and, therefore, as a ruler, he is inferior to his father, who at least was capable of independent judgment. The fourth generation of the lineage is inferior to his predecessors in every psychological respect, most of all because the great-grandson does not appreciate the effort or recognize the personal qualities that it took to originally build the state, and imagines that his family, to whom his subjects abjectly defer, ruled solely because people admired and respected their noble lineage. This fourth-generation ruler also considers himself superior to his fellow tribesmen, who originally shared his family's ʿasabiyah. He despises them as inferiors, causing them, in turn, to scorn him and revolt.

Ibn Khaldun attributes these psychological changes to generational shifts rather than ascribing them to effects of the physical or social environment, so that in this case the individual ruler is not portrayed as a child of custom but as a victim of inexperience and ignorance. Ibn Khaldun assumes that these psychological changes are as inevitable as the loss of ʿasabiyah, the decline in military capacity, the deterioration in physical and mental health, and the disappearance of asceticism and religiosity. Yet he never explicitly links the shifting assumptions of these successive generations of monarchs to their policies, as they distanced themselves from or killed tribal supporters, hired mercenary troops, abandoned themselves to luxurious living, and generally adopted policies emblematic of pre-Islamic imperial dynasties. In failing to theorize how these two explanations for dynastic cycles might be associated, Ibn Khaldun again leaves the reader scrambling for an explanation, as he sometimes does elsewhere in the *Muqaddimah* when he fails to correlate closely related ideas.

Once again, one might say he has bequeathed an additional puzzle for later generations of philosophical historians to unravel.

Integral to his generational model was one additional but critically important assumption that Ibn Khaldun introduces almost as afterthought when he discusses the dynamics of generational change. He says that while some people within a troubled dynasty may notice the signs of decline and senility, they are wrong to imagine that these conditions were due to negligence or that they could be reversed through the actions of individuals. "This is not so," he declares. Making clear to readers just how much he believed in what modern Western scholars would describe as a type of structuralist interpretation of historical change, he says that dynastic decline, like the earlier evolution of tribal society, was a natural, evolutionary process. It was, as he mentioned earlier, an organic process of growth, vitality, and decay inherent in dynasties as well as in all living things. It was, he repeats once again, inevitable. "Once senility has afflicted a dynasty," he writes, "it cannot be reversed... We have explained that it is natural [*tabī'ī*] for senile traits to affect a dynasty... If then," Ibn Khaldun concludes, "senility is something natural in (the life of) the dynasty, it must develop in the same way natural things come about, exactly as senility affects the temper of living beings."[103] Some modern scholars have found fault with Ibn Khaldun's schema precisely for this reason. It is, they argue, antihumanistic.[104] Certainly it is the polar opposite of Thomas Carlyle's Great Man theory, explained in his work *On Heroes, Hero-Worship and the Heroic in History*. Even when Ibn Khaldun describes tribal leaders who possessed superior *'asabiyah*, he attributes their success to social processes rather than individual brilliance.

And yet, without warning, in the midst of this deterministic account of change caused by altered social environments and evolving psychological stages, he suddenly interjects God as a prime mover of his dialectical model. Having explained the natural processes of social change, he stops, almost as if he has emerged from a reverie, and insists that it is God who invests men with the superior *ʿasabiyah* that culminates in *mulk* or monarchy. Likewise, he says, God decides when to deprive men of kingship by inducing moral decline. He causes men to indulge in immoral and unethical behaviors that destroy their political integrity, resulting in a total loss of royal authority. Someone else, whom Ibn Khaldun does not here identify, will assume power in these individuals' stead. Conjuring the Quranic variant of the Sodom and Gomorrah tableau, Ibn Khaldun quotes the Quran 17.16, which states: "When we want to destroy a village, we order those of its inhabitants who live in luxury to act wickedly therein. Thus, the word becomes true for it, and we do destroy it."[105] This leads Ibn Khaldun to conclude, "God has the power to do what he wishes. If he wants them [dynasties] to disappear He causes them to do so, and brings forth a new creation. That is not difficult for God."[106] Here al-Ghazali's God demonstrates his absolute power, not just to set cotton alight but to destroy kingdoms!

It is almost inexplicable that Ibn Khaldun would make such a stunningly antithetical statement while he was in the midst of elaborating his carefully constructed, philosophically informed dialectical model, for it invokes a moral political universe he subsequently rejects out of hand when he analyzes monarchy. It would be truly inexplicable, not to say unpardonable, if he were a philosopher. After all, he spent more than twenty years in Cairo revising the *Muqaddimah*. Yet he was not, as mentioned earlier, a philosopher or a rigorously systematic thinker, and the revisions he made in Egypt appear to have largely consisted of adding information about the eastern Muslim world. Considering the overwhelmingly rationalist nature of the *Muqaddimah*, it seems unlikely he abruptly inserted this brief but dissonant moral and religious subsection of the text to mollify conservative 'ulama'. Given his personality, that seems improbable. Instead, Ibn Khaldun was probably reflexively expressing a long-internalized matter of faith, as he did when he ratified al-Ghazali's notion of causation. It is almost as if he experienced a moral spasm, a type of autonomic religious impulse. While the sudden appearance of an immanent God here is momentarily disorienting, Ibn Khaldun's abrupt insertion of a deus ex machina into the explanation of North African history again typifies the compartmentalized nature of the sprawling *Muqaddimah*. His insertion reminds scholars committed to philosophical history they really must take him at his word and labor to improve his newly conceived historical science in many different respects.

SENILE DEMENTIA

Having explained his generational dynastic model in both its social and psychological dimensions—and subsequently repeated and enlarged on the social model several times over—Ibn Khaldun describes what he considers to be the three possible means by which a new dynasty arises as an established sedentary regime declines into political senility. Despite his seeming preoccupation with the rise and fall of tribal dynasties, his first example involves nothing more complex than the phenomenon of provincial governors asserting themselves as central government collapses. He illustrates this process with two examples from Islamic history: the 'Abbasid and Iberian Umayyad dynasties. As the 'Abbasids entered their senile phase and deeded their authority to ministers and slave troops, the Iranian Muslim

Samanids of Bukhara (819–999) became independent rulers in Mawarannahr; Arab Hamdanids (ca. 905–1004) gained control as two separate dynasties over northern Iraq and Syria; and the Turkic Tulunids (868–905) came to power in Egypt, exemplifying the disappearance of Arab Muslim social cohesion and military power and the rise of independent sultanates, many of which, as Ibn Khaldun lamented, were ruled by non-Arab lineages. In Iberia, the Iberian Umayyads (711–1031) disintegrated and were succeeded by the Arab Muslim *muluk al-tawa'if*, the *reyes de taīfas*, the "kings of factions," provincial governors of the Umayyads. Ibn Khaldun does not suggest any of these sultanates possessed either 'asabiyah or other bedouin moral or intellectual traits, although they obviously had military skills.[107] Indeed, he specifically says that these kings of factions emerged in Iberia because earlier Umayyad Arab 'asabiyah had been lost. Andalusia experienced the same kind of ethnic or racial degradation that had earlier befallen the 'Abbasids, and while these petty Andalusian rulers did not possess 'asabiyah themselves, they were able to rule for a period using clients and Berber mercenaries because no groups or tribes with 'asabiyah could still be found in Iberia that were capable of challenging them.[108]

The history Ibn Khaldun cites here has little to do with his dialectical tribal model. First of all, the 'Abbasid caliphs, who he regards as the last legitimate Arab Muslim rulers, governed or at least reigned for more than five centuries, far more than the 120 years he assigns to a typical four-generation tribal dynasty. Byzantine and Sasanid dynasties were similarly long-lived. In accounting for survival of such regimes, Ibn Khaldun ignores his tribal dialectical model in favor of an imperial one. "When a dynasty is firmly established," he writes, it could dispense with 'asabiyah. It could rule without this sense of social cohesion because once it has endured for "multiple generations," or with "multiple progeny," after a time people would forget the ruler's origins, accept his leadership, and submissively follow his orders. "It is as if," Ibn Khaldun observes, "obedience to the government were a divinely revealed book." "People will fight with them in their behalf," he says of these subjects, "as they would fight for the articles of the faith."[109] In this instance he seems to be proposing an idea of legitimacy similar to what the German sociologist Max Weber proposed when he analyzed what he described as the charisma of success. After subjects had come to accept the dynasty's legitimacy, its rulers could sustain their control even longer, Ibn Khaldun writes, because they employed clients who had long since absorbed the now dissipated ʿasabiyah of the dynasty. "Something of the sort," he says, "happened to the ʿAbbasids."[110]

In certain cases, however, the transmutation of provincial governors into regional dynasts could represent nothing more than a resuscitation of the old dynasty. Ibn Khaldun allows for the possibility that in cases when a ruling family has multiple descendants, some of these men might have retained a degree of the original ʿasabiyah. While the members of the ruling lineage descend into senility, their relatives, who have lived at some distance from the capital and have not participated in its decadent, emasculating life, still possess vigor, social cohesion, and a wellspring of nobility required for kingship. It seems likely that some of these men governed in the regime's provinces. Whether or not they have been active members of the regime, or as tribesmen simply continued to live in the countryside, relatives long excluded from government could, he argues, exploit the opportunity presented by their fatally weakened relatives to seize power. Like the dynastic cycles, but within a single extended family, this process could conceivably repeat itself ad infinitum, as the new rulers eventually descended into luxurious impotence, always assuming of course that a sufficient reservoir of disadvantaged kinsmen exist who had remained undefiled by urban life.

Unlike these examples of dynastic succession, Ibn Khaldun's third category of successor states represents exactly what he suggests will occur in his dialectical model, a new cycle of tribal conquest. Alluding to his model, he says that in some cases new dynasties originate when someone from among peoples, *umam*, or tribes, *qaba'il*, successfully revolts against a senile regime and establishes a new sedentary dynasty. Such individuals are successful either because of their ideology or because they possesses superior ʿ*asabiyah* among their people. Ibn Khaldun differentiates this kind of tribal dynasty from that of a former provincial governor by saying that whereas former governors were content to erect a new dynasty within their existing kingdom, tribal rebellions overwhelmed existing states. Where such rebellions were successful, they embodied his model of natural social and political evolution that carried a tribe with ʿ*asabiyah* from rural simplicity to sedentary kingship.

As examples of successful tribal revolts he cites the triumph of the Saljuq Turks over the Ghaznavids, the ʿAbbasid victory over the Umayyads, the Fatimid conquest of Egypt, the Mongol or, in his terms, the Tatar conquest of Iran, and finally and most importantly the Berber revolutions in the Maghrib and Ifriqiyah, which provided him with most of the data for his model: the Almoravids (Lamtunah Berbers) against their Maghrawah Berber rulers, the Almohads (Harga-Masmudah Berbers) against the Almoravids, and the Marinids (Zanatah Berbers) against the Almohads. To complicate matters, and Ibn Khaldun's theories have never been as simplistic as they commonly have been represented, here—but nowhere else in the *Muqaddimah*—he says these multiple Berber states represented a single extended example of different branches of the same people seizing power after their relatives have lived through the natural process of conquest, settlement, and degeneration.[111] Readers having earlier absorbed the four-generation dialectic model then have to stop and imagine the innumerable generations these accumulated Berber states represented.

Collating all Ibn Khaldun's scattered comments about cycles of tribal conquests and subsequent collapse, it is possible to formulate a clearer idea of what he imagined or knew to be the pattern and causes of these events. First of all, it has to be said that his fundamental notion of tribal *ʿasabiyah* is a concept fraught with problems when it is used to explain the trajectory of North African dynastic history. In the history of North African tribal states, there is little evidence of such feeling over a broad geographical settlement area of the tribe's members, and this is actually consistent with Ibn Khaldun's conviction that kinship alone did not generate this sense of group solidarity. Constant common experience was also required. In none of his North African examples did a tribe begin its rise to power as an entire population spontaneously acclaiming a religious leader or noble head of a prestigious house. Instead religious missionaries and/or powerful heads of tribal houses or families initiated the actual process of conquest. Ibn Khaldun fails to state this explicitly, but he clearly implies that *buyutat*, houses, lineages, or heads of families, formed the nucleus of North African tribal dynasties. In Ibn Khaldun's schema the *shaikh* of a powerful or famous house possessed superior *ʿasabiyah*. He mentions that individual *qabilah*s might contain different houses, each with its distinct *ʿasabiyah,* and in an Arabic verse he quotes, a poet refers to one such house that consisted of near relations: "The Banū Kaʿb, our closest blood relatives, our cousins, both the old and young men."[112] Such houses, which quite likely consisted of both pastoralists, who possessed the necessary camels and horses for mounts, and farmers, consisted of varying numbers of individuals living in relatively close proximity. In terms of ʿasabiyah, that is, close and meaningful kinship relations, the extended house, whose members lived in close proximity, was the social unit closest to the camp group, the pastoral tribal segment with close kinship ties and shared experience.[113] Ibn Khaldun reported that the number of individual houses varied greatly from one tribe to another, and in his historical account of North Africa, he mentions hundreds of *buyutat* that he evidently felt had played a significant role in the region's history. In doing so, he highlights the pivotal role of these houses in North Africa's atomized social and political history. This view of tribal dynastic evolution is also consistent with more recent or better-documented cases of tribal dynastic history.[114]

Instead of an ʿasabiyah-fueled uprising of an entire tribe or tribal confederation, the "natural" progress from nomad or tribesmen to city Ibn Khaldun describes while developing his model, he elsewhere realistically and accurately attributes to decades of brutal warfare led by an individual house and driven, psychologically at least, by rapacity. Perhaps after individual tribal segments or members of other tribes were bludgeoned into submission and began to campaign with and profit from their association, they acquired a sense of common ʿasabiyah. That is difficult to say and impossible to prove. Ruthless brutality rather than a kind of spontaneous cinematic acclamation appears to have been the rule in the early history of North African tribal dynasties. All the instances of successful tribal rebellions and conquests he cites, Ibn Khaldun attributes to leaders who spent decades imposing their authority over the countryside before they were capable of staging attacks on cities. Even then the lingering legitimacy of senile rulers allowed them to fend off raids for years before they succumbed. The Marinids, he notes, spent thirty years trying to seize Fez from the Almohads before taking another thirty years to seize the Almohad capital of Marrakesh. The fact that Muslims overran Byzantine and Iranian territories more quickly than Berber tribes conquered North African states was attributable, he insisted, to the unique spiritual exception of Muhammad's prophecy that proved his rule.[115]

As for the generational dialectic of new tribal dynasties, readers once again must take the initiative to integrate Ibn Khaldun's depiction of environmentally determined social and political change with his assertion that members of the dynasty underwent a contemporaneous psychological evolution in four generations. Attentive readers might reasonably conclude that the first and final generations of rulers corresponded to the first and fourth stages or generations of profound social alterations in tribes and political transformation of the state. It is not, however, something that Ibn Khaldun has discussed, nor has he sought to relate how rulers' distinct psychologies affected these social and political processes. Nonetheless, a final revision of his dialectical model ultimately ought to include a synthesis of the structural and psychological changes he describes and at least suggest how they interacted with each other.

In his model of conquest, social change, and dynastic cycles, Ibn Khaldun abstracted traits he observed in the history and present conditions of North African states. Detached from its North African context, it exerts the seductive appeal of Marx's nineteenth-century dialectic, offering a simple, philosophically persuasive explanation and perhaps also a prediction of complex, tumultuous events. His model is, in actuality, neither so simple nor so persuasive when scrutinized carefully. Nonetheless, as a model it raises fundamental questions about the processes of tribal conquest, rule, and subsequent collapse in the history of the Middle East, Central Asia, and China. In general outline the Mongol successor states of Yüan China (1271–1368) and Ilkhanid Iran (1256–1353) seem, at a distance at least, to exemplify the process Ibn Khaldun describes in his model, as each powerful Mongol regional dynasty disintegrated within a century as rulers and some fellow tribesmen shed their bedouin traits and adopted the urban cultures of their respective territories. Mongols in China became sedentary sinicized rulers, and in Iran they settled and became Islamized and Iranized monarchs.[116] Meanwhile steppe Mongols of the Central Asian Chagatai Khanate retained their bedouin habits and culture.[117] The psychological or generational variant of Ibn Khaldun's model of dynastic cycles seems particularly relevant when considering the rise and fall of Chinese dynasties, whether tribal or not.[118] Like Ibn Khaldun's psychology of generational change, the Chinese model attributes dynastic change to personal qualities rather than social evolution.

Nonetheless, a fundamental question arises when trying to use Ibn Khaldun's model to understand the rise and fall of these two Mongol successor states—or sultanates of North Africa. This question concerns an aspect of tribal dynasties that Ibn Khaldun only partly addresses, the inherently unstable nature of tribal governance. This trait deserves to be considered another axiom, another critical element of the overall nature of tribal societies. In his model he assumes that after a particular house leads his followers in a successful conquest, he and his patrilineal descendants will continuously rule the state, at least until it declines into political senility. "It should be known," he writes, "that the first (perceptible) consequence of a dynasty's senility is that it splits." At that final stage states will break up into two or more parts. "The process of splitting," he remarks, "may [even] lead to the formation of more than two or three dynasties that are not controlled by members of the (original) ruling family. This was the case with the *reyes de taïfas* in Spain and with the non-Arab rulers in the East. It was also the case in the Sinhājah Zīrid realm in Ifrīqiyah. In the latter (years) of the Sinhājah dynasty, every castle in Ifrīqiyah was in the possession of an independent rebel . . . This was the case with every dynasty."[119]

Ibn Khaldun thus introduces the idea of political fragmentation as an effect and not as a cause of dynastic decline. Yet one of the conspicuous features of tribal states is the lack of a stable system of succession or legitimacy, since any male tribesmen could seize power or act independently in the provinces. In both the Mongol and North African cases decline was not solely a matter of internal decay driven by the evolution of tribal dynasties. It also was driven by tribal military units or families, which competed with one another within a particular dynasty or tribal confederation. This was true in China and Iran, and it was also the case, for example, of the multiple Hafsid rulers or the factional struggles among the Marinids, in which Ibn Khaldun participated during his early residence in Fez. If Ibn Khaldun ever considered including chronic political instability as an integral part of tribal nature he might, though, have found it difficult to reconcile with his central notion of '*asabiyah*. It could only be done if it were generally recognized that his idea of social cohesion characterized individual families and not widely dispersed tribes.

Ibn Khaldun's model, therefore, while stimulating, suggestive, and remarkable in so many respects, leaves readers wanting more, including a detailed analysis of the history of the Almoravids or

Almohads or the Marinid, Hafsid, and ʿAbd al-Wadid states he knew firsthand. To really test his model—in Central Asia, Iran, or North Africa—detailed case studies are necessary. He frequently cites examples from Berber dynasties to illustrate his thesis. Yet he does not provide specific examples of ethnic intermarriage, physical and moral decline of previously vital tribesmen, or the progressively deteriorating psychological states of particular Berber rulers, even though his generalizations persuasively suggest he has personally witnessed examples of these phenomena in North Africa. Nor does he try to examine if the four-generational model exactly or approximately fits any of his Berber dynasties. Once again he could point to his caveat that founders of sciences are not responsible for resolving all their unresolved issues, and he has a point. The *Muqaddimah* was an enormous undertaking!

Instead he devotes the remainder of the *Muqaddimah* to providing a remarkably full account of the politics, sedentary society, economics, and culture of the urban phase of tribal rule, abstracted from his experience and knowledge of North Africa, Andalusia, and Egypt. It is a semiautobiographical analysis of his own environment that resembles in many respects the ambitious eighteenth-century European works of political economy, without the political agenda of Montesquieu or the moral and economic advocacy of Adam Smith. Like these men's works, however, it is a synchronic study of man rather than a narrative history of a dynasty or state.

5

THE RATIONAL STATE AND THE LAISSEZ-FAIRE ECONOMY

HAVING ANALYZED THE nature of bedouin society and explained the fundamental dynamics of the tribal dialectical model, Ibn Khaldun shifts his attention to the model's postconquest phase and studies sultanates and their urban economy. He leaves rural North Africa behind, never attempting to provide a "thick description" of a particular Berber house, tribe, or clan; not even alluding to his protectors at the Ibn Salamah desert fortress, where he wrote the *Muqaddimah*.[1] In keeping with the philosophical nature of his new historical science, his account of state and city is also topical and analytical rather than personal or humanistic. Individuals, who find a place in his memoir, are rarely mentioned in the *Muqaddimah*.

Ibn Khaldun's treatment of politics and urban economics offers additional salient examples of the complex relationship between his goal of further explaining his dialectical model and his desire to offer a comprehensive account of Islamic North Africa. Thus, in discussing sultanates and their cities, he supplements his earlier schematic account by providing some criteria to measure the evolution of tribal regimes from simplicity to complexity, from dynamism to senility, and he occasionally attributes the decline of these regimes both to state economic policies and also to the growth of luxurious urban economies. Otherwise Ibn Khaldun devotes much of his account of sultanate regimes to explaining their essentially pragmatic nature, and in his analysis of their economies he offers elaborate accounts of cities' economic systems, only occasionally linking this account with the dialectical dynamics of his model. While contributing in certain respects to illustrating the schematics of the model, his political and economic studies represent nearly independent contributions to his science of man in North Africa. Complicating Ibn Khaldun's rigorously rationalist analysis of states and cities are his periodic summaries of *nasihat* or advice literature, in which he softens his pragmatic, sometimes cynical commentaries on monarchical rule and urban life with idealized suggestions for administering governments or improving cities. The irony in these latter passages is that anyone considering such advice might soon reflect that it seems quixotic to take to heart ideas, however admirable, however useful, however compassionate, considering his belief that the cyclical social processes he describes are natural, inevitable, and irreversible.

THE ORIGINS AND FUNCTIONS OF MONARCHY

Mulk, monarchy or kingship, Ibn Khaldun reiterates in these chapters, is the joint product of societal and chiefly ʿ*asabiyah*. In his evolutionary model, kingship is "prior to" and "necessary for" the towns and cities that exemplify sedentary society. Ibn Khaldun explains this sequence by saying that when bedouins were still nothing more than rural tribesmen, they did not require or build cities. Given their bedouin social nature, he observed, Arabs were more concerned with their camels than the proper construction of cities, an allusion to pre-Islamic Arabia and also to the Hilal Arab tribal confederation that had ravaged North Africa. Yet once a particular tribe evolved from a state of rural primitiveness and overran a sedentary kingdom, its chiefs, its once and future monarchs, required cities for two reasons. First, following initial military triumphs fellow tribesmen wanted to enjoy the alluring fruits of their victory, urban luxuries that were long the distant objects of their desire. They wished to live, that is, in comfortable, prosperous urban environments. Second, new monarchs required cities for protection and defense. Cities were necessary places of refuge and bases for further operations against the enemies of new dynasties. Therefore, monarchs either occupied existing cities near former tribal territories or, lacking cities, as was the case in many areas of North Africa, they built their own. Here Ibn Khaldun undoubtedly had in mind Fez and Marrakesh, which the Almoravids and Almohads developed as capitals.[2]

Once the new dynasty was firmly established, its territorial expansion depended on a number of factors, all of which Ibn Khaldun links with ʿasabiyah. The breadth of the regime's conquests was directly dependent on the number of its tribal followers who shared this sense of social cohesion. First, it could not occupy territory beyond what its loyal core of tribesmen could safely garrison. Second, it was difficult if not impossible for a new dynasty to conquer and administer territories occupied by other tribes, that possessed their own ʿasabiyah. Early Arab Muslims learned this to their cost, he writes, when they tried to pacify North Africa, which had innumerable Berber tribes. One historian reported, he notes, that Berbers in the Maghrib revolted twelve times before Arab Muslims pacified them, a figure that was no more than a formulaic placeholder for continuous trouble in the region. In contrast, it was easy, Ibn Khaldun writes, to control highly urbanized territories, where ʿasabiyah had long since dissipated. This was true of fourteenth-century Iberia, Syria, Iran, and Egypt. He reports that in Egypt, a country he knew well after more than twenty years' residence in Cairo, *mulk* was stable and its Turkic sultan was secure owing to the lack of tribes who might otherwise cause trouble.³

As was the case in Egypt, sultans or otherwise titled independent Berber chiefs had ruled North Africa since the eleventh century. Ibn Khaldun's clear-eyed characterization of these rulers reveals how committed he was to a rational, practical analysis of Muslim politics. In outlining the basic elements of his political theory, Ibn Khaldun made clear, first of all, that he would not discuss political utopias, *siyasah madaniyah*. In saying this, he undoubtedly had in mind the ideal city or state of Greek philosophers and al-Farabi. The most uncompromisingly philosophical of Greco-Islamic rationalists, al-Farabi, in his Greek-derived work *On the Perfect State*, declared that the ideal ruler of a city or a state should be a philosopher, or, failing that, a philosopher ought to be found who would advise the actual ruler in order to establish a perfect state devoted to the realization of an ethical society, a society that mirrored the perfection of nature.⁴ Al-Farabi's type of city, Ibn Khaldun observes, represented a utopian ideal rather than the reality of an actual social organization. The monarchy and cities Ibn Khaldun knew and describes comprised a complex amalgam of the Islamic ideal and the pragmatic power state.⁵

He tells his readers he intended to discuss two types of what he terms *siyasah ʿaqliyah*, rational politics, the Iranian and the Muslim. He termed the Iranian or Persian variant the *siyasah al-fars*, the politics or government of Fars, an unambiguous reference to the last great pre-Islamic Iranian or Persian dynasty, the Sasanids, who like their predecessors the Achaemenids, ruled from Fars province in southern Iran.[6] Ibn Khaldun shared Muslim intellectuals' respect for Sasanids, especially the great emperor Khusrau I, known in different sources as Chosroes/Kasra or Anushirwan the Just (531–579).[7] He describes the Sasanid dynasty as one concerned for the public interest whose policies were guided by an unnamed philosophy, presumably an allusion to Zoroastrian moral and ethical precepts. Ibn Khaldun's second type of rational politics was, he said, one all rulers, including Muslims, practiced. In this type, public interest was secondary to the question of how rulers could maintain themselves through the exercise of power. Muslim rulers, sultans, practiced such rational politics by combining a concern for Islamic law, *shariʿah*—as much as they were able—with norms, *qawanin*, that derived from the nature of social organization. His latter category represented one variant of what later came to be termed *natural law*.[8]

He introduces his analysis of the sultanate, the prevailing Muslim political structure in the fourteenth century, by contrasting it with the Muslims' idealized original Islamic state of the Rashidun or Rightly Guided Caliphs, and he does so explicitly in order to clarify the differences between caliphs and sultans. In the course of discussing Iranian rational politics, he remarked that once Islam emerged, its law made all other laws or norms irrelevant, since it regulated all human affairs. Sunni Muslims believed that God established the Caliphate, or, as it was otherwise termed, the Imamate, to oversee religious affairs as well as governance, and they agreed that leaders of the Muhammad's Quraysh branch of the Mudar tribal group ought to be appointed to this office. "It has become clear," Ibn Khaldun writes, "that to be caliph in reality means acting as a substitute for the Lawgiver [Muhammad] with regard to the preservation of the religion and the political leadership of the world."[9] Arab Muslims chose the

Quraysh, he emphasizes, because of the tribe's superior ʿasabiyah, which far exceeded the social integrity or cohesion of other Arab tribes. Shiʿahs, on the other hand, later gave the term *Imam* a special meaning, designating descendants of ʿAli, the first cousin and son-in-law of the Prophet and the fourth Rashidun caliph, as infallible beings, which led to a system of hereditary succession in their community. Some Shiʿi extremists, known as *ghulah*, regarded these *Imams* as divine or God incarnate, mistakenly so in Ibn Khaldun's conservative Sunni view, who denounced these Shiʿahs for violating "the norms of reason and the faith of Islam." in promoting a doctrine, which resembled Christian tenets of the divinity of Christ.[10]

The original Rashidun Caliphate or Imamate was preferable to monarchy in Ibn Khaldun's eyes, not merely because caliphs were concerned with the spiritual health and ultimate salvation of their people but also because these men appointed ʿulamaʾ, who enforced religious laws. Caliphs appointed imams (prayer leaders), muftis (legal scholars), *qadis* (religious judges), *shurtahs* (police), *adalah*s (witnesses), the latter a category of legal functionaries whom Ibn Khaldun denounced in Cairo, and *hisbah*s (market supervisors).[11] Like most Sunni Muslims, he looked back on the Rashidun Caliphate as the Islamic golden age. He also saw this as a period when these early Arab Muslims were marked by original bedouin traits of his model: social integrity, physical vitality, and simple religiosity. Even the civil war between ʿAli and Muʿawiyah, he says, was fought over different interpretations of religious truth rather than material gain, an indication, he implies, that the edifying, restraining power of Islam continued to suffuse Arab Muslim bedouin life during this era. Not until the Umayyad Caliphate did Arab Muslims begin to abandon their desert traditions and adopt monarchical trappings and habits as they became enmeshed in world affairs, intermarried with non-Arabs, and indulged their acquisitive instincts. The restraining influence of Islam dissipated to an even greater degree in later ʿAbbasid years.[12]

With the rise of independent sultanates based on "superiority and force," in the tenth century C.E., the Muslim world entered a new phase in which ʿulamaʾ were marginalized, and to explain this development Ibn Khaldun invoked both philosophy and sociology. Alluding to ʿulamaʾ complaints that they, the rightful "heirs of the prophets," as Muhammad is reported to have described them, were being wrongly excluded from royal councils, Ibn Khaldun says they are wrong to imagine they should influence sultanate regimes, thus continuing the critical roles they had played in the caliphates. The sultan's monarchical authority was not derived from divine law; rather it issued from the "nature of society and human existence ... The nature of society," he continued, "does not require that jurists [muftis] and scholars [ʿulamaʾ] have any share (in authority)."[13] Once again the importance of something's nature can be seen to be central to Ibn Khaldun's argument, as it is throughout the *Muqaddimah*. Sultanates had specific natures, just as caliphates did. They were power states of rational politics. In North Africa sultans, the former tribal chiefs of noble lineage, possessed superior ʿasabiyah, and therefore rightfully exercised sole authority in these states.[14] They might consult ʿulamaʾ on religious law, but they would not seek their advice on politics.[15] If sultans deigned to invite Muslim religious scholars and functionaries into their counsels, they did so only as a courtesy and a sign of their regard for Islam—regard not faith. Then to add lower-class insult to religious injury, Ibn Khaldun also said that "common people" as well as sultans had "no compelling need for the things religious (officials) have to offer. They are needed only by those special people who take a particular interest in their religion." This explained, he said, why ʿulamaʾ rarely became wealthy.[16]

The inherent realpolitik nature of sultanate regimes represented only part of Ibn Khaldun's justification for approving the marginalization of the religious classes. He also denounced the social integrity of the ʿulamaʾ, reasoning it was legitimate to exclude them from government because they had long since lost their ʿasabiyah, their independence and their ability to defend themselves. This had occurred, he believed, because during the centuries of sedentary culture of the Umayyad and ʿAbbasid caliphates, the character of religious officials progressively deteriorated as they became typically corrupt creatures of imperial states, and it was the descendants of these people who held offices under the new Arab, Iranian, Turkic, and Berber sultanates. Not only were these individuals socially and morally corrupt, they also were unrelated with the new rulers and consequently did not share their social identity, their ʿasabiyah.

If he is taken at his word, Ibn Khaldun despised these new kinds of professional, sedentary religious officials and teachers, a class, after all, to which in some measure he also belonged. He writes with special contempt of "weak, indigent, and rootless" teachers in his era. He portrays them as deracinated individuals, insignificant, marginal people, unlike the noble companions of the Prophet in the Rashidun era, powerful tribesmen who possessed the original Arab Muslim ʿasabiyah and ably governed the community. Contemporaries of the Prophet, these men had received the Quran as an immediate oral revelation, for which they fought and died. In sad contrast to early practice, later government officials living in luxurious sedentary surroundings were too proud to teach and ceded religious education to men of inferior social status. Simultaneously the nature of Islam itself changed and evolved into a faith of dry, complex legal texts. As it evolved, Ibn Khaldun implies, the faith lost its original spiritual energy.[17]

What led Ibn Khaldun to write with such fervor about the ossification of Islam's spiritual vitality and the deteriorating integrity of its teachers is difficult to say, considering his deeply engaged commitment to the study and practice of Islamic law. Or perhaps it was his familiarity with Maliki juridical practice that prompted his comment. He was critical, as will be seen, of the quality of North African religious education and he thought Maliki law to be conservative and intellectually stunted because of the influence of bedouin culture. Based on his memoir, he became disenchanted with, well, appalled by, the Muslim judiciary in Cairo, but earlier he had been personally familiar with many members of the clerical class in North Africa and Andalusia. Some 'ulama', like his close friend Sharif al-Tilimsani, he seems to have greatly admired.

Even if Ibn Khaldun entertained contradictory feelings about Islamic law, there is no mistaking his conclusions about the nature of monarchy in his era. He portrays North African rulers, like the Iranian and Turkic sultans who had arisen in the last days of the 'Abbasid Caliphate, as autonomous Muslim monarchs who could, if they chose to do so, patronize Islamic institutions and occasionally invite 'ulama' to tea. Otherwise they could act according to their self-defined political interests. Having drawn this austere portrait of tribal monarchs, Ibn Khaldun then indicates how he thought such men ideally ought to govern, by quoting an entire *nasihat namah*, literally a letter of advice, which a general of the seventh 'Abbasid caliph, al-Ma'mun (813–833) wrote to his son 'Abdallah b. Tahir, who had been appointed as governor of

Egypt and the surrounding territories. The letter constitutes a classic example of this royal advice genre. It contains a typical list of aphorisms or maxims for the new governor, ranging from religious and moral policy (modeling himself on the Prophet by implementing Islamic law and protecting the poor), to administrative measures (carefully supervising the administration by appointing capable judges and district officials), to matters of personal conduct (not abusing his authority by acting moderately in all things, being slow to anger, and having pure intentions, suppressing egotism). Before all else the father advises his son ʿAbdallah to please God and protect the Muslim community as well as his Jewish and Christian subjects. This letter was, Ibn Khaldun concludes, the best thing ever written on the subject of rational politics of Muslim sultans, and it contains both religious and practical moral injunctions. It was consistent with Ibn Khaldun's seeming idealistic preference for benign, morally righteous, autocratic rule.[18] It also seems as irrelevant to his political analysis as was his sudden insertion of God as the cause of the social and political changes of his dialectical model, for it was an essentially ethical document. Like other educated Muslims, Ibn Khaldun had undoubtedly internalized such ideals, which may have seemed especially compelling in his time, considering the sordid reality of many sultanate regimes.

Yet, considering that monarchy was "required by the nature of society and human existence," as he said throughout the *Muqaddimah*, Ibn Khaldun had no patience for considering the relationship of government institutions to religious laws, even if, in his theory of the rational state, sultans ought to implement them if at all possible. If readers wanted to consider such matters, which were fundamental to the Rashidun Caliphate but only tangentially relevant to sultanates, Ibn Khaldun advised them to read the work by the eleventh-century political theorist al-Mawardi. He, on the other hand, begins his description and analysis of monarchy and its institutions with his own *nasihat,* his own advice, which, apart from a fleeting allusion to God's creation, does not contain a single reference to belief, piety, religious law, or morality. His catalogue of royal duties represents what he seems to regard as urgent prescriptions for political survival, a bias anyone familiar with North African politics would understand.

Central to these injunctions is his raison d'être for monarchy, the Aristotelian notion, perhaps taken directly from al-Farabi's work, of ensuring the survival of a human community by protecting it from internal dissension and external threat. Beyond this basic responsibility the ruler had to persuade people to act in their own best interests, protect property, regulate the economy, including the operation of the mint, and, most difficult of all, he had to persuade people to submit to him while understanding he enjoyed all the glory of the regime while they had none. To achieve these goals he ought to employ people who shared his *'asabiyah,* whether they were men of the sword or the pen, military commanders or bureaucrats. Ibn Khaldun's successful monarchy was always socially at least an *'asabiyah* state.[19]

Or was it? Well, at first it always was for Ibn Khaldun, but later, after "many generations" of rulers, powerful dynasties might forswear *'asabiyah,* implicitly contradicting his dynastic tribal model of four generations. He attributes their ability to function independently of their tribesmen to two major factors. First, a subservient population accorded legitimacy to members of a successful dynasty, who sometimes acquired a sacral quality in their subjects' eyes merely because of their success. Second, a dynasty might employ officials and troops of different ethnicities to sustain their power, just as the 'Abbasids did in later years when they enlisted Iranian bureaucrats and purchased Turkic slave troops. He does not explicitly cite a third factor, which, however, played a major role in the stability of his rational states. This was the bureaucracy, whose offices Ibn Khaldun discusses not as individual examples of particular Arab Muslim or Berber regimes but as generic cases of monarchical government. Here there were no muftis or *qadi*s, no religious teachers or moral guardians. Instead he considers the function of officials who traced their lineage to sedentary, pre-Islamic empires and the monarchical eras of Arab Muslim history in the Umayyad and ʿAbbasid caliphates: *wazir*s, *hijab*s, or doorkeepers, *diwan*s, or finance ministers, and learned secretaries. Apart from Ibn Khaldun's desire to be comprehensive and his seeming interest in describing and commenting on offices as a kind of mirror for princes' guidance, his underlying reason for doing so is to use the account to classify the relative bedouin or sedentary status of particular North African and Muslim regimes. Here he returns directly and specifically to his model.

First in importance was the *wizarah*, the office of *wazir*, the *umm al-khitat al-sultaniyah wa-l-rutab al-mulukiah*, or "mother of offices and royal ranks." Found in many pre-Islamic empires, the *wazir* was a chief minister who supervised all state affairs. Ibn Khaldun dates the appointment of a *wazir* in Islamic era governments to the "moment" in a dynasty's history when it has completed the transition from a bedouin or tribal regime to a sedentary, monarchical one. Once again taking seventh-century Arab Muslim history as an example and guide, he says that during Muhammad's lifetime and the following Rashidun Caliphate the position did not exist, essentially because Muslims, then still in an illiterate bedouin state, made decisions orally in council. Besides, he adds, during these years the Muslim community was a religious enterprise, not a monarchical state, and therefore had no political concerns that required a government bureaucracy.

A transition occurred as the Arab Muslim Empire expanded and tribesmen settled and began administering conquered territories. They required help with correspondence and accounting, for which they employed Jews, Christians, or non-Arab clients. When the original caliphate gave way to more imperial rule in the Umayyad era; the pre-Islamic position of *wazir* reappeared. It remained the preeminent administrative position throughout the Umayyad century. Under the ʿAbbasids, the *wazir* became an even more powerful position, even to the extent that Harūn al-Rashid's Iranian Barmakid *wazir*, Jaʿfar b. Abdullah, held the title of sultan and exercised complete control over matters of both the pen and the sword. As the ʿAbbasid Caliphate declined and non-Arabs came to dominate the office of *wazir*, its function began to alter. Nonetheless, in North Africa, after an early history as a Berber tribal power, the Fatimid Ismaʿili's expanded, conquered, settled, and resurrected this and other Umayyad and ʿAbbasid offices.

Subsequently the Almohad Berbers did the same. They revived the office of *wazir*, but only after they, like the Umayyads before them, had distanced themselves from their original bedouin condition and become a *mulk*, a monarchical state that required separate government functions with distinct titles. While initially the Almohad *wazir* fulfilled the same duties as his predecessors, the term subsequently became synonymous, Ibn Khaldun reports, with *hajib*, the doorkeeper. This development signaled a further sclerosis of the dynasty's original bedouin social arteries and an additional elaboration of its monarchical character, for doorkeepers historically had been charged with keeping the general public away from the ruler, whether caliph or sultan. In this particular case the doorkeeper seems to have been responsible only for ceremonial practices at court, so perhaps the position did not at first signal the dynasty had entered its senile phase, as he suggests was commonly the case in dynastic histories. Perhaps this did occur later when Almohad rulers elevated the importance of this office, for Ibn Khaldun believed that only when rulers put severe entry restrictions in place had they entered their final dynastic phase.[20] At that he point, he says, rulers wanted to keep commoners and even others at a distance, a policy he associates here with a change in their personality. He characterizes this change to a monarch's adoption of "strange, peculiar . . . royal character qualities."[21] While he does not say so, this change presumably occurred in the second or third generation of his Buddenbrooks-like depiction of the four generations of tribal monarchs.[22]

As for other North African dynasties use of these two positions, the Hafsids of Ifriqiyah, whom Ibn Khaldun knew well, employed an official who fulfilled the duties of the *wazir* but was called the Shaikh of the Almohads, a title that suggests a continuously evolving political transition from tribal leadership of the *shaikh* or chieftain to sedentary kingship. He leaves no doubt the transition had taken place, probably with the help of Andalusian émigrés who had flocked to Tunis, for he says that Hafsid rulers enjoyed a broadly dispersed *mulk*. At some point the Hafsids had broken formerly with the camaraderie of tribal ʿ*asabiyah* and appointed a *hajib* whose first duties were clerical but who later controlled access to the sultan. Ibn Khaldun reports that following the reign of the twelfth Hafsid monarch, the *hajib* controlled the government for a time, until a later ruler abolished the office and restored a semblance of the original Hafsid rule, a development that represents an unacknowledged example of human intervention to sustain the life of a dynasty.[23] Elsewhere he adamantly insisted no one was capable of arresting dynastic decay. Twelve Hafsid rulers might not represent twelve generations, but the number still suggests a dynastic history that was one exception, one of many, to Ibn Khaldun's rule of four. Readers of the *Muqaddimah* must continually remind themselves that Ibn Khaldun's model is a model and not a universally valid explanation for North African history.

Based on their administrative offices, Ibn Khaldun implicitly locates the Marinids of Fez and the ʿAbd al-Wadids of Tilimsan on opposite ends of the bedouin–*mulk* development spectrum. He says the Zanatah Marinid dynasty employed both a *wazir* who oversaw military operations and an official who performed the function of a *hajib*, although given this man's Berber title of *mizwari*, it was a sign they had not been thoroughly Arabized, even if they had achieved a degree of royalty. The ʿAbd al-Wadids, in contrast, used none of these titles. Nor did they even have separate government departments, a fact Ibn Khaldun attributed to their bedouin character.

In contrast to the office of *hijabah*, whose function seemed to vary from one dynasty to another, all three truly sedentary dynasties Ibn Khaldun discusses had elaborate *diwan*s or financial bureaus. An office first modeled on Byzantine and Iranian examples and carrying an Iranian title, the *diwan*, Ibn Khaldun states, represented one of the three pillars of *mulk*. Nonetheless, in the case of the Almohads, a member of the ruling family usually held this office, just as members of the family also usually served the dynasty as *wazir*s and also as *hakim*s or city magistrates. The Almohads, that is, even if they had attained *mulk*, still functioned as a family or tribal enterprise to a significant degree. In contrast, the Hafsids employed Andalusian aristocratic émigrés for this important work, such as members of one Banu Saʿid house, previously members of the landed gentry near Granada. In better days some of the family had supervised financial matters in Andalusia. The identity of the men who staffed the Marinid *diwan* is not known, but a member of the Marinid branch of the Zanatah Berbers probably occupied the office, since members of the ruling family served as city magistrates.

Ibn Khaldun also includes a section on the *diwan* of state correspondence, the secretary, which was not, he remarks, required by *mulk,* for dynasties that still retained bedouin traits did not require skilled scribes and secretaries. His account of this office, which enjoyed high status under the ʿAbbasids, seems transparently autobiographical, for Ibn Khaldun performed the duties of a court secretary on several occasions, however briefly. Perhaps it is not surprising, therefore, that he should take more care in describing the office of the *sahib al-inshaʾ*, the chief secretary, than any of these other more important posts. In this instance Ibn Khaldun quotes a Damascene Umayyad official's epistle, another *nasihat namah,* briefly cited in the introduction to this work. It is difficult to avoid thinking that Ibn Khaldun was thinking of himself when he included this text, which stipulated secretaries must possess high social status, literary skills, intelligence, and cultural sophistication—and, yes, modesty. One of the secretarial functions he mentions is that of *tawqiʿ*, sitting before the ruler in public audiences and recording his decisions on petitions in the most concise and stylistically perfect form.[24] Marinids, Nasrids, and Hafsids certainly employed such men; the ʿAbd al-Wadids, with no defined government offices, presumably did not.

As a relatively primitive, semi-bedouin dynasty, it is also unlikely that any ʿAbd al-Wadid rulers appointed an *almiland* or admiral, what Ibn Khaldun considered to be one of the "ranks of the state" in the monarchical institutions of Ifriqiyah and the Maghrib.[25] The Umayyad caliph ʿAbd al-Malik b. Marwan (685–705), initiated a Muslim naval tradition in North Africa when he ordered a shipyard constructed in Tunis to prepare for the invasion of Sicily. Later ships from both Andalusia and North Africa enabled Muslims to occupy most Mediterranean islands and conducted raiding operations as far north as Genoa in 934–935. Fatimids and Iberian Umayyads also organized fleets to attack one another in the tenth century. The balance of power in the eastern Mediterranean gradually turned in the eleventh century because, Ibn Khaldun believed, both Fatimid and Iberian Umayyad dynasties became "infirm" just as northern European Christian crusading states entered the area in force. Only in Ifriqiyah and the Maghrib did Muslims sustain their naval efforts.

Chiefs of the Banu Maymun house operating from Cadiz led Almoravid fleets, sometimes numbering nearly one hundred ships, and in the twelfth century the Almohads, building on their predecessors' efforts, surpassed their naval operations, led by the son of a Berber who had served Roger II of Sicily. As the Almohads declined in their turn, Muslim naval affairs in the western Mediterranean deteriorated once again to be briefly resurrected for the last time by the Marinid ruler of Fez Abu l-Hasan (r. 1331–1351) who had occupied Tunis in Ibn Khaldun's day. By the time Ibn Khaldun wrote, Muslim sea power in the western Mediterranean had evaporated. In his opinion, this was due to the rise of bedouin influence in North Africa and the decay of state structures there, and the resurgence of northern Mediterranean Christian states. Yet, Ibn Khaldun wistfully notes, the concept of a Muslim admiralty had survived, along with shipbuilding knowledge, and the office would, according to a book of predictions, be revived to lead a successful conquest of Europe.[26]

Ibn Khaldun does not identify *amir*s, in his terms military commanders, as head of a distinct monarchical office, even when he alludes to times when they controlled governments. He does, however, include an essay on the tactical history of Muslim campaigns that amounts to another *nasihat* or advice text. Apart from once again demonstrating his encyclopedic range of knowledge and desire to be comprehensive, the essay is important for two reasons. In it he reiterates his belief in the power of ʿ*asabiyah* in a combat situation by arguing that if two sides to a conflict are more or less evenly matched, then if one consists of a force sharing a single powerful ʿ*asabiyah* while the other is composed of many distinct social or ethnic groups, the single cohesive army is likely to prevail, while the coalition probably will disintegrate. In saying this he seems to have been reflecting on the social and therefore military difference between rural tribes and atomized city populations composed of small family units. Yet having restated his profound belief in the power of social cohesion, Ibn Khaldun goes on to conclude that victory in battle was never certain because it depended on what he terms "hidden" factors. Under this heading he included a commander's tactical intelligence in exploiting the terrain and surprising his opponent or simply trickery, spreading rumors that affect the enemy's morale. In addition he cites what amounts to divine intervention as a factor that sometimes determined victory in battle. This latter factor he corroborates by citing Muhammad's conquests, in which his multiple victories over panicked unbelievers could be understood only as a divine gift.[27]

Ibn Khaldun said earlier that dynasty and monarchy had the same relationship to society as form has to matter; the form is the shape that preserves the existence of matter. Taking the bureaucratic offices of monarchy as a separate subject, he might also have said, but does not, that such positions represented the necessary accidents of a dynasty while certain outward features might be regarded as transient ephemera. It is to these latter elements that he turns, following his characterization of sultanates or rational states and identifications of their typical institutions, to descriptions of banners, thrones, mints, embroidered silk cloth, tent walls, and prayer enclosures. Terming them *sharat*, emblems, Ibn Khaldun speaks of these emblems as inevitable and, in the case of mints, necessary features of monarchy. Except for the mint, all of these emblems certainly fall under the category of what he would have termed *contingent accidents*. Muslims copied them, he asserts, from pre-Islamic dynasties or Byzantine and Iranian clients, already infected with habits of "ostentation and luxury," who taught Muslims how to use these emblems to increase monarchical prestige.[28] As is the case with other aspects of his model, he draws a parallel between the Arab Muslim adoption of these customs and their acceptance by Berbers. In each case simple bedouins, initially unfamiliar with or hostile to sedentary society, did not indulge in ostentatious display, only doing so as they conquered and settled in cities and acclimatized themselves to a luxurious life.

Such was the case with the display of flags or banners and the beating of drums and sounding of trumpets. Early Arab Muslims shunned such display because, Ibn Khaldun reports, they knew it had nothing to do with religious truth. With the rise of the monarchical Umayyad and imperial ʿAbbasid caliphates, all that changed. Similarly in North Africa, tribal confrontations had traditionally featured poets advancing before battle formations, singing verses eulogizing heroic tribal ancestors, but flags became common in the ʿAbbasid era, if not before. Fatimid armies displayed them, as did Almohads and Marinids. Ibn Khaldun personally learned that his contemporary the Marinid Abu l-Hasan sometimes displayed one hundred silk flags and had one hundred drums beaten in processions. Similarly, Muslim rulers from the Umayyads onward used ornate thrones, elaborate gold seals, splendid *tiraz* cloth with rulers' names woven in with gold thread, elaborate, decorated tents, and elaborate prayer enclosures that distinguished and separated rulers from their Muslim subjects. Finally, Muslims began issuing their own coinage, the only "emblem" Ibn Khaldun identifies as "necessary to monarchy." It was, he said, the sedentary institution Muslims universally adopted, beginning in the late seventh century, only omitting the practice of picturing rulers because of the simplicity of Islam and the bedouin nature of early Arab Muslims.[29]

Summarizing these emblematic features of monarchy, Ibn Khaldun concludes, "Such was the [simple] attitude of dynasties at the beginning, when they still had a low standard of living and preserved the bedouin outlook. But when their political eyes were opened and they looked toward (all) the aspects of royal authority and perfected the details of sedentary culture and the ideas of ostentation and pomp, they adopted all the external attributes (of royal authority) and exhausted all the possibilities in this respect. They disliked the idea that anyone else might share in them, and they were afraid that they might lose them and that their dynasty would be deprived of the effect of them."[30]

He concludes with the following Quranic verse: "The world is a garden and God watches over everything." Perhaps, but was he an immanent deity when it came to fourteenth-century politics, not, with a very few exceptions, based on the evidence in the *Muqaddimah*.

URBAN ECONOMIES

Having examined *mulk,* the pragmatic sultanate, Ibn Khaldun turns to the monarch's city. In keeping with his philosophical or, in modern terms, sociological approach to the study of human society, Ibn Khaldun generalizes about urban society and economy rather than writing biographically about a particular city. He could have presumably described Tunis, Fez, or Granada in great detail, but he offers no such information about these or any other North African or Andalusian city. Readers of his urban chapters will not find evocative descriptions of *suqs* or bazars, mosques and monuments, or colorful sketches of social or ethnic types. Instead he devotes his attention to a topical analysis of occupations and a schematic depiction of economic relations, one remarkable in every way for its time. It is implicit in his account that he is principally concerned with the traits of North African cities during monarchical rule. Yet it is likely that he derived at least some of his observations from Cairo, where he spent more than two decades of his adult life. The only exception Ibn Khaldun makes to his generalized account of urban life is his pious description of three Muslim ritual centers: Mecca, Medina, and Jerusalem.

He implicitly exempts these ritual centers from the inexorable life and death cycle of ordinary dynastic cities, whose fortunes rose and fell with a royal lineage, and, in doing so, illustrates once more the separation he largely observed between religious and philosophical issues in the *Muqaddimah*. These cities constituted special cases, as God chose them to be devotional centers. Quoting a *hadith* from the canonical collection of the ninth-century compiler of canonical traditions al-Bukhari (810–870), Ibn Khaldun demonstrates that Mecca, the House of Abraham, Jerusalem, the

House of David, and Medina, the House of the Prophet Muhammad, were the best places on earth.[31] His account of the three cities is entirely given over to historical and religious questions, not to the social and economic issues that otherwise concern him when he discusses the generic city. In that vein one of his most telling comments is an offhand dismissal of pre-Islamic ritual sites in Iran, Greece, and Arabia, which were not, he writes, worth considering, since these sites had not been sanctioned by Islamic religious law. He was not, therefore, obliged to discuss them. He refers readers interested in these non-Islamic ritual centers to historical accounts, much as he earlier suggested that if they were concerned with the marginal role of religious law in rational states they could consult al-Mawardi or other authors of administrative texts. In neither case was he prepared to expend effort describing such an irrelevant subject.

Ibn Khaldun devotes his study of ordinary cities to analyses of occupations or crafts and economic relations, and he finds that their evolution imitated the bell-shaped curve plotted by the evolution of monarchical institutions and the increased prevalence of emblems, rising from bedouin simplicity to the height of sedentary complexity before descending to senile impotence. While he conducts his discussion within the broad framework of his dialectical model, it does not all fit together so nicely. Take the case of Andalusia, always Ibn Khaldun's measure of a dynamic civilization in the Muslim west. He assumed the number and sophistication of crafts to be an accurate measure of urban development, remarking that these skills or occupations only became well established when sedentary society persisted in a region for an extended period, as it had, he says, in contemporary Andalusia. Referring presumably to Granada, he writes that in Andalusian cities all the principal crafts were still flourishing, even though the population of Spain no longer equaled the number of inhabitants in eastern Mediterranean centers. Andalusian crafts included architecture, construction, metal and craft manufacture, cooking, dancing, and singing, and all others demanded by a people living in luxury. He attributes the flourishing of these cities to the stability of a sequence of dynasties, stretching from early Gothic rulers, through the Iberian Umayyads to their atomized successors, the *Tawā'if* states. He compares Andalusian sedentary society favorably with Iraq, Syria, and Egypt, whose cities also, he asserts, benefited from enduring dynastic rule.

After only brief reflection, readers will realize Ibn Khaldun is discussing the persistence of dynamic Andalusian urban society through different dynasties and many, many generations, rather than the four stages of his North African tribal model. The explanation for this seeming inconsistency lies in his view that Granada and other Andalusian cities belonged to the same category as the great urban centers that endured over centuries or even millennia in Iraq, Iran, Syria, and Egypt. In these regions fertile riverine regions supported major population centers and entrenched dynasties that could survive without ʿasabiyah because relatively few powerful tribes existed to threaten these powerful regimes. Cairo represented for Ibn Khaldun an especially apposite example of such a city. In contrast, North African cities such as Fez and Marrakesh rose and declined in importance and cultural vitality with the tribes that founded them or took them as their capitals. Throughout the *Muqaddimah* he distinguishes between North Africa's pallid sedentary culture and flourishing cities in the Middle East and even other unnamed urban centers known to exist in India and China. This observation serves as another reminder that Ibn Khaldun did not compose a universally valid philosophy of history, but instead offered a model to explain the turbulent society and history of his homeland. Otherwise, it could be invoked as an historical guide only in regions such as Iran, Afghanistan, or Central Asia, the historic home of powerful tribes.

Ibn Khaldun took the relative strength of *sana'i'*, occupations, professions, or crafts, to be the bellwether of the economic strength of cities. He considered it as one form of livelihood, *ma'ash,* which included hunting and gathering, agriculture, commerce, and the government extraction of wealth through taxation. The first three were "natural" ways of making a living, while the use of government power to obtain wealth he classified as "unnatural," although, as will be seen, he intended that label to be philosophical rather than pejorative. Hunting and gathering and agriculture Ibn Khaldun regarded not only as natural but also primitive occupations, largely practiced by rural tribes or bedouins. Like bedouins themselves these occupations were "prior to and older than sedentary life." Invented by the primordial man, Adam, they were innately natural and simple and required no thinking or philosophical/scientific thought. While implicitly conceding agriculture required careful cultivation and a range of special skills, he says it was not practiced or even known by most urbanites, whose crafts were complex.[32] A few weak and humble sedentary inhabitants did practice agriculture, but they were presumably bereft of speculative intelligence.[33] Apart from agriculture bedouins practiced only crude variants of a few simple crafts, those of the carpenter, blacksmith, tailor, and butcher.

After *mulk* or monarchy was fully realized and sedentary society developed, cities fostered the development of innumerable crafts and the proliferation of craftsmen. Ibn Khaldun's account of crafts constituted a fundamental part of his urban analysis. In it he describes, first, what he considered to be crafts of particular social and intellectual significance for a flourishing sedentary society; second, he discusses the economic significance of craftsmen as creators of economic value. Generally, these urban crafts were, unlike bedouin skills, composite or complex. They were taught and acquired through habit until the form of some skill was acquired through repetition and then memorized. Unlike bedouins' crude, unchanging, and undeveloped crafts, urbanites continued refining their skills over several generations. In the process they gradually brought them from potentiality to actuality, *min al-quwah ilā l-fiʿl,* to use two of his Aristotelian-derived philosophical idioms, until they were perfect. As urban society expanded and luxuries proliferated, more crafts developed to include glassblowers, goldsmiths, perfumers, cooks, coppersmiths, weavers of *tiraz* brocade cloth, owners of public baths, teachers of all kinds, and book producers. The latter craft, Ibn Khaldun notes, was demanded by those who enjoyed the urban luxury of intellectual pursuits, including the poetical habit, the calligraphic habit, the scientific habit, the juridical habit, the mystical habit, and the linguistic habit, to name Ibn Khaldun's own most important intellectual indulgences. Eventually in later generations, urban crafts evolved to luxurious and decadent extremes.[34]

Crafts, Ibn Khaldun says, could be divided into two categories: necessary and noble occupations. He considered the necessary skills to be architecture, carpentry, weaving, and tailoring. Architecture, the "first and oldest craft of sedentary society," was practiced extensively in moderate temperate zones. A composite craft par excellence, it demanded a range of skills and was essential to new dynasties, as their monarchs built towns and erected large monuments. Carpentry was also a "necessity of society," but one employed in later generations of a city to construct luxury products. Carpenters, Ibn Khaldun notes in a typical, intellectually engaging aside, needed to know geometry, which explains why all Greek geometricians were carpenters, including Euclid (b. 300 B.C.E.), the author of *The Book of Principles*, and Apollonius (262–190 B.C.E.), who studied with Euclid and wrote a work on conic sections, *The Conic*, an aspect of mathematics Ibn Khaldun considers separately under the sciences. Tailoring, another necessary craft, was required of people in temperate climates, since they needed to keep warm. It was not necessary for bedouins, he notes, as they simply used uncut cloth.

Noble crafts included midwifery and medicine, as well as writing, book production, teaching—fundamental for individual intellectual growth and the development of the sciences—and singing. Singing, however, constituted the vocal announcement of impending political collapse, the cultural sign of impending senility, the last and unnecessary craft to appear in a fully developed society and one devoted solely for pleasure.[35] Midwifery ranked so high because skills of childbirth were necessary to maintain the human species, a consideration that leads Ibn Khaldun to refute the different theories of both al-Farabi and Ibn Sina on the question of whether humanity might ever become extinct. Medicine was essential considering the prevalence of disease among sedentary city dwellers, since they lived a luxurious life, taking little exercise and consuming a variety of foods. "I once," Ibn Khaldun remarks to illustrate such excess, "counted forty different kinds of vegetables and meats in a single dish," and it was well known, he remarks, that food, which generated noxious vapors, caused all disease.[36]

In contrast to midwifery and medicine, writing, book production, teaching, and logic represented mental crafts. These were skills at the core of Ibn Khaldun's intellectual being and his discussion of them is more obviously autobiographical than other sections of the *Muqaddimah*. He ranks writing above other crafts because it provided information about what he termed the noblest aspects of thought: ʿ*ulum wa maʿarif,* science and knowledge, basically what he considered the *Muqaddimah* to exemplify. The process of writing involved a mental effort in which one first apprehended the shape of letters and then their meaning, thus stimulating abstract thought or what Ibn Khaldun here and elsewhere terms *al-nazar al-ʿaqli,* intellectual speculation. This rational skill allowed individuals to understand the sciences, which eventually enabled their souls, humans' unique trait, to evolve from potentiality to actuality and to become pure intellect, the highest form of humanity. Writing numerical calculations contributed to this intellectual maturation, as it required deductive reasoning. It was one of the most important crafts that catalyzed this process, which allowed the rational soul to achieve its potential and enable it to practice the philosophical speculation that yielded true knowledge.[37]

In addition to considering the philosophical benefits of writing, Ibn Khaldun discussed Arabic calligraphy as a distinct craft. His treatment of the subject is consistent with his general accounts of the societies and cultures of Arab Muslim and North African history. Thus the quality of writing depended on the state of social organization, *ijtimaʿ,* and society, ʿ*umran,* in any given city; the larger the population, the more developed its crafts and the more perfect the quality of writing. After its crude beginnings in Arabia, Arabic calligraphy attained its greatest polish in ʿAbbasid Iraq where a particularly elegant form of handwriting became standardized. After the tenth century the calligraphic arts were taken up in Cairo, where they continued to Ibn Khaldun's day. In North Africa forms of the old eastern scripts Arabs introduced at Qayrawan in the seventh century C.E. were later forgotten, as

Andalusian émigrés and refugees began settling in North Africa during Almoravid times. With the collapse of the Almohads the quality of writing suffered, to be revived somewhat by the Marinids, but in Ibn Khaldun's time the decline of sedentary culture and corruption of ruling dynasties meant that writing everywhere in North Africa outside Fez had deteriorated in both appearance and accuracy.[38]

The craft of book production had experienced a similar fate by Ibn Khaldun's day. While previously flourishing in the powerful dynasties and substantial cities of Iraq and Andalusia, the craft, which had been concentrated in the most populous cities, declined. As in the case of writing and every other craft associated with urban life, Ibn Khaldun attributed this situation to the decay of North African sedentary society and the desert attitude of Bedouins there. No longer, he writes, did copyists in the Maghrib of his day retain scholarly concern for accuracy, so that even *hadith* collections were badly and incorrectly copied. The virtual collapse of fine book production with legible script and reliable texts also affected the quality of legal and even religious scholarship generally, which, he lamented, had virtually ceased to exist in the Maghrib, even though it survived in Andalusia to a limited degree.

Scientific instruction was also a craft, implicitly the preeminent one, as it utilized other noble crafts. Based on knowledge of all the basic principles in a particular science, it was an essential occupation, since all matters of the senses had to be taught. The fact that every field possessed its own technical vocabulary demonstrated, he argued, that scientific instruction required teachers. Just take speculative theology, jurisprudence, Arabic philology, or any other subject, all of which possessed idiosyncratic terminology, which had to be learned. The easiest way to transmit knowledge of this specialized vocabulary and scientific subjects, Ibn Khaldun insisted, was to teach students how to express themselves and debate scientific issues. By doing so, they would acquire a clearer understanding of these subjects. Unfortunately, he reported, many students were never forced to speak during classes; instead they were compelled to memorize data, imagining that by doing so they would acquire what Ibn Khaldun terms the "scientific habit." Memorization, however, did not, he dismissively notes, produce knowledge. "Good habits," Ibn Khaldun concludes, referring to the Socratic or dialectical process, "add insight to the intellect of a man and enlightenment to his thinking."[39]

The contrast between educational training of Maghrib inhabitants and Tunisians demonstrated the truth of his argument, Ibn Khaldun adds. In the Maghrib, where scientific instruction had declined, students enjoyed little guidance. Consequently, they studied for sixteen years and might not master a subject even then. In Tunis, students studied for five years. He attributed this to the fact that scientific subjects had not been taught in Fez and other cities of the Maghrib since the collapse of education in Cordoba and Qayrawan, perhaps mentioning Cordoba in this context because of the emigration of so many Andalusian scholars to North Africa. The problem, of course, as Ibn Khaldun repeats yet one more time, was due to the dominant bedouin society of North African regions.

Scientific education had also disappeared in Andalusia, having slowly declined over the previous century. Ibn Khaldun reports that in his day Andalusians, that is, Granadans, studied only Arabic philology and literature but that philosophical studies had not survived. His rare reference to philosophical studies here evidently alludes to the achievements of Ibn Rushd, Ibn Bajja, and others, a brief rationalist interlude that did not long continue after their deaths, except in Paris. He attributed this dismal intellectual environment to the deterioration of the size and dynamism of Andalusian society as the Christian Reconquista proceeded. Only in the eastern Islamic world, Egypt, Iran, and Central Asia, did scientific instruction continue to thrive among Muslims. "The sciences are numerous," Ibn Khaldun concludes, "only where the population is large and sedentary society highly developed."[40]

Ibn Khaldun does not correlate the rise and decline of these and other crafts with particular generations of specific dynasties. He does not indicate, for example, just when he thought calligraphy or book production in the Almoravid, Almohad, or Marinid dynasties reached the apex of the sedentary curve that simultaneously marked the end of their ascension to urban florescence and the beginning of their dissolute descent into senility and annihilation. The appearance of singing, which normally meant the setting of poems to music, was the one definite marker he offered for identifying the moment when senility was first manifest.

Singing was, he asserts, the last craft to appear in a sedentary society, because it was exclusively devoted to pleasure. It was also the first to disappear when a society collapsed.[41] In the course of making this point, he also explored the art of music, explaining its technical aspects: rhythmic modes, the appeal of harmony, and even the nature of its pleasure. "Everyman," he writes, "desires beauty in the objects of vision and hearing, as a requirement of his nature. Beauty in the objects of hearing is harmony and the lack of discordance in the sounds . . . The transition from a sound to a sound one-half, one-third, or some other fraction of it, must take place in a harmonious manner according to the rules established by musicologists."[42] Here is the craft of music, Ibn Khaldun explained with the same care he takes when describing the midwife's exact role in childbirth. In neither case do these engaging accounts directly contribute to his dialectical model, although they exemplify sedentary culture and add piquant details to his comprehensive account of fourteenth-century North African Muslim society.

Apart from his careful discussion of music, which in the *Muqaddimah* he lists as one of the philosophical sciences, Ibn Khaldun dwells on the religious question of whether it was permitted to recite the Quran in a melodious manner. Maliki law, he reports, did not permit it and he agrees with Imam Malik's opinion that melodious singing was out of place in the practice of religious devotions, which ought to stimulate awe and remind humans of their transient life and salvation. Nonetheless, he notes with seeming approval that not only non-Arabs—read Iranians—took great pleasure in music but even Arab Muslims, after their ascetic, puritanical early phase, also came to enjoy music. In saying this, Ibn Khaldun seems to be alluding to court or secular performances, and he remarks that Arabs of these later years also had Iranian and Byzantine singers brought to them in their recently occupied cities. As usual it was the 'Abbasids, whose cultural achievements he always praises, who were said to have cultivated singing, perfecting this now widely accepted craft. Elaborate dancing and singing performances were staged in Baghdad and elsewhere throughout the Islamic world, including Andalusia. From Seville especially it was transmitted to North Africa, where only traces of it could still be found, owing to the decline of society and the weakness of existing dynasties. Ibn Khaldun's comments here serve once again to illustrate his seemingly conflicted feelings about tribal simplicity and urban floescence. Who is speaking here: Ibn Khaldun the Maliki legal scholar or Ibn Khaldun the sophisticated urbanite? They both are!

URBAN ECONOMICS

Architecture and midwifery, carpentry and writing, tailoring and teaching were essential crafts, one category of sedentary societies Ibn Khaldun earlier identified as essential accidents. Their presence or absence, simplicity or complexity, offered a basic guide to the dynamism and prosperity of any given sedentary society. Men and women who practiced these and multitudinous other crafts constituted one of the three classes who produced wealth and/or substantially influenced the urban economy. The two others were the political and religious elite and wealthy merchants and property holders. Individuals from all three groups were driven by the same innate desire for profit or the need to provide for themselves. This was a "natural" instinct of human beings and constitutes Ibn Khaldun's first principle or premise of economic life. This constituted the first of many economic principles he introduced to explain economic growth and urban prosperity, and it represented the economic dimension of the forces that drove the formation of primordial society. Here Ibn Khaldun almost seemed to forget his stages of urban growth and decay as he analyzed urban economics.

Among these three groups, Ibn Khaldun rated craftsmen the highest in importance as economic actors in sedentary societies. Craftsmen, he asserted, produced most of the wealth of urban societies. Speaking of them, he writes, "Gains and profits in their entirety or for the most part, are values realized from human labor."[43] By making this statement, he introduced a labor theory of value, often believed, like the discipline of historical sociology, to have originated in Europe, in this case with Adam Smith, Ricardo, and Marx. All craftsmen, Ibn Khaldun writes, generated *kasb*, or earnings, the *qimah*, or value, realized from labor. Still, Ibn Khaldun did not advance a simple labor theory of value, which he does not characterize as a theory but as a statement of fact. He does not, that is, assert that labor, which was required to produce a product, constituted its sole value. Supply and demand, the scarcity of labor, the complexity of the product, and hoarding also contributed to a product's value and final price.

Ibn Khaldun did not separately consider teachers, men like himself, but he includes them in the same category as religious officials such as *qadi*s and *mufti*s. He notes that since the value of a craft depended on demand, most religious officials never prospered. These officials were, after all, paid by the state, whose rulers determined whether or not they fulfilled an urgent public need. Monarchs in a rational state, as he had already indicated, could choose whether or not to honor or humor 'ulama'. He says that whatever an individual ruler's attitude, monarchs never treated religious officials equally with government officials or craftsmen, however noble their spiritual purpose. Contributing to their modest income, he believed, was the fact that religious scholars, who believed in the nobility of their profession, did not usually act to improve their lot by obsequiously flattering monarchs.[44] Whether or not philosophers were willing to do so is another matter. Were al-Farabi, Ibn Sina, and Ibn Rushd high-income earners? Probably not! Well, Ibn Sina, he has said, was rich, evidently from inherited wealth.

Apart from craftsmen, traders and merchants could also earn a living and create value, even if honest traders were rare and their occupations demanded traits that destroyed virtue and manliness.[45] "Commerce [*tijarah*]," Ibn Khaldun writes, "means the attempt to make a profit [*ribh*] by increasing capital," that is, by "buying goods at a low price and selling at a high price."[46] Traders could do so either by marketing or by hoarding. They might sell rare commodities they acquired through long-distance trade, and North African trade with the Sudan was most dangerous and potentially the most lucrative long-distance commerce. They could also profit by hoarding merchandise in anticipation of rising prices in times of scarcity or by exploiting market fluctuations. To maximize their profit, they ought to realize that it was preferable to trade in goods required by the general population than to sell luxury products to the few. Traders and the entire economy suffered, including government tax receipts, he added, alluding to deflationary problems, if the prices for goods remained low for long periods of time. Nonetheless, when it came to grain, the significance of low prices for the entire population in the cause of social stability outweighed the goal of commercial profit.[47]

In discussing the acquisition of profit the realistic, politically experienced Ibn Khaldun reported that high ranking officials and clerics could indirectly derive profit from the labor of their productive citizens, even if they were not productive individuals themselves. "Ranks," as he titled one section, "are useful in securing property."[48] Men with *imarah,* or political power, did so either by demanding free labor from social inferiors or by using their position to unjustly impeach wealthy merchants and confiscate their property—a very, very common occurrence in Islamic societies. What could one expect in sultanates, after all, for "government decisions," Ibn Khaldun says matter-of-factly, "are as rule unjust, because pure justice is found only in the legal caliphate."[49] Some *'ulama'* were also able to siphon profit from craftsmen and others by exploiting their pious reputations. Ibn Khaldun, who earlier observed that clerics produced little of value themselves, said that nonetheless ʿulamaʾ were able to convince common people that when they gave clerics presents they served God. In consequence these individuals quickly became wealthy. Ibn Khaldun reported he had observed this phenomenon in both cities and in the desert, where people who "sit at home," doing no work, accumulated wealth from merchants and farmers.[50]

Having introduced a labor theory of value in descriptions of natural and unnatural economic actors, Ibn Khaldun outlined a dynamic account of the functioning of the urban economy. He based his account on two additional principles or premises. First, even though individuals naturally and egotistically sought their own economic advantage, acting alone they could not realize all they needed or desired. In this case Ibn Khaldun restates in economic terms a principle he had earlier invoked to explain the necessity for *mulk* or kingship, the Aristotelian or Greco-Islamic belief that humans must cooperate in order to survive. He probably read one version of this theory in al Farabi's work *On the Perfect State*, where al-Farabi writes, offering his own description of the division of labor: "In order to preserve himself and to attain his highest perfection every human being is by his very nature in need of many things, which he cannot provide all by himself; he is indeed in need of people who each supply him with some particular need of his. Everybody finds himself in the same relation to everybody in this respect. Therefore, man cannot attain the perfection, for the sake of which his inborn nature has been given to him, unless many (societies) of people who cooperate come together who each supply everybody else with some particular need of his, so that as a result of the contribution of the whole community all the things are brought together which everybody needs in order to attain perfection."[51]

Not only did people have to associate in order to ensure physical survival and prevent social chaos; they also needed to deal with each other in order to further their economic well-being. By doing so they would be able both to satisfy their needs and also produce wealth on a scale many times greater than what individuals could accomplish by themselves. "What is obtained through the co-operation of the group of human beings," Ibn Khaldun argued, "satisfies the need of a number many times greater (than themselves)."[52] To illustrate the multiplying effect of a division of labor, he cites what he considers to be the simplest form of economic activity, agriculture, saying that when multiple individuals—farmers, carpenters, herdsmen, blacksmiths—cooperated in farming activities, they could produce many times greater amounts of food than what they personally required.[53]

His second premise, restated repeatedly throughout the *Muqaddimah,* is that economic development varied directly with population, 'umran. To illustrate this principle in general terms, he situates Maghrib's cities on a spectrum from the most to the least populous. Marinid Fez was then the most populous and the most prosperous of these cities, while others, such as Tilimsan, lagged far behind in both categories. He drives the point home by testifying from personal experience that all social classes in Fez lived better than those in Tilimsan, Oran, and other smaller towns. This included, he said, beggars, who in Fez during the 'Id festival asked for luxuries and delicacies, something that would astonish and offend residents of other towns. "I saw them beg for many kinds of luxuries and delicacies such as meat, butter cooked dishes and butter, garments and utensils."[54] He added, thus dating this passage of the *Muqaddimah* to his stay at the Ibn Salamah fortress, that he had heard astonishing stories about the prosperity in Cairo and Egypt. "Many of the poor in the Maghrib even want to move to Egypt... because they hear that the prosperity in Egypt is greater than anywhere else."[55]

In explaining urban prosperity, Ibn Khaldun links the growth of population of newly settled or constructed cities to a rise in demand and production, as craftsmen produced goods for the expanding market. "A large population," he writes, "yields large profits because of the large amount of (available) labor, which is the cause of (profit)."[56] The affluence such producers realized increased demand within the city, and as the population continued to grow, so did demand, not only for necessities but, increasingly, for luxuries. New crafts developed to satisfy increased demand, and, in consequence, as happened with the division of labor in agriculture, "profits are again multiplied in the town."[57] Cairo and other great cities of the east illustrated the process Ibn Khaldun outlined here. One obvious question to be raised about Ibn Khaldun's compelling argument about the effect of these economic multipliers is that he seems to assume that everyone who migrated to these cities became a craftsmen of some type, even though he has explained in a separate passage how most tribesmen, bedouins, who moved into cities from the near countryside did not usually possess sufficient income needed to prosper in a complex, expensive urban environment.[58] Modern anthropological and social studies have shown how such tribesmen often became part of the *lumpenproletariat* when they migrated to cities.

Monarchs were active economic agents in sedentary societies, and their policies paralleled the experience of their tribal followers, influencing the prosperity of the state, initially for good and, later, increasingly for ill. In discussing the economic impact of the state, Ibn Khaldun now returned to discuss the fiscal role of the *diwan*, the finance minister, who levied and collected taxes and disbursed funds. As he performed these important functions, the *diwan* represented, Ibn Khaldun estimated, one-third of the authority of the monarch.[59] Concerning revenues, Ibn Khaldun identifies three principal types: customs, land or property taxes, and levies on subject tribes. Additionally he alludes to a number of unspecified taxes on markets and business transactions, which were commonly levied in Muslim cities of this and earlier ages. "At the beginning of the dynasty," he observes, "taxation yields a large revenue from small assessments. At the end of the dynasty, taxation yields a small revenue from large assessments."[60] He attributed this economic phenomenon to the fact that taxes were lightly assessed at the beginning of a new dynasty, when the new rulers, still mentally tribal chiefs, were imbued with bedouin virtues of simplicity, moderation, and restraint. Unprepossessing *shaikhs* did not require large revenues for personal expenditures and relied on their own tribesmen for their military manpower.

Apart from collecting taxes at varying rates, monarchs exerted a pervasive influence on the economy in a number of ways. Above all, it had to be recognized, Ibn Khaldun argues, that government spending was critical for urban economic prosperity. The dynasty represented, he said, "the world's greatest marketplace," alluding to the wealth and potential spending power enjoyed by members of the regime, who had siphoned profit from the productive classes. In his analysis of government spending, which like the labor theory of value, seems to predate an important, and in this case Keynesian, strain of modern economics, Ibn Khaldun argued that since members of a regime controlled the single largest pool of money in a state, their expenditures were crucial for the economic health of the society. If members of the dynasty and court hoarded their wealth, they would set in motion a cyclical process of economic decline. Business would suffer from a fall in demand and a consequent lack of capital, leading ultimately to a decline in tax revenue and, eventually, a fall in government income.[61]

A government could also damage or pervert the economy if it interfered in the market by engaging in commerce, hoping thereby to increase its revenues. In what was essentially an argument for a laissez-faire economic policy, Ibn Khaldun argued that apart from exposing state revenues to the uncertain fluctuations in the economy, a ruler who entered the market would damage the business of farmers and merchants, who lacked the kind of capital the state controlled. With sufficient funds to dominate a particular market, monarchs could also buy goods at low prices and, given their quasi-monopolistic position, they could sell to captive merchants at higher prices, eventually driving them out of business. The ruler could thus, he concludes, cause "corruption of society and confusion in the state."[62] Iranians, he noted in one of his many favorable if sometimes idealistic or naive asides about the Sasanid Empire, chose only just rulers and forbade them from seizing agricultural land or becoming merchants.

Ibn Khaldun also developed a distinct theory of prices, which included the influence of the state, along with two other factors: the supply of agricultural produce and the demand for crafts or goods within the city. As is consistent with his discussion of crafts and urban prosperity generally, his analysis stressed the importance of population density. The first part of his argument concerning food prices seems the least convincing, although it may have been based on his own observation, for he surmised that the prices for food in major cities were initially low because individuals took care to procure their own supplies, usually stocking large reserves, thus providing surpluses that drove down prices. In smaller towns, he argues, prices were higher and reserves were smaller, simply because of the smaller population. He does not suggest, however, that the amount of food relative to the population differed significantly among cities. The second part of his theory is far more compelling. In it he observed that as cities developed and their economies became more complex, luxurious, and expensive, the cost of food rose along with the price of other goods.[63]

Finally, Ibn Khaldun took into account how the cost of agricultural labor affected food prices in all types of cities, and the example he chose to illustrate this relationship was Andalusia or, more particularly, the sliver of Iberian land still held by Muslims in Granada. In that region where the soil was relatively poor and was, perhaps then as it is now, much given over to olive trees, producing food demanded greater labor and more expenditure than in wealthier areas of Iberia controlled by Christians. Knowledge of his family's former estates in Seville and his visit to the city must have heightened his awareness of the especially fertile agrarian lands in and around that city. Consequently, in Andalusia food had become expensive, and rulers, presumably the Nasrids of Granada, provided food rations in the pay they gave to soldiers when they participated in anti-Christian jihads, implying that common soldiers could not otherwise afford to provision themselves because of exorbitant prices.

Luxury products made by craftsmen cost a great deal in cities, and, like agricultural produce, rose in price as the population increased and luxurious living became commonplace. Luxury goods were always expensive, Ibn Khaldun observed, because of the labor required to produce them. Their prices also rose when demand of a rising population exceeded supply. People in increasingly prosperous cities also drove up prices because they controlled so much surplus income they were willing to pay more for goods than they were worth in terms of the labor craftsmen needed to produce them. Then, finally, if members of the dynasty did not hoard their considerable income, he reported they alone with their enormous spending power could drive up the prices of luxury goods.

In his account of the urban economy, Ibn Khaldun provided some socioeconomic data for the disintegration of the tribal state, but it is easy to forget his dialectical model as he devotes most of his economic analyses solely to fleshing out his comprehensive account of urban economics. Nonetheless, in the course of demonstrating how a complex division of labor and rising population interacted to produce ever-greater urban prosperity Ibn Khaldun stops to remind the reader that several generations of prosperous sedentary life could ultimately result in the debilitating moral and physical decay of a formerly cohesive and robust tribal population. "When the people of a society acquire luxury and prosperity," he observes, "it naturally leads them to adopt the traits of sedentary society."[64] This meant tribesmen now quiescent urbanites, gradually embraced a whole range of luxuries, to which they became addicted, and when their consumption reached its limit and they desired no more goods or foodstuffs, they then sought to satisfy unnamed desires—presumably including music and dance among other more disreputable habits! Their ever-greater pursuit of wealth and pleasure not only impoverished many of them financially, but, as he has described earlier, it also polluted their souls and tainted their faith. Immorality reigned openly in the city as people abandoned their bedouin social values. Many dissolute individuals now swarmed the streets, and this new social milieu enmeshed members of elite families and children of the dynasty, whose education had been neglected.[65] Some of these wastrels may have lounged about in the shadows of decorative orange trees, whose inedible fruit Ibn Khaldun took to be a horticultural marker of dynastic senility.

Simultaneously, as tribal chiefs morphed into authoritarian monarchs, they adopted economic policies that accentuated the economic woes of the population and ensured the financial collapse of the dynasty. First, monarchs themselves adopted urban customs and indulged in the luxuries that required greater and greater income. Second, these rulers had to raise revenue for paying mercenary troops, who replaced the formerly vigorous but now sedentary and militarily inexperienced tribesmen who had brought the dynasty to power. These expenses led them continually to increase taxes on all members of the population until their demands became so heavy all productive classes ceased to work or do business. This caused a downward economic spiral, driven by falling revenues and the imposition of still more taxes to compensate for lost revenue, which in turn discouraged new economic activity. Many taxes were not only excessive but also unjust according to religious law, although in this case Ibn Khaldun has already explained why rulers felt they could ignore such strictures. Monarchs not only acted unfairly; they also used their power unjustly to infringe on or confiscate property. These activities further weakened merchants' incentives to conduct business, leading some to flee to other states.[66] Finally, when rulers destroyed all economic incentive, their states collapsed, along with the towns and the sedentary society they had created and nurtured.

A MORAL ECONOMY?

Ibn Khaldun's abstracted portrait of political realities and economic relations bears little resemblance to al-Farabi's "Perfect

THE RATIONAL STATE 249

State," or to an Islamic City of God. He marginalizes both philosophers and clerics while analyzing his rational state and its economy. Yet it is characteristic of this as well as other sections of the *Muqaddimah* that Ibn Khaldun shows himself to be conflicted, offering a stringent account of political and economic realities while retaining a powerful sense of regret that sultans in particular were not guided by a moral code. As was earlier suggested, it is as if while writing, his moral instinct or religious ethics occasionally breached the barrier of his intellect, spilling over, incongruously or not, into the argument. The mirror for princes' advice format typifies his idealistic outbursts, exemplified by quoting the entire letter that the 'Abbasid caliph wrote to his son, the governor of Egypt.

Ibn Khaldun offered a similar type of moral advice, but about the economy, in a section titled "Injustice [*zulm*] Ruins Society." The injustice Ibn Khaldun refers to in this section is a ruler's attack on property, which becomes prevalent, he says, during a dynasty's final stage, when it tries desperately to increase its revenue. In these remarkable pages he advises that a successful economy depended on men perceiving economic relations as an aspect of a moral universe, which was manifested, he indicates, in the tenets of Muslim religious law, a law he has said largely ceased to be observed in sultanate regimes. Having noted that Muhammad was thinking of property violations when he forbade injustice, Ibn Khaldun says Muslim canonical law generally, not solely its Maliki variant, emphasized five principles: (1) *din*, religion; (2) *'aql*, the intellect; (3) *nafs*, the soul; (4) *nasl*, progeny; and (5) *mal*, property.[67]

The Quran and *Sunnah* contained, he says, too many references to these principles to mention or to quote any of them accurately, an intriguing comment, suggesting perhaps that there were scarcely any books at the Ibn Salamah desert fortress where he wrote the *Muqaddimah*. Thus instead of citing one of these two sacred Islamic sources, he recalled al-Masʿudi's account of pre-Islamic Iranian tradition and quotes a tale the historian related about the Sasanid ruler Bahrām ibn Bahram (274–293), who was criticized by his chief Zoroastrian cleric for his unjust policies. The story, illustrating how the monarch's policies had precipitated depopulation, was meant to remind Bahram, the cleric said, that *mulk* should act according to religious law. Monarchs preserved the law, and policies defined by the law protected property and allowed farmers to survive, flourish, and provide income to the state. Yet Bahram had unjustly seized farms from their owners and granted these lands to state officials, who never cultivated the properties and did not even pay the land tax. The remaining productive farmers then had to pay disproportionate taxes to compensate for these absentee landlords, leading these farmers eventually to abandon their lands. Consequently the economy was ruined, soldiers could not be paid, and the spiraling crises attracted ambitious foreign rulers to prey on the now-weakened Iranian state. The moral of this story, Ibn Khaldun observes, is that injustice ruins society.[68]

Only powerful state authorities, Ibn Khaldun asserts, were capable of injustice, which encompassed not only confiscation of property, as in the Iranian example, but an entire range of arbitrary acts. These unjust acts included forced labor, collecting taxes not sanctioned by religious law, infringing on property rights in any way, including mandatory sales of property at artificially low prices and reselling the same at equally unjustified high prices, and generally denying people their—unspecified—rights. Unjust acts affected all peddlers, craftsmen, professions, and classes equally. They led to a reduction in capital, merchant bankruptcy, interruptions in trade, unemployment, a precipitous decline in state revenue, and, finally, the decay of urban society and the dissolution of the dynasty. In other, philosophical, terms Ibn Khaldun liked to use, he once again remarks that when the matter, society, decays, its form, the monarchy, inevitably disintegrates.[69] Owing to the catastrophic consequences of unjust state policies, Ibn Khaldun concluded that canonical law forbade such practices. He conceded the law permitted cunning, *mukayyisah*, in commercial sales, but he insisted that it forbade the political classes from illegally depriving people of their property.[70]

By attributing the economic collapse of the state to misguided or morally corrupt monarchs who ignored fundamental Quranic principles, Ibn Khaldun seems to reimagine what he has theorized about the final stage of his dialectical model. As he described that stage, monarchs inevitably evolved to become corrupt, self-aggrandizing rulers, men of the fourth generation who had little knowledge or understanding of their ancestor's state formation. In explaining the model, he does not suggest that moral failure caused economic collapse but ascribes deteriorating conditions to natural social and psychological processes. Questions of justice or injustice are simply not relevant. His seeming wish here to regard monarchical policy as a moral or ethical question seems to represent another instance of his apparent difficulty in separating rational analysis from his deeply internalized Islamic faith and nostalgia for the imagined moral qualities of the first Arab caliphate. It is not only that Ibn Khaldun seems deeply conflicted. In such moments he seems more completely and emotionally human.

In lieu of a more introspective memoir, it is only possible to pose rather than satisfactorily resolve such issues. Yet, whatever is personally opaque, the fundamental principles of Ibn Khaldun's economic analysis are clear. He advanced the following economic ideas. First, after noting humans' fundamental egotistical motivations, which necessitated the rise of the ruler and formation of the state, he asserted the primacy of labor as the principal source of profit or value and indicated that the division of labor had a multiplier effect, generating wealth far beyond the value of each individual craftsman. He outlined this idea most clearly when he discussed different occupations or crafts that contributed to agricultural production in words almost exactly the same as those Adam Smith used in 1776. Second, he emphasized the critical function of state spending, emphasizing the negative economic implications of monarchies "unnaturally" extracting wealth from productive classes without disbursing these funds back into the economy. Third, he analyzed pricing mechanisms and warned against the economic danger of consistently low prices, a danger that might be tolerated for social reasons in the case of foodstuffs. Fourth, he warned against the distorting economic effects of monarchs and state officials engaging in commerce, citing, as he so often does, an Iranian example of public policy, Sasanid prohibitions against such practices. Fifth and finally, he warned against tyrannical economic policies such as property seizures and excessive taxation that would destroy profit margins for all economic actors and vitiate incentives for future production and trade. In contrast, light taxation would offer people the incentive of certain profits.

Taken together with his dialectical model of tribal-urban dynamics Ibn Khaldun's analyses of sultanate politics and urban economics constitutes a comprehensive science of man in Islamic North Africa. Given his originally declared ambition to record every aspect of life after the cataclysm of the plague, Ibn Khaldun produced an account that is often numbingly prolix and repetitive, full of ambiguities, uncertainties, omissions, and outright contradictions. Yet, taking the *Muqaddimah* all in all, it is a remarkable and original achievement, unprecedented in any society at this time and unequaled until Europeans began asking similar questions about man and society in the eighteenth century. Less remarkable is the fact that Ibn Khaldun's ambition to found a new science of philosophical history entirely failed. It is tempting to imagine what he might have said about the work's reception during his lifetime. Perhaps he would have remarked something similar to what David Hume is reported to have quipped when his book *A Treatise of Human Nature* failed to attract interest following its publication in 1739 and 1740, that it fell "dead-born" from the press.[71] The *Muqaddimah* suffered a similar stillbirth and, as will be seen, experienced a resurrection only in later European society, whose nature differed considerably from the fourteenth-century Mediterranean as well as from Europe's own Middle Ages.

6

THE SCIENCE OF MAN

IN THE *Muqaddimah* Ibn Khaldun developed what he considered to be a universally valid science of man and applied this new philosophical science to formulate a comprehensive account of "nature of human society and human existence" in fourteenth-century North Africa and Andalusia. Given the nature of the two distinct societies in his homeland, he framed his account within a dialectical model that explained the underlying dynamic of the region's history. He thought the model he developed also could be applied to Arab Muslim history of the first three caliphates, which he considered analogous to the tribal-urban dynamic he identified as determining the politics of his homelands. Ibn Khaldun was not, however, a philosopher of history, and he did not suggest his dialectical model was universally valid. He was adamant that historians could not make simplistic generalizations about one place and time and apply them to other eras and geographies where conditions were distinctly different. He makes this clear, for example, when he says that his model did not apply to the great urban civilizations of the eastern Mediterranean, because of the strength of their sedentary culture and the absence of indigenous tribes with powerful ʿasabiyah. Considering the strength of his convictions and the scope of his intellectual achievement, important questions remain regarding his legacy and the significance of his ideas. Briefly, the *Muqaddimah* had little discernable influence on the human sciences then or now, but European scholars from the Enlightenment onward applied the same philosophical ideas and logical methods as they sought knowledge anew by studying the nature of man and the essence or structure of human society.

IBN KHALDUN'S SCIENCE OF MAN IN THE MIDDLE EAST AND EUROPE

Not a single scholar can be identified in the Islamic world or in Europe who explicitly embraced Ibn Khaldun's new science, his philosophically informed historical methodology that took the study of human society as its principal subject. Only a few individuals are known to have adopted his dialectical model to explain the past or predict the future. Ibn al-Khatib in Andalusia and scholars in Syria, Egypt, Iran, and elsewhere composed important historical works during and immediately after Ibn Khaldun's lifetime, but given the nature of the *Muqaddimah* and the kind of political and institutional support for scholarship that existed in his time, it is not surprising Ibn Khaldun's new science was widely ignored.[1] It was and is a rigorously demanding discipline. Ibn Khaldun wrote for an elite scholarly audience, not even for the literate public and certainly not for the crowd who, he said, relished entertaining narratives! Roundly dismissing the work of nearly all Muslim historical scholars, he insisted they abandon chronologies, the structure of *hadith* historiography, in favor of topical analyses of human societies. Muslim historians were also expected to master fundamental Greco-Islamic philosophical concepts and, using them, apply rigorous logical standards of proof to verify historical information.

If historians did not acclaim Ibn Khaldun's new science, neither did royal patrons, who in Ibn Khaldun's case were limited to the Hafsid ruler of Tunis and the Mamluk rulers of Egypt. Quite apart from his prickly relations with the Tunisian ruler and a prominent Maliki scholar in the city, Ibn Khaldun had not produced a work that spoke to the pride or piety of these men: the *Muqaddimah* was neither a grand history of Hafsid rulers nor a work chronicling the devotion or heroism of the Muslim community. Nor did the *Muqaddimah* or the larger *Kitab al-ʿibar* offer much to gratify Mamluk sultans. They could find sycophantic praise only in Ibn Khaldun's memoir, where it was perfunctory and presumably remained unread. Yet the possible or likely response by Ibn Khaldun's scholarly and political contemporaries to his work is largely a matter of conjecture, as there are few indications it was widely known or appreciated in his time or later in the Arabic-speaking world. A number of scholars did use Ibn Khaldun's work in limited ways for information about particular topics, particularly his important history of the Berbers, but no one who did appears to have adopted or even praised his methods, if indeed anyone understood them.

In Cairo where he lived for more than two decades and had time, therefore, to influence scholars, Ibn Khaldun was a controversial figure, criticized by some and lauded by others. As mentioned earlier, some who attended his lectures in the city praised his presentations, but otherwise he seems to have made little impression on Muslim intellectuals there. The prolific, imaginative scholar Taqi-al-Din al-Makrizi (1364–1442) is one of the few individuals who could in some respects be called a disciple. A man whom Ibn Khaldun may have influenced to become a historian, al-Makrizi enthusiastically praised the *Muqaddimah* in words that reflect his appreciation for its breadth and depth, writing that it was "a unique work of its kind . . . [that] reveals the truth of things, events and news; it explains the state of the universe and reveals the origin of all things in an admirable, plain style."[2] Ibn Khaldun may have influenced al-Makrizi to compose works on diverse and unusual topics, including coins and famines. The Egyptian scholar also wrote analytically about Egyptian economics and society, sometimes even using Ibn Khaldun's philosophical vocabulary, as when he spoke of "conditions of existence and the nature of society." Yet while it seems fair to describe al-Makrizi as, in a limited sense, Ibn Khaldun's intellectual protégé, it is not evident that he or any other Egyptian scholar understood the philosophical basis of the *Muqaddimah*.[3] Al-Makrizi did not found a new school of historical studies in Cairo, which would have probably required an institutional basis, an educational institution, that included history and philosophy in its curriculum. It is difficult to imagine that any institution in the medieval Muslim or Christian world, except possibly a *madrasah* in fifteenth-century Timurid Samarqand, would have been inclined to support a curriculum of philosophical history as a distinct discipline.[4]

Otherwise Ibn Khaldun had a discernable influence in the precolonial Islamic world principally in the Ottoman Empire, when some scholars feared Ibn Khaldun's dialectical model foretold an imminent collapse of the empire. Four valuable manuscripts written during Ibn Khaldun's lifetime and many copied later are extant in Turkey, which remains the center of Ibn Khaldun studies in the twenty-first century.[5] The *Muqaddimah* was first translated into Ottoman Turkish in 1598, well after Ottomans had conquered

Egypt and appropriated many historical texts, and scholars in Istanbul began discussing ideas from the the work in the late seventeenth century. The geographer and historian Katib Çelebi (1609–1657) was the first Ottoman scholar known to have invoked Ibn Khaldun's analogy of human and political life spans.[6] Later Mustafa Naʿima (d. 1716), a disciple of Çelebi, appropriated some of his dialectical ideas, including the antagonistic relations between tribes and sedentary societies. Ibn Khaldun's ideas became even more widely known in eighteenth-century Ottoman circles, including, for the first time, an adoption of his critical historical methods by Munecimbaşı (d. 1702). Most Ottomans were, however, interested in the implications of Ibn Khaldun's cyclical dialectic and his emphasis on the fundamental importance of kingship in his essentially secular account of sultanate governments, of which the Ottoman Empire represented the Muslim world's most successful example. Here, after all, was a "rational state" of his model, a pragmatic sultanate whose rulers governed according to their *qununs/kanuns*, administrative laws such as Ibn Khaldun administered at the *mazalim* court in Marinid Fez.[7] Ultimately, however, Ibn Khaldun's methodology never took hold in Ottoman historical circles any more than it had in Egypt. No Ibn Khaldun historical school ever developed in Istanbul, or elsewhere in the Middle East in precolonial times, or, really, in the contemporary world.

Apart from Ottoman scholars perhaps the single most intriguing Middle Eastern use of Ibn Khaldun's ideas was the seventeenth-century work of Muhammad b. ʿAbd al-Wahhab al-Ghassani al-Andalusi, the ambassador of the Moroccan ruler Mulay Ismaʿil Sharif (r. 1672–1727). In 1690–1691 he traveled to the Spain of Carlos II to ransom Moroccan Muslim captives. Introducing his memoir of the trip, the *Rihlah al-wazir fi iftikak al-asir (Journey of the Minister for the Release of the Captive)*, he spoke of "things that stun the mind and dazzle the intellect" he observed in Spain. Al-Ghassani, as his *nisbah* al-Andalusi implies, was descended from an Andalusian Muslim family, and he wrote evocatively about his family's homeland with the warmth and melancholy that typified North African Muslim writers' image of a now-lost but elysian Andalusia. Yet, rather than merely regretting Andalusia's loss, which many, many Arab Muslims still wistfully express in the twenty-first century, al-Ghassani instead recounted the original Arab conquest of Iberia and predicted a renaissance of Muslim power in the peninsula. Whatever wonders could be seen in Spain, al-Ghassani wrote, the decline of Christian society was obvious and its collapse inevitable, unless, that is, Spaniards embraced Islam.

Al-Ghassani repeated a well-established Muslim trope when he imagined Andalusia as an Arab Muslim golden age, but he offered an altogether novel explanation for the coming demise of Christian Spain. He invoked Ibn Khaldun's North African model to demonstrate the incipient disintegration of Christian states and society, the only known instance of a Muslim author applying Ibn Khaldun's theory to predict historical events. Perhaps it was no more than a rhetorical flourish to please his sultan, the ruthless Mulay Isma'il, who was known to execute his servants for petty offenses, real or imagined. Al-Ghassani believed that peasants in certain Spanish districts resembled Ibn Khaldun's Berber bedouins, a simple, vigorous rural people. Spanish cities, on the other hand, exemplified urban centers that had already entered the decadent final phase of Ibn Khaldun's model. Probably thinking of Madrid's inhabitants, he reported city dwellers lived a luxurious, indolent life, ruled by a physically weak monarch who had never fought a battle. Only northern Europeans, the Dutch, English, and French, exhibited vigorous, aggressive instincts. Detecting no obvious *'asabiyah* in Christian Spain, al-Ghassani condemned its moral laxity, exemplified by bizarre Christian religious festivals. Given decadent Christian morals, it was obvious that the dynamic Ibn Khaldun proposed to explain North African history would inevitably occur in Spain, unless Christians converted to Islam. Then, more or less abandoning Ibn Khaldun's thesis, al-Ghassani in the end just predicted his sultan, Mulay Isma'il, would reenact the original Muslim conquest and recover Iberia for Islam.[8]

European interest in Ibn Khaldun began, however, not in Spain but in France, and was directly connected with Ottoman scholarship. D'Herbelot (1625–1695) a French orientalist, who relied on a bibliographic dictionary by Katib Çelebi, introduced Ibn Khaldun's name to Europe in his *Bibliotèque orientale* (1697), but only in the nineteenth century did it become widely known among scholars, after French and German Arabists began translating the *Muqaddimah* and commenting on the text. Antoine Isaac Sylvester de Sacy (1758–1838), a Persian and Arabic scholar, published a biography of Ibn Khaldun in 1806, and subsequently translated some passages of the *Muqaddimah* and carefully described the nature of the work.[9] Not surprisingly the first European scholar to fully engage with Ibn Khaldun's ideas was Austrian Islamicist and Ottoman historian Joseph von Hammer-Purgstall (1774–1856). In 1812 von Hammer-Purgstall published a book devoted to the decline of Arab Islam, in which he cited Ibn Khaldun's theories and called him, presciently, the "Montesquieu of the Arabs."[10] He might, upon reflection, have referred to Montesquieu as the Ibn Khaldun of the Europeans, given these men's dates and the fact that Ibn Khaldun was the first man to analyze the nature of societies in a synchronic study rather than composing a traditional narrative of events. Still, in identifying Ibn Khaldun with the prestigious French jurist and scholar, von Hammer-Purgstall accurately identified his importance in world historical scholarship.

In 1858 E. Quatremère published the Arabic text of the entire *Muqaddimah*, which was followed by M. de Slane's French translation, completed a decade later. These two works stimulated what has become in the twentieth and twenty-first centuries a flood of Western, Turkish, and modern Arab studies of Ibn Khaldun's work. Nearly all authors of these works have treated the *Muqaddimah* as a brilliant but idiosyncratic artifact of Arab Muslim culture, views exemplified by the British historian Arnold Toynbee's astonished admiration, which he recorded in his multivolume history of civilization, *A Study of History* (1934-1961). After favorably comparing Ibn Khaldun with Thucydides and Machiavelli, Toynbee wrote, "In the prolegomena *(Muqaddimat)* to his *Universal History* he has conceived and formulated a philosophy of history, which is undoubtedly the greatest work of its kind that has ever been created by any mind in anytime or place."[11] Toynbee wrongly characterized the *Muqaddimah* as a philosophy of history, but his comment is valuable because it is symptomatic of the treatment of the *Muqaddimah* as an exotic product of a foreign civilization, rather than as an important milestone in an intellectual tradition that linked Greeks with Muslims and Europeans in a common philosophical culture. Despite such praise and its intellectual pedigree, the *Muqaddimah* has not been absorbed into the mainstream of Western scholarly life but continues to be held, admiringly, at arm's length. It is not included in historiographical studies that begin with Herodotus and conclude with twentieth-century Western scholars, even though intellectually it is part of that tradition. Therefore, Ibn Khaldun's methodology, his new science of man, has no more become part of the Western historical or critical intellectual curriculum than it has found a home in the Muslim world. The exceptions to this generalization are very few.[12]

Contrasted with the lack of attention given to Ibn Khaldun's methodology has been the proliferation of studies of his dialectical model, devoted mainly to analyses of the concept of ʿasabiyah and occasionally to his economic observations. Anthropologists and historians have sometimes used his model to discuss tribal societies or dynasties, but most scholars have been content to analyze and to admire different sections of the *Muqaddimah*. The recurring theme of modern scholarship throughout the world has been Ibn Khaldun's apparent modernity, an idea that reflects a lack of understanding of Ibn Khaldun's philosophical lineage. Most of all he has been seen as a sociologist, a view frequently advanced in the nineteenth century and now widely accepted and promoted in the Muslim world.[13] Muslims have sometimes described him as the founder of an "eastern" or Arab sociology, and a few individuals have attempted to demonstrate he stimulated the development of the discipline in Western Europe. Most thoughtful scholars have, however, been content to describe Ibn Khaldun as a precursor of Western sociological thought, while not explaining why his science of man seems so remarkably similar to later European social analysis. The reasons for the resemblance have already been indicated here, the common philosophical inheritance of Ibn Khaldun and European social and political theorists.

THE SCIENCE OF MAN IN EUROPE

Put simply, first of all, Greek philosophy, encompassing logic, physics, mathematics, music, rhetoric, poetry, and metaphysics, served as the intellectual basis of the European social sciences, just as this fund of ideas and analytical methods enabled Ibn

Khaldun to create a historical science and then construct an intellectually cohesive model to explain the dynamics of North African and earlier Arab Muslim history. Ibn Rushd, the twelfth-century Andalusian Aristotelian, personified the earliest intellectual link between the philosophical cultures of North Africa, Andalusia, and Europe. It was Ibn Rushd, whose works were read in Paris by Thomas Aquinas and later in North Africa or in Andalusia by Ibn Khaldun, who, in refuting al-Ghazali's occasionalist theology, revitalized rationalist thought in the Muslim world. He articulated the ideas of nature and causation that were central to Ibn Khaldun's thought and the ideas of so many Enlightenment and post-Enlightenment thinkers.[14] "For it is self-evident, he [Ibn Rushd] argues, that existing things possess certain natures or properties, which determine the kind of actions associated with them and even the definitions appropriate to them, 'Hence if an existing entity did not have a nature proper to it, it would not have a name or definition proper to it, then all things would be reducible to one thing and not one thing at the same time.' ... Now, reason ... is the faculty which apprehends entities or events as possessing certain determinate natures."[15]

Given the primacy of the University of Paris in the European acquisition of Greek philosophy, it is not surprising that a Frenchman, Charles-Louis de Secondat, Baron de Montesquieu (1689–1755), would be the first European Ibn Khaldun, the first European to develop a science of human society comparable in some respects to the work of his Arab Muslim predecessor. More to the point, Montesquieu derives his synchronic study of European and Asian societies and polities from the same philosophical perspective as his Arab predecessor. Indeed, "the defining characteristic of the *Spirit of the Laws* is Montesquieu's unrelenting search for the basic causes underlying what exists. He believed that very little in the world of man is the product of pure chance, and this perspective opened up for him the prospect of a new science modeled on the natural philosophy that so demystified the realm of nature . . . Like Aristotle before him, to whose work Montesquieu's own treatise may be fruitfully compared, he set out to address the overall nature and prospects of government."[16]

Time, place, politics, society, and culture separated the two men, but only to a degree. Both were members of the social elite, both trained as lawyers, both understood politics, while instinctually preferring scholarship. Both men had studied Greek philosophy, if not always the same texts.[17] While pious, both men also constructed rationalist, secular sciences of man that combined analysis with advice. Montesquieu echoed Ibn Khaldun's notion of a rational state and implicitly invoked Aristotle's politics when he insisted that when he discussed virtue, it was not a Christian but a political virtue and when he discussed the "good man" he meant the political man and not the Christian one.[18] Both were publically proud to have created radically original, scientific accounts of human society. Both also wrote massive, complex, sprawling works, which deserve the bon mot that the nineteenth-century French scholar Emile Faguet used when he described Montesquieu's *Esprit des Lois* as "less a text than an existence."[19]

Just as Ibn Khaldun proudly announced his creation of a new Greco-Islamic science, Montesquieu famously asserted the *Esprit des Lois* was *Prolem sine matre creatum,* "a work with no mother." Pointing out that human science lagged far behind natural science, which meant for eighteenth-century Europeans the science of Newton, he sought the basic causes of existence. "Montesquieu, as Aristotle had already tried to realize it, intended to find the final causes underlying the diversity of empirical reality, which are inherent in the intelligible order of things."[20] Like Ibn

Khaldun, he rejected the idea that knowledge consisted in assembling facts, in his case laws and customs, and dismissed anecdotal accounts, what Ibn Khaldun described as crowd-pleasing entertainments. "I began," Montesquieu wrote in his preface, "by examining men, and I believed that, amidst the infinite diversity of laws and mores, they were not led by their fancies alone," further noting, "I did not draw my principles from my prejudices but from the nature of things."[21] By the "nature of things," he meant both the nature of human beings, who were, he insists, capable of understanding their own nature when instructed, as well as laws and governments. "Laws," he proclaims in his opening sentence, "taken in the broadest meaning, are the *necessary* relations deriving from the *nature* of things."[22] In Greco-Islamic terms, laws constituted necessary accidents.

Montesquieu thus took as his starting point the concept of nature, which Galen and, after Galen, Ibn Khaldun, had insisted was the basis of all scientific investigation. In addition the Frenchman subscribed to his own version of determinism, which is suggested by the full title of his work: *The Spirit of the Laws, or the Relation Laws Should Bear to the Constitution of Each Government, the Customs, the Climate, the Religion, the Commerce etc. to which the Author Has Added Some New Examinations on Roman Laws, Concerning Inheritances, on French Laws, and on Feudal Laws*. While his views on the relation of human agency to historical change are not consistent through all his writings, Montesquieu more often than not expressed his belief in a type of structural history in which various physical social and political factors determined a society's political nature and, therefore, its historical trajectory. "Many things," he writes, "govern men: climate, religion, laws, the maxims of government, examples of past things, mores and manners; a general spirit is formed as a result."[23]

Sometimes he draws a dichotomy that partially resembles Ibn Khaldun's model, arguing that, on the one hand, "The barrenness of the land makes men industrious, sober, inured to work, courageous and fit for war," while, on the other, "the fertility of a country gives, along with ease and softness... a certain love for the preservation of life."[24] In any event Montesquieu had already expressed his belief that history was determined by underlying causes in his earlier work *Considerations on the Causes of the Greatness of the Romans and Their Decline* (1734). "It is not chance that rules the world. Ask the Romans... There are general causes, moral and physical which act in every monarchy, elevating it, maintaining it or hurling it to the ground. All *accidents* are controlled by these causes. And if the chance of one battle—that is, a particular cause—has brought a state to ruin, some general cause made it necessary for that state to perish from a single battle. In a word, the main trend draws with it all particular *accidents*."[25]

A French contemporary of Montesquieu's, Charles Bonnet, wrote to him: "Newton discovered the laws of the physical world. You, monsieur, have discovered the laws of the intelligent world."[26] Émile Durkheim (1858–1917), the late nineteenth-century founder of French sociology, believed Montesquieu was the first person since Aristotle to understand that social phenomena were realities. He was wrong about Montesquieu's primacy, which belonged to Ibn Khaldun, but right about his belief in the reality of societies and political institutions. In some respects it is relatively easy to identify the sources of Montesquieu's ideas, first of all in Aristotle's *Physics* and *Politics* and Plato's *Laws*, among a catalogue of other classical and European sources, including Ptolemy, Galen, Pliny, Plutarch, Livy, and Leibniz. Unlike Ibn Khaldun, he did not outline a research methodology, so even though Bonnet, Durkheim, and many others who read the *Esprit des Lois* saw he had developed a science of man, Montesquieu does not analyze the predictive concept of nature or describe Aristotle's *Organon*, much less does he dwell on specific types of proof or criticize the works of others for their faulty reasoning. "By nature," Montesquieu writes, "I have not at all a censorious spirit."[27] This is one of several ways he differs from Ibn Khaldun, who was never shy in this regard. Another contrast is Montesquieu's focus on political systems and laws rather than society itself. Nonetheless, these differences do not invalidate the idea that these men developed their synchronic sciences of society by reaching into the same reservoir of philosophical knowledge. Two other European examples illustrate these parallel intellectual worlds in fourteenth-century North Africa and eighteenth- and nineteenth-century Europe: a group of eighteenth-century Scottish intellectuals and, most important, Montesquieu's nineteenth-century French compatriot, Durkheim.

Apart from composing his great work, Montesquieu also markedly influenced the next chapter in the philosophically inspired study of society in Europe, which took place, as improbable as it might seem, in eighteenth-century Scotland, hitherto an impoverished backwater of European culture and society. In Scotland, as in France, philosophy inspired the creation of a science of man and society. There *The Spirit of the Laws* helped to catalyze the ferment of the Scottish Enlightenment, a philosophically driven intellectual florescence whose most notable figures were the philosopher David Hume and the political economist Adam Smith. In Scotland "Montesquieu's *piece de resistance* was the idea of *ésprit*, the anthropological-cultural analysis of politics. Here was a 'system of political knowledge,' as Hume celebrated it, showing that 'the laws have, or ought to have, a constant reference to the constitution of governments, the climate, the religion, the commerce, the situation of each society.'"[28] The work of an unjustifiably lesser-known figure, John Millar (1753–1828), a student of Adam Smith and a professor of law at Glasgow University, exhibits Montesquieu's influence most clearly. In his important work "The Origins of the Distinctions of Ranks," he wrote:

> In searching for the causes of those peculiar systems of law and government which have appeared in the world, we must undoubtedly resort, first of all, to the differences of situation, which have suggested different views and motive of action to the inhabitants of particular countries. Of this kind, are the fertility or barrenness of the soil, the nature of its productions, the species of labour requisite for procuring subsistence, the number of individuals collected together in one community, their proficiency in the arts . . . The variety that frequently occurs in these, and such other particulars, must have a prodigious influence upon the great body of people; as by giving a peculiar direction to their inclinations and pursuits, it must be productive of correspondent habits, dispositions and ways of thinking.[29]

Not surprisingly given these opinions, Millar reiterated Ibn Khaldun's critique of the traditional historian's preoccupation with narrative history, what Millar termed "that common surface of events, which occupies the details of the vulgar historian."[30]

However physically isolated Scotland may have seemed at this period, its intellectuals participated in a European, principally French rationalist culture and had done so at least since the late fifteenth century, when some Scots studied and taught at the University of Paris, where the works of Aristotle and Ibn Rushd were part of the curriculum. When in 1474 the French king Louis

XI approved the teaching of the works of Aristotle, Ibn Rushd, Thomas Aquinas, Duns Scotus, and others at the University of Paris, two Scotsmen had already studied and taught there. Others were to follow, such as the influential scholar John Mair, who studied at the College of Montaigu in Paris, where first Erasmus and later Ignatius Loyola also matriculated. Mair, who took a PhD at the college, had published books on philosophy and logic before he returned to Scotland, first to Glasgow and later in 1523 to Saint Andrews. Other Scots followed Mair to Paris and Saint Andrews, thus establishing a philosophical tradition, which initially was subsumed within a Scottish variant of speculative theology, an integration of Aristotelian logic into Christian theology. The tradition was similar in many respects to the theological arguments of Thomas Aquinas or the Ash'ari strain of Islamic theology.[31] Many of these Scottish theologians were probably intellectually indistinguishable from Ibn Khaldun's friend Sharif al-Tilimsani.

While most of these early scholars participated in what is now regarded as a fairly bleak tradition of scholasticism, by the seventeenth century some individuals began to value a broader range of Aristotle's thought, including considering how Aristotle discussed moral philosophy in the *Nicomachean Ethics*. By this time, too, Scottish scholars began to read the original Greek texts, which became widely available when philosophical studies began to shake off their scholastic constraints in the eighteenth century. Then, and particularly in the work of Francis Hutcheson (1694–1746), a professor of philosophy at the University of Glasgow, studies of moral philosophy increasingly dealt with questions of human nature and the issues that had engaged Ibn Khaldun and Montesquieu. "Hutcheson's concept of an original constitution of our nature was taken over by Hume," and with Hume Scottish philosophy emerges from its Christian chrysalis en route to its flight in Adam Smith's *Wealth of Nations*.[32] By the end of the eighteenth century, Edinburgh came to be known as the "Athens of the North," a public recognition of Scottish intellectuals' philosophical commitment and public engagement with social and political issues.

The Scottish Enlightenment was an intellectual florescence that saw the emergence of natural philosophers, such as the chemist and physician Joseph Black (1728–1799), but it is usually associated with Black's friends David Hume and Adam Smith. With these two men and many lesser-known figures such as John Millar and the historian William Robertson, "the philosophical analysis of human nature and the 'empirical' analysis of human societies, human history and the natural world merged in a distinctive synthesis that led to the rise of the human and social sciences."[33] Precisely, and that merger of *logos* and *peira* is what had earlier led Ibn Khaldun to invent these sciences. Like Montesquieu, Hume and Smith lived in a radically different environment from that which Ibn Khaldun inhabited, but as philosopher and philosophically trained political economist, they shared the same intellectual universe and debated many similar fundamental questions. More than anything else they were preoccupied with questions of nature, human and social nature, and the trajectory of human society from the earliest times to the present. In his *A Treatise of Human Nature* Hume wrote: "all sciences have a relation, greater or less, to human nature ... Even *Mathematics, Natural Philosophy,* and *Natural Religion* are in some measure dependent on the science of Man."[34]

Hume bears the least resemblance to Ibn Khaldun in the sense he was a philosopher, not a historical sociologist like Montesquieu, or a moral philosopher turned political economist like

Adam Smith, or a sociologist like Émile Durkheim. As a philosopher he considered some of the same ideas Ibn Khaldun used to explain his dialectical model, foremost among these was the question of nature, in his case human rather than social nature. He discussed this in his major early work *A Treatise of Human Nature* (1739–1740), subtitled an *Attempt to Introduce the Experimental Method of Reasoning into Moral Subjects*. Hume, like Ibn Khaldun and Montesquieu, believed he was revolutionizing the human sciences. By explaining "the principles of human nature," he wrote, "we in effect propose a compleat system of the sciences, built on a foundation almost entirely new, and the only one upon which they can stand with any security."[35]

Hume believed his monumental treatise laid the foundations for a complete system of sciences because human nature encompassed "principles" that "explained the origin and basic workings of morality."[36] He based his analysis of human nature on two premises. First, humans were motived by instinct or passion not reason. Second, human nature comprised two types of virtues, natural or inherent and acquired. Natural virtues included benevolence, humanity, sympathy, and the single most powerful instinct, self-interest, the virtue his friend Adam Smith accepted and made a central motivating force of political economy. Hume believed that taken together these natural virtues, these inherent or instinctual qualities of human nature, generated a social morality of mutual obligation. Then, as society evolved from a primitive state to more complex forms, natural virtues stimulated the development of artificial virtues required to mediate, dampen, or resolve conflicts, such as property rights and legal systems of justice. Furthermore, Hume concluded and Adam Smith concurred: "It is universally acknowledged that there is a great uniformity among the actions of men, in all nations and ages, and that human nature remains still the same in its principles and operations."[37] Nonetheless, Hume insisted that while the fundamental virtues of human nature could not be altered, people's personalities would still differ if they were exposed to distinct circumstances and particularly to novel ideas. Habitual study could alter or more importantly "refine" people's nature—as it could for Ibn Khaldun. Reading his *Treatise,* he hoped, would have such an effect.[38]

Ibn Khaldun, a social theorist but not a philosopher, did not attempt to analyze what Hume terms the principles of human nature. Nor did he concern himself with moral and ethical implications of human nature that concerned eighteenth-century Scottish intellectuals. He did, of course, believe, with Hume, that human society required political institutions, monarchy, to moderate individual passions, including self-interest, the instinct that necessitated the original formation of what he called *human social organization.* If asked, he might have agreed bedouins and urbanites acted from emotion or instinct rather than reason. As he reminded his readers on several occasions, he firmly believed that humans inherited identical intellectual capacities, but he spoke about intelligence or native capabilities rather than moral traits or virtues. As has been seen, Ibn Khaldun was also convinced that humans would differ if exposed to contrasting environments or ideas, which they would absorb through sustained effort or habit. In discussing education he emphasized that memorization, *hifz,* led to the acquisition of traits, *malakat,* whether poetical, scientific, juridical, or mystical, which explained the reality of different personalities in human society.[39]

Hume, for all his extraordinary range of thought on a multitude of subjects, did not develop the comprehensive science of man, whose basis he felt he had assembled in *A Treatise of Human*

Nature. In his final work, *Essays Moral, Political, and Literary,* a compendium of essays written between 1741 and 1760, he presented a view of primordial society very similar to Ibn Khaldun's, writing that man was compelled to establish a politically organized society for the sake of "peace . . . safety [and] mutual intercourse." In the essay he also characterized both government and the clergy as regrettable necessities, portraying them very much in Ibn Khaldun's terms as necessary accidents that were required to keep the peace.[40] He wrote his principle historical work, *The History of England* (1754–1762), as a narrative, and the work is not in any sense a philosophical history or a work of historical sociology. Nonetheless, he argued that historical accounts provided the basis for philosophical knowledge, writing that history's "chief use is only to discover the constant and universal principles of human nature."[41]

In his history Hume's philosophical training is on view primarily where he rigorously applied a logical critique of accepted ideas, resembling Ibn Khaldun's technique for finding an historical report questionable if it was contrary to the laws of nature.[42] He adopted Montesquieu's Aristotelian-derived typology of despotisms, monarchies, and constitutional regimes, and seems to have shared the Frenchman's fundamental political conservatism. Yet he never appears to have considered composing a synchronic model like *The Spirit of the Laws* in which he would draw out all the implications of his analyses of human nature, perhaps because, as he said to one of his friends, his ambition for "system making" had waned after *A Treatise of Human Nature* had been so poorly received when first published.

Scottish system building was left to Hume's close friend Adam Smith (1723–1790). As explicitly as Ibn Khaldun, Smith invoked philosophy as the analytical basis for a science of man. In an early essay on "The History of Astronomy," Smith declared his belief in the fundamental explanatory power of philosophy in terms that echo Montesquieu's goal of abstracting principles from the seeming chaos of reality. "Philosophy is the science of the connecting principles of nature. Nature seems to . . . abound with events which appear solitary and incoherent . . . Philosophy, by representing invisible chains which bind together all these disjointed objects, endeavours to introduce order into this chaos of jarring and discordant appearances, to ally this tumult of the imagination, and to restore it, when it surveys the great revolutions of the universe, to that tone of tranquility and composure, which is both more agreeable."[43]

Smith wrote this essay as a young man, but he still valued it at the end of his life, for it was one of a very few of his unpublished works he wanted preserved and published. Smith was known to admire French rationalist thought. He embraced what he termed the *esprit systématique,* while stressing that what he wanted to see in a science of man was French rationalism married to English empiricism. In this he was a successor to Galen for medicine and Ibn Khaldun for history, and Smith was known to the governor of Massachusetts as the man who succeeded where everyone else had failed in creating a system that identified principles of the human community.[44]

Smith is a well-documented thinker, as well attested as Ibn Khaldun, an individual whose philosophical training and practical knowledge led him to construct a persuasive model of society. Like Ibn Khaldun, who believed scientific teaching was one of the elite crafts, Smith thought the philosopher occupied a unique place in society.[45] Like Hume he was educated in Scottish universities during a period when philosophy dominated the final three years of the five-year curriculum. In Glasgow, after courses in Latin and Greek in the first two years, Smith would have studied logic and metaphysics in his third year, moral philosophy in the fourth, and natural philosophy in the fifth. Part of his education included an introduction to Newtonian physics and Euclidian geometry, whose proofs appealed to him for the same reason Ibn Khaldun and other Greco-Islamic rationalists admired them: their rigorous logical certainty. Intellectually Smith and Ibn Khaldun inhabited the same philosophical world, however different their economic, social, and political environments. Among other differences, Scotland's own bedouins, the Highland clans, had been decimated and rendered powerless at and immediately following the Battle of Culloden in 1746. Smith began his lifelong commitment to a science of man with lectures on rhetoric in 1748 only three years after the clans had occupied Edinburgh in September 1745.[46]

Smith developed his study of speech, known to Ibn Khaldun as *Kitab al-Khitabah,* the art of persuasion through analogical reasoning and the seventh part of Aristotle's *Organon,* as a rigorously logical argument. His own method of persuasion in arguing for a modern, polite, and refined variant of rhetoric was in fact mathematical, derived from his knowledge of Euclidian geometry. He began, as he later began many sections of the *Wealth of Nations,* with an axiom, that rhetoric was most effective when "used with propriety."[47] Smith developed elaborate, evolutionary theories of language, demonstrating among other things that it became more abstract as society grew to become more complex. He and Ibn Khaldun shared classically derived notions about the necessity of language for social communication and cooperation, but an elaborate comparison of points on which they agreed or disagreed on any subject is less relevant here than Smith's mode of argument. As much or more than Ibn Khaldun's emphasis on *burhan* and logical methodology, Smith developed his science of man with a dialectical method, "In which the design of the writer is to Lay Down a proposition and prove this by different arguments which lead to that conclusion."[48]

The systematic, philosophical basis of Smith's *Wealth of Nations* was recognized by many of his contemporaries, even if most people have forgotten this fact, just as most scholars no longer recall the philosophical basis of sociology.[49] Whatever the myriad differences that separated Ibn Khaldun and his times from Smith and his era, Smith's *Wealth of Nations* represents what Ibn Khaldun would term philosophical history. Dugald Stewart (1753–1828), another stalwart of the Scottish Enlightenment, wrote an essay in 1793 interpreting Smith's life and thought in which he said, "In Mr. Smith's writings, whatever be the nature of the subject, he seldom misses an opportunity . . . in tracing from the principles of human nature, or from the circumstances of society, the origins of the opinions and institutions he describes." Stewart could have been describing Ibn Khaldun in this passage. Stewart continued by alluding to Smith's *History of Astronomy* and reporting Smith had told him he had always planned to produce histories of other sciences on the same methodological plan.[50] Smith largely based his explanation of the logic or trajectory of historical change on two of Hume's premises concerning human nature. These were, first, that human nature remained constant over time and space and, second, that self-interest was one of its most important intrinsic elements. Self-interest was in turn the motivating force, or as he expressed the idea in his *History of Astronomy*, "the connecting principle," behind the division of labor, the fundamental source of wealth in *The Wealth of Nations* and, as has been seen, in Ibn Khaldun's economics.

It was, Smith argued, exactly the division of labor, not innate human differences, that produced distinct human personalities.

"The difference of natural talents in different men is, in reality, much less than we have been aware of; and the very different genius which appears to distinguish men of different professions, when grown up to maturity, is not upon many occasions so much the cause, as the effect of the division of labour. The difference between the most dissimilar characters, between a philosopher and a common street porter, for example, seems to arise not so much from nature, as habit, custom, and education."[51] Ibn Khaldun, of course, expressed virtually the same sentiment in the fourteenth century. The bedouin and the urbanite inherited the same capabilities and grew to differ owing to their distinct environments and education. Smith, presumably, would have said the same about the rude Highland clansmen and polished Edinburgh intellectuals such as Hume, Stewart, and himself!

Ibn Khaldun's and Smith's understanding of human nature and their analysis of how people's natural acquisitive instincts produced wealth through the division of labor are markedly similar. Smith's example of how pin making, once an individual craft, had developed into a complex industry employing a variety of specialists virtually reproduces Ibn Khaldun's analysis of how wealth was exponentially created in an agricultural economy, where different craftsmen cooperate to produce farming implements and crops.[52] It is only one of several common threads in their economic arguments, which include, most obviously, their shared notions of taxation, the role of capital, and, perhaps above all, the importance of a laissez-faire economy, in which governments do not participate or interfere in business. They also differ in many ways, perhaps most obviously in their attitude toward merchants as a class and the promise of commerce. Ibn Khaldun, after all, did not live in an "improving society" influenced by Enlightenment ideals.[53] Nonetheless, both approached the study of politics and economies with the same *esprit systématique*. Smith's prize student, John Millar, wrote that Smith deserved to be known as the Newton of the science of politics.[54] Well since Newton was an Englishman, fair enough, but if Millar had read the *Muqaddimah*, what then would he have said—of both men?

ÉMILE DURKHEIM AND THE ANNALES

Hume, Smith, and Millar derived their concepts and methodology from philosophy to formulate philosophical, economic, and social analyses. The intellectual vigor of the Scottish Enlightenment, however, declined in the late eighteenth century, and apart from a few men such as Millar, its dominant philosophical influence ceased to yield new synchronic studies of man. It is possible to detect the traces of this tradition in the histories of the influential William Robertson (1721–1793), the principal of the University of Edinburgh and a friend of Hume. Robertson exhibits his philosophical heritage of logic and concern with something's nature in several of his works, although he never explicitly discusses historical methodology. In his *Historical Disquisition . . . on India,* for example, he includes an appendix in which he discusses the *nature* of Indian/Hindu society and speaks, at one point, of basing conclusions on inductive reasoning.[55] His analysis of societies in his more famous work *The History of America* has prompted one modern scholar to label him a historical anthropologist, for the same reason Ibn Khaldun has so often been seen as a sociologist, his application of philosophy to the study of social systems.[56] Still it was not Robertson or any other Scot but Émile Durkheim (1858–1917) who most closely resembled Ibn Khaldun in creating a new philosophical methodology by exploiting fundamental Aristotelian ideas to construct anew a science of man valid for the study of any society.

Durkheim came to the study of society as a scholar who had begun his formal academic career at age twenty-four as a lecturer in philosophy, the dominant discipline in late nineteenth-century French higher education. Between 1883 and 1884 he presented a series of lectures required of a new professor in which he both defined philosophy and also surveyed a variety of philosophical issues. These Sens lectures contained no obvious hint of his later sociological ideas, nor any suggestion he was particularly committed to Aristotle's thought, which became obvious only later.[57] They do reveal his fundamental understanding of classic, that is, Greek, philosophical principles, including logic and scientific methodology, his commitment to a combination of rational and empirical thought, and concern with the concept of nature.[58]

Durkheim's knowledge of Aristotle's thought was critical for his development of sociology. His general familiarity with Aristotle's writings is evident in the Sens Lectures, and there is little doubt he knew the Organon as well as the *Nicomachean Ethics*, the *Politics*, and the *Metaphysics*. As a student he first heard from his teacher Émile Boutroux Aristotle's dictum, which Ibn Khaldun also cited, that each science had to have its own principles, its special subject of investigation, the *mawdu* of Ibn Khaldun's *Muqaddimah*.[59] More important than this early association is Durkheim's allusion in his 1888 lecture on sociology to "The illustrious Example of Aristotle, who was," he said, "the first to see society as a natural fact." He went on to remark, "In the eighteenth century the same idea was indeed reborn with Montesquieu and Condorcet."[60] The idea that society represented an entity, a natural fact, was the foundational concept of Durkheim's sociology, and in *The Rules of the Sociological Method* he attributed the origin of sociology to "the great philosophical doctrines."[61] In his 1903 essay "Sociology and the Social Sciences," he wrote that the ultimate goal of sociology was the "philosophical part of the science."[62]

Durkheim's familiarity with Montesquieu, the subject of his Latin thesis, and his knowledge of Aristotle's works explain why his approach to the study of society so closely resembles Ibn Khaldun's philosophical methodology.[63] Both Ibn Khaldun and Durkheim wanted to establish sciences of man using Greek and predominantly Aristotelian assumptions, concepts, and methods. In "Sociology and the Social Sciences" Durkheim outlined the "Principal Divisions of Sociology" and said the main goal of his first category, "Social Morphology," is "the study of the geographic base of various peoples in terms of its relationships with their social organizations."[64] Durkheim did not express his "social morphology" in axiomatic terms, but his formulation was close to Ibn Khaldun's when he remarked, whether rural or urban, "This territory, its dimensions, its configuration, and the composition of the population which moves upon its surface are naturally important factors of social life, they are its substratum and, just as psychic life in the individual varies with the anatomical composition of the brain, which supports it, collective phenomena vary with the constitution of the social substratum."[65] Ibn Khaldun would have characterized these variable collective phenomena as accidents!

Elsewhere, Durkheim wrote in terms that sound like a paraphrase of part of the *Muqaddimah*, "The goal of sociology is to explain social phenomenon in terms of their hidden essences." He argued that societies, like the rest of the world, are subject to laws that *"derive necessarily from their nature and that express it."*[66] In *Rules for the Sociological Method,* he also stated "society is not a mere sum of individuals. Rather, the system formed by their association represents a specific reality which has its own characteristics."[67] Society, that is, represents an essence or nature distinct from the individual natures of its inhabitants. These arguments essentially paraphrased Montesquieu's observation that "laws express the nature of things." Ultimately, as with Ibn Khaldun, Durkheim's conception of society as a discrete entity also represents an argument about causation, a social not an individual phenomenon.

Durkheim's emphasis on "hidden essences" and the nature of societies also virtually reproduces Ibn Khaldun's ideas—or those of Aristotle—and when he discussed "collective phenomena" or what he called "social facts" he seemed to be discussing necessary accidents. The latter phenomena were Durkheim's principal concern; they were the subjects of sociology. He identified them as "life itself," or, more precisely, as the various aspects of what he terms "social psychology": religion, morality, law, linguistics, aesthetics, and so forth. Durkheim coined the term because he believed these collective phenomena were to geography or social morphology what psychology was to biology. And his explanation used the idea of structure in a physical sense that anticipates its later use in history and the social sciences. "In biology," he wrote, "while anatomy (also called morphology) analyzes the structures of living beings and the mode of composition of their tissues and organs, physiology studies the functions of these tissues and organs."[68] Durkheim's ultimate goal was to see in "species" of various classes of "social facts," "the unity of the genus." That is, he wanted to see the particular in the universal and hoped thereby to establish "general laws of which the very diverse laws established by the special sciences are only particular forms."[69]

Durkheim, like Ibn Khaldun, advocated comparison as a fundamental step in the logical process that scholars had to use in order to determine the truth about societies. He believed that only through comparison, more particularly through comparative history, could sociologists study the various institutions that concerned them. "We have only one way," he wrote, "to demonstrate that a logical relationship (for example, a causal relationship) exists between two facts; we would have to compare cases in which they are simultaneously present and absent to see if the variations which they present in these different combinations of circumstances bear witness to the dependence of one on the other. Experiment," he concludes, "is fundamentally just a form of comparison; it consists in making fact vary, of producing it in various forms, which are subsequently methodologically compared."[70] Comparison for both men yielded knowledge in two ways. First, it allowed scholars to generalize, to move from a perception of many species to an understanding of a particular genus, and, second, it permitted them to test the veracity of evidence against what they knew about the nature of a particular society.

Durkheim's philosophical or methodological assumptions represented a reprise of Ibn Khaldun's ideas, and his characterization of the two distinct forms of social solidarity echoed Ibn Khaldun's contrasting portrayal of bedouin and urban societies—only the projected consequence of city life was radically different. Durkheim posited two forms of social solidarity: mechanical and organic. Mechanical solidarity, a term that seems inappropriate for the society it describes, existed in small, socially undifferentiated societies whose members were closely related and shared common beliefs. Such societies, Durkheim theorized, possessed a kind of common conscience. Organic solidarity, a term that seems more appropriate for his simple society, Durkheim used to characterize complex urban social organizations. These were societies whose people lacked common kinship ties but recognized their economic interdependence, giving them a shared sense of purpose, based on the division of labor. Legal systems regulated social behavior in organic societies, rather than retribution and violence that resolved disputes in mechanical societies.

Durkheim's environment differed radically from Ibn Khaldun's. Late nineteenth-century France had a large agrarian population, but bands of nomadic pastoralists did not threaten its cities. Nonetheless the contrast Durkheim drew between these two types of societies, which just as easily could be labeled as rural and urban, strongly resembles Ibn Khaldun's contrasting depiction of rural tribes and sedentary urbanites. Durkheim's collective conscience is virtually identical to Ibn Khaldun's 'asabiyah, and his idea that complex societies lack kinship bonds but are integrated by a division of labor matches Ibn Khaldun's portrayal of urban populations. Durkheim's idea that legal systems regulated social relationships in complex societies but not in simple ones also echoed Ibn Khaldun's belief in the distinction between customary and bureaucratic legal systems. He thought that formal legal systems, rather than representing progress, contributed to the dependence and passivity of city dwellers. The two social theorists diverge in their views when it comes to the social integrity and vitality of complex, presumably urban societies. Ibn Khaldun indicated his craftsmen were economically interdependent, but he did not suggest they also consciously valued this relationship or that it compensated for the loss of tribal social cohesion and personal freedom. His North African tribes, he said, did not believe this.

THE ANNALES

While Émile Durkheim established sociology as an academic discipline, it was left to one of his students, Marc Bloch (1886–1944), along with his colleague Lucien Febvre (1878–1956), to found a school of historical interpretation, the Annales School, which, after five centuries, finally approximated Ibn Khaldun's idea of a school of philosophical history. Bloch came of age as a young scholar at a time when Durkheim assaulted traditional French historical preoccupation with the individuals and political history.[71] Beginning in 1903 and continuing at an intense level for the following five years, Durkheim had published his critique of narrative history through articles in his journal, *Année Sociologique*, founded in 1886. His disciple, the economist François Simiand, was especially active in spreading Durkheim's ideas of social analysis and was one of the individuals responsible for denouncing traditional historical narrative, in a very Ibn Khaldun-like phrase, as *l'histoire événementielle*, the history of events. The Annales School has been described as the most "scientistic" school of historical interpretation, but scholars who use the term, while discerning its traits of structural analysis, do not seem to appreciate its philosophical origins, which indeed, Bloch does not explicitly identify. Bloch himself has been described by some scholars as a historical sociologist who believed in the explanatory power of structure, that is, nature, the hallmark of philosophical history and its intellectual offspring, sociology. Structure remanded social attributes such as law and even daily human activities, to the status of necessary accidents. These included language, as Bloch demonstrates in his work *Feudal Society*, where, without invoking Aristotle's terminology, he attributes feudal vocabulary to the medieval social structure.[72]

His debt to the philosophically inspired ideas of Émile Durkheim and intellectual resemblance to Ibn Khaldun is unmistakable in many ways that comprised part of the early twentieth-century French debate on the proper conduct of historical research. First, he embraced Montesquieu's and Durkheim's perception of society as a social fact and the related concept of a collective mentality. Lucien Febvre, the cofounder of the Annales School, reported that Durkheim's sociology was the discipline that had the greatest effect on Bloch, and in his late work, *The Historian's Craft*, Bloch, in the course of describing the subject of history, quotes Febvre to the effect that the history was not concerned with individual man, "not man, never again man. [But] Human societies, organized groups."[73] In adopting this idea, Bloch embraced the notion of social causality, nearly identical to Ibn Khaldun's embrace of Aristotle's and Galen's belief that an entity's nature determined its trajectory. Second, as Febvre's comment implies, Bloch and more explicitly Braudel accepted Durkheim and Simiand's denunciation of narratives devoted to individuals and events in favor of enduring underlying structures. François Simiand, the Durkheimian economist, was one of the sources for Braudel's phrase *l'histoire événementielle*, the history of events, which Braudel and Ibn Khaldun dismissed as a form of knowledge. Third, Bloch also discussed the question that preoccupied Ibn Khaldun and attracted Durkheim's attention, social cohesion. In his work *Feudal Society* he analyzed the nature of social cohesion in medieval Europe. Beginning with the solidarity of the kinship group, which could be found in Ibn Khaldun's rural tribal ʿasabiyah and Durkheim's mechanical solidarity, he went on to discuss "vassalage as a substitute for the kinship tie," in the manorial system. Fourth, Durkheim, and Bloch also shared Ibn Khaldun's equation of population growth with economic development and an increase in the division of labor.

Bloch's work on feudalism also contains an important methodological element that typified both Ibn Khaldun and Durkheim's methodology: the comparative method. Thus in the penultimate chapter of *Feudal Society,* titled "Feudalism as a Type of Society," Bloch includes "A Cross-Section of Comparative History" that he devoted to pointing out the commonalities shared by European and Japanese society.[74] In *The Historian's Craft* Bloch discussed comparison in a different sense, not as a means of identifying the species as a constituent of a newly broadly defined genus, but as a method, which Ibn Khaldun also emphasized, of distinguishing truth from falsehood in an historical report.[75] "The historian," Ibn Khaldun wrote, "must compare similarities and differences between the present and the past . . . He must know the causes of the similarities in certain cases and the differences in others . . . Then he must check transmitted information with the basic principles [the natures] he knows."[76] Bloch wrote, in a section titled "Toward a Logic of the Critical Method," "Rightly understood, critical comparison is not content to collate evidences from the same plane of time. A human phenomenon is always linked to a chain which spans the ages."[77] When preparing to lecture before the Collège de France in 1933, he described himself professionally "as a comparative historian of European societies."[78]

Marc Bloch's societal bias and devotion to the comparative method made his historiography and that of some Annales School disciples echo Ibn Khaldun's desiderata for philosophical history. The fundamental assumptions are the same, even if Bloch's Aristotelianism was mediated through Émile Durkheim. Bloch was more insistent on the importance of considering individual personalities, but in his final work, 1944's *The Historian's Craft*, he wrote, "For all individual originality has its limits. The style of Pascal belongs to him alone; but his grammar and the stock of his vocabulary belong to his time."[79]

In the case of Fernand Braudel, however, the scholar who is often seen as Bloch's preeminent successor, the philosophical core of Bloch and Durkheim almost disappears. In the *Mediterranean* (1949), his earliest and perhaps still perhaps most famous work, his tripartite structure of environmental structure, social conjuncture, and superficial events presents the appearance of a logically constructed study, but Braudel does not connect the three through causation. The idea of something's nature as a cause is completely absent. He does not phrase his arguments with the logical vocabulary found in the *Muqaddimah* or Durkheim's works, except briefly when discussing transhumance, when he remarks any logical study should begin with this basic agricultural situation, for "all transhumance is the result of a demanding agricultural situation."[80] Readers of Ibn Khaldun might expect this comment to be followed by an extended discussion of environmental determinism of social groups, but Braudel, who evidently read Ibn Khaldun only later, uses logical in the common sense of sequence rather than its philosophical meaning of causation. In any event, the philosophical or sociological rigor of Durkheim and Bloch is altogether absent in the *Mediterranean*, a work that remains, in the words of the French critic Claude Lefort, one of *pointillisme*.[81] With pointillism we seem to have come if not full circle at least to 1376, the year before Ibn Khaldun wrote the *Muqaddimah*.

CONCLUSION

A Question of Knowledge

IN WRITING THE *Muqaddimah* Ibn Khaldun felt he had accomplished two goals. He had, first, developed a new science of philosophical history, and, second, he used his methodology to explain the dynamics of North African and Andalusian history. In his desire to create a historical science that would yield genuine knowledge, he introduced his ideas with a blizzard of words and phrases to convey the vital importance of probing beneath surface appearances, *safahat*, to identify deep, *ʿamiq*, or deep-rooted, *ʿariq*, truths underlying events and determine the causes and ultimate origins of "existing things," *kaʾinat*. Among other terms, he also uses *batin*, the interior, to emphasize the necessity of penetrating to the heart or core of something. The word is commonly associated with the Sufi spiritual quest for the vital soul or spiritual essence. Like Sufis, philosophical historians were also searching for essences or natures, but essences in the external, material world. These were the *haqaʾiq*, "true natures," "essences," or "realities," and their associated accidents in the visible world of physical objects and human societies. Beyond this *logos* or rationalism needed to determine the enduring nature of human social organizations, historians had to practice *peira,* empirical testing of information about every known facet of geography, human society, and political structures. His book, Ibn Khaldun concludes, had accomplished this and was "unique for incorporating remarkable sciences and hidden wisdom."[1]

Ibn Khaldun included several ritualistic asides in the *Muqaddimah* as he celebrated his achievement in creating a new "science of man." He understood he had produced something both unique and enduring when he applied his science to analyze and describe North African societies and explain their histories. In illustrating how historical studies could be transformed from arid narratives to philosophically meaningful analyses and conceptualizations, he offered scholars an opportunity to discern substance and meaning in historical reports and social observations. His dialectical model, characterization of rational or sultanate politics, and analysis of urban economies constitute three distinct sections of the *Muqaddimah* that stand alone as major intellectual achievements. Beyond these one can point to dozens of observations he makes about society, politics, and intellectual life of his time, many of them only slightly disguised autobiographical anecdotes that he expresses as generalizations. The *Muqaddimah,* thus, for all its many inconsistencies, contradictions, and sometimes numbingly prolix summaries of knowledge, retains its appeal as a remarkably original, acute, and expansive study of man written by an exceptional individual, who by every evidence, possessed a luminous intelligence and a powerful, enduring, egoistic devotion to scholarship that was evidently aided by a prodigious memory.

The *Muqaddimah* may also be viewed as a testament to the fertility of Muslim scholarship and the breadth of accumulated

Muslim knowledge in the fourteenth century. Franz Rosenthal has been quoted in the introduction to the effect that Ibn Khaldun's work encapsulates the sum total of Islamic scholarship at this period. The *Muqaddimah* is not quite so all-inclusive as that, but it does contain a remarkable range of information, which is evidently the result of Ibn Khaldun's stated intent to be comprehensive. Given its range, it seems likely Ibn Khaldun was trying replicate the encyclopedic nature of al-Masʿudi's history—if not the great historian's logical failures—which had, he writes, become a reference work for earlier historians. The *Muqaddimah* could be used as a basis for compiling an encyclopedia of Muslim religious, philosophical, and literary learning in an era not known for its cultural florescence. A systematic study of the topics Ibn Khaldun discusses and sources he mentions, an enormous task, would also represent an important means of trying to develop a better idea of how he developed his ideas. However original as a work of historical sociology or as an innovative study of politics and economics, Ibn Khaldun largely derived the data of the *Muqaddimah* from existing sources.

In many cases Ibn Khaldun's intellectual debts are obvious, including his seemingly arcane summary of the traits of conic sections. Euclid's geometry, for example, was widely known and studied even by committed *ʿulama* such as the Maliki scholar al-Tilimsani. Nearly all Greco-Islamic rationalists appreciated geometry for its intellectual discipline as much as officials valued this knowledge for its practical uses. In other instances the source of his information is not always so immediately clear. Consider one of the topics that Ibn Khaldun touches on in the course of writing the *Muqaddimah,* the role of the *adib,* the liberally educated man, as *katib* or secretary. Having emphasized such men must be selected from highly educated, upper-class individuals who write well, he cites an epistle of an Umayyad official, who describes the desirable skills and morality for individuals who hold such offices.[2] Ibn Khaldun's source for this essay is not known, but later in the text when he provides an essay on *adab* or belles lettres, he mentions four scholars he considers the founders of this discipline, which involved, he said, "knowledge of the poetry and history of the Arabs as well as the possession of some knowledge of every science."[3]

Two of these men were exceptionally prolific *adib*s and possible sources not only for this Umayyad epistle but for a good deal of Ibn Khaldun's discussion of Arabic language, literature, literary criticism, and even some scientific subjects. One, al-Jahiz (776–868), was well known, an independent scholar of Ethiopian descent, who thrived as an *adib* in ʿAbbasid Baghdad during its rationalist Mutazili days. Known for works on Arabic language, such as his work on literary criticism, *Kitab al-bayan wa-l-tabyin (The Book of Elegance of Expression and Clarity of Exposition)*, al-Jahiz was a classic type of an intellectually liberal literary *adib*.

The Iranian Ibn Qutaybah (828–889) was a second important ʿAbbasid era intellectual. He was a *qadi* and later a teacher in Baghdad, who wrote on a variety of literary, theological, and practical scientific works. His essays were well known in late ninth-century Andalusia. An important figure, "his adab, which comprises an ethos and a culture in which are united all the intellectual currents of ʿAbbasid society at the beginning of the 3rd/9th century, and ... displays an intent to popularize, at least for a certain literate public, a kind of humanism."[4] Ibn Qutaybah wrote a classic *adab* treatise titled simply *Adab al-katib (The Culture/Education of the Secretary)*. The book is unusual as a piece of *adab* writing in its concern for practical, scientific knowledge, and it represents one important source for the dissemination of such knowledge throughout the Arabic Islamic world. In his introduction he wrote:

> In addition to my works [which provide linguistic, literary and religious training], it is indispensable for the [secretary] to study geometrical figures for the measurement of land in order that he can recognize a right, acute and an obtuse triangle... and the different sorts of quadrangles, arcs and other circular figures, perpendicular lines, and in order that he can test his knowledge on the land and not on the [survey] registers, *for theoretical knowledge is nothing like practical experience.*
>
> The Persians [i.e., the Sasanians] used to say that he who does not know the following would be deficient in his formation as state secretary... He who does not know the principles of irrigation... [measuring] the varying lengths of days, the revolution of the sun, the rising points [on the horizon] of stars, and the phases of the moon and its influence... constructing arched stone bridges... the nature of the instruments used by artisans and craftsmen; and the details of accounting.[5]

Ibn Khaldun's appreciation of Ibn Qutayba's book offers a hint at how he may have come by some of the seemingly esoteric scientific information he discussed in the *Muqaddimah*. He refers to hundreds of other works, which a serious *adib* and committed scholar like himself read to acquire information. Yet it is also important to recognize that in creating a new philosophical science, he implicitly claimed a far more distinguished self-worth than an identity as a particularly well-informed secretary. What he admired more than anything else was the ability to acquire true knowledge and, with it, an elevated level of humanity. His repeatedly expressed admiration for scholars alerts readers to his own intellectual purpose. The question of knowledge lies at the heart of the *Muqaddimah*.

After noting that God had implanted intelligence or reason, *idrak*, in the human soul, Ibn Khaldun defines knowledge as a perception, *tasawwur*, of the essences, *haqa'iq or mahiyat*, of things.[6] Students, he implies, initially acquired such philosophical knowledge through dialectical discussion, *jadaliyah*. Having attained this intellectual level, an individual scholar's next mental step was to identify the essential accidents associated with the subject of his perception or study. Elsewhere Ibn Khaldun expresses this somewhat differently by saying humans were distinguished from the animals by their ability to perceive universals, by comparing similar individual objects with one another. An example of this thought process is the instance when someone perceives that all individual humans constitute a species, thus sharing an essence or nature. This is the process Ibn Khaldun can be said to have followed by treating the distinct Arab Bedouin and Berber species as the genus *bedouin*s.[7] Fundamentally, Ibn Khaldun was describing how comparison leads to generalization or abstraction, yielding a conclusion that Aristotle defined as scientific knowledge. Ibn Khaldun himself concludes that the "treasury of human science, the locus of these perceptions or abstractions, is the soul of man."[8]

The mental processes Ibn Khaldun describes are those he used in constructing his dialectical model. He did not merely summarize existing factual information such as dynastic lists; he created knowledge of universals and abstract principles, by perceiving "existence as it is, with is various genera, differences, reasons and causes," which, he evidently believed, would allow him as well as other rationalists to acquire a "pure intellect and perceptive soul."[9] Then, in a slightly different context he argues that the "degree to which a human being is able to establish an orderly causal chain determines his degree of humanity."[10] Some individuals, he remarks, can perceive only two or three levels of causation, while others manage five or six. The example of chess, he suggests, may help the student understand his point, as some players can plan as many as five moves in advance, while the less intelligent cannot. He allows, however, that his analogy is not perfect as chess is a habit, an acquired skill, whereas an understanding of causal chains is innate or "something natural."[11] Readers are probably meant to assume that Ibn Khaldun could easily imagine five chess moves in advance, an ability that also enabled him to synthesize knowledge, therefore ensuring his membership in a humanist pantheon of Greco-Islamic rationalists. Indeed, he suggests that rationalists who attained these abstract levels of rational thought realized a kind of philosophical immortality of the kind Ibn Rushd described when he remarked that "when mind is set free from its present conditions it appears as just what it is and nothing more: this alone is immortal and eternal."[12]

Similar intellectual abilities also powered the initial stages of prophethood, which represented another type of immortality, the unique status of God's messenger. As has been seen, Ibn Khaldun distinguished spiritual and rational knowledge. Humanity at large "knew" God and his creation not directly but through the Quran, while prophets alone enjoyed divinely mediated access to God and the world of the angels. Yet it was the power of reason, he argued, that also allowed talented individuals with a certain type of soul to achieve degrees of "spiritual thought," enabling them to approach the divine world.[13] As is so often the case with other discussions in the *Muqaddimah*, however, Ibn Khaldun does not stop, as a philosopher might, to compare these complex ideas of philosophical and spiritual thought. A first and obvious distinction between them is that philosophers could reach the highest plane of intellect—and humanity—solely through reason, while prophets could attain the most exalted and final stage of spiritual knowledge only if they were chosen by God.

Ibn Khaldun made another and unappreciated distinction between philosophical and religious approaches to knowledge. Apart from its logical rigor, he thought philosophical sciences enjoyed an advantage over religion—and history, too—in one fundamental respect. His comment on the differences constitutes one of the most important passages in the *Muqaddimah*. "Differences occur in the religious sciences," he observed, "because of the differences among the various religions, and in the historical sciences because of differences in the outward character of historical information... The philosophical sciences do not show (such) differences. They have developed uniformly, as required by the very nature of thinking, which is concerned with the perception *(tasawwur)* of existing things as they are, whether corporeal, spiritual, celestial, elemental or material. These sciences show no differences."[14] *'Unsur,* the elemental here, refers to the four classical elements: earth, air, fire, and water.

Philosophers, he thus argued, always used the same axioms and logical reasoning to study common issues of human existence. In saying this, Ibn Khaldun might be imagined to be mortgaging the integrity of his faith in favor of some type of ecumenical spiritual relativism, but this is almost certainly not what he means to imply. He has revealed the theological depth and emotional force of his Islamic faith, as well as pointedly dismissed the spiritual validity of other religions. If pressed about the meaning of this passage, he would almost certainly deny the validity of the messages in the books of other faiths, even while acknowledging their existence. These observations about the universality of philosophical questions are critical, though, for in making them Ibn Khaldun essentially asserted that in his social analysis he belonged to a rationalist lineage of scholars that began with Plato, Aristotle, and Galen, continued with al-Farabi, Ibn Sina, and Ibn Rushd, and would emerge again in the future, as it did with Montesquieu, Hume, Smith, and Durkheim. His philosophically based analysis of human and political natures, politics, and economics demonstrated his engagement with the same issues previously debated by Greek and Greco-Islamic thinkers, which Europeans were to turn to again during the Enlightenment and onward into modern times.

This intellectual lineage also documents the extraordinary longevity and influence of Greco-Islamic ideas and logical argument, including the notion of a primordial society, the concept of someone's or something's nature, and the application of logically trained intelligence to the study of historical and sociological evidence. Historical works and religious treatises might differ from one society and time to another, but rationalist scholars who sought to develop definitive studies of humanity over the course of more than two millennia persisted in their attachment to certain *muqaddimat*, certain fundamental Greco-Islamic axioms or premises. Most of all they continued to value the concept of nature or essence, which Aristotle defined and explained at length in his *Physics*. Natures were inductively perceived truths that explained the movement or direction—of a physical form or a society—and for Ibn Khaldun as well as his European intellectual descendants, historical and social knowledge was, in the first instance, the product of this understanding.

Philosophical knowledge is one thing; self-knowledge is another. In an era and culture when literary introspection and emotional displays were rare, it would be unrealistic to expect Ibn Khaldun either to unburden himself of his hopes, fears, or dreams or publicly reflect on his sense of self. It is difficult to reconstruct an emotional life for nearly any individual, but at least when it comes to Ibn Khaldun's complex public identity the evidence is not veiled, like the faces of Sinhajah Berber tribesmen. It is openly displayed in his memoir and throughout the *Muqaddimah*. He considered himself to be and sometimes functioned as an *adib* and a secretary, but he also consciously worked as a scholar of both the religious and rational sciences. He sometimes alludes in his memoir to his scientific work. As a student trained in Maliki law as well as Greco-Islamic philosophy, he was indisputably both a traditional, *naqli,* and a rational, *'aqli,* scientist, the first based on the Quran and Sunnah and the second on humans' ability to think.

More problematic than his obvious professional and scholarly identities was Ibn Khaldun's attitude toward his ethnicity or race. He was proud of his Yemeni Arab lineage as a member of the Banu Khaldun family, which traced its descent from a renowned chief, who, he reports, was one of the Companions of the Prophet.[15] Even though he never returns to the first pages of his memoir where he trumpets his family's status, Ibn Khaldun valued, even revered, Arab Muslims of the Prophet's generation. It was those spiritually authentic, vital individuals Ibn Khaldun relates, who internalized Muhammad's message and fought for the faith. These men taught a simply expressed, compelling Islam, in contrast to the complex, dry textual versions offered later by corrupt, deracinated professional teachers, long accustomed to comfortable, sedentary life. Then there was the 'Abbasid caliph's sister, who, he writes, could never have defiled herself with an Iranian *mawali* because she was still close to the Arab Bedouinism of the first Arab Muslim generation. Sometimes—often rather—he seems to have ached to experience this same spiritual vitality in his own era. Certainly he failed to find it in the Maliki courts in Cairo, whose practices, he must at some point have reflected, demonstrated the accuracy of his model that described how corruption afflicted advanced urban societies.

Ibn Khaldun's contradictory feelings about Arabs are on display throughout the *Muqaddimah*. He looked back from his own century to the first Arab Muslim generation and denounced Arab Muslims for destroying the sedentary society of Yemen, Iran, and any other urban society they conquered, and he also repeatedly extolled the cultural florescence of the ʿAbbasid centuries. Yet he decried the loss of Arab Muslim *ʿasabiyah*, as caliphs compromised Arab integrity by employing Iranians and Turks, leading ultimately to the collapse of the second Arab caliphate, whose culture he valued so highly. Then he wrote bitterly about Arabs of his day, who exemplified the worst aspect of generic bedouin behavior, and except for his occasional reference to the earliest Arab Muslims and the sister of the ʿAbbasid caliph, he applied the term *Arab* in the *Muqaddimah* only to the Banu Hilal and similar tribes, whom he excoriated for their destructive rampages in North Africa as well as for their dishonesty.

As a member of the urban Arab Muslim social elite, did Ibn Khaldun agonize over his contradictory characterizations of his fellow Arab Muslims? It should be recalled Ottoman Turks called themselves Ottomans, their legitimizing dynastic identity, while speaking contemptuously about Turks in the Anatolian countryside. Babur, the founder of the Mughal Empire of India and himself part Turk and part Mongol, identified himself dynastically as a descendant of Timur, a Timurid, while using the term *turk* as a pejorative adjective, referring to rustic, undisciplined, and uncivilized people of any ethnicity or race, Turk, Mongol, or

Afghan, who lived in the countryside. In this genealogical spirit, if asked, Ibn Khaldun, an Arab without dynastic pretensions, may have emphasized his family identity as a Banu Khaldun or possibly his family's status as Tunisian or Andalusian, while denouncing the Hilal Arabs or their Berber counterparts.

Did he imagine himself to be one of the disreputable, deracinated teachers he denounced in the *Muqaddimah*? If he was concerned or even thought about the implications of his different statements, it is not recorded in any of his writings. On the surface it seems difficult to reconcile his statements about Arabs, just as his conflicting religious and philosophical assumptions about causation cannot be simply explained away. Yet, once again it is relevant to observe that Ibn Khaldun recorded many contradictory statements in the *Muqaddimah*. He gave religious explanations to religious questions and rational answers to questions about society, politics, and economics, never stopping to reconcile obvious contradictions. His failure to do so may be partly seen to be a result of his intent to compose an encyclopedia of Arab Muslim knowledge as well as to reform the historical profession. First, he summarizes religious knowledge, then philosophy. In other instances his elaborate descriptions contain information that contradict arguments in his model. Perhaps finally the best way to accept these and the other seeming inconsistencies in his writings is to agree with F. Scott Fitzgerald when he wrote: "The test of a first-rate intelligence is the ability to hold two opposed ideas in the same mind and still have the ability to function."[16] By this measure, Ibn Khaldun's ability to hold a number of opposing ideas at the same time would testify to a remarkable intelligence, which itself would contradict his assertion that human nature was everywhere the same—except for naturally talented chess players, where this is demonstrably not true.

CHRONOLOGY

ISLAMIC WORLD, EGYPT AND NORTH AFRICA, IBERIA
(Caliphates/Dynasties in bold print)

Islamic World	Egypt and North Africa	Iberia
622–632 Muhammad's Prophecy		
Rightly Guided Caliphs		
632–634 Caliphate of Abu Bakr		
634–644 Caliphate of 'Umar	642 Arab Muslims occupy Alexandria	
644–656 Caliphate of 'Uthman		
656–661 Caliphate of 'Ali First *fitnah* and Kharijis in Iraq		
Umayyad Caliphate of Damascus, 661–750		
661–680 Caliphate of Mu'awiya	670 Qayrawan founded: Arab Muslim military camp near Tunis	

(continued)

Islamic World	Egypt and North Africa	Iberia
685–705 Caliphate of Marwan	698 Arab Muslims occupy Carthage	
705–715 Caliphate of Al-Walid		711 Arab/Berber Muslim armies invade Iberia
750 Massacre of the Umayyads	739–740 Berber revolt in North Africa and Iberia	732 Charles Martel defeats Muslims at Poitiers in France
'Abbasid Caliphate of Baghdad, 750–1258		
754–775 Caliphate of Mansur and origins of Greco-Islamic translation movement		
—Baghdad founded 762		756–809 Emirs of Cordoba
775–785 Caliphate of al-Mahdi		
	777–814 **Rustamids of Tahert**	
786–809 Caliphate of Harun al-Rashid		—765–856 Umayyad campaigns in Andalusia
	789–814 **Idrisids of Fez**	
813–833 Caliphate of al-Ma'mun	800–909 **Aghlabids of Qayrawan**	
833–842 Caliphate of al-Mu'tasim	868–905 **Tulunids of Egypt**	
		856–1031 **Western/ Iberian Umayyad Caliphate**

Islamic World	Egypt and North Africa	Iberia
847–861 Caliphate of al-Mutawakkil	908 Fatimid campaigns in North Africa	
—867–911 **Saffarids of Sijistan**	969–1171 **Shi'i Fatimids of Egypt**	1031 rise of the *Muluk al-tawa'if*, the "kings of factions"
—875–1005 **Samanids of Khurasan and Mawarannahr**	—1031 Banu Hilal and Banu Sulaym Bedouins to North Africa	1086–1147 **Almoravids**
		—1186 Ibn Rushd born in Cordoba
—935–1055 **Shi'i Buyids in Baghdad**	1031–1147 **Almoravid Berbers of Fez**	
		1147–1269 **Almohads**
—977–1186 **Ghaznavids of Iran, Afghanistan, and India**	1130–1269 **Almohad Berbers of Marrakesh**	1085 Christian Reconquista of Toledo
	1250–1517 **Mamluks of Egypt**	
1258 Mongols occupy Baghdad, 'Abbasid Caliph killed		1236 Reconquista of Cordoba
	1229–1574 **Hafsid Berbers of Tunis**	
1360–1405 Timur in Central Asia, Iran, India		1248 Reconquista of Seville
	1258–1420 **Merinid Berbers of Fez**	

(continued)

Islamic World	Egypt and North Africa	Iberia
1401 Timur occupies Damascus, meets with Ibn Khaldun		1231–1492 **Nasrids of Granada**, Christian Reconquista 1492
	1332 Ibn Khaldun born in Tunis	

NOTES

PREFACE

1. Ibn Khaldun, *The Muqaddimah*, vol. II, trans. Franz Rosenthal (Princeton: Princeton University Press, 1958), 295/259. Hereafter cited as the letter *M* followed by the volume number and the page references, first to Rosenthal's translation and second to Quatremère's Arabic text (as M, II, 295/259).
2. Ibid., I, introduction, lxxxv.
3. Ibid., lxxxvi.
4. For an instructive list of studies of Ibn Khaldun in a visual format, see the Yale University Library exhibition: *Ibn Khaldūn: An Exhibition at Sterling Memorial Library, March to May 2008*. Online, 2009, Yale University Library. Commentaries that accompany each pictured text offer an excellent introduction to the range of scholarship on Ibn Khaldun.

INTRODUCTION · PRINCIPLES AND PURPOSE

1. M, I, 65/52.
2. Ibid., 63–65/51–53. Ibn Khaldun's friend Ibn al-Khatib (1313–1374), the multitalented Granadan *wazir*, wrote a scientific treatise on the plague titled *Muqni'at al-sa'il 'an marad al-ha'il*, which W. B. Ober and N. Alloush discuss in their article "The Plague at Granada: Ibn al-Khatib and Ideas of Contagion," *Bulletin of the New York Academy of Medicine* 58, no. 4 (May

1982): 418–424. Ibn al-Khatib guessed that seven-tenths of the population died of the plague; the figure, however exaggerated, at least suggests the scope of the calamity.

3. M, I, 64/51.

4. For a discussion of the "victory of Aristotelianism" in Greco-Islamic philosophy, see Dimitri Gutas, *Greek Thought, Arabic Culture* (London: Routledge, 1998), 95–104.

5. "Since Aristotle requires scientific propositions to be about universals, he refuses to allow singular statements about particulars to be part of science." T. H. Irwin, *Aristotle's First Principles* (Oxford: Clarendon Press, 1992), 119.

6. Ibn Khaldun characterizes philosophical history either as ʿilm or *fann*. ʿIlm means knowledge, and it is commonly used in a phrase for a particular scientific subject such as arithmetic, ʿilm al-hisab. Fann generally connotes a scientific discipline. See Anis Hamadeh, "The Concept of Science in Early Islamic History," *Periodica Islamica* 6, no. 1 (1996): 7–14. Ibn Khaldun uses the Arabic term *hikmah* rather than the Arabicized Greek word *falsafah* to categorize his new historical science. At different times in their history, Muslims employed *hikmah* to designate religious scholarship as well as Greek-derived rationalism. Nonetheless, Muslim philosophers commonly used *hikmah* as a synonym for *falsafah*, and in his foreword Ibn Khaldun unmistakably intends *hikmah* to refer to Greco-Islamic philosophy.

7. M, I, 78/62.

8. Ibid., 11/6.

9. For an excellent introduction to Islamic historiography, see R. Stephen Humphreys, *Islamic History: A Framework for Inquiry* (Princeton, NJ: Princeton University Press, 1991). Humphreys appropriately characterizes Ibn Khaldun as an exceptional scholarly figure and therefore omits him from his study of traditional Muslim historians (ibid., 135).

10. Ibn Khaldun, like many other philosophically educated Muslims, was familiar with at least some of Galen's writings, but no evidence exists to suggest the nature or structure of his science was inspired by Galen's example.

11. R. J. Hankinson, "The Man and His Work," and Teun Tieleman, "Methodology," in R. J. Hankinson, ed., *The Cambridge Companion to Galen* (Cambridge: Cambridge University Press, 2008), 10–11, 61.

12. Tieleman, "Methodology," in Hankinson, *The Cambridge Companion to Galen*, 62, 51–52.

13. Ibid., 54. See also Sabine Vogt, "Drugs and Pharmacology," in Hankinson, *The Cambridge Companion to Galen*, 315–316.

14. For sources of these comments, see Tieleman, "Methodology," 49–65; R. J. Hankinson, "Epistemology," 157–183; and Ben Morison, "Logic," 66–115, in Hankinson, *The Cambridge Companion to Galen*.

15. M, I, 13/7–8.

16. He briefly discusses the incidence of plagues at the end of dynasties as a result of overly dense or heavily concentrated urban populations. In this context he cites it as one of many possible diseases common to the decadent phase of dynasties. In this respect it can be seen as part of his categorization of the traits of corrupt tribal dynasties. See Chapter 4, where these traits are discussed. He does not return specifically to the devastating plague of his era. M, II, 135–137/124–126.

17. M, I, cxiii.

18. *'Ibar* means admonitions, lessons, or examples and is derived from the Arabic root *'abara*—to cross over, to interpret, to illustrate. The word is commonly used in Arabic titles.

19. M, III, 481/434.

20. Its full title—one of its titles—is *al-Ta'rif bi-Ibn Khaldun wa-rihlatuhu garban wa-sharqan/Biography of Ibn Khaldun and Report on His Travel in the West and the East*. See Abdesselam Cheddadi's discussion of the text in his edited dual-language edition with French translation and Arabic text, *Ibn Khaldun Autobiographie* (Algiers: CNRPAH, 2008), 11–14; hereafter cited by the letter A followed by the page number (as A, 11–14).

21. Ross E. Dunn, *The Adventures of Ibn Battuta, a Muslim Traveler of the Fourteenth Century* (Berkeley: University of California Press, 1989). For a commentary on the traditional *rihlah* genres, see especially Dale F. Eickelman and James Piscatori, eds., *Muslim Travelers: Pilgrimage, Migration, and the Religious Imagination* (Berkeley: University of California Press, 1990).

22. See Franz Rosenthal's seminal article "Die arabische Autobiographie," *Studia Arabica* 1 [*Analecta Orientalia*], no. 14 (1937): 1–40; the essay by M. J. L. Young, "Arabic Biographical Writing," in *Religion, Learning and Science in the 'Abbasid Period*, ed. M. J. L. Young, J. D. Latham, and R. B. Serjeant

(Cambridge: Cambridge University Press, 1990), 168–188; and Dwight Reynolds, *Interpreting the Self: Autobiography in the Arabic Literary Tradition* (Berkeley: University of California Press, 2001).

23. For an introduction to al-Mawardi's ideas, see Erwin I. J. Rosenthal, *Political Thought in Medieval Islam* (Cambridge: Cambridge University Press, 1968), 27–37.

24. M, I, 414–428/364–376.

25. Ibid., II, 22/18.

26. Ibid., 22/18.

27. Ibid., I, 468–469/411.

28. A, 20; A. Huici Miranda, "Ibn Hayyān," in Bearman et al., *Encyclopaedia of Islam*, http://referenceworks.brillonline.com/entries/encyclopaedia-of-islam-2/ibn-hayyan-SIM_3196.

29. See, for example, Otto Zwartjes, Ed de Moor, and G. H. van Gelder, eds., *Poetry, Politics and Polemics: Cultural Transfer between the Iberian Peninsula and North Africa* (Amsterdam: Rodopi, 1996).

30. M, III, 340/295.

31. Ibid., II, 28/23–24.

32. Ibid., 328–329/289–291. Ibn Khaldun distinguishes God's just use of rank to ensure social stability as something "essential" (*dhat*) from an individual's obsequious grasping for rank as something "accidental" (*'arad*), "as is the case of all evils decreed by God." He goes on to say, "Much good can fully exist only in conjunction with the existence of some little evil, which is the result of matter [*mawadd*]." In accounting for the existence of evil, Ibn Khaldun uses the philosophical terminology of "accidents," the Aristotelian concept alluded to above and explained below. He may have derived this argument from Muslim speculative theology, which used logic to substantiate religious doctrine. See Chapter 2.

33. M, I, 29/19.

34. Ibid.

35. Ibid., II, 196–197/172–173 and 343–344/304–305.

36. Ibid., I, 14/8, and III, 481/433–444.

37. An instructive list of variant logical meanings of the use of the word *muqaddimah* in Arabic sources is contained in Ilai Alon and Shukri Abed, *Al-Fārābī's Philosophical Lexicon,* vol. 1: Arabic Text (Cambridge: Cambridge

University Press, 2007), 350–358. See also Joep Lameer, *Al-Fārābī and Aristotelian Syllogistics* (Leiden: Brill, 1994), 70n6, quoting al-Khwarizmi's *Mafātīh* to the effect: "A muqaddama is a statement which is put forward in (constructing) a syllogism." See also multiple entries in Lameer's index.

38. Alon and Abed, *Al-Fārābī's Philosophical Lexicon*, vol. 1, 347–350.
39. For the range and complexity of this concept, see ibid., 235–239.
40. Abū Nasr al-Fārābī, *On the Perfect State*, ed. and trans. Richard Walzer (Chicago: Great Books of the Islamic World, 1998), 368n196.
41. Alon and Abed, *Al-Fārābī's Philosophical Lexicon*, vol. 1, 382 and 327.
42. Avicenna, *The Physics of the Healing*, ed. and trans. Jon McGinnis (Provo, UT: Brigham University Press, 2009), 2. See especially bk. I, "On the Causes and Principles of Natural Things."
43. M, III, 157/125 and n. 752, a reference to Ibn Sina's work *Kitāb al-najāh*.
44. Al-Fārābī, *On the Perfect State*, 430. "The term *ijtimāʿ* (='formation of a society,' 'association as such') seems to render the Aristotelian term *koinōnia*."
45. M, I, 89/68–69.
46. Ibid., 328/291.
47. Ibid., 302–304/270–272.
48. Jonathan Barnes, ed., *The Cambridge Companion to Aristotle* (Cambridge: Cambridge University Press, 1995), 97–101. As Barnes and other commentators have observed, Aristotle's usages are not always either clear or consistent.
49. Avicenna, *The Physics of the Healing*, bk. I, 14.
50. M, I, 9/4.
51. Ibid.

1 · IBN KHALDUN'S WORLD

1. M. Talbi, "Ifrīkiya," and G. Yver, "al-Maghrib," in Bearman et al., *Encyclopaedia of Islam*, http://referenceworks.brillonline.com.proxy.lib.ohio-state.edu/entries/encyclopaedia-of-islam-2/ifrikiya-COM_0354 and http://referenceworks.brillonline.com.proxy.lib.ohio-state.edu/entries/encyclopaedia-of-islam-2/al-maghrib-COM_0614. The latter article on the

Maghrib is an especially valuable essay on the region's history, population, settlement patterns, and intellectual life.

2. For an introduction to North Africa in the early fourteenth century see Dunn, *The Adventures of Ibn Battuta*, 13–40.

3. M, II, 266/230–231.

4. Ibn Battuta visited and praised the city in 1325. See Dunn's evocative account, *The Adventures of Ibn Battuta*, 35–38.

5. Ibid., 296.

6. John Clarke's contemporary study of seminomadism offers considerable insight into environmental and population patterns of interior North Africa. See his article, "Studies of Semi-Nomadism in North Africa," *Economic Geography* 35, no. 2 (April 1959): 95–108.

7. M, I, 250–251/222. Many modern anthropological studies of North African and Middle Eastern tribes describe mixed pastoral nomadic and agricultural populations. Ibn Khaldun's typically generalized account of rural tribesmen alludes at least in part to a similar mixed economy. Roy H. Behnke Jr. offers an excellent introduction to the social and economic complexity of tribal life in the late twentieth century among bedouins in eastern Libya in his book *The Herders of Cyrenaica* (Urbana: University of Illinois Press, 1980).

8. M, II, 49/43. For a sense of this verse, see Ibn Khaldun's discussion of "Contemporary Bedouin Poetry" (ibid., III, 412–440), and for a modern taste of poetry sung in tribal conflicts, similar in many fractious ways to Ibn Khaldun's North Africa, see Steven C. Caton's intriguing study, *Peaks of Yemen I Summon* (Berkeley: University of California Press, 1993).

9. Michael Brett and Elizabeth Fentress, *The Berbers* (Oxford: Blackwell, 1997), 6.

10. M, II, 266/265–266.

11. While Ibn Khaldun and other commentators agree on the anarchic and destructive nature of the Banu Hilal and the devastation they visited on North Africa, the origin and composition of this complex tribal group or confederation is not well documented. See Brett and Fentress, *The Berbers*, 132–142.

12. M, I, 305/272.

13. A, 255.

14. M, I, 303/270. See also Chapter 4 for the traits of sedentary culture. Complete lists of North African tribes also have to include other ethnic

groups, such as small populations of Kurds, who migrated to North Africa following the Mongol conquest of Baghdad in 1258. See *Ibn Khaldun, Le Livre des Examples II Histoire des Arabes et des Berbères du Maghreb*, ed. and trans. Abdesselam Cheddadi (Paris: Gallimard, 2012), 929–930.

15. See William D. Phillips Jr. and Carla Rahn Phillips, *A Concise History of Spain* (Cambridge: Cambridge University Press), 2010, especially chap. 1, "The Land and Its Early Inhabitants."

16. For an introduction to Andalusia's political history, see Hugh Kennedy, *Muslim Spain and Portugal* (Harlow, UK: Longman, 1996).

17. M, I, 356/317 and 238–243/205–209.

18. Ibid., III, 460. For pictures of the palaces and gardens in both North Africa and Andalusia, see Christopher Tadgell, *Islam, from Medina to the Magreb and from the Indes to Istanbul* (New York: Routledge, 2008), 196–269.

19. Brought home to the author in a conversation with an Algerian in the fall of 2013, who spoke emotionally of Muslims' persisting nostalgia for Andalusia.

20. M, II, 355/316.

21. Ibid., 290/254, and III, 300–302/260–261 and 364–366/319–320.

22. Ibid., II, 350–351/309–311.

23. A, 18.

24. This précis of North African history is based principally on the book of Jamil M. Abun-Nasr, *A History of the Maghrib in the Islamic Period* (Cambridge: Cambridge University Press, 1987), and articles in the *Encyclopaedia of Islam*.

25. Ibn Khaldun includes a section on town planning in the *Muqaddimah*, which emphasizes a city's ideal physical setting. M, II, 243–249/210–215. Rosenthal notes some of the likely sources for some of his material in M, II, 246/212, n. 39.

26. M, III, 461/411. This poet is not identified.

27. For an accessible introduction to this important movement in Iraq as well as in North Africa, see Ira M. Lapidus, *A History of Islamic Societies*, 2nd ed. (Cambridge: Cambridge University Press, 2009). See references in the index of this book.

28. M, I, 333/296. In the twentieth century Europeans sometimes characterized Moroccan tribal groups as "systems of organized anarchy." Quoted by David Montgomery Hart in his article "Segmentary Systems and the Role

of the 'Five Fifths' in Tribal Morocco," *Revue de l'Occident musulman et de la Méditeranée* 3 (1967): 71.

29. For an anthropologist's discussion of some of these issues, see Dale Eickelman, *The Middle East and Central Asia: An Anthropological Approach* (Upper Saddle River, NJ: Prentice Hall, 2002).

30. See Chapter 4, where this question is discussed. Richard Tapper provides one of the best modern anthropological discussions of the nature of kinship relations within various tribal segments in his description of tribes in northwestern Iran. See his book *Pasture and Politics: Economics, Conflict and Ritual among the Shahsevan Nomads of Northwestern Iran* (London: Academic Press, 1979), especially chap. 3, "The Nomadic Community I: Kinship and Affinity." In his *The Herders of Cyrenaica*, Roy H. Behnke Jr. discusses the usage of the term *qabilah* among the bedouins of eastern Libya (see especially 109–110 and 137–138). Hart provides a careful modern analysis of Moroccan tribal structures in his article "Segmentary Systems," 65–95. I am indebted to Professor Emilio Spadola of Colgate University for this reference. Hart does not discuss Ibn Khaldun's terminology in this article. He does, however, discuss the concept of a tribe in his book *Qabila* (Amsterdam: Het Spinhuis 2001).

31. Brett and Fentress, *The Berbers*, 6.

32. M, II, 114/104. See M. Talbi, "Rustamids," in Bearman et al., *Encyclopaedia of Islam*, http://referenceworks.brillonline.com.proxy.lib.ohio-state.edu/entries/encyclopaedia-of-islam-2/rustamids-SIM_6348.

33. D. Eustache chronicles the fragmentation that bedeviled this tribal state in his article "Idrīsids," in Bearman et al., *Encyclopaedia of Islam*, http://referenceworks.brillonline.com.proxy.lib.ohio-state.edu/entries/encyclopaedia-of-islam-2/idrisids-SIM_3495.

34. Abun-Nasr, *A History of the Maghrib in the Islamic Period*, 51–52.

35. Ibid., 51.

36. G. Marçais and J. Schacht, "Aghlabids or Banu 'l-Aghlab," in Bearman et al., *Encyclopaedia of Islam*, http://referenceworks.brillonline.com.proxy.lib.ohio-state.edu/entries/encyclopaedia-of-islam-2/aghlabids-or-banu-l-aghlab-COM_0024.

37. For a lucid introduction to the origin, evolution, and varieties of Islamic law, see N. J. Coulson, *A History of Islamic Law* (Edinburgh: Edinburgh University Press, 1991).

38. M, II, 350/310 and 283/246.

39. Regarding the Arabization of North Africa, see M, I, 64/52, and William Marçais, "Comment l'Afrique du Nord a été arabisée," in *Articles et Conférences, Publications de l'Institut des Etudes Orientales à Alger, XXI*, ed. William Marçais (Paris: Adrien-Maisonneuve, 1901), 171–192.

40. Ibn Khaldun's own detailed narrative account of the history of these two major Berber states is easily accessible in Abdesselam Cheddadi's French translation of Ibn Khaldun's history of the Berbers in his *Le Livre des Exemples*, especially 1073–1367.

41. M, I, 316/281.

42. Ibid., 321–322/285–286.

43. Ibid., 53/41 and 471/413–414.

44. Ibid., 471–472/413–415.

45. Ibid., II, 15/12 and 66/59.

46. Ibid., 134/123.

47. Josef Puig Montada provides a concise summary of Ibn Bajjah's and Ibn Tufayl's ideas in his essay "Philosophy in Andalusia: Ibn Bājja and Ibn Tufayl," in *The Cambridge Companion to Arabic Philosophy*, ed. Peter Adamson and Richard C. Taylor (Cambridge: Cambridge University Press, 2005), 155–179. Taylor briefly discusses Ibn Rushd in the same volume in his essay "Averroes: Religious Dialectic and Aristotelian Philosophical Thought," 180–200. Ibn Rushd's writings are discussed in greater detail in Chapter 2.

48. See M. Shatzmiller, "Marīnids," in Bearman et al., *Encyclopaedia of Islam*, http://referenceworks.brillonline.com.proxy.lib.ohio-state.edu/entries/encyclopaedia-of-islam-2/marinids-SIM_4966.

49. M, I, 252/223–224.

50. Ibid., 295/263.

51. Ibid., 331/294.

52. Ibid., 368/326. See H. R. Idris, "Hafsids," in Bearman et al., *Encyclopaedia of Islam*, http://referenceworks.brillonline.com.proxy.lib.ohio-state.edu/entries/encyclopaedia-of-islam-2/hafsids-SIM_2625.

53. M, II, 24/19–20.

54. Ibid., 283/247.

55. Ibid., 290/254.

56. Ibid., 77/68.

57. Ibid., I, 275–276/246–247.

2 · THE TWO PATHS TO KNOWLEDGE

1. Al-Fārābī, *On the Perfect State*, 472.
2. Majid Fakhry, *A History of Islamic Philosophy*, 3rd ed. (New York: Columbia University Press, 2004), 286–293; Majid Fakhry, *Averroes (Ibn Rushd)* (Oxford: Oneworld, 2001), 161–164.
3. See Alon and Abed, *Al-Fārābī's Philosophical Lexicon*, vol. 2, 847, and references to rhetoric and dialectic in the index of Alon and Abed's volume.
4. M, III, 114–115/90.
5. Ibid., 115–116/90–92.
6. Ibid., 116–117/92.
7. He describes these scholars in his memoir (A, 31 passim).
8. Ibid., 36–37.
9. Ibid., 32.
10. Ibid., 32 and 37–40.
11. M, I, xliv; G. C. Anawati, "Fakhr al-Dīn al-Rāzī," in Bearman et al., *Encyclopaedia of Islam,* http://referenceworks.brillonline.com/entries/encyclopaedia-of-islam-2/fakhr-al-din-al-razi-COM_0206.
12. See M, III, 29/22, where Ibn Khaldun praises the abridgement of four prominent speculative theologians, noting al-Razi's preference for logical argument.
13. Ibid., I, 386/343.
14. Ibid., II, 436/385.
15. Ibid., 438/387.
16. Ibid., 438/387.
17. Ibn Khaldun, nonetheless, includes a brief account of Christianity and its history, organization, and theology in ibid., I, 472–481/415–422.
18. Ibid., III, 3/1.
19. Ibid., 34/27.
20. Ibid., I, 199/178.
21. Ibid., 192/171.
22. Ibid., 192/171.
23. Ibid., 192–193/172.
24. Ibid., 203/181.

25. Ibn Khaldun's attitude to Sufism continues to spark debate, at least among Western scholars. James Winston Morris, an Arabic Islamicist and specialist on the thought of the Andalusian mystic Ibn ʿArabi, cites Ibn Khaldun's brief treatise on Sufism to portray him as sympathetic to early Sufi beliefs and practices but unrelentingly hostile to later manifestations of this devotional, mystical aspect of the Islamic faith. See his article "An Arab Machiavelli? Rhetoric, Philosophy and Politics in Ibn Khaldun's Critique of Sufism," *Harvard Middle Eastern and Islamic Review* 8 (2009): 242–291. Historian Allen James Fromherz argues, or strongly implies, that Ibn Khaldun was a practicing Sufi. See his book *Ibn Khaldun: Life and Times* (Edinburgh: Edinburgh University Press, 2011). Ibn Khaldun's treatise on Sufism, cited in the introduction, discusses the role of the Sufi *shaikh* rather than expressing a spiritual commitment. See also Alexander D. Knysh, *Ibn ʿArabi in the Later Islamic Tradition* (Albany: SUNY Press, 1999), 184–197.

26. M, III, 81/64.

27. Ibid., 83/65.

28. Ibid., 80/63.

29. Ibn Khaldun particularly cites Galen's work *De usu partium* (*On the Use of the Parts*) (ibid., I, 90/70). Mark J. Schiefsky discusses this work in his essay "Galen's Teleology and Functional Explanation," in *Oxford Studies in Ancient Philosophy*, ed. D. Sedley (Oxford: Oxford University Press, 2007), 33:369–400. For a discussion of Galen's concept of soul, see Pierluigi Donini, "Psychology," in Hankinson, *The Cambridge Companion to Galen*, 184–209.

30. M, I, 210/187–188.

31. Ibid., III, 34/27.

32. Ibid., 53/42.

33. Ibid., 28/22.

34. Discussions of technical logical terminology and the logic of al-Farabi, whom Ibn Khaldun repeatedly cites in the *Muqaddimah*, may be found in Joep Lameer's book *Al-Fārābī and Aristotelian Syllogistics*. See especially chap. 2, "The Syllogism and Its Kinds."

35. M, III, 35/28.

36. Ibid., 38/30 and 154/123.

37. Ibid., 257/219–220.

38. Ibid.

39. Ibid., 50/40.
40. Ibid., 154/122.
41. Ibid.
42. Ibid., 252/215.
43. Ibid., 49/39 and 61/48. Ibn Khaldun summarizes what he considers to be the essential characteristics of the original Muslim faith, speculative theology, orthodox theologians, and the Muʿtazilah on 34–110/7–86.
44. Frank Griffel, *Al-Ghazālī's Philosophical Theology* (New York: Oxford University Press, 2009), 98–99. See Griffel's chapter, "Al-Ghazālī on the Role of *falsafa* in Islam."
45. M, III, 146/116.
46. Ibid., 153–154/121–122.
47. Ibid., 54/44.
48. Ibid., 53/42.
49. Ibid., 250/213.
50. Ibid., 247/211.
51. Ibid., 249–250/213.
52. Ibid., II, 196/173.
53. Ibid., 195/171.
54. Ibid., III, 261/224.
55. Ibid., 263/226.
56. Ibid., 262/225.
57. Ibid., 245/208.
58. Ibid., 156/124 and 169/135–136.
59. Ibid., 280/241.
60. Ibid., 32/25.
61. Ibid., 23/17.
62. Ibid., 22/16.
63. Ibid., 32–33/25–26.
64. James Gleick, *Isaac Newton* (New York: Random House, 2004), 112.
65. Griffel, *Al-Ghazālī's Philosophical Theology*, 134–135.
66. Lucid introductions to Hume's ideas may be found in David Fate Norton and Jacqueline Taylor, eds., *The Cambridge Companion to Hume* (Cambridge: Cambridge University Press, 2011). See especially Martin Bell's essay "Hume on Causation," 147–176, in that volume.
67. Griffel, *Al-Ghazālī's Philosophical Theology*, 211.

68. Ibid., 155.
69. M, III, 36–37/29.
70. Ibid., 39 and n. 314. Rosenthal notes that this idea, which al-Ghazali also cites, can be found in the famous early Persian treatise on Sufism by al-Hujwiri, *Kashf al-mahjūb*, trans. R. A. Nicholson (Leiden: E. J. W. Gibb Memorial Series, 1911), 18.
71. Fakhry, *Averroes (Ibn Rushd)*, 26.
72. M, III, 309/268.
73. Ibid., 145/114.
74. Ibid., 145/114–115.
75. Ibid., 145/114.
76. Ibid., 308–309/268.
77. Ibid., 309/269.
78. Ibid., 111/86–87.
79. Ibid., II, 436/385.
80. Ibid., 412–413/364–365, and III, 138–139/109.
81. Alon and Abed, *Al-Fārābī's Philosophical Lexicon*, vol. 2, 789.
82. Ibn al-Khatib noted that Ibn Khaldun had studied Ibn Rushd's works, without specifying which books he summarized. M, I, introduction, xliv. Ibn Khaldun also specifically talks about philosophers studying Ibn Rushd's abridgements of Aristotle's texts (ibid., III, 254/217).
83. Ibid., 147/116–117 and 153/121–122.
84. Majid Fakhry discusses Ibn Rushd's studies of Aristotle's *Physics* in *Averroes*, chap. 5, "The Physical Structure of the Universe."
85. Charles E. Butterworth, *Philosophy, Ethics and Virtuous Rule: A Study of Averroes' Commentary on Plato's "Republic,"* Cairo Papers in Social Science, vol. 9, monograph 1 (Cairo: American University in Cairo Press, 1986).
86. For an introduction to Greek philosophical works translated into Arabic in Baghdad between the eighth and tenth centuries, see Gutas, *Greek Thought, Arabic Culture*.
87. Majid Fakhry, *Al-Fārābī, Founder of Islamic Neoplatonism* (Oxford: Oneworld, 2002), 45.
88. M, III, 138/109, where Ibn Khaldun uses these two terms in his discussion of man's ability to think.
89. Ibid., 147/116–117.
90. Ibid., 130–131/102.

91. Ibid., 137/108.
92. Ibid., 137/108 (translator's italics).
93. Hankinson, *The Cambridge Companion to Galen*, 11.
94. R. J. Hankinson, "Philosophy of Science," and C. C. W. Taylor, "Politics," in Barnes, *The Cambridge Companion to Aristotle*, 120, 235–238.
95. Avicenna, *The Physics of the Healing*, 45.
96. Hankinson, "Philosophy of Science," 120.
97. M, III, 147.
98. Fakhry, *Averroes (Ibn Rushd)*, 27.
99. W. D. Ross and J. O. Urmson, "Nicomachean Ethics," in Barnes, *The Complete Works of Aristotle*, 2:1799.
100. Hankinson, "Philosophy of Science," 109.
101. Ibid., 113.
102. For a series of definitions, see Alon and Abed, *Al-Fārābī's Philsophical Lexicon*, 256–263.
103. R. Rashed and B. Vahabzadeh, *Omar Khayyam the Mathematician* (New York: Biblioteca Persica Press, 2000), 218. See also Bijjan Vahabzadeh, "KHAYYAM, OMAR vi. as Mathematician," in *Encyclopædia Iranica Online,* http://www.iranicaonline.org/articles/khayyam-omar-vi-mathematician, where the author remarks, "Khayyam ... understands mathematical concepts in accordance with Aristotelian philosophy."
104. M, II, 28/24.
105. Ibid., III, 311/271. See his entire editorial on the subject of "science" in Islam in ibid., 311–315/270–274.
106. Fakhry, *Averroes (Ibn Rushd)*. See especially chaps. 10 and 11, "Averroes and the Latin West" and "Averroes and Aquinas."
107. For an introduction to this important figure and others of his school, see Fakhry, *A History of Islamic Philosophy*, 314–322.

3 · A SCHOLAR-OFFICIAL IN A DANGEROUS WORLD

1. A, 60.
2. Ibid., 62–67, where Ibn Khaldun enthusiastically identifies scholars and the works they had studied at the Marinid court at Fez.
3. Ibid., 62.

4. For valuable information on this scholar and his family, see especially H. Bencheneb, "al-Sharīf al-Tilimsānī," in Bearman et al., *Encyclopaedia of Islam*, http://referenceworks.brillonline.com.proxy.lib.ohio-state .edu/entries/encyclopaedia-of-islam-2/al-sharif-al-tilimsani-COM_1043.

5. A, 64.
6. Ibid., 67.
7. Ibid., 72.
8. Ibid. For the verse, see page 276 of the second appendix.
9. Ibid., 62.
10. Ibid., 72–73.
11. M, II, 99–100/89–90.
12. Ibid., 99/90.
13. Nasrid *mawlid*s, celebrating the birth of the Prophet, were lavish affairs. Ibn al-Khatib recounts this one in great detail. It took place during the month of *rabī'* I, 764, or from December 19, 1362, until January 17, 1363. If celebrated on the usual date, the twelfth of *rabī'*, it would have taken place on the thirty-first, and, as an honored guest, Ibn Khaldun almost certainly attended. Ibn al-Khatib's description of the Alhambra, the sumptuous banquet, and recitation of laudatory *qasidah*s offers valuable insight into the scale of Nasrid court festivals. See Antonio Fernández-Puertas's carefully annotated account, "El Mawlid De 764/1362 De La Alhambra Segun El Manuscripto De Leiden y La *Nufāda III* Editada," in *Ibn al-Jatib Y Su Tiempo*, ed. Celia del Moral and Fernando Velázquez Basanta (Granada: Universidad de Granada, 2012), 161–203. Interestingly, Ibn al-Khatib's account describes the lions of the lion fountain as made of copper, *min al-nahas*, rather than marble (see 173n55).
14. Ibid., 181–183.
15. A, 80.
16. Ibn Khaldun reports his mission occurred in 765, which began in November of 1363.
17. A, 80. For additional information on this man, Ibrahim ibn Zarzar or Zarvar, see Walter J. Fischel, *Ibn Khaldun and Tamerlane* (Berkeley: University of California Press, 1952), 80–81.
18. Alexander Knysh, "Ibn al-Khatib," in *The Literature of Al-Andalus*, ed. María Rosa Menocal, Raymond P. Scheindlin, and Michael Sells (Cambridge: Cambridge University Press, 2000), 358–371. I am indebted to the author for

his analysis of Ibn al-Khatib's historical work, which is encapsulated here. See also Muhsin Ismail Muhammad, "El Método De Investigación Histórica De Ibn al-Jatib," in Moral and Basanta, *Ibn al-Jatīb Y Su Tiempo*, 71–83.

19. See note 2.

20. Later in Cairo Ibn Khaldun corresponded with this man regarding an anti-Muʿtazili Maliki text and other matters (M, II, 447, n. 106; A, 176–179). Ibn Zamrak wrote a number of the verses that are inscribed in various sections of the Alhambra palace. See, among other sources, Nasser Rabbat, "The Palace of the Lions, Alhambra and the Role of Water in Its Conception," *AARP/Environmental Design* 2 (1985): 64–73; D. Fairchild Ruggles, "The Eye of Sovereignty: Poetry and Vision in the Alhambra's Lindaraja Mirador," *Gesta* 36, no. 2 (1997): 180–189.

21. M, III, 459/409.

22. A, 82.

23. Ibid., 83.

24. Cheddadi includes a late-nineteenth-century print of Bijayah in his edition of Ibn Khaldun's memoir (ibid., 94).

25. For Ibn Khaldun's description of his attempt to raise funds from the Berber tribes of the region, which includes his account of the chaotic, internecine Hafsid conflicts at this time, see ibid., 93.

26. Ibid., 98.

27. Ibid., 145.

28. Ibid.

29. Ibid., 147.

30. Ibid., 147–154.

31. Ibid., 157. For an introduction to Mamluk Cairo, see Dunn, *The Adventures of Ibn Battuta*, 45–51; Humphreys, *Islamic History*, chap. 7, "The Fiscal Administration of the Mamluk Empire," and multiple references to Mamluk topics in Humphreys's index; and various issues of the *Mamlūk Studies Review*, available online at the *Mamlūk Studies Resources* website of the Middle East Documentation Center of the University of Chicago.

32. A, 162–165.

33. Ibid., 185.

34. Ibid., 164.

35. Ibid., 157.

36. Mohammad Abdullah Enan, *Ibn Khaldūn: His Life and Works* (New Delhi: Kitab Bhavan, 1997), 66–67.

37. Amid a vast number of publications on the *waqf* institution, see especially Richard Van Leeuwen's *Waqf and Urban Structures* (Leiden: Brill, 1999) for its analysis of the relation of *waqf*s and state power in early Ottoman Damascus.

38. A, 182.

39. Morimoto Kosei, "What Ibn Khaldun Saw: The Judiciary of Mamluk Egypt," *Mamlūk Studies Review* 6 (2002): 112.

40. Ibid.

41. Ibid., 121.

42. A, 198–199.

43. Ibid., 201. Enan is one of the few scholars who, in his biography, noticed this important section (*Ibn Khaldūn*, 75).

44. A, 201.

45. Ibid., 225.

46. Ibid., 245.

47. Ibid., 255.

4 · THE METHOD AND THE MODEL

1. M, I, 6/2.
2. Ibid., II, 411–19/364–370.
3. Ibid., 413/365.
4. Ibid., I, 6/2.
5. Ibid., 76/61 and 73/58.
6. Ibid., 371/329.
7. Ibid., 72/58.
8. Ibid., 15/8.
9. Ibid., 76–77/61; Marc Bloch, *The Historian's Craft* (New York: Vintage Books, 1953), 110.
10. M, I, 56/43–44 (my italics).
11. Ibid., 72/57 and 63/50.
12. Ibid., 63/51 and 56/44.
13. Ibid., 63/50 and 57/44.

14. Ibid, 63/50.
15. Ibid., 58/46.
16. Ibid., 9/4 and 7/3.
17. Ibid., 15–16/8–9 and 71–72/56–58.
18. Ibid., 6/2.
19. Ibid., 9/4.
20. Ibid., 71/57.
21. Ibid., II, 88.
22. Ibid., I, 7/3.
23. Ibid., 358–359/320–321.
24. Ibid., II, 158/143.
25. Ibid., I, 76/61.

26. Ibid., 11/6. In this phrase Ibn Khaldun clearly distinguishes society, ʿumran, from civilization, tamaddun, thus clarifying the use of the two terms discussed in the introduction.

27. Franz Rosenthal discusses the title, a matter of debate, and suggests, on the basis of grammar, that Ibn Khaldun intends the phrase *al-mubtada' wa-l-khabar* to connote a logical connection between primordial human social organization and subsequent human history (M, I, 13, n. 28). Rosenthal's observation is correct and provides a grammatical confirmation of Ibn Khaldun's idea of priority discussed above.

28. Ibid., 12–13/7–8.
29. Ibid., 85/68.
30. Ibid., II, 433/382.
31. Ibid., I, 89/68.
32. Ibid., 93/72–73.
33. Ibid., 91/71.

34. For an introduction to Islamic geographical knowledge and theories, see J. Brian Harley and David Woodward, eds., *Cartography in the Traditional Islamic and South Asian Societies,* vol. 2, book 1, *The History of Cartography* (Chicago: University of Chicago Press, 1992).

35. M, I, 167, 172/149.
36. Ibid., 174–175/155–156.

37. Nor is levity a noticeable trait of historians, but for insight into bawdy, careless behavior of Central Asia Turks, which also challenges Ibn Khaldun's

philosophical theory on climate and ebullient behavior, see the account of Babur, the founder of the Mughal Empire of India, who describes jolly/debauched Timurid soirees known either as the *suhbat* or *majlis* in landlocked Central Asia. See "The Timurid Symposium," in Stephen F. Dale, *The Garden of the Eight Paradises, Babur and the Culture of Empire in Central Asia, Afghanistan and India (1483-1530)* (Leiden: Brill, 2004), 179–186.

38. M, I, 177–183/157–165.
39. Ibid., 302/270.
40. Ibid., 254/225.
41. Ibid., 253/225.
42. See ibid., 210; Pierliugi Donini, "Psychology," in Hankinson, *The Cambridge Companion to Galen*, 187–188.
43. M, I, 183/165.
44. Ibid., 179–180/160–161.
45. See Chapter 2 of this volume, which is partly based on this final *Muqaddimah*, which is found in ibid., 184–245.
46. Ibid., 247/220.
47. Ibid., 252–253/224. Like so many eighteenth- and nineteenth-century European social theorists, Ibn Khaldun posits human development from a simple tribal state to complex settled and/or urban society. Yet rather than a single human trajectory that typified European thought, he posits a recurring pattern of evolutionary development as one tribe succeeds another in his dialectical model.
48. J. C. Ackrill, "Categories," in Barnes, *The Complete Works of Aristotle*, 1:22.
49. M, I, 249/220.
50. Ibid., 252–253/224.
51. Ibid., II, 267/230–231. For a sense of the attitudes of tribesmen toward sedentary society, see the detailed study by Lois Beck of the Qashqa'i, one of the large Iranian tribal confederations. *Nomad, A Year in the Life of a Qashqa'i Tribesman in Iran* (Berkeley: University of California Press, 1991).
52. M, I, 253/224.
53. Ibid., II, 280/243.
54. Ibid., I, 347/309.

55. See, for example, the seminal work by Neil J. Smelser, *Social Change in the Industrial Revolution: An Application of Theory to the British Cotton Industry* (Chicago: University of Chicago Press, 1959), which exemplifies the analytic power and humanistic weakness of sociological analysis.

56. M, I, 302–305/270–273.

57. See especially ibid., 302–305/270–274, where Ibn Khaldun dwells on the plundering habits of Arab tribes, particularly the Banu Hilal and Banu Sulaym.

58. Ibid., II, 199–200/175–176.

59. Ibid., I, 307/275.

60. Ibid., 304–305/272–273.

61. This is an instance, one of many in the *Muqaddimah*, when Ibn Khaldun's comments in different sections of the work have to be carefully parsed in order to determine or approximate his ultimate intent and meaning. Here they illustrate his conflicted feelings about the vital but destructive nature of bedouins and the cultured but doomed character of urban life, which is discussed in the conclusion.

62. See ibid., 249–310/220-277, for all twenty-eight premises.

63. Ibid., 264/235.

64. Ibid., 265/236.

65. For a note on the spelling *ʿibbida,* see ibid., 276, n. 78.

66. For information on this important family of Iranian Buddhist converts to Islam, see Kevin van Bladel, "Barmakids," in Fleet et al., *Encyclopaedia of Islam,* http://referenceworks.brillonline.com.proxy.lib.ohio-state.edu/entries/encyclopaedia-of-islam-3/barmakids-COM_24302.

67. M, I, 267/238 and 276–278/245–247.

68. Ibid., 321/285.

69. Ibid., 320–321/284–285.

70. Ibid., 258/229.

71. Ibid., 257–258/229. See also Ibn Khaldun's examples of "Contemporary Bedouin Poetry III" (416–440/362–390) and note how it contrasts in subject and tone with the urban Maghribi verse he quotes later (ibid., III, 466–475/417–429).

72. Ibid., I, 258/229.

73. Ibid., 284/252.

74. See Ibn Khaldun's somewhat schizophrenic discussion of the qualities of rulership or *malaka,* an account that veers from the need for ruthless authority to an emphasis on compassionate, mild rule (ibid., 380–388/337–344).

75. Ibid., 291/259.
76. Ibid., 381/338.
77. Ibid., 381–382/338–339.
78. Ibid., 308–310/276–277.
79. Ibid., 287–290/255–258.
80. Ibid., II, 300/264.
81. Ibid., 291/255.
82. Ibid., I, 278–279/247–248. See H. H. Joachim, "On Generation and Corruption," in Barnes, *The Complete Works of Aristotle,* 1:512–555. See also H. H. Joachim, ed., *Aristotle, on Coming to Be and Passing Away* (New York: Georg Olms Verlag, 1970), 265–266.

83. M, I, 345/308. A search of Arabic translations of Euclid's works might be useful here. Whether or not Ibn Khaldun meant these different logical terms to convey subtle variations in his arguments is not clear.

84. Ibid., 353/314.
85. Ibid., 293–294/261–262.
86. Ibid., 284/252–253.
87. Ibid., II, 118–119/108.
88. In his book *A History of the Maghrib in the Islamic Period,* Jamil M. Abun-Nasr offers ample evidence of the nasty, vicious reality of tribal warfare and conquest in North Africa as he chronicles the history of its dynasties.

89. M, II, 299–300/264–265.
90. Ibid., I, 351/312.
91. Beginning with his description of the dynasty's second generation, Ibn Khaldun does not attempt to specify exactly which change occurred in each generation. He merely indicates that conditions steadily worsened from the second generation to the tribal dynasty's later phases. See ibid., II, 291–301/255–265, where he provides his most complete and compelling account of the social deterioration of newly sedentarized tribes and the physical disintegration of the capital city.

92. Ibid., 302–303/267.
93. Ibid., I, 274/243–244.
94. Ibid., 267/238.
95. Ibid., 341–342/303–305.
96. Ibid., 341/303, and ibid., II, 292–297/256–561. See also ibid., 373–377/333–337, for his discussion of the "craft" of medicine, where he analyzes the pernicious effects of well-fed, underexercised urban inhabitants and contrasts them with bedouins, who eat small amounts of simple foods and physically exert themselves in hunting or in connection with other aspects of their daily life.
97. Ibid., I, 353–355/314–317.
98. Ibid., II, 119–121/108–109.
99. Ibid., 293–294/257–259.
100. Ibid., I, 343–355/305–317.
101. W. W. Rostow, *The Stages of Economic Growth: A Non-Communist Manifesto* (Cambridge: Cambridge University Press, 1960).
102. M, I, 279/248.
103. Ibid., II, 117/107. See also ibid., I, 378/336–337.
104. See, for example, the comments of Hayden V. White in his essay "Ibn Khaldun in the World Philosophy of History," *Comparative Studies in Society and History* 2, no. 1 (1959): 110–128; and Johan H. Meuleman, "La causalité dans la Mudqaddimah d'Ibn Khaldun," *Studia Islamica* 74 (1991): 105–142.
105. M, II, 294/258–259.
106. Ibid., 301/265.
107. Ibid., 128–129/118.
108. Ibid., I, 313–316/278–281.
109. Ibid., 314/279.
110. Ibid., 314–315/279–280. See Said Amir Arjomand's discussion of Max Weber's theory in the context of Shi'i Iran in *The Shadow of God and the Hidden Imam* (Chicago: University of Chicago Press, 1984).
111. M, I, 298/265–266. This is a rare instance when Ibn Khaldun talks of the Berbers as a single related group or community rather than as distinct tribes or houses.
112. Ibid., 284/253 and 428/377.

113. The Norwegian anthropologist Fredrik Barth offers a detailed account of the intimate kinship relations within the camp group of an Iranian tribe, as well as illustrating what the Western term *tribe* meant when discussing its sections. He describes his fieldwork in *Nomads of South Persia: The Basseri Tribe of the Khamseh Confederacy* (Boston: Little Brown, 1961).

114. See, for example, Madawi al Rasheed, *Politics in an Arabian Oasis* (London: I. B. Tauris, 1991), where a partly sedentarized member of the Shammar tribal confederation maneuvered over many years in a bewilderingly complex process to become a dynastic ruler with an imposing physical base that exhibited his political status.

115. M, II, 134–135/123–125.

116. For introductions to these Mongol dynasties, see Herbert Franke and Denis Twitchett, eds., *The Cambridge History of China* (Cambridge: Cambridge University Press, 1994), vol. 6; and J. A. Boyle, ed., *The Cambridge History of Iran* (Cambridge: Cambridge University Press, 1968), vol. 5.

117. John W. Dardess provides information about tensions between traditional Mongols of the Chaghatai Khanate and their partly sinicized brethren in his book, *Conquerors and Confucians: Aspects of Political Change in Late Yüan China* (New York: Columbia University Press, 1973).

118. I am indebted to Professor Lillian Li for this reference, which Owen Lattimore discusses in *Inner Asian Frontiers* (New York: American Geographical Society, 1940).

119. M, II, 114–117/103–106.

5 · THE RATIONAL STATE AND THE LAISSEZ-FAIRE ECONOMY

1. An allusion to Clifford Geertz's influential work *The Religion of Java* (Chicago: University of Chicago Press, 1960).

2. M, II, 235–237/201–204.

3. Ibid., I, 332–336/295–302, and II, 266–267/229–231. A twentieth-century observer might reflect that the relative ease of conquering urban societies and the difficulty of subduing tribal territories was partly exemplified in the rapid Soviet occupation of Czechoslovakia in 1968 and its failure to subdue Afghanistan in the 1980s.

4. Al-Farabi, *On the Perfect State*, 229–259. As Richard Walzer observes, al-Farabi seems to have had in mind a broader society or state more often than a city, as al-Farabi sometimes also uses the term *al-umma al-fadilah*, the perfect community (see 430, ns. para. 2).

5. M, II, 137–139/126–128.

6. Ibid., 138/127. In Quatremère's 1858 edition Iran or Persia is rendered as *Fārs* or *Fars* and the kings of Iran or Persia as *mulūk Fārs* or *mulūk Fars*, except when they appear as *mulūk al-ʿajam*. *Kisra*/Chosroe is often used to refer to any of the Sasanid monarchs, who are also sometimes just identified as *qaisar* or Ceasar. Parvaneh Pourshariati analyzes the Sasanid Empire and the Arab Conquest of Iran in her book *Decline and Fall of the Sasanian Empire* (London: I. B. Tauris, 2008).

7. In India Ibn Khaldun's near-contemporary Zia al-Din Barani (1285–1357) also invoked Iranian models when trying to rationalize the administration of the notably pragmatic/ruthless rulers of the Delhi Sultanate. See Mohammed Habib, *The Political Theory of the Delhi Sultanate (Including a Translation of Ziauddin Barani's Fatawa-i Jahandari, circa 1358-9 A.D.)* (Allahabad: Kitab Mahal, 1961).

8. M, II, 138–139/127–128.

9. Ibid., I, 448/394.

10. Ibid., 406/358.

11. Ibid., 449/394.

12. See Ibn Khaldun's analysis of "the transformation of the caliphate into royal authority [*mulk*]" (ibid., 414–428/364–377).

13. Ibid., II, 5/3, and I, 459/403.

14. Ibid., I, 459–460/402–403.

15. Ibid., 460/403.

16. Ibid., II, 334/295. This observation represents an element of Ibn Khaldun's modified labor theory of value discussed below.

17. I infer this from a brief but suggestive passage at the conclusion of his critique of teachers (ibid., 60/47). Ibn Khaldun's attitudes on this subject are opaque, but in his discussion of Islamic Law he criticizes the lack of critical reasoning and the multiplication of textual sources that made independent judgment difficult. In saying this, he may be reiterating his feeling that the original dynamism of the early Arab Muslim community had been lost. He

also depicts his own Maliki legal school as a conservative, textual tradition, whose scholars merely cite traditions rather than speculating about religious principles. See ibid., III, 31–32/24–25.

18. Ibid., II, 139–156/128–142.
19. Ibid., 3–4/1–2.
20. Ibid., 13/10 and 111–113/100–103.
21. Ibid., 111–113/112–103.
22. This is yet another but compelling example of the segmented nature of the *Muqaddimah* in that Ibn Khaldun does not explicitly associate these changes with the evolution of monarchical psychological states he outlined earlier. Readers have to make these connections for themselves.
23. Ibid., 16–17/13.
24. Ibid., 27/23.
25. As Franz Rosenthal notes, the word is an Arabicized version of the Catalan *almirant* (ibid., 38, n. 516).
26. Ibid., 37–46/32–40.
27. Ibid., 73–89/65–78.
28. Ibid., 50/44.
29. Ibid., 55/48. Ibn Khaldun includes a precise and extensive account of Muslim mints and coinage after making his preliminary remarks.
30. Ibid., 73/65.
31. Ibid., 249–266/215–229.
32. Ibid., 316–317/278–279 and 356–357/317–318, where Ibn Khaldun offers slightly variant descriptions of agriculture.
33. Ibid., 335/296.
34. Ibid., 348/308.
35. Ibn Khaldun lists the craft of teaching separately under "Scientific Instruction," perhaps because of its pivotal importance. He does not include teaching when he gives a brief list of crafts, which is intended to be illustrative rather than exhaustive (ibid., 355/316). Nonetheless, it belongs in his category of noble occupations.
36. Ibid., 376/336.
37. Ibid., 406–407/362–363.
38. Ibid., 386–387/345–346.
39. Ibid., 432/382.

40. Ibid., 434/383.
41. Ibid., 405/361.
42. Ibid., 398–399/355–356.
43. Ibid., 314/275.
44. Ibid., 334–335/295–296.
45. Ibid., 342–344/301–305. Muslim writers often distinguished between prestigious long-distance traders and petty local merchants. See the comments of Sir John (Jean) Chardin, the Huguenot merchant who traded in seventeenth-century Iran and India, in *Travels in Persia 1673–1677* (Mineola, NY: Dover Books, 1988), 279–280.
46. M, II, 336/297.
47. Ibid., 337/298 and 340–343/301–304.
48. Ibid., 326/287.
49. Ibid., 285/249.
50. Ibid., 327/288. I have occasionally heard pious Afghan Muslims express similar sentiments about poorly educated village clerics, characterizing them as parasites.
51. Al-Farabi, *On the Perfect State*, 229.
52. M, II, 271/235.
53. Ibid., 271/235. The Chinese legalist philosopher Han Fei Tzu made a similar if less fully developed observation about self-interest and the division of labor in the third century B.C.E. See Han Fei Tzu, *The Complete Works of Han Fei Tzu*, ed. and trans. Wen-Kuei Liao (London: A. Probsthain, 1939), 2:44–45. I am indebted to Professor Thomas Rawski of the University of Pittsburgh for this reference.
54. M, II, 274/237–238.
55. Ibid., 274/238.
56. Ibid., 282/246.
57. Ibid., 273/236.
58. Ibid., 279–280/243–244.
59. Ibid., 23/19.
60. Ibid., 89/79.
61. Ibid., 103/93–94.
62. Ibid., 95/85.
63. Ibid., 276–279/239–243.

64. Ibid., 292/256.
65. Ibid., 291–297/255–261.
66. Ibid., 107/97–98.
67. Ibid., 107/97.
68. Ibid., 104–105/97 and 94–95.
69. Ibid., 104/94.
70. Ibn Khaldun excoriates the characters of most merchants, for whom, he writes, deceit is the norm and manliness the exception (ibid., 343–344/304–305).
71. David Fate Norton and Jacqueline Taylor, eds., *The Cambridge Companion to Hume* (Cambridge: Cambridge University Press, 2011), 24.

6 · THE SCIENCE OF MAN

1. See especially Abdesselam Cheddadi's chapter "La reception de l'oeuvre," in his important book *Ibn Khaldun L'homme et le théorticien de la civilization* (Paris: Éditions Gallimard, 2006), 169–188.

2. Enan, *Ibn Khaldūn*, 98–102. See Cengiz Tomar's analysis of the Arab response to Ibn Khaldun and his work, "Between Myth and Reality: Approaches to Ibn Khaldun in the Arab World," *Asian Journal of Social Science* 36, nos. 3–4 (2008): 590–611; and F. Rosenthal, "al-Makrīzī, Taqī al-Dīn," in Bearman et al., *Encyclopaedia of Islam*, http://referenceworks.brillonline.com.proxy.lib.ohio-state.edu/entries/encyclopaedia-of-islam-2/al-makrizi-SIM_4838.

3. See Bruce Craig, ed., *Mamlūk Studies Review* 7, no. 2 (2003), Middle East Documentation Center, University of Chicago, http://mamluk.uchicago.edu/Mamluk Studies Review VII-2-2003.pdf. This issue is entirely devoted to a study of Maqrizi's work. See also Li Guo's article "Mamluk Historical Studies: The State of the Art," *Mamlūk Studies Review* 1 (1997): 15–43.

4. Not long after Ibn Khaldun's death Ulugh Beg, the Timurid governor of Samarqand, sponsored astronomical and mathematical research that, momentarily at least, made the city the center of scientific research in both the Muslim and Christian worlds. See, among numerous other works, Ahmad Dallal, "Science, Medicine and Technology," in John Esposito, ed., *The Oxford History of Islam*, (Oxford: Oxford University Press, 1999), 161–183.

5. Rosenthal includes a typically erudite and insightful discussion of *Muqaddimah* manuscripts. See "The Textual History of the *Muqaddimah*," in M, I, lxxviii–cix.

6. Cornell Fleischer, "Royal Authority, Dynastic Cyclism and 'Ibn Khaldunism' in Sixteenth Century Ottoman Letters," *Journal of Asian and African Studies* 18, nos. 3–4 (July–October 1983): 198–220.

7. Ottoman legitimacy was not, however, a simple matter. It shifted over time according to circumstances. For a thoughtful discussion of this process, see Hakan T. Karateke, "Legitimizing the Ottoman Sultanate: A Framework for Historical Analysis," in Hakan T. Karateke and Maurus Reinkowski, eds., *Legitimizing the Order: The Ottoman Rhetoric of State Power* (Leiden: Brill, 2005), 13–54.

8. Nabil Matar, "Spain through Arab Eyes, 1573–1691," in *Europe Observed*, ed. Kumkum Chatterjee and Clement Hawes (Lewisburg, PA: Bucknell University Press), 143–172. Matar includes a full translation of al-Ghassani's text in his *In the Lands of the Christians* (New York: Routledge, 2003).

9. A. I. Silvestre de Sacy, *Chrestomatie arabe, ou Extraits de divers écrivains arabes* (Paris: Ulan Press, 2012).

10. Enan, *Ibn Khaldūn*, 151; J. Hammer-Purgstall, "Extraits d'Ibn Khaldun," *Fundgruben des Orients* (Vienna) 6 (1818): 301–307, 362–364. See also Muhammad Mahmoud Rabi, "Previous Studies of Ibn Khaldun's *Muqaddima*," in his book *The Political Theory of Ibn Khaldun* (Leiden: Brill, 1967), 1–10.

11. Toynbee, *A Study of History* (New York: Oxford University Press, 1962), 3:321–328.

12. See the preface for a brief discussion of important studies of Ibn Khaldun's work.

13. See, for example, Fuad Baali, *The Science of Human Social Organization: Conflicting Views on Ibn Khaldun's (1332–1406) Ilm al-Umran* (Lewiston, NY: Edward Mellen Press, 2005); Saleh Fabirzadeh, *Sociology of Sociology: In Search of Ibn Khaldun's Sociology: Then and Now* (Tehran: Soroush Press, 1982); and Mahmoud Dhaoudi, "Ibn Khaldun: The Founding Father of Eastern Sociology," *International Sociology* 5, no. 3 (1990), 319–335.

14. Aquinas came to criticize certain aspects of Ibn Rushd's Aristotelianism and found other, Byzantine Greek, texts of Aristotle's works.

15. Fakhry, *Averroes (Ibn Rushd)*, 26–27.

16. David Carrithers, "An Appreciation of *The Spirit of the Laws*," in *Montesquieu's Science of Politics*, ed. David R. Carrithers, Michael A Mosher, and Paul R. Rahe (Lanham, MD: Rowman and Littlefield, 2001), 6, 4.

17. Montesquieu's knowledge of classical and postclassical philosophers and social thinkers, including Aristotle and Plato most prominently, is obvious from his text. Unfortunately his commentaries on Aristotle have been lost. Robert Shackleton alludes to Montesquieu's study of Aristotle and Galen in his definitive biography, *Montesquieu* (Oxford: Oxford University Press, 1961), 264–303.

18. Montesquieu, *The Spirit of the Laws*, ed. and trans. Anne M. Cohler, Bascia C. Miller, and Harold Stone (Cambridge: Cambridge University Press, 2011), xli.

19. Carrithers, "An Appreciation of *The Spirit of the Laws*," 18.

20. Simon Goyard-Fabre, *Montesquieu la nature, les lois, la libertè* (Paris: Presses Universitaires de France, 1993), 22–45, cited in Balázs Fekete, "The Unknown Montesquieu," *Iustum Acquum Salutare* 1 (2009): 155.

21. Montesquieu, *The Spirit of the Laws*, xliii.

22. Ibid., 3 (my italics).

23. Ibid., 310.

24. Ibid., 287.

25. Montesquieu, *Considerations on the Causes of the Greatness of the Romans and Their Decline*, ed. and trans. David Lowenthal (Indianapolis, IN: Hackett Publishing. 1999), 169 (my italics).

26. Carrithers, "An Appreciation of *The Spirit of the Laws*," 9.

27. Montesquieu, *The Spirit of the Laws*, xliii.

28. David Hume, *An Enquiry Concerning the Principles of Morals* [1751], quoted by Fania Oz-Salzberger in "The Political Theory of the Scottish Enlightenment," in *The Scottish Enlightenment*, ed. Alexander Broadie (Cambridge: Cambridge University Press, 2003), 171.

29. John Millar, "The Origin and Distinction of Ranks," in *John Millar of Glasgow 1735–1801*, ed. William C. Lehmann (Cambridge: Cambridge University Press, 1960), 175. Millar's work deserves to be better known, especially his essays "The Social Consequences of the Division of Labour" and "The Relationship between Morality and Economics," both of which are included in Lehmann's volume.

30. Peter Burke, *The French Historical Revolution* (Oxford: Blackwell, 1969), 6–7.

31. For a concise introduction to Scottish rationalist thought, see Alexander Broadie, *The Tradition of Scottish Philosophy* (Savage, MD: Barnes and Noble Books, 1990).

32. Ibid., 95.

33. Aaron Garrett, "Anthropology: The 'Original' of Human Nature," in Broadie, *The Scottish Enlightenment*, 79.

34. David Hume, *A Treatise of Human Nature*, 4, quoted in Norton and Taylor, *The Cambridge Companion to Hume*, 386.

35. Hume, *A Treatise of Human Nature*, 6, quoted by Terence Penelhum in "Hume's Moral Psychology," in ibid., 241.

36. Terrence Penelhum, "Hume's Moral Psychology," in ibid.

37. David Hume, *A Treatise of Human Nature*, quoted in Andrew S. Skinner's "Economic Theory," in Broadie, *The Scottish Enlightenment*, 180. Hume did not believe it was possible to explain the commonalities of human beings' nature, which nonetheless could be observed throughout history. Ibn Khaldun, never a philosopher, did not try to identify the various emotional or intellectual strands common to all people. He wanted only to emphasize that while humans were endowed with the same capabilities, their personalities and intellects altered with circumstance.

38. Norton, "An Introduction to Hume's Thought," in Norton and Taylor, *The Cambridge Companion to Hume*, 34.

39. M, II, 426/376, and III, 394/347.

40. Nicholas Phillipson, *Adam Smith* (New Haven, CT: Yale University Press, 2010), 68–69.

41. Hume, *An Enquiry Concerning Human Understanding*, section 65, quoted by H. M. Hopfl in his essay "From Savage to Scotsman: Conjectural History in the Scottish Enlightenment," *Journal of British Studies* 17 (Spring 1978): 39.

42. Norton and Taylor, *The Cambridge Companion to Hume*, 458.

43. Adam Smith, *History of Astronomy*, in *The Essential Adam Smith*, ed. Robert L. Heibroner (New York: Norton, 1987), 31. See also Herbert F. Thomson, "Adam Smith's Philosophy of Science," *Quarterly Journal of Economics* 79, no. 2 (May 1965): 212–233.

44. Phillipson, *Adam Smith*, 4.

45. Thomson, "Adam Smith's Philosophy of Science," 218; Phillipson, *Adam Smith*, 220–221.

46. M, III, see especially 141 and 332–341 for Ibn Khaldun's discussion of literature and speech.

47. Phillipson, *Adam Smith*, 92, 89.

48. Ibid., 100.

49. Ibid., 214.

50. Dugald Stewart, "Account of the Life and Writings of Adam Smith LL.D," in *Collected Works*, ed. William Hamilton (Edinburgh: Constable, 1854–1858), 10:19–20.

51. Adam Smith, *The Wealth of Nations* (Hollywood, FL: Simon and Brown, 2010), 13.

52. Ibid., 8.

53. For intriguing references to this "improving spirit," see John Galt's 1821 novel, *Annals of the Parish*, ed. Jame Kinsley (Oxford: Oxford University Press, 1972), the source of John Stuart Mill's word *utilitarian*.

54. Phillipson, *Adam Smith*, 216.

55. Robertson's brief Indian work is titled *An Historical Disquisition Concerning the Knowledge which the Ancients Had of India* (Edinburgh: Basil, 1792). In it he repeatedly alludes to philosophical knowledge and reasoning, as in the following statement: "Science, when viewed as disjoined from religion . . . is employed in contemplating either the operation of the understanding, the exercise of our moral powers, or the nature and qualities of external objects. The first is denominated logic; the second ethics; the third physics, or the knowledge of nature" (297).

56. William Robertson, *The History of America* (London: T. Cadell and J. Balfour, 1792). See especially E. Adamson Hoebel, "William Robertson: An 18th Century Anthropologist-Historian," *American Anthropologist* 62 (1960): 648–655.

57. For an especially forceful assertion of Aristotle's influence on Durkheim, see Donald A. Nielsen, *Three Faces of God: Society, Religion and the Categories of Totality in the Philosophy of Émile Durkheim* (Albany, NY: SUNY Press, 1999), and Douglas F. Challenger, *Durkheim through the Lens of Aristotle: Durkheimian, Postmodernist, and Communitarian*

Responses to the Enlightenment (Lanham, MD: Rowman and Littlefield, 1995).

58. Emile Durkheim, *Durkheim's Philosophy Lectures*, ed. and trans. Neil Gross and Robert Alun Jones (Cambridge: Cambridge University Press, 2011). See especially part 1, which deals with the object of philosophy, its relationship to science, and the divisions of the discipline.

59. "Influences upon Durkheim's View of Sociology," in Émile Durkheim, *The Rules of the Sociological Method*, ed. Steven Lukas and trans. W. D. Halls (New York: Free Press, 1982), 259.

60. Émile Durkheim, "Course in Sociology, Opening Lecture," in *Émile Durkheim on Institutional Analysis*, ed. and trans. Mark Traugott (Chicago: University of Chicago Press, 1994), 45.

61. Durkheim, *Rules of Sociological Method*, ed. Stephen Lukas and trans. W. D. Halls, 159.

62. Durkheim, "Sociology and the Social Sciences," in Traugott, *Émile Durkheim on Institutional Analysis*, 82.

63. W. Watts Millar, ed., and Emma Griffiths, trans., *Montesquieu quid secundatus scientiae politicae instituendae contulerit* (Oxford: Durkheim Press, 1997).

64. Durkheim, "Sociology and the Social Sciences," in Traugott, *Émile Durkheim on Institutional Analysis*, 83.

65. Ibid., 79.

66. Warren Schmaus, *Durkheim's Philosophy of Science and Sociology of Knowledge* (Chicago: University of Chicago Press, 1994), 58, 60 (my italics).

67. Durkheim, *The Rules of the Sociological Method*, 129.

68. Durkheim, "Sociology and the Social Sciences," in Traugott, *Émile Durkheim on Institutional Analysis*, 80.

69. Ibid., 82.

70. Ibid., 85.

71. Carole Fink describes Bloch's training and friendships with a galaxy of young men who became important scholars in a range of humanistic and scientific disciplines. See her biography *Marc Bloch: A Life in History* (Cambridge: Cambridge University Press, 1991), 26.

72. Marc Bloch, *Feudal Society*, cited by R. Colbert Rhodes in "Émile Durkheim and the Historical Thought of Marc Bloch," *Theory and Society* 5, no. 1 (January 1978): 55.

73. Febvre's observation about Durkheim's influence is quoted by C-E. Perrin, "L'oeuvre historique de Marc Bloch," trans. R. C. R, *Revue historique* 199 (1948): 183–184. It is cited by Rhodes, "Émile Durkheim and the Historical Thought of Marc Bloch," 46–47 and 71n6. See also Marc Bloch, *The Historian's Craft*, trans. Peter Putnam (New York: Vintage Books, 1964), 26n3.

74. Susan Friedman discusses Marc Bloch's evolving attitude to the comparative method in her book *Marc Bloch, Sociology and Geography* (Cambridge: Cambridge University Press, 1996). See also William H. Sewell Jr., "Marc Bloch and the Logic of Comparative History," *History and Theory* 6 (1967): 208–218.

75. M, I, 56/44.

76. Ibid., 56/44.

77. Bloch, *The Historian's Craft*, 122. Durkheim stated that comparison is the only way of demonstrating that "one phenomenon is the cause of another," and described the form of "indirect experimentation" practiced by students of human society as the "comparative method" and the only methodology suitable for sociology. Durkheim, *The Rules of the Sociological Method*, 147.

78. Marc Bloch, unpublished letter of December 28, 1933, to Etienne Gilson, cited by Rhodes, "Émile Durkheim and the Historical Thought of Marc Bloch," n. 82.

79. Bloch, *The Historian's Craft*, 122.

80. Fernand Braudel, *The Mediterranean and the Mediterranean World in the Age of Philip II*, trans. Siân Reynolds (New York: Harper Torchbook, 1976), 95.

81. Claude Lefort, "Histoire et sociologie dans l'oeuvre de Fernand Braudel," *Cahiers internationalaux de sociologies* 13 (1952): 124.

CONCLUSION · A QUESTION OF KNOWLEDGE

1. M, I, 14/8.

2. Ibid., II, 29–35/24–30; see Rosenthal's note 504 on page 29.

3. Ibid., III, 340–341/296.

4. G. Lecomte, "Ibn Kutayba," in Bearman et al., *Encyclopaedia of Islam*, http://referenceworks.brillonline.com.proxy.lib.ohio-state.edu/entries/encyclopaedia-of-islam-2/ibn-kutayba-COM_0333.

5. Gutas, *Greek Thought, Arabic Culture*, 111–112 (author's italics).

6. M, III, 281/241–242.
7. Ibid., II, 413/365.
8. Ibid., III, 281/242.
9. Ibid., II, 413/365. See Ibn Khaldun's entire section on "Man's Ability to Think," ibid., 411–419/364–370, and for the special role of logic, read his advice to students, ibid., III, 295–298/254–258.
10. Ibid., II, 416/367.
11. Ibid., 416/367.
12. Quoted by Oliver Leaman in his work *Averroes and His Philosophy* (Oxford: Clarendon Press, 1988), 90 (my italics). Leaman suggests that Ibn Rushd's arguments mean that "the species of the human intellect can be regarded as eternal" (91).
13. See Ibn Khaldun's discussion of prophecy (M, I, 194–202/173–181).
14. Ibid., III, 282/243.
15. A, 17.
16. F. Scott Fitzgerald, "The Crack Up," *Esquire*, February 1936.

GLOSSARY

adib—a cultured individual

ahl al-maʿmūr—settled people/population

ahwāl al-ʿumrān wa-l-tamaddun—conditions of society and civilization

ʿalīm (pl. ʿulamāʾ)—one learned in the religious sciences; a member of the clerical class

ʿarad (pl. aʿrād)—accident

ʿarad dhātī—essential accident

ʿasabiyah—group feeling

badāwah/bidāwa—desert/rural life, bedouinism

bādiyah (pl. bawādin)—semidesert, peasantry; pl. nomads, bedouins

badw—desert; nomads, bedouins

baidāʾ—desert, steppe, wilderness

bait (pl. buyūtāt)—family, house, tent

burhān (pl. barāhīn)—demonstration, absolute or *apodictic* proof

dhāt (pl. dhawāt)—being or essence

dhātī—essential

falsafah—philosophy

faqīh (pl. fuqahāʾ)—religious law scholar

fass—Aristotle's *Organon*

faylasūf (pl. falāsifah)—philosopher

fiqh—jurisprudence

fitnah—revolt, disturbance, civil war

ghair mutamaddin—uncivilized

hadar—a civilized/settled region with towns and villages

hadārah—sedentariness

hadarī—sedentary

hadith—reports of the Prophet Muhammad

hakīm (pl. hukamāʿ)—sage, philosopher

hasab—measure, value

hayy—clan (?)

hikmah—wisdom, philosophy

ijāzah—certificate of expertise in some branch or text of the Islamic sciences

ijtimāʿ—human social organization, human community, social group

ʿilm (pl. ʿulūm)—science, knowledge, perception

ʿilm al-tabīʿī—natural philosophy, physics

imām—prayer leader in a mosque; Imåm—leader of the Shīʿī branch of Islam

istidlāl—deduction, demonstration, reasoning, syllogism

istiqrāʾ—induction

jihād—effort or striving (for spiritual perfection) or for the defense or expansion of Islamic sovereignty

kasb—earnings, profit

madanī—urban, urbanized

māddah (pl. mawādd)—substance, matter

madhhab—Islamic legal school, such as Ibn Khaldun's Maliki school

madīnah—town, city

madrasah—a seminary or Muslim religious college
māhiyah—essence, nature
mamluk—"possessed"; a military slave, Egyptian dynasty
maʿmūr—settled, sedentary
mawlid—celebration of the prophet's birth
mulk—sovereignty, kinship, monarchy
muqaddimah (pl. muqaddimāt)—introduction; premise
mutamaddin—civilized, cultured
qabīlah (pl. qabāʾil)—tribe, tribal confederation
qādī—a judge of religious law
qiyās—syllogism, deductive logic
sanāʾiʿ—crafts, occupations
sharīʾah—the "straight path," Islamic law
surah (pl. suwar)—form, shape
tabaqah—rank or class
tabīʿah—nature, essence
tabīʿī—natural
tāʾifah (pl. tawāʾif)—group, band, party, tribal segment; sect
tamaddun—civilization
ʿulamāʾ (s. ʿalīm)—Muslims learned in the religious sciences
ummah (pl. umam)—people, community
ʿumran badawi—tribal culture
ʿumran hadari—urban culture

BIBLIOGRAPHY

PRIMARY SOURCES

Al-Fārābī, Abū Nasr. *On the Perfect State*. Edited and translated by Richard Walzer. Chicago: Great Books of the Islamic World, 1998.

Apollonius. *Apollonius of Perga Conics*. Bks. I–IV. Translated by Catesby R. Taliaferro. Santa Fe, NM: Green Lion Press, 2013.

Averroes (Abū al-Walīd Muhammad ibn Ahmad ibn Rushd). *Middle Commentary on Aristotle's De Anima*. Translated by Alfred L. Ivry. Provo, UT: Brigham Young University Press, 2002.

Avicenna (Ibn Sina). *The Metaphysics of the Healing*. Translated by Michael E. Marmura. Provo, UT: Brigham Young University Press, 2005.

———. *The Physics of the Healing*. Bks. I–IV. Edited and translated by Jon McGinnis. Provo, UT: Brigham Young University Press, 2009.

Barnes, Jonathan, ed. *The Complete Works of Aristotle*. Princeton, NJ: Princeton University Press, 1984.

Durkheim, Émile. "Course on Sociology: Opening Lecture in *Émile Durkheim on Institutional Analysis*." Edited and translated by Mark Traugott. Chicago: University of Chicago Press, 1978, 43–71.

———. *Durkheim's Philosophical Lectures: Notes from the Lycée de Sens Course, 1883–1884*. Edited and translated by Neil Gross and Robert Alun Jones. Cambridge: Cambridge University Press, 2011.

———. *Émile Durkheim on Institutional Analysis*. Edited and translated by Mark Traugott. Chicago: University of Chicago Press, 1978.

———. *Rules of Sociological Method*. Edited by Steven Lukas. Translated by W. D. Halls. New York: Free Press, 1982.

———. "Sociology and the Social Sciences." In *Émile Durkheim on Institutional Analysis*, edited and translated by Mark Traugott. Chicago: University of Chicago Press, 1978, 71–88.

Euclid. *Euclid's Elements*. Edited by Dana Densmore. Translated by T. L. Heath. Santa Fe, NM: Green Lion Press, 2002.

al-Gūrgānī, Alī. *Kitāb al-taʿrifāt [A Book of Definitions]*. Beirut: Librairie Du Libnan, 1978.

Ibn Khaldun. *Autobiographie*. Edited and translated by Abdesselam Cheddadi. Algiers: CNRPAH, 2008.

———. *Le Livre des Exemples II Histoire des Arabes et des Berbères du Maghreb*. Edited and translated by Abdesselam Cheddadi. Paris: Gallimard, 2012.

———. *The Muqaddimah*. Translated by Franz Rosenthal. Princeton, NJ: Princeton University Press, 1958.

———. *Prolégomènes D'EBN-KHALDOUN*. Edited by M. Quatremère. Paris: Benjamin Duprat, 1858.

———. *Shifāʾ al-Sāʾil fī tahdhīb al-masāʾil [The Healing of Seekers]*. Edited by M. al-Tanji. Beirut: al-Matbaʿah al-kāthulīkīyah, 1959.

———. *Tarīkh Ibn Khaldūn*. Beirut: Ibn Hazm, 2003.

Ibn Tufayl. *Ibn Tufayl's Hayy Ibn Yaqzān*. Chicago: University of Chicago Press, 2003.

Montesquieu. *Considerations on the Causes of the Greatness of the Romans and Their Decline*. Edited and translated by David Lowenthal. Indianapolis, IN: Hackett Publishing, 1999.

———. *The Spirit of the Laws*. Edited and translated by Anne M. Cohler, Basia C. Miller, and Harold S. Stone. Cambridge: Cambridge University Press, 2011.

Rousseau, Jean-Jacques. *The Confessions*. London: Penguin, 1953.

Smith, Adam. *The Wealth of Nations*. Hollywood, FL: Simon and Brown, 2010.

Tzu, Han Fei. *The Complete Works of Han Fei Tzu*. Edited and translated by Wen-Kuei Liao. London: A. Probsthain, 1939.

SECONDARY SOURCES

Abun-Nasr, Jamil M. *A History of the Maghrib in the Islamic Period*. Cambridge: Cambridge University Press, 1987.

Adamson, Peter, and Richard C. Taylor, eds. *The Cambridge Companion to Arabic Philosophy*. Cambridge: Cambridge University Press, 2005.

Alatas, Syed Farid. *Ibn Khaldun*. New Delhi: Oxford University Press, 2013.

———, "Ibn Khaldun and Contemporary Sociology." *International Sociology* 21, no. 6 (November 2006): 782–795.

Al-Azmeh, Aziz. *Ibn Khaldun: An Essay in Reinterpretation*. London: Frank Cass, 1981.

Alon, Ilai, and Shukri Abed. *Al-Fārābī's Philosophical Lexicon*. Vol. 1, Arabic Text; vol. 2, English Translation. Cambridge: Cambridge University Press, 2007.

Anawati, G. C. "Fakhr al-Dīn al-Rāzī." In Bearman et al., *Encyclopaedia of Islam*, 2nd ed. http://referenceworks.brillonline.com/entries/encyclopaedia-of-islam-2/fakhr-al-din-al-razi-COM_0206.

Arjomand, Said Amir. *The Shadow of God and the Hidden Imam*. Chicago: University of Chicago Press, 1984.

Baali, Fuad. *The Science of Human Social Organization: Conflicting Views of Ibn Khaldun's (1332–1406) Ilm al-Umran*. Lewiston, NY: Edward Mellen Press, 2005.

———. *Society, State and Urbanism: Ibn Khaldun's Sociological Thought*. Albany: State University of New York Press, 1988.

Baeck, Louis. "Ibn Khaldun's Political and Economic Realism." In *Joseph A. Schumpeter, Historian of Economics*, edited by Laurence S. Moss. London: Routledge, 1996.

Barnes, Jonathan, ed. *The Cambridge Companion to Aristotle*. Cambridge: Cambridge University Press, 1995.

Barth, Fredrik. *Nomads of South Persia: The Basseri Tribe of the Khamseh Confederacy*. Boston: Little Brown, 1961.

Barthold, W., and D. Sourdel. "al-Barāmika." In Bearman et al., *Encyclopaedia of Islam*, 2nd ed. http://referenceworks.brillonline.com.proxy.lib.ohio-state.edu/entries/encyclopaedia-of-islam-2/al-baramika-COM_0099.

Bearman, P., Th. Bianquis, C. E. Bosworth, E. van Donzel, and W. P. Heinrichs, eds. *Encyclopaedia of Islam*. 2nd ed. Brill Online, 2015.

Beck, Lois. *Nomad: A Year in the Life of a Qasqa'i Tribesman in Iran*. Berkeley: University of California Press, 1991.

Behnke, Roy H., Jr. *The Herders of Cyrenaica*. Illinois Studies in Anthropology, no. 12. Urbana: University of Illinois Press, 1980.

Bencheneb, H. "al-Sharīf al-Tilimsānī." In Bearman et al., *Encyclopaedia of Islam*, 2nd ed. http://referenceworks.brillonline.com.proxy.lib.ohio-state.edu/entries/encyclopaedia-of-islam-2/al-sharif-al-tilimsani-COM_1043.

Bloch, Marc. *The Historian's Craft*. New York: Vintage Books, 1953.

Boyle, J. A., ed. *The Cambridge History of Iran*, vol. 5. Cambridge: Cambridge University Press, 1968.

Braudel, Fernand. *The Mediterranean and the Mediterranean World in the Age of Phillip II*. Translated by Siân Reynolds. New York: Harper Torchbook, 1976.

Brett, Michael, and Elizabeth Fentress. *The Berbers*. Oxford: Blackwell, 1997.

Broadie, Alexander. "Scottish Philosophy in the 18th Century." *Stanford Encyclopedia of Philosophy* (Fall 2009). http://plato.stanford.edu/archives/fall2009/entries/scottish-18th/.

———. *The Tradition of Scottish Philosophy*. Savage, MD: Barnes and Noble Books, 1990.

———, ed. *The Scottish Enlightenment*. Cambridge: Cambridge University Press, 2003.

Burke, Peter. *The French Historical Revolution*. Oxford: Blackwell, 1969.

Butterworth, Charles. *Philosophy, Ethics and Virtuous Rule: A Study of Averroes' Commentary on Plato's "Republic."* Cairo Papers in Social Science, vol. 9, monograph 1. Cairo: American University in Cairo Press, 1986.

Carlyle, Thomas. *On Heroes, Hero-Worship and the Heroic in History*. Berkeley: University of California Press, 2007.

Carrithers, David. "Montesquieu's Philosophy of History." *Journal of the History of Ideas* 47, no. 1 (January–March 1986): 61–80.

Carrithers, David W., Michael A. Mosher, and Paul A. Rahe, eds. *Montesquieu's Science of Politics*. Lanham, MD: Rowman and Littlefield, 2001.

Caton, Steven C. *Peaks of Yemen I Summon*. Berkeley: University of California Press, 1993.

Challenger, Douglas F. *Durkheim through the Lens of Aristotle: Durkheimian, Postmodernist, and Communitarian Responses to the Enlightenment*. Lanham, MD: Rowman and Littlefield, 1995.

Chaouch, Khalid. "Ibn Khaldun, in Spite of Himself." *Journal of North African Studies* 13, no. 3 (September 2008): 279–291.

Chardin, Sir John (Jean). *Travels in Persia 1673–1677*. Mineola, NY: Dover Books, 1988.

Cheddadi, Abdesselam. *Actualite d' Ibn Khaldun: Conferences et entretiens*. Temara: Maison de Arts des Sciences, et des Lettres, 2000.

———. *Ibn Khaldūn L'homme et le théoricien de la civilization*. Paris: Éditions Gallimard, 2006.

Clarke, John I. "Studies of Semi-Nomadism in North Africa." *Economic Geography* 35, no. 2 (April 1959): 95–108.

Coulson, N. J. *A History of Islamic Law*. Edinburgh: Edinburgh University Press, 1991.

Craig, Bruce, ed. *Mamlūk Studies Review* 7, no. 2 (2003). Middle East Documentation Center, University of Chicago. http://mamluk.uchicago.edu/Mamluk Studies Review VII-2-2003.pdf.

Daiber, Hans. *Bibliography of Islamic Philosophy*. Leiden: Brill, 1999.

Dale, Stephen F. *The Garden of the Eight Paradises: Babur and the Culture of Empire in Central Asia, Afganistan and India (1483–1530)*. Leiden: Brill, 2004.

Dallal, Ahmad. "Science, Medicine and Technology." In *The Oxford History of Islam*, ed. John Esposito. Oxford: Oxford University Press, 1999.

Daoudi, Mahmoud. "Ibn Khaldun: The Founding Father of Eastern Sociology." *International Sociology* 5, no. 3 (September 1990), 319–335.

Dardess, John. *Conquerors and Confucians: Aspects of Political Change in Late Yüan China*. New York: Columbia University Press, 1973.

Dunn, Ross E. *The Adventures of Ibn Battuta, a Muslim Traveler of the Fourteenth Century*. Berkeley: University of California Press, 1989.

Eickelman, Dale. *The Middle East and Central Asia: An Anthropological Approach*. 4th ed. Upper Saddle River, NJ: Prentice Hall, 2002.

Eickelman, Dale, and James Piscatori, eds. *Muslim Travelers: Pilgrimage, Migration and the Religious Imagination*. Berkeley: University of California Press, 1990.

Elinson, Alexander. "Making Light Work of Serious Praise: A Panegyric *zajal* by Lisān al-Dīn ibn al-Khatīb." *eHumanista* 14 (2010): 83–104.

Enan, Mohammad Abdullah. *Ibn Khaldūn: His Life and Works*. New Delhi: Kitab Bhavan, 1997.

Endress, Gerhard, and Jan A. Aertsen, eds. *Averroes and the Aristotelian Tradition*. Leiden: Brill, 1996.

Eustache, D. "Idrisids." In Bearman et al., *Encyclopaedia of Islam*, 2nd ed. http://referenceworks.brillonline.com.proxy.lib.ohio-state.edu/entries/encyclopaedia-of-islam-2/idrisids-SIM_3495.

Fabirzadeh Saleh. *Sociology of Sociology: In Search of Ibn Khaldun's Sociology: Then and Now*. Tehran: Soroush Press, 1982.

Fakhry, Majid. *Al-Fārābī, Founder of Islamic Neoplatonism*. Oxford: Oneworld, 2002.

———. *Averroes (Ibn Rushd)*. Oxford: Oneworld, 2001.

———. *A History of Islamic Philosophy*. 3rd ed. New York: Columbia University Press, 2004.

Fekete, Balázs. "The Unknown Montesquieu." *Iustum Acquum Salutare* 5 (2009): 151–159.

Fernández-Puertas, Antonio. "El Mawlid De 764/1362 De La Alhambra Segun El Manuscripto De Leiden y La *Nufāda III* Editada." In *Ibn al-Jatib Y Su Tiempo*, edited by Celia del Moral and Fernando Velázquez, 161–203. Granada: University of Granada, 2012.

Fındıkoğlu, Z. Fahri. *Türkiyede ibn Haldunızm 60 [Altmışıncı] Doğum Yili Münasebetiyle Fuad Köprülü Armaganı Mélanges Fuad Köprülü* (Istanbul, 1957).

Fink, Carole. *Marc Bloch: A Life in History*. Cambridge: Cambridge University Press, 1991.

Fischel, Walter J. *Ibn Khaldun and Tamerlane*. Berkeley: University of California Press, 1952, 80–81.

———. *Ibn Khaldun in Egypt*. Berkeley: University of California Press, 1967.

Fleet, Kate, Gudrun Krämer, Denis Matringe, John Nawas, and Everett Rowson. *Encyclopaedia of Islam*. 3rd ed. Brill Online, 2015.

Fleischer, Cornell. "Royal Authority, Dynastic Cyclism and 'Ibn Khaldunism,' in Sixteenth Century Ottoman Letters." *Journal of Asian and African Studies* 18, nos. 3–4 (July–October 1983): 198–220.

Forcada, Miquel. "Ibn Bājja and the Classification of Sciences in Al-Andalus." *Arabic Sciences and Philosophy* 16 (2006): 287–307.

Franke, Herbert, and Denis Twitchett, eds. *The Cambridge History of China*. Vol. 6. Cambridge: Cambridge University Press, 1994.

Friedman, Susan. *Marc Bloch, Sociology and Geography*. Cambridge: Cambridge University Press, 1996.

Fromherz, Allen James. *Ibn Khaldun*. Edinburgh: Edinburgh University Press, 2011.

Galt, John. *Annals of the Parish*. 1821. Edited by Jame Kinsley. Oxford: Oxford University Press, 1972.

Garthwaite, Gene R. *Khans and Shahs: A History of the Bakhtiyari Tribe in Iran*. London: I. B. Tauris, 2009.

Gearhart, Suzanne. "Reading De l'Esprit des Lois: Montesquieu and the Principles of History." *Yale French Studies* 59 (1980): 175–200.

Geertz, Clifford. *The Religion of Java*. Chicago: University of Chicago Press, 1960.

Gellner, Ernest. *Saints of the Atlas*. London: Weidenfeld and Nicolson, 1969.

Gibb, H. A. R. "The Islamic Background of Ibn Khaldun's Political Theory." *Bulletin of the School of Oriental and African Studies* 7, no. 1 (1933): 22–31.

Gleick, James. *Isaac Newton*. New York: Random House, 2004.

Gohlman, William E. *The Life of Ibn Sina*. Albany: SUNY Press, 1974.

Griffel, Frank. *Al-Ghazālī's Philosophical Theology*. New York: Oxford University 2009.

Guo, Li. "Mamluk Historical Studies: The State of the Art." *Mamlūk Studies Review* 1 (1997): 15–43.

Gutas, Dimitri. *Avicenna and the Aristotelian Tradition*. Leiden: Brill, 1988.

———. *Greek Thought, Arabic Culture*. London: Routledge, 1998.

Habib, Mohammed. *The Political Theory of the Delhi Sultanate (Including a Translation of Ziauddin Barani's Fatawa-i Jahandari, circa 1358-9 A.D.)*. Allahabad: Kitab Mahal, 1961.

Hamadeh, Anis. "The Concept of Science in Early Islamic History." *Periodica Islamica* 6, no. 1 (1996): 7–14.

Hammer-Purgstall, J. "Extraits d'Ibn Khaldun." In *Fundgruben des Orients*, vol. 6. Vienna, 1818, 301–307, 362–364.

Hankinson, R. J., ed. *The Cambridge Companion to Galen*. Cambridge: Cambridge University Press, 2008.

Harley, J. Brian, and David Woodward, eds. *Cartography in the Traditional Islamic and South Asian Societies*. Vol. 2, bk. 1, *The History of Cartography*. Chicago: University of Chicago Press, 1992.

Hart, David Montgomery. "Faulty Models of North African and Middle Eastern Tribal Structures." *Rervue du monde musulman et de la Méditerranée* 68–69 (1993): 225–238.

———. *Qabila*. Amsterdam: Het Spinhuis, 2001.

———. "Segmentary Systems and the Role of Five Fifths in Tribal Morocco." *Revue de L'Occident musulman et de la Méditerranée* 3 (1967): 65–95.

D'Herbelot, Barthelemy. *Bibliotèque orientale*. Paris: Dufour & Roux, 1776.

Hetherington, Norris S. "Issac Newton's Influence on Adam Smith's Natural Laws in Economics." *Journal of the History of Ideas* 14, no. 3 (July–September 1983): 497–505.

Hoebel, E. Adamson. "William Robertson: An 18th Century Anthropologist-Historian." *American Anthropologist* 62 (1960): 648–655.

Hopfl, H. M. "From Savage to Scotsman: Conjectural History in the Scottish Enlightenment." *Journal of British Studies* 17 (Spring 1978): 19–40.

Horrut, Claude. *Ibn Khaldun un islam des "Lumières"?* Brussels: Éditions Complex, 2006.

Al-Hujwiri, 'Alī b. 'Uthman al-Jullābī. *Kashf al-mahjūb*. Translated by R. A. Nicholson. Leiden: E. J. W. Gibb Memorial Series.

Humphreys, R. Stephen. *Islamic History: A Framework for Inquiry*. Princeton, NJ: Princeton University Press, 1991.

Idris, H. R. "Hafsids." In Bearman et al., *Encyclopaedia of Islam*, 2nd ed. http://referenceworks.brillonline.com.proxy.lib.ohio-state.edu/entries/encyclopaedia-of-islam-2/hafsids-SIM_2625.

Irwin, T. H. *Aristotle's First Principles*. Oxford: Clarendon Press, 1992.

Ivry, Alfred L., ed. and trans. *Averroës Middle Commentary on Aristotle's De Anima*. Provo, UT: Brigham Young University Press, 2002.

Al-Jabri, Mohammed 'Abed. *Arab-Islamic Philosophy, a Contemporary Critique*. Translated by Aziz Abbassi. Austin, TX: Center for Middle Eastern Studies, 1999.

———. *Falsafat al-tarikh ʿinda Ibn Khaldun.* Casablanca: Dar Al-Thaqafah, 1971.

———. *La Pensée de Ibn Khaldoun: la Assabiya et l'État. Grandes lignes d'une Théorie Khaldounienne de l'histoire musulmane.* Paris: Édima, 1971.

Joachim, H. H., ed. *Aristotle, on Coming to Be and Passing Away.* New York: Georg Olms Verlag, 1970.

Jones, Robert Alun. "Ambivalent Cartesians: Durkheim, Montesquieu, and Method." *American Journal of Sociology* 100, no. 1 (July 1994): 1–39.

Karateke, Hakan T. "Legitimizing the Ottoman Sultanate: A Framework for Historical Analysis." In *Legitimizing the Order: The Ottoman Rhetoric of State Power*, edited by Hakan T. Karateke and Maurus Reinkowski, 13–54. Leiden: Brill, 2005.

Kennedy, Hugh. *Muslim Spain and Portugal.* Harlow, UK: Longman, 1996.

al-Khashab, Ibrāhīm ʿAlī. *Tārikh al-adab al-ʿArabī fī al-Andalus.* Cairo: Dār al-Fikr al-ʿArabī, 1970.

Knysh, Alexander D. *Ibn ʿArabī in the Later Islamic Tradition.* Albany: SUNY Press, 1999.

Kosei, Morimoto. "What Ibn Khaldūn Saw: The Judiciary of Mamluk Egypt." *Mamluk Studies Review* 6 (2002): 109–131.

Lacoste, Ives. *Ibn Khaldun: The Birth of History and the Past of the Third World.* London: Verso, 1984.

Lameer, Joep. *Al-Fārābī and Aristotelian Syllogistics.* Leiden: Brill, 1994.

Lapidus, Ira M. *A History of Islamic Societies.* 2nd ed. Cambridge: Cambridge University Press, 2009.

Lattimore, Owen. *Inner Asian Frontiers.* New York: American Geographical Society, 1940.

Lawrence, Bruce, ed. *Ibn Khaldun and Islamic Ideology.* Leiden: Brill, 1984.

Leaman, Oliver. *Averroes and His Philosophy.* Oxford: Clarendon Press, 1988.

———. *An Introduction to Classical Islamic Philosophy.* Cambridge: Cambridge University Press, 2002.

Lecomte, G. "Ibn Kutayba," In Bearman et al., *Encyclopaedia of Islam,* 2nd ed. http://referenceworks.brillonline.com.proxy.lib.ohio-state.edu/entries/encyclopaedia-of-islam-2/ibn-kutayba-COM_0333.

Lefort, Claude. "Histoire et sociologie dans l'oeuvre de Fernand Braudel." *Cahiers Internationalaux de sociologies* 13 (1952): 122–131.

Lehman, William C. *John Millar of Glasgow.* Cambridge: Cambridge University Press, 1960.

Lopez, Jerónimo Páez, et al. *Ibn Jaldūn Entre al-Andalus y Egipto.* Granada: GPD, 2008.

Mahdi, Muhsin. *Ibn Khaldun's Philosophy of History.* London: George, Allen & Unwin, 1957.

Mann, Thomas. *Buddenbrooks.* New York: Vintage Books, 1994.

Marçais, G., and J. Schacht. "Aghlabids or Banu 'l-Aghlab." In Bearman et al., *Encyclopaedia of Islam,* 2nd ed. http://referenceworks.brillonline.com.proxy.lib.ohio-state.edu/entries/encyclopaedia-of-islam-2/aghlabids-or-banu-l-aghlab-COM_0024.

Marçais, William. "Comment l'Afrique du Nord a été arabisée." In *Articles et Conférences, Publications de l'Institut des Etudes Orientales à Alger, XXI,* edited by William Marçais, 171–192. Paris: Adrien-Maisonneuve, 1901.

Maróth, Miklós. "Aristoteles und Ibn Khaldun, Zur Enstehung einer Aristotelischen Geschichtsphilosophie." In *Aristoteles Werk und Wirkung,* edited by Jürgen Wiesner, 390–408. Berlin: De Gruyter, 1987.

Marquet, Y. "Ikhwān al-Safa'." In Bearman et al., *Encyclopaedia of Islam,* 2nd ed. http://referenceworks.brillonline.com.proxy.lib.ohio-state.edu/entries/encyclopaedia-of-islam-2/ikhwan-al-safa-COM_0356.

Matar, Nabil. "Spain through Arab Eyes, c. 1573–1691." In *Europe Observed,* edited by Kumkum Chatterji and Clement Hawes, 123–143. Lewisburg, PA: Bucknell University Press, 2008.

Menocal, Maria Rosa, Raymond P. Scheindlin, and Michael Sells. *The Literature of Al-Andalus.* Cambridge: Cambridge University Press, 2000.

Meuleman, Johan H. "La causalité dans la Muqaddimah d'Ibn Khaldun." *Studia Islamica* 74 (1991): 105–142.

Millar, John. "The Origin of the Distinction of Ranks." In *John Millar of Glasgow*, edited by William C. Lehmann, 173–322. Cambridge: Cambridge University Press, 1960.

Millar, W. Watts. "Durkheim's Montesquieu." *British Journal of Sociology* 44 (1993): 693–712.

Millar, W. Watts, and Emma Griffiths, trans. *E. Durkheim, Montesquieu. Quid Secundatus Politicae Scientiae Instituendae Contulerit, with a Commentary by W. Watts Millar*. Oxford: Durkheim Press, 1997.

Miranda, A. Huici. "Ibn Hayyān." In Bearman et al., *Encyclopaedia of Islam*, 2nd ed. http://referenceworks.brillonline.com.proxy.lib.ohio-state.edu/entries/encyclopaedia-of-islam-2/ibn-hayyan-SIM_3196.

Amir-Moezzi, Mohammad Ali. "al-Tūsī," In Bearman et al., *Encyclopaedia of Islam*, 2nd ed. http://referenceworks.brillonline.com.proxy.lib.ohio-state.edu/entries/encyclopaedia-of-islam-2/al-tusi-SIM_7653>.

Moral, Celia del, and Fernanado Velázquez Bassanta. *Ibn Al-Khatīb Y Su Tiempo*. Granada: Universidad De Granada, 2012.

Morris, James Winston. "An Arab Machiavelli? Rhetoric, Philosophy and Politics in Ibn Khaldun's Critique of Sufism." *Harvard Middle Eastern and Islamic Review* 8 (2009): 242–291.

Mortera, Emanuele Levi. *Dugald Stewart, Selected Philosophical Writings*. Exeter, UK: Imprint Academic, 2007.

al-Najjār, ʿAbd al-Halīm. *Tarikh al-adab al-ʿarabi*. Cairo: Dār al-Maʿārif, 1968.

Nasser, Nassif. "Le maître d'Ibn Khaldūn: Al-Ābilī." *Studia Islamica* 20 (1964): 103–114.

Nielsen, Donald A. *Three Faces of God. Society, Religion and the Categories of Totality in the Philosophy of Émile Durkheim*. Albany: SUNY Press, 1999.

Norton, David Fate, and Jacqueline Taylor, eds. *The Cambridge Companion to Hume*. Cambridge: Cambridge University Press, 2011.

Ober, W. B., and N. Alloush. "The Plague at Granada: Ibn al-Khatib and Ideas of Contagion." *Bulletin of the New York Academy of Medicine* 58, no. 4 (May 1982): 418–424.

Perrin, C-E. "L'oeuvre historique de Marc Bloch." Translated by R. C. R. *Revue historique* 199 (1948): 161–188.

Phillips, William D., Jr., and Carla Rahn Phillips. *A Concise History of Spain*. Cambridge: Cambridge University Press, 2010.

Phillipson, Nicholas. *Adam Smith*. New Haven, CT: Yale University Press, 2010.

Piaget, Jean. *Le structuralisme*. Paris: Presses Universitaires de France, 1972.

Pines, Solomon. "The Societies Providing for the Bare Necessities of Life According to Ibn Khaldun and the Philosophers." *Studia Islamica* 24 (1971): 125–138.

Plato. *The Republic*. Mineola, NY: Dover Books, 2000.

Pourshariati, Parvaneh. *Decline and Fall of the Sasanian Empire*. London: I. B. Tauris, 2008.

Powers, David. *Law, Society and Culture in the Maghrib*. Cambridge: Cambridge University Press, 2002.

Rabbat, Nasser. "The Palace of the Lions, Alhambra and the Role of Water in Its Conception." *AARP/Environmental Design* 2 (1985): 64–73.

———. "Was al-Maqrizi's Khitat a Khaldūnian History?" *Der Islam* 89, nos. 1–2 (November 2012): 118–140.

Rabi, Muhammad Mahmoud. *The Political Theory of Ibn Khaldun*. Leiden: Brill, 1967.

Rashed, R., and B. Vahabzadeh. *Omar Khayyam, the Mathematician*. New York: Biblioteca Persica Press, 2000.

Rasheed, Madawi al-. *Politics in an Arabian Oasis*. London: I. B. Tauris, 1991.

Redman, Deborah A. "Adam Smith and Isaac Newton." *Scottish Journal of Political Economy* 0, no. 2 (May 1993): 210–230.

Reynolds, Dwight. *Interpreting the Self, Autobiography in the Arabic Literary Tradition*. Berkeley: University of California Press, 2001.

Rhodes, R. Colbert. "Emile Durkheim and the Historical Thought of Marc Bloch." *Theory and Society* 5, no. 1 (January 1978): 45–73.

Richter, Melvin. "An Introduction to Montesquieu's 'An Essay on Causes That May Affect Men's Minds and Characters.' " *Political Theory* 4, no. 2 (May 1976): 132–138.

Robertson, William. *The History of America*. London: T. Cadell and J. Balfour, 1792.

———. *An Historical Disquisition Concerning the Knowledge which the Ancients Had of India*. Edinburgh: Basil, 1792.

Rosenthal, Erwin I. J.. *Political Thought in Medieval Islam*. Cambridge: Cambridge University Press, 1968.

Rosenthal, Franz. "al-Makrīzī, Taqī al-Dīn," In Bearman et al., *Encyclopaedia of Islam*, 2nd ed. http://referenceworks.brillonline.com.proxy.lib.ohio-state.edu/entries/encyclopaedia-of-islam-2/al-makrizi-SIM_4838.

———. "Die arabischie Autobiographie." *Studia Islamica I [Analecta Orientalia]* 14 (1937): 1 40.

Rostow, W. W. *The Stages of Economic Growth: A Non-Communist Manifesto*. Cambridge: Cambridge University Press, 1960.

Ruggles, D. Fairchild. "The Eye of Sovereignty: Poetry and Vision in the Alhambra's Lindaraja Mirador." *Gesta* 36, no. 2 (1997): 180–189.

Sacy, A. I. Silvestre de. *Chrestomatie arabe, ou Extraits de divers écrivains arabes*. 2 vols. Paris: Ulan Press, 2012.

Schatzmiller, M. "Marinids." In Bearman et al., *Encyclopaedia of Islam*, 2nd ed. http://referenceworks.brillonline.com.proxy.lib.ohio-state.edu/entries/encyclopaedia-of-islam-2/marinids-SIM_4966.

Schiefsky, Mark J. "Galen's Teleology and Functional Explanation." In *Oxford Studies in Ancient Philosophy 33*, edited by D. Sedley, 369–400. Oxford: Oxford University Press, 2007.

Schmaus, Warren. *Durkheim's Philosophy of Science and the Sociology of Knowledge*. Chicago: University of Chicago Press, 1994.

Sewell, William H., Jr. "Marc Bloch and the Logic of Comparative History." *History and Theory* 6 (1967): 208–218.

Shackleton, Robert. *Montesquieu*. Oxford: Oxford University Press, 1961.

Shehaby, Nabil. *The Propositional Logic of Avicenna*. Dordrecht: D. Reidel, 1973.

Skinner, Andre. "Economics and History—the Scottish Enlightenment." *Scottish Journal of Political Economy* 12 (1965): 1–22.

Smelser, Neil J., *Social Change in the Industrial Revolution: An Application of Theory to the British Cotton Industry*. Chicago: University of Chicago Press, 1959.

Smith, Adam. *History of Astronomy*. In *The Essential Adam Smith*, edited by Robert L. Heibroner. New York: Norton, 1987.

Spengler, Joseph J. "Economic Thought of Islam: Ibn Khaldun." *Comparative Studies in Society and History* 6, no. 3 (April 1964): 268–306.

Sterns, Justin. "Two Passages in Ibn Al-Khatib's Account of the Kings of Christian Iberia." *Al-Qantara* 25, no. 1 (2004): 157–182.

Stewart, Dugald. "Account of the Life and Writings of Adam Smith LL.D." In *Collected Works*, edited by William Hamilton. Edinburgh: Constable, 1854–1858. 11v.

Swingewood, Alan. "Origins of Sociology: The Case of the Scottish Enlightenment." *British Journal of Sociology* 21, no. 2 (June 1970): 164–180.

Tadgell, Christopher. *Islam: From Medina to the Magreb and from the Indes to Istanbul*. Abingdon, UK: Routledge, 2008.

Talbi, M. "Ibn Haldūn et le sens de l'histoire." *Studia Islamica* 26 (1967): 73–148.

———. "Ibn Khaldūn." In Bearman et al., *Encyclopaedia of Islam*, 2nd ed. http://referenceworks.brillonline.com.proxy.lib.ohio-state.edu/entries/encyclopaedia-of-islam-2/ibn-khaldun-COM_0330.

———. "Rustamids." In Bearman et al., *Encyclopaedia of Islam*, 2nd ed. http://referenceworks.brillonline.com.proxy.lib.ohio-state.edu/entries/encyclopaedia-of-islam-2/rustamids-SIM_6348.

Tapper, Richard. *Frontier Nomads of Iran*. Cambridge: Cambridge University Press, 1997.

———. *Pasture and Politics: Economics, Conflict and Ritual among the Shahsevan Nomads of Northwestern Iran*. London: Academic Press, 1979.

Thompson, Herbert F. "Adam Smith's Philosophy of Science." *Quarterly Journal of Economics* 79, no. 2 (May 1965): 212–233.

Tomar, Cengiz. "Between Myth and Reality: Approaches to Ibn Khaldun in the Arab World." *Asian Journal of Social Science* 36, nos. 3–4 (2008): 590–611.

Toynbee, Arnold. *A Study of History*. New York: Oxford University Press, 1962.

Vahabzadeh, Bijjan. "KHAYYAM, OMAR vi. As Mathematician," *Encyclopædia Iranica Online*. http://www.iranicaonline.org/articles/khayyam-omar-vi-mathematician.

van Bladel, Kevin. "Barmakids." In Fleet et al., *Encyclopaedia of Islam*, 3rd ed. http://referenceworks.brillonline.com.proxy.lib.ohio-state.edu/entries/encyclopaedia-of-islam-3/barmakids-COM_24302.

Veitch, John. "Philosophy in the Scottish Universities," *Mind* 2, no. 5 (April 1877): 74–91.

Walzer, Richard. "Aspects of Islamic Political Thought: Al-Farabi and Ibn Khaldun." *Oriens* 16 (1963): 40–60.

Weir, Shelagh. *The Bedouin*. London: World of Islam Festival Publishing, 1976.

Weiss, Dieter. "Ibn Khaldun on Economic Transformation." *International Journal of Middle East Studies* 20, no. 1 (February 1995): 29–37.

White, Hayden V. "Ibn Khaldun in the World Philosophy of History." *Comparative Studies in Society and History* 2, no. 1 (1959): 110–128.

Wiesehöfer, Josef. *Ancient Persia*. London: I. B. Tauris, 1996.

Wightman, W. P. D., and J. C. Bryce, eds. *Adam Smith, Essays on Philosophical Subjects, Vol. III of the Glasgow Edition of the Works and Correspondence of Adam Smith*. Indianapolis: Liberty Fund, 1982.

Yale University, "Ibn Khaldūn." Yale University Library. www.library.yale.edu/neareast/exhibitions/IbnKhaldun.html.

Young, M. J. L., J. D. Latham, and R. B. Serjeant. "Arab Biographical Writing." In *Religion, Learning and Science in the ʿAbbasid Period*, edited by M. J. L. Young, J. D. Latham, and R. B. Serjeant, 183–237. Cambridge; Cambridge University Press, 1990.

Yver, G., E. Lévi-Provençal, and G. S. Colin. "al-Magh̲rib." In Bearman et al., *Encyclopaedia of Islam*, 2nd ed. http://referenceworks.brillonline.com.proxy.lib.ohio-state.edu/entries/encyclopaedia-of-islam-2/al-maghrib-COM_0614.

Zalta, Edward N., ed. *The Stanford Encyclopedia of Philosophy*. http:/plato.stanford.edu.

Zwartjes, Otto, Ed de Moor, and G. H. van Gelder, eds. *Poetry Politics and Polemics: Cultural Transfer Between the Iberian Peninsula and North Africa*. Amsterdam: Rodopi, 1996.

INDEX

'Abbasah, al-: relation with an Iranian *mawali*, 20, 297; as symbol of pure Arabism, 20-21
'Abbasid Caliphate: Barmakid/Iranian *wazir*, 219; bureaucracy, 218, 219, 222; decline, 15, 191, 197-198, 214, 225; as exception to model, 198; fail to control the Maghrib, 46; Greco-Islamic translation movement, 81, 110; high culture, 107, 178, 233, 237, 291-292, 298; influencing Iberian Umayyads, 47; *mawali*s in, 20, 180; *nasihat nama* of, 249; persecuting anti-Mutazili *'ulama'*, 92; Persian cultural inheritance, 189; use of Iranians and Turks, 217-218; victory over Umayyads, 200
'Abd al-'Azim, 41-42
'Abd al-Malik b. Marwan, 15, 223
'Abd al-Mu'min, 65-66
'Abd al-Wadids (Zanatah Berbers/Zayyanids), 68, 69, 71, 116, 127, 137, 138, 140; allied with Granada and Castile, 70; nature of state, 221-222; origins, 70; rule in Tilimsan, 70; wars with Marinids, 70
Abili, Muhammad b. Ibrahim al-, 80-81, 106
Abstraction. *See* Aristotle; Ibn Khaldun; Philosophy
Abu 'Abdallah (Hafsid of Bijayah), 137
Abu 'Abdallah Muhammad b. Muhammad, 122
Abu Bakr. *See* Almoravids
Abu Bakr, 14
Abu Hammu II, 70, 122
Abu 'Inan, 69, 119, 121, 125. *See also* Marinids
Abu l-Hasan, 69, 79, 120, 223. *See also* Marinids
Abu Muslim b. Khaldun, 110
Abu Salim, 125

Abu Yaʻqub Yusuf, 66
Abu Zakariya' Yahya, 70
Accidents (*ʻarad*): defined, 3, 29, 115; essential and contingent, 29–30, 116, 225; Greco-Islamic concept, 3, 115; in Ibn Khaldun's thought, 5; as Marx's superstructure, 29; in methodology, 154; relation to nature or essence, 29, 154; in sultanates, 225
Achaemenids, 210. *See also* Iran
Adab, 119, 291; Ibn al-Khatib's writings, 133
*Adalah*s. *See* Rashidun Caliphate
*Adib*s: ʻAbbasid era, 291–292; criteria, 19; Ibn al-Khatib as an ideal, 132; Ibn Khaldun as, 19, 124, 126, 130, 293, 297; Ibn Khaldun's father, 18; Ibn Ridwan, 79
Afghanistan, 230
Aghlab, Ibrahim b. al- (Aghlabid), 53
Aghlabid dynasty, 53–54
Agriculture: division of labor in, 242, 264; and the environment, 175; Ibn al-Khatib writing on, 133; as a primitive craft, 230; in temperate climates, 168
Agriculturalists: bedouins, 28, 37; in North Africa, 37. *See also* Economics
Al-Akhdar Bedouins, 141
Alchemy, 97–98
Alexandria, 43, 45, 107, 143
Algeria, 33, 35, 37

Alhambra, 41. *See also* Granada; Nasrids of Granada
ʻAli, 212
Almohads: *ʻasabiyah* of, 59, 65, 181; capital city, 117, 209; conquests, 64–65; data for Ibn Khaldun's model, 57, 200; decline, 68, 192, 203, 223, 234, 236; Ibn Khaldun's characterization of, 63–64; legacy, 67–68; nature of state, 68, 116, 189, 220, 221, 223, 226; origins, 62–63; philosophical patronage, 58, 66; role of religion, 46; theology, 61, 63, 66, 69, 82. *See also* Ibn Tumart, Muhammad
Almoravids: abandoning Fez and building Marrakesh, 60, 209; allied with *ʻulama*,' 61; Andalusians employed by, 234; *ʻasabiyah* of, 181; conquests, 46, 61, 64, 65; data for Ibn Khaldun's model, 200, 205; fleets, 223; legacy, 62, 67–68; and Maliki law, 63, 122; nature of state, 57, 58–62; rule in Iberia, 61–62; theology, 58, 60–61, 81
Amiland. *See* Almoravids
Amirs: in Egyptian law courts, 145; as military commanders, 224. *See also* Sultanate
Andalusi, Muhammad b. ʻAbd al-Wahhab al-Ghassani al-, 258–260
Andalusia: Arabs in, 44–47; *ʻasabiyah* in, 72–73; Banu Khaldun in, 18; Berbers in, 38, 44, 47–49,

62; bureaucrats and scholars from, 62, 68, 79–80, 221, 222; civilization (*tamaddun*) in Iberia compared with North Africa, Egypt, Syria, and Iraq, 35, 40–43, 229; crafts, 228; Damascene Umayyads in, 46, 53; decline of scholarship, 235; diet, 172; environment, 40–41; Iberian Muslims' influence in North Africa, 17, 42, 62, 71, 78; Ibn Khaldun in, 33; Ibn Khaldun's nostalgia for, 21, 260; Ibn Khaldun's positive view of, 42, 72–73; Maliki clerics in, 62; Muslim nostalgia for, 42; philosophy in 66–67; plague, 78; population decline, 236; *zajal* verse, 41. *See also* Almohads; Almoravids; Christian Reconquista; Iberian Umayyads; Ibn al-Khatīb; Ibn Rushd, Abu Walid

Ankara, 149

Annales School, 10, 151, 154, 278, 284, 287. *See also* Bloch, Marc; Braudel, Fernand; Febvre, Lucien; Simiand, François

L'Année Sociologique, 284. *See also* Annales School; Bloch, Marc; Durkheim, Émile

Ansari, Abu 'Abdallah, Muhammad al-, 79

Anushirwan (Chosroes), 211. *See also* Iran; Sasanids

Apodictic proof. *See* Philosophy

Apollonius, 232. *See also* Euclid

Aquinas, Saint Thomas, 131, 269

Arab Bedouins. *See* 'Abbasah, al-; Bedouins;*'Umran badawi*

Arabia, 16, 39, 209, 228, 233

Arab Muslims: Arab essence, 21; attack on rational sciences, 75; attitude to Greek and Persian knowledge, 75–76; Banu Hilal and Banu Sulaym tribesmen destroying civilization of, 39–40, 56–57, 70, 116, 171, 178, 299; conquests in North Africa, 43–45; converting Berbers, 44; historical parallels with sultanates, 13–16, 44; Ibn Khaldun's Arab lineage, 16, 45, 297; rule in Andalusia, 44, 47–49; rule in North Africa, 17, 43–44; social terminology, 49–50; traits of early, 44, 211–213, 225; treatment of Berbers, 45, 210; Yemeni Arabs, 16, 43, 55. *See also* Bedouins

Aragon, 40

Aristotle: attitude to history, 2, 111; *Categories*, 4, 175; compared with Montesquieu, 264, 266; essence (*dhat*), 24, 32; Ibn Khaldun's knowledge and critique of, 67, 94, 107; *Kitab al-burhan*, 90, 112; *Kitab al-maqulat*, 111; *koinonia*, 26; metaphysics, 93, 94 102, 108, 110, 279; Muslims' "First Teacher," 2, 76; nature, 112, 153; *Nicomachean Ethics*, 114, 269, 279; on accidents, 29–30, 116, 153–154; on

Aristotle *(continued)*
deduction and induction, 114–115; on nature, movement, and growth, 26, 29, 112–113, 296; *Organon*, 108, 109, 112, 114, 115, 118, 119, 267, 275, 279; *Physics*, 24, 102, 108, 109, 110, 114, 115, 152, 296; *Politics*, 2, 279; *Posterior Analytics*, 115; potentiality to actuality, 231; primordial society, 26, 165–166, 175, 217, 298; *Rhetoric*, 2, 72, 123; use of syllogisms, 23, 111, 112; works studied in Paris, 67, 131, 263, 268–269; *See also* Ibn Rushd, Abu Walid; Methodology; Nature; Philosophy

'Asabiyah: Almoravid, 59; as an axiom, 179; among Berber tribes, 46; in a camp group, 202; clients sharing, 180; critique of Ibn Khaldun's use of term, 59, 85, 179–180, 201–202; defined, 26–27; lack of in Andalusia, Egypt, Syria, and Iran, 72–73, 198, 210; legitimacy without, 217–218; loss in corrupt towns, 190; and monarchy (*mulk*), 208–209; multiple households, 183; not required in an imperial or rational state, 199, 217–218; presence in Andalusia and eastern Mediterranean cities, 72–73; Rashidun Caliphate possession of, 214; religion and, 50, 181; sine qua non of tribal conquest, 181; superior *'asabiyah*, 182–183, 191; *'ulama'* loss of, 214. *See also* Dialectical model

Ash'ari, Abu l-Hasan al-: critiquing Mutazili thought, 92; role in speculative theology, 89–90

Ashraf /sharif (eminent), 52, 129

'Asqalani, Ibn Hajar al-, 143

Astrology, 96

Atlas Mountains, 34, 36, 37, 63

Autobiography (*al-Ta'rif bi-Ibn Khaldun*). *See* Ibn Khaldun

Avempace. *See* Ibn Bajjah

Averroes. *See* Ibn Rushd, Abu Walid

Averroism, 67

Avicenna. *See* Ibn Sina

Avila, 80

Awlad 'Arif tribe, 140

Awrabah Berbers. *See* Idrisids

Axioms, 4, 24, 114, 115, 163, 179, 296; basis of dialectical model, 163–176, 179; religious, 90–91. *See also* Dialectical model; *Muqaddimah*; Philosophy

Ayyubids, 148

Azhar, al-, 143. *See also* Cairo

Babur, 298
Baghdad, 15, 42, 46, 63, 81, 90, 237, 291
Bahram b. Bahram, 250. *See also* Sasanids
Banu Hilal. *See* Arab Muslims; Bedouins
Banu Khaldun. *See* Ibn Khaldun
Banu Maymun of Cadiz, 223

Banu Saʿid of Granada, 222
Banu Sulaym. *See* Arab Muslims
Barmakids. *See* ʿAbbasid Caliphate
Barquq, Sultan (Mamluk), 142, 148
Basra, 52
Battle of Culloden, 275
Baybarsiyyah *khanagah* in Cairo, 87
Bayezid, 149
Bedouins: Arab and Berber compared to Kurds, Mongols, Turks, and Turcomans, 39–40, 150, 172; as "barbarous communities," 116, 176–177; *bedouin-mulk* development spectrum, 218–226; crude crafts of, 42; as generic term, 27, 38–39; as noble savages, 171; Scottish, 275. *See also* Arab Muslims; Berbers; Dialectical model; *ʿUmran badawi*
Beiro River, 40
Berbers: in Andalusia, 44, 47–48; antithetical to urban society, 35, 38; *ʿasabiyah* of, 27; Banu Hilal and Kutamah, 55–56; compared to Arab Muslims, 14, 177; compared to Mongols, 39; conversion to Islam, 44; distinct culture of, 38, 53; data for Ibn Khaldun's model, 206; economic dependence on cities, 176; environment, 167; Fatimids and, 55; as generic bedouins, 27–28, 64, 116; Ibn Khaldun collects taxes from, 138; Ibn Khaldun's history of, 11–12, 141, 163, 256; individuality, 38; Khariji Rebellion, 45–47; later states, 68–72; monarchies, 17, 46, 57–68, 218, 219, 225; as Muslims, 38, 53; nature of society, 50, 172; origins, 38; poets, 38; population in North Africa, 11–12; praise of, 12; relations with Arab Muslims, 38, 44–45, 48–49, 54, 209; religion in Berber states, 46, 57, 60; revolts, 46–47, 200; states of, 51, 214; subjugated by Arab Muslims, 43; terminology, 49; tribal politics, 50; as ungovernable, 49. *See also* ʿAbd al-Wadids; Almohads; Almoravids; Bedouins; Hafsids; *Khariji*; Marinids
Biblical prophets, 85
Bijayah (Bougie), 120, 125; Ibn Khaldun at, 136, 137; teaching Maliki law, 138
Biskra(h) Oasis, 138, 139
Black, Joseph. *See* Scottish Enlightenment
Bloch, Marc, 10: accidents, 284; Annales School, 284; *ʿasabiyah*, 285; comparative history, 286; comparative method, 154–155, 286; *Feudal Society*, 284; *The Historian's Craft*, 285–287; historical sociologist, 284; influenced by Aristotle, Durkheim, and Galen, 284–286; nature, 284; resembling Ibn Khaldun, 285, 286; social cohesion, 285; social structure, 284

Bonnet, Charles, 266. *See also* Montesquieu, Charles-Louis de Secondat
Book of Roger, 166
Boutroux, Émile, 279
Braudel, Fernand, 174, 285, 287; not a philosophical historian, 287; *pontillisme*, 287. *See also* Annales School
Brownian motion, 140. *See also* Bedouins
Buddenbrooks' dynamic, 193
Bukhari, Muhammad al-, 227
Burhan. *See* Philosophy
Buyutat, 49–50, 64, 183, 191, 201–202
Byzantine Empire, 75

Cairo: climate of, 169; flourishing scientific culture in, 117; Ibn Khaldun's praise for, 142; lack of *'asabiyah*, 229; Maliki law, 79, 99, 144–146, 215, 298; prosperity of, 242; urban civilization, 72, 243
Caliphates. *See* 'Abbasid Caliphate; Rashidun Caliphate; Umayyad Caliphate
Carlos II of Spain, 258
Castile, 33, 65, 69, 70
Categories. *See* Aristotle
Causality, 101–104, 285; Aristotelian, 102; al-Ghazali on, 102–103; Greco-Islamic, 101–102; Ibn Rushd on, 103
Çelebi, Katib, 258.

Central Asia: *'asabiyah* in, 27; scientific instruction in, 236; tribal society of, 55, 124, 230
Ceuta, 128
Chess, 294, 299
China, 17, 39, 167, 205; cities in, 229; Mongol successor state, 204
Christianity, 17, 44, 84, 95, 167, 219; *'asabiyah* in Christian Spain, 259; Christian Berbers, 53; condemned by Moroccan ambassador, 260; hostility to philosophy, 76, 107; Ibn Khaldun asked to convert to, 131; Ibn Khaldun's hostility to Christian presence, 84; Ibn Khaldun visiting church in Jerusalem, 148; intellectual renaissance in Christian lands, 131; and metaphysics and physics, 75, 77; not considered relevant by Montesquieu, 264
Christian Reconquista, 42, 45, 61, 78, 123, 130, 223, 248
City of God, 249
Civilization, defined, 28–29. *See also* Towns; *'Umran hadari*
Climate. *See* Environment
Comparison. *See* Annales School; Methodology; Philosophy
Condorcet, Marquis de, 279
Conic sections, 7, 232
Constantine (city), 128
Cordoba, 4, 40–41, 47–48, 61, 116
Crafts. *See* Economics

Crusaders, 142
Cycle, cyclical. *See* Dialectical model

Damascus, 15, 36, 46, 47, 222; Ibn Khaldun's visit, 148–149. *See also* Iberian Umayyads
Deduction (*istidal*), 105, 114, 115. *See also* Philosophy
Dhat. See Philosophy
D'Herbelot, Barthélem, 260
Dialectical discussion: for education, 235; in Islamic law, 100
Dialectical model, 7; 'asabiyah in, 26–27, 65, 179–184, 186, 191–192, 196, 200–202; axioms of society, 164–176, 179, 184–185, 204; brutality of conquest, 188; superior 'asabiyah, 182–183, 201–202; causation and, 101–102; contradictory religious explanation, 195–197; contrasting effect of rural and urban environments, 8, 34, 170–173; critique of, 201–206; as cyclical and dialectical, 5; environment and, 8, 34, 166–169; evidence for, 43, 51, 65, 67, 68, 120, 127; exceptions to 'asabiyah model, 198–199, 229; *Fitnah* of al-Nasiri as case study, 147–148; form and matter in tribal governments, 184; and generations, 5, 186–195; the idealized *shaikh*, 187; military skills, 181–182, 190; moral failure and economic collapse, 251; nature of tribal/bedouin society, 174–179; prosperity and decline, 247–248; psychology of kingship, 193–195; rapacity as proximate cause, 176–177; regional successors, 199; senile dementia, 192, 195, 196, 197; similarity to Marx, 5, 203–204; stages of, 184–195, 228; structuralism, 195; theology as irrelevant, 101; tribal chief to decadent monarch, 190–191; tribal politics as unexplained factor, 204–205; tribal successor states, 200–201. *See also* 'Asabiyah; Axioms; Environment; Human social organization; Ibn Khaldun; *Muqaddimah*
Diet, 170–173. *See also* Dialectical model; Environment
Diwan, 218, 221, 222, 243, 244
Duns Scotus, 269. *See also* Aristotle; Scottish Enlightenment; University of Paris
Durkheim, Émile, 2, 267, 271, 278–283; *L'Année Sociologique*, 284; 'asabiyah, 283; compared with Ibn Khaldun, 153, 280–283, 285; on Condorcet, 279; idea of nature, 153; influenced by Aristotle, 278, 279; legal systems, 283; on Montesquieu, 279, 280; narrative denounced 266; philosophy and sociology, 279; *The Rules of the Sociological Method*, 279; rural and urban societies, 282; Sens

Durkheim, Émile *(continued)*
lectures, 279; social cohesion/solidarity, 282–285; society as a natural fact, 279; species and genus, 281; use of comparison, 281–282
Dutch, 259

Ebro River, 40
Economics: agricultural labor and prices, 246; axioms/premises of, 241–243; capital and profit, 239–241; corruption and, 248; crafts/occupations, 230–237; the cunning merchant, 251; derived profit, 240–241; *diwan* and, 243–244; exponential growth, 243; Fez and economic data, 128; Fez and Tilimsan compared, 242; government spending, 244–245; Islamic, 248–252; labor theory of value, 9, 238–240; laissez-faire, 245; luxury products, 246–247; morality, 248–251; population and economic growth, 9, 36, 229, 233, 242–243, 245, 246, 247, 285; prices, 240, 245–246; property rights and, 250–251; Sasanid example, 250; status of *'ulama'*, 239; taxation, 244, 248; urban, 9–10, 11; value of a craft, 239–240; wealth producers, 238. *See also* Dialectical model
Edinburgh. *See* Scottish Enlightenment

Education, 74–117; Adam Smith on, 277; in Andalusia, 43, 235–236; Andalusia and North Africa compared, 42; bedouin and urbanite, 277; decadence and, 247; decline in the Islamic world, 214; educational theory, 234–235; in Fez, 235; *hajj* and religious education, 63; Maghrib and Tunisia contrasted, 236; memorization criticized, 272; Muslim heartland, 67; in Paris, 236; Qayrawan, 54; in Tunis, 235. *See also* Ibn Khaldun; Ibn al-Khatib
Egotism and society, 238, 241
Egypt: climate in, 169; compared to North Africa, 35; Fatimids in, 55–56; Ibn Khaldun revising *Muqaddimah* in, 162; Maliki law in, 99; personality traits of Egyptians, 169; prosperity of, 242–243; reception of the *Muqaddimah*, 256–258; scientific instruction in, 236. *See also* Cairo
Elements. *See* Euclid
English, 167, 259. *See also* Andalusi, Muhammad b. ʿAbd al-Wahhab al-Ghassani al-
Environment, 26, 34–35, 39, 49; climate and civilization, 167–168; the Egyptian case, 169; regions, 166; settlement patterns, 167; temperate zone and moderation, 167–169; urban versus rural, 170. *See also* Dialectical model

Ephemeral accidents. *See* Philosophy
Esprit des Lois. See Ibn Khaldun;
    Montesquieu, Charles-Louis de
    Secondat
Esprit systématique. See Smith,
    Adam
Essence. *See* Nature; Philosophy
Essence of humanness. *See* Ibn Sina
Ethnicity. *See* Ibn Khaldun
Euclid, 110, 123, 232, 275, 290
Europe, philosophical culture,
    262–263
Extraordinary method. *See* Ibn
    Khaldun; Methodology

Falsafa, falasifa. See Philosophy
Faqih, 18, 124
Farabi, al-, 81, 94, 111; attacked by
    al-Ghazali, 93, 102; comments on
    Aristotle's *Physics*, 108; on
    division of labor, 241; Ibn
    Khaldun's critique of, 94;
    influencing Ibn Sina, 108; on the
    intellect, 107; on logic and
    certainty, 108; *On the Perfect
    State*, 108; possible influence on
    Ibn Khaldun, 107; on supremacy
    of reason, 75, 93, 105, 106; on the
    utopian state, 26, 210, 217
Fatimids: conquests, 52, 53, 56;
    *daʻiyah*s, 55; decline, 223;
    government, 219; punishing Zirids
    with Banu Hilal and Banu
    Sulaym, 56; use of emblems, 225.
    See also Shiʻah

Febvre, Lucien, 285. *See also* Annales
    School
Fez: Arabization, 53; bedouin culture
    of, 229; climate, 169; exemplifying
    decline of towns, 72, 235; Ibn
    Khaldun in, 119–128; Marinid
    capital, 119; population and
    prosperity, 242. *See also* Marinids
Fiqh. See Maliki law
"First Teacher." *See* Aristotle
Fitnah: first, 45; "*Fitnah* of al-Nasiri,"
    147–148. *See also* Mamluks
Fitzgerald, F. Scott, 299
Form and matter/substance. *See*
    Philosophy
Four Elements, 97, 295
Four Generations. *See* Dialectical
    model
France, 44, 283; Aristotelian thought
    in, 67; Collège de France, 286; Ibn
    Khaldun studied in, 260; Ibn
    Rushd's works studied in Paris,
    117; and Scotland, 267; as vigorous
    society, 259
Fuqahah. See Faqih; Maliki law

Galen, 6, 77; causes of illness, 172; on
    geometry, 4, 110; and Ibn Khaldun
    and Montesquieu, 3, 152–153, 154,
    156, 265, 296; *logos* and *peira*, 3–4,
    156, 288–289; on nature and
    universals, 112; on the nature of
    the soul, 88–89
Genil River, 42
Genoa, 223

Genus and species. *See* Philosophy
Geometry: Adam Smith's use of, 275; Greek geometricians, 232; practical use of, 292; studied by al-Tilimsani, 123; synonym for premise, 185; value of geometric proofs, 14, 110, 114–115. *See also* Euclid
Germanic tribes (Visigoths), 44
Ghazali, Abu Hamid Muhammad b. Muhammad al-: on causality, 102–103, 169, 196, 197; condemned by Almoravids, 61, 81, 122; conservative Sunni orthodoxy, 77, 95; critique of philosophers, 93, 94; influencing Ibn Khaldun, 77, 83; rationalist/speculative theology, 67, 84, 89, 90, 92, 93, 94, 122; respected by Almohads, 61, 67, 81; *The Revival of Religious Sciences*, 61; Sufism, 88, 122; *Tahafut al falasifah*, 93, 102; using logic, 93. *See also* Sufis/Sufism
Ghaznavid Turks, 200
Ghulah. *See* Shi'ah
Ghuzz, 167
Gibraltar, 16, 34, 128
Glasgow, 268, 269, 274
Granada: Andalusia's second golden age, 132; economy, 228–229; education declines, 235; Ibn Khaldun at, 41, 128–132; *mawlid* in, 129; poetic praise for, 41, 173. *See also* Ibn al-Khatib; Nasrids of Granada
Great Man theory, 195

Greco-Islamic thought. *See* Aristotle; Farabi, al-; Galen; Ibn Rushd, Abu Walid; Ibn Sina
Greeks and Greek philosophy, 131, 261–262, 269
Guadalaviar (Turia) River, 40
Guadalquivir River, 40
Gudalah (Sinhajah Berbers). *See* Almoravids

Hadhrami, al-, 16. *See also* Ibn Khaldun
Hadith: in Almoravid and Almohad theology, 60, 63, 122; corrupt *hadith* in North Africa, 234; fundamental to Islamic faith, 83, 92, 100; Ibn Kaldun critiques *hadith* scholarship, 95–96, 161, 255–256; Ibn Khaldun teaches *hadith* in Cairo, 146; taught to Ibn Khaldun, 79; used to sanctify the holy cities, 227
Hafsids, 68, 69, 116, 120, 125, 137, 206; as Almohads, 68, 70; Andalusian personnel, 70, 221; *'asabiyah* compromised, 220; bureaucracy, 220–222; employing Banu Khaldun, 18; employing Ibn Khaldun, 141–142; fragmented political structure in fourteenth century, 71, 140; history, 70–71
Hajib (hijabah), 22
Hakam II, b. 'Abd al-Rahman al-, 48
Hakims, 221
Hamdanids, 198

INDEX

Hammer Purgstall, Joseph von, 260
Hanafi law, 54
Hargah Berbers, 64
Harun al-Rashid, 20, 53
Hashimis. *See* Prophet Muhammad
Hayy (clan), 50
Herodotus, 261
Hijaz, 14, 56, 59, 98, 170, 181
Hikmah/hukuma', 2, 26
Historical sociology, 6
History, philosophical, 2–4. *See also* Dialectical model; Ibn Khaldun; Methodology
House of David. *See* Jerusalem
House of the Prophet. *See* Medina
Human nature: Adam Smith on, 276–277; constant of, 8–9, 27, 165, 241, 299; environmental influence upon, 34; Ibn Sina on, 25; rural and urban compared, 27–28, 170–173; in the Scottish Enlightenment, 270; *A Treatise of Human Nature* (Hume), 270–273, 296. *See also* Dialectical model; Methodology; Philosophy
Human social organization: in Greco-Islamic thought, 26; necessity of, 26, 166, 241. *See also* Aristotle; Dialectical model
Hume, David, 2, 102, 253, 267, 274, 278; causality, 102; compared to Ibn Khaldun, 272; *A History of England*, 273; philosophical use of history, 273; on primordial society, 273; *A Treatise of Human Nature*, 253, 270–273; use of history, 273; view of human nature, 270, 272. *See also* Aristotle; Scottish Enlightenment
Hutcheson, Francis, 269–270

Iberia, dynastic history, 229. *See also* Andalusia
Iberian Umayyads: Arab dominance, 44, 46–49; collapse, 61, 198, 223; culture, 47–48, 187; history, 47–48; Iberian golden age, 41; influence in North Africa, 47, 53, 56, 191; loss of *'asabiyah*, 198; relations with Berbers, 48; state, 47–48. *See also* Civilization; Towns; Umayyad Caliphate
Ibn Bajjah, 66
Ibn Battuta: describing Sijilmasa, 37; travel narrative, 12
Ibn Hayyan, Abu Marwan, 17. *See also* Andalusia
Ibn Khaldun: on accidents, 112, 115–116; achievement, 6–7, 288–289; in Andalusia, 128–132; on Arab Bedouins destroying civilization, 57; Arab Muslim identity, 11; autobiography, 12–13, 118–119; Banu Khaldun, 16–17, 43, 45, 118, 125, 129, 130, 131; Berber identity, 38; Cairo years, 78, 142–148, 256; career as scholar-official, 19, 118–149; causality, 96, 101–104; civilization defined, 28–29; compared with Adam

Ibn Khaldun *(continued)*
Smith, 275–276; compared with Durkheim, 280–283; compared with Galen, 3; compared with Marx, 5; comparison of North Africa and Andalusia, 73; contradictions, 22–23, 299; critique of Maliki law, 215; critique of metaphysics, 76; critique of Shi'ahs and Sufis, 95–96; critique of tribal dynasties, 73; dialectical discussion and knowledge, 293; distinguishing philosophical from religious knowledge, 295; education,18–19, 74, 77–82, 272; emotional life, 13, 143; ethnicity, 297–299; experience with bedouin society, 136–142; family, 1, 13, 16–19, 80, 81, 119, 142–143; faith, 82–101; friendship with *'ulama'*, 215, al-Ghazali's influence, 67, 77; *hadith* proofs criticized, 95, 162, 255; history as a philosophical discipline, 2–3, 289; imprisoned in Fez, 125; intellectual lineage, 6, 107–109, 261–263, 295–296; *ijazah*s (teaching certificates), 146; Islamic education, 77–79; judicial career in Cairo, 144–145; knowledge and the soul, 294; knowledge defined, 292–295; knowledge of Aristotle, 67, 107; lament for Andalusia and North Africa, 73, 116–117; legacy as an historical theorist, 253, 289; *logos* and *peira*, 3–4, 156, 270, 288–289; Maliki scholar, 19, 79, 84, 146; at the Marinid court, 119–128; marriage, 18; meeting Timur/Tamerlane, 148–150; on monuments, 41; *nasihat namah*, 217; on nature, 112–114; personality, 16, 126–128, 136; as philosopher, 22, 254; philosophical apologia for a new science, 22; philosophical education, 80–81; philosophy as key to knowledge, 116; poetry, 13, 130, 142; political environment, 71; précis of Islamic history, 149; purpose of *Muqaddimah*, 1–4, 7, 43, 254–255, 288; reception of *Muqaddimah* in Islamic world, 255–260; refuting metaphysics, 94; relations with Ibn al-Khatib, 129, 130, 132, 136; religion and philosophy, 74–76, 83, 101, 103 104, 249; reputation in Cairo, 143–144; self-knowledge, 296–299; social attitudes, 19, 20–21, 96–98; Sunni orthodoxy, 95, 212; tribal terminology, 49–50; in Tunis, 33, 119, 140–141; visiting Damascus, Jerusalem, and Ghaza, 148; writings, 10–14; Yemeni ancestors, 45, 297. *See also* Dialectical model; Ghazali, Abu Hamid Muhammad b. Muhammad al-; Islam; Methodology; *Muqaddimah*; Nature; Philosophy

Ibn al-Khatib, Lisan al-Din, 129, 134, 255; chronicles Nasrid court, 134;

education, 132; as historian, 134–135; on historic, organic cycles, 185; historiography, 134–135; importance for Ibn Khaldun, 132; position in Granada, 132–133; *rihlah*s, 12, 134; as scholar-official, 132–133; tragic fate, 133–134, 139–140; treatise on the plague, 133; victim of politics, 133–134, 139–140

Ibn Marzuq, Muhammad b. Ahmad, 126

Ibn Qutaybah, Abu Muhammad al-Dinawari, 292

Ibn Ridwan, Abu Qasim Abu Allah b. Yusuf, 79

Ibn Rushd, Abu Walid: on accidents, 29, 116; Aristotelian scholarship, 66–67, 107; on causality, 103, 114, 153, 263; criticized by Ibn Khaldun, 72; essay on religion and philosophy, 74–75; and Ibn Khaldun, 66–67, 77, 80, 81, 107, 111, 112; influence in France and Italy, 117, 263; influence on Thomas Aquinas and Christian theology, 29, 67, 69, 263; read by Scottish philosophers in Paris, 268; on supremacy of reason, 75, 93. *See also* Aristotle; Farabi, al-; Ibn Khaldun

Ibn Sina (Avicenna): on accidents, 29, 115; on alchemy, 97–98; attacked by al-Ghazali, 93, 102; "essence of humanness," 25, 27; as a Greco-Islamic philosopher, 22, 25, 77, 81, 94; influence on Ibn Khaldun, 108–109, 112; on nature, form, and essence 112–113, 153; philosophical terminology, 113; *The Physics of the Healing*, 25, 109; read in North Africa, 119, 123; summarizing Euclid, 110

Ibn Tashfin, 61

Ibn Tufayl, Abu Bakr Muhammad, 66

Ibn Tumart, Muhammad: condemning Almoravid legalism, 64; legacy, 66; personifying simple tribal leader, 63; studies in Baghdad, 90; theology of Quran and *hadith*, 63

Ibn Zamrak, 133, 140

Ibn Zarzar, Ibrahim, 131

Ibrahim b. al-Aghlab, 53

Idris b. Abdullah, 52

Idrisi, Muhammad al-, 166

Idrisids, 52–53, 54, 60; legitimacy, 52; as tribal coalition, 52–53

*Ijazah*s, 146

Ijtima'. *See* Human social organization

Il-Khanid Mongols, 82, 204

'*Ilm*, 2. *See also* Philosophy

Imam, 52, 64, 211; in Shi'i Islam, 212

Imamate, 212

Immanent God, 197, 226

India, 167, 168, 229, 278, 298

Induction (*istiqra'*), 3, 114. *See also* Deduction; Philosophy

Insha', *sahib al-*, 222

Intellect: levels in philosophy, 105–106; no place in faith, 77, 91, 93; in rural and urban populations, 8, 171

Intellectual lineage. *See* Ibn Khaldun

Intellectual sciences, 105–117. *See also* Islam; Philosophy

Intermarriage, 189, 190, 206.

Iran: flourishing urban and scientific culture in, 117; *mawali* in, 20, 297; Mongol dynasty of, 204; non-Islamic ritual centers, 228; scientific instruction in, 236; *siyasah al-Fars*, 210; sultanates in, 214. *See also* Samanids of Bukhara; Sasanids

Iraq, 46, 67, 168, 198; calligraphy in, 233; flourishing sedentary society, 34, 35, 168, 229, 234; legal school, 98–99; Maliki law in, 98–99

Islam: augurs, 87; dream visions, 88–89; *hadith*, 83; Ibn Khaldun's fundamental beliefs, 82–84; knowledge, 294; ossification of Maliki law, 215; piety, 84–89; prophets, 84–85; religious sciences, 82–84; soothsaying, 86; Sufism, 87–88; theology, 89–95; vital Islam, 14, 73, 164, 215, 297

Isma'ilis, 52, 53, 55, 63, 64, 219. *See also* Fatimids; Shi'ah

Isnad, 160. *See also* Hadith

Israelis/Israelites, 163, 184

Italian Renaissance, 68. *See also* Ibn Rushd, Abu Walid

Italians, 1

Jahiz, Abu 'Uthman 'Amr al-Basri al-, 291

Jerusalem, 227–228. *See also* '*Umran hadari*

Jews, 53, 131, 219

Jihad: in Andalusia, 44, 62, 246; in North Africa, 44

Justinian, 75

Juwayni, Abu l-Ma'ali al- (Imam al-Haramayn), 90. *See also* Speculative/rationalist theology

Kalam. See Speculative/rationalist theology

Katibun, 19

Khariji: doctrines, 45–46; revolt in North Africa, 45–47; link with Rustamids, 51; origins in Basra, 51

Khattab, 'Umar b. al-: comparison to Christians, 75; destroying Sasanid books, 76

Khurasan, Iran, 117

Kitab al-burhan, 90

Kitab al-'ibar, 11, 57, 147, 256; content, 161–163; first draft, 141; knowledge of in Cairo, 143; relation to the *Muqaddimah*, 11–12

Kitab al-Muwatta'. See Muwatta', al-

Kitab al-shifa (*The Book of the Healing*). *See* Ibn Sina

Knowledge, 74, 288, 293; philosophical 293–294; religious, 294–295

Koinonia, 26.

Kurds, 69, 174

Kutumah Berbers, 38, 50, 55

INDEX

Labor theory of value. *See* Economics
Lamtunah (Sinhajah) Berbers. *See* Almoravids
Laws, 266; administrative, 258; Durkheim on, 280, 281; Hume on, 267–268; inheritance, 100, 110; Montesquieu on, 265; of nature, 273; religious, 75, 104, 211, 212; sultanate, 187, 216. *See also* Ibn Khaldun; Maliki law
Lefort, Claude, 287
Leibniz, 266
Libya, 33, 35
Lisbon, 40
Livy, 266
Logic. *See* Philosophy
Logos (rationalism). *See* Galen; Methodology
Louis XI, 268–269
Lubab al-Muhassal fi usul al-din (Compendium on the Principles of Theology), 81. *See also* Ibn Khaldun; Razi, Fakr al-Din al-; Tusi, Nasir al-Din al-
Luxury. *See* Economics

Machiavelli, 134, 261
Madrasah, 66, 70, 122, 123, 144, 145–146, 257
Madrid, 259
Maghrib: education declines, 235; Ibn Khaldun lamenting decay of, 71; political fragmentation of, 72
Mahdi, 63–64, 66, 95–96, 161. *See also* Ibn Khaldun

Mair, John, 269
Makrizi, Taqi al-Din al-, 256–257
Malaga, 79
Mali, 58
Malik b. Anas. *See* Maliki law
Maliki law: bedouin legal school, 99, 116, 215; condemning *kalam*, 61; dialectics, 100; embraced by Almoravids, 60–62; founder, 54; history in North Africa, 54, 55, 56, 60, 99; Ibn Khaldun's study of, 19, 78, 98–99, 120, 135, 146, 297; *al-Maliki*, 79, 143; as Maliki jurist in Cairo, 144–145, 148, 298; Qayrawan, 116; and singing, 237; subjects of, 100; taught by Ibn Khaldun in Tunis, 141; traits, 54, 77, 78, 79, 101, 124
Mamluks, 78, 146, 169, 256; *Fitnah* of al-Nasiri, 147–148; Ibn Khaldun's meeting in Granada, 129; patronizing Ibn Khaldun, 142–143, 144; rulers in Cairo, 142
Ma'mun, Abu al-'Abbas 'Abdallah al-, 215–216
Mann, Thomas, 193
Mansur, 'Abd al-Ja'far b. Muhammad al-, 110
Maqqari, Abu Abdallah Muhammad al-, 120
Marinids (Zanatah Berbers): calligraphy in, 234; conquests, 69, 70, 203; nature of state, 68–69, 124, 140, 205, 221–222; savage bedouin origins, 69; use of

Marinids (Zanatah Berbers) *(continued)*
emblems, 226. *See also* Abu 'Inan; Abu l-Hasan; Fez
Marrakesh, 117, 229
Marrakushi, Ibn al-Banna' al-, 81, 110; granting *ijazahs* to Ibn Khaldun, 146
Martel, Charles, 44
Marx: compared to Ibn Khaldun's dialectic, 5, 203; labor theory of value, 239; "superstructure" and accident, 29
Masmudah Berbers. *See* Almohads; Hargah Berbers
Mas'udi, 'Ali b. al-Husayn al-: historian of Iran, 250; Ibn Khaldun's attempt to emulate, 1–2, 6–7, 290; Ibn Khaldun's critique of, 160; as Muslim historian, 1–2, 156, 159
*Mawalı*s: Arab attitude toward, 45; *'asabiyah* of, 180; Berbers, 45; Iranians, 45, 297
Mawarannahr. See Central Asia
Mawardi, al-, 14–15, 217, 228. *See also* Sultanate
Mawlid: in Andalusia, 129, 130; in Fez, 126; in Granada, 173
Mazalim court, 126, 127, 258. *See also* Marinids
Mecca, 18, 52, 55, 60, 146, 227
Medina, 54, 78, 146, 227–228
Merchants. *See* Economics
Metaphysics, 10, 75, 92, 102, 108, 110, 262; Adam Smith, 275;

al-Ghazali's critique, 93; Ibn Khaldun's critique, 76, 94. *See also* Philosophy
Methodology, 3–4, 6, 13, 80, 152–157, 160; accidents, 153–154; comparison, 25, 154–155, 282, 286, 293; critique of Muslim historians, 157–160, 255–256; critique of *'ulama'* as historians, 160–161; deductive logic in, 154; encyclopedic knowledge required, 155; "extraordinary method," 151; Galen's method, 3–4, 156, 288–289; history as philosophical subject, 2–3, 152, 160; identifying the nature of society, 25, 153; logical proofs, 154–155; method and model, 151; philosophical speculation, 152; presentism denounced, 156; search for underlying causes, 152, 288; similarity to Annales School, 151–152; truth (*haqq*) and fiction (*batil*), 154. *See also* Galen; Ibn Khaldun; Nature; Philosophy
Millar, John, 268, 270, 278
Modernity, 262
Monarchy. *See Mulk*
Mongols, 28, 40, 149, 162; compared to Arab and Berber bedouins, 39, 40, 44, 176; successor states, 204
Montaigu College, 269. *See also* Paris; Scottish Enlightenment
Montesquieu, Charles-Louis de Secondat: accidents, 265, 266;

Aristotelian political typology, 273; compared to Aristotle, 264; compared to Galen, 265; concept of nature, 265; education, 264, 269; environment and personality, 266; *Esprit de Lois*, 8; influence of philosophy, 263, 274; laws, 265; parallels with Ibn Khaldun, 263, 264, 265, 267, 271; rationalist analysis, 264; search for underlying causes, 264; sources, 266–267; stimulating Scottish Enlightenment, 267; underlying causes, 266

Moral economy. *See* Ibn Khaldun

Moral philosophy. *See* Hutcheson, Francis

Mu'awiyah, b. Abi Sufyan, 212

Mudar, 211. *See also* Quraysh

Muhammad V of Granada (Nasrid), 129, 130, 133, 136, 140

Mulaththamun, al-. *See* Almoravids

Mulay Isma'il Sharif of Morocco, 258, 259, 260

Mulk, 185, 219, 221, 227, 241; 'Abbasid Caliphate as, 15; Almohads and, 219; *'asabiyah* as necessary quality, 183, 208; bureaucracy, 218, 221; cities and, 230; form and matter, 184, 224; God and, 296; Hafsid, 220; Mamluk, 210; al-Mawardi on, 217; military, 224; monarchs and bedouins, 221–222; as a natural institution, 183; nature of, 190–191, 208, 219–221; necessity for, 208, 217, 241; need for cities, 209; offices required by, 222; the pragmatic sultanate, 227; Sasanian, 250; tribal *shaikh* to monarch, 183. *See also* Sultanate

Mulla Sadra, Sadr al-Din Muhammad Shirazi, 117

Muluk al-tawa'if (*reyes de taifas*), 61, 198, 229. *See also* Andalusia

Munecimbaşı, 258. See also *Muqaddimah*; Ottomans

Muqaddimah: as autobiography, 10–11; comprehensive knowledge, 1, 109, 290; contents, 10–12, 163–164; European discovery of, 260–262; first draft, 11, 140–141; knowledge of in Cairo, 143; legacy, 253; Moroccan use of, 258–260; not syllogistic, 115; Ottoman interest in, 257–258; philosophical meaning, 23; relation to the *Kitab al-'ibar*, 161; source of information, 290–292; structure, 22–23, 161–163, 173–174, 299; viewed by Western scholars, 261

Muqatilah tribes, 191

Muslims. *See* Arab Muslims; Berbers

Mu'tazilah, 92, 291

Muwahiddun, al-. *See* Almohads

Muwashshah poetry, 134

Muwatta, al-, 78, 146

Na'ima, Mustafa, 258

Nasihat literature, 208, 215, 217, 222, 224

Nasrids of Granada, 33, 48, 72, 129, 131, 136, 138, 222; Ibn Khaldun's praise for as a golden age, 132. *See also* Ibn al-Khatib; Muhammad V

Natural occupation. *See* Economics

Nature: Aristotle's concept, 112–114, 153, 154; basis of Ibn Khaldun's methodology, 5, 24, 112, 153; Durkheim's appropriation of, 153; Galen's emphasis on, 3, 154; Greco-Islamic meaning, 112–114; Hume's use of, 270–272; Ibn Sina on, 112–113; Montesquieu's discussion of, 265; natures and potentials, 25, 153; persistence of philosophical concept, 296; "prior by nature," 24. *See also* Aristotle; Dialectical model; Galen; Methodology

Negroes, 168

Neoplatonism, 66, 67, 81, 107, 275, 278; among Almohads, 66; Ibn Rushd's critique of, 107

Newton, 264, 266, 278; Newtonian physics, 275; and religion, 101; stature in the Enlightenment, 264, 266

Nicomachean Ethics. See Aristotle

Nisba, 16

North Africa, 49–73; Arab conquests, 43–45; Berbers limit of urban growth, 35, 116; cities, 35–37; geography, 34–38; history, 51–73; Ibn Khaldun's lament for, 234; *Khariji* Rebellion, 45–47; rural/tribal population, 38–40, 49; tribal poets, 225; tribal politics, 49–51. *See also* Maghrib

Objective reality, 3. *See also* Philosophy

Occupations. *See* Economics

Old/New Testaments, 166

Oran, Algeria, 37, 242

Orange trees, 248

Organon. See Aristotle; Philosophy

Ottomans: as a sultanate, 258; studies of the *Muqaddimah*, 257–258; and Turks, 298. *See also* *Muqaddimah*

Paris, 67; Ibn Rushd's works studied at, 29, 67, 131, 263; rationalist studies, 236, 263; Scots studying at College of Montaigu, 269; Thomas Aquinas's use of philosophy in, 29, 131

Pascal, 287

Pastoral nomads. *See* Arab Muslims; Bedouins; Berbers; Mongols; Turks/Turcomans

Pedro the Cruel of Seville, 17, 130, 131

Peira. See Galen; Methodology

Persians. *See* Iran

Philosophy: abstractions, 9, 106, 111, 293; apodictic proof (*burhan*), 24, 90, 93, 108, 154, 155, 186, 276; axioms/*muqaddimat*, 164; comparison, 25, 281, 282, 293; essence (*dhat*), 24, 29, 90, 112–113,

288, 293; faith and reason, 74–75; form (*suwar*) and matter/substance (*mawadd*), 30–31, 224, 251; the four sciences, 109–110; idea of nature, 24, 112, 274; intellectual speculation, 83, 94, 101, 152, 233; knowledge, 293–294; logic, 3, 61, 90, 104, 110, 111, 160; mathematical premises, 185; movement and rest, 113–114; potentiality (*quwah*) to actuality (*fiʻl*), 25, 231, 233; priority, 24, 175–176; species and genus, 158, 282, 286, 293; superior to history and theology, 295–296; syllogism, 23, 24, 111, 112, 114, 115; terminology, 23–31; universals, 86, 104, 111, 112, 114, 293. *See also* Axioms; Intellect; Methodology; *Muqaddimah*; Nature

Phoenicia, 35

Physics. *See* Aristotle; Nature; Philosophy

Piety. *See* Islam

Plato, 6, 66, 67, 75, 92, 107, 172, 266

Platonic Academy, 75

Pliny, 266

Plutarch, 266

Pointillism. *See* Annales School; Braudel, Fernand

Poitiers, 44

Polis, 26, 112

The Politics. See Aristotle; Farabi, al-

Population: Andalusia, 62, 229; composition in North Africa, 38, 72. *See also* Economics

Portugal, 33

Posterior Analytics. See Aristotle

Pre-Islamic cities, 2, 209, 228

Primordial origin of states. *See* Aristotle

Prophethood, 294

Prophet Muhammad: *hadith*s of, 161; *mawlid*s in Fez and Granada, 126, 129; model for Almoravids and Almohads, 59, 64; and Rightly Guided Caliphs, 14, 211–212; as seen in dialectical model, 174, 192; source of spiritual knowledge, 83–88, 90; and *ʻulama*ʼ 213–214; vital Islamic teachings, 297

Ptolemy, 266; on astrology, 96; on geography, 149, 167

Qabilah: Awlad ʻArif, 140; *buyutat* in, 183, 201; varying meanings of, 49–50

Qalʻat Ibn Salamah, 140, 207

Qamhiyah *madrasah*, 145. *See also* Cairo

Qanun (*kanun*), 161, 258

Qayrawan, 36, 51, 52, 54, 59; badly sited, 44; calligraphic arts decline, 233; center of Maliki scholarship, 36, 116; education declines, 235; Maliki jurists in, 56; original settlement, 36, 39; religious center during Aghlabid era, 54

Quatrèmere, Étienne Marc, 261

Quraysh, 211–212

Rashidun Caliphate (Rightly Guided Caliphs): *'asabiyah* of, 214; evolution from tribe to monarchy, 14; Ibn Khaldun's idealized view of, 14–15, 211–212, 216; justice in, 240; religious officials, 212; simplicity of, 218; *'ulama'* in, 212; *wazir* in, 218

Rational politics/state. *See* Iran; Montesquieu, Charles-Louis de Secondat

Razi, Fakr al-Din al-, 82, 94; critique of Ibn Sina, 82; speculative theologian, 82, 84, 89

Realpolitik. *See* Sultanate

Reconquista. *See* Christian Reconquista

Religion and tribal conquest. *See* Ibn Khaldun

Rhetoric: Adam Smith, 275–276; Aristotle, 2; Ibn Khaldun, 275.

Ricardo, 239

Rif Mountains, 34

Rihlah genre, 2, 12, 134, 259

Robertson, William, 278. *See also* Scottish Enlightenment

Roger II of Sicily, 223

Rome, 35, 37, 38, 147

Rosenthal, Franz, 8

Rousseau, 12

Rustam, 'Abd al-Rahman b. Rustam b. Bahram (Rustamid), 51

Rustamids, 51–52

Sacy, Silvestre de, 260

Sahara, 34, 37

Saint Andrews University: philosophy at, 268–269; scholars compared to al-Tilimsani, 269

Saladin, 142

Salghatmish *madrasah*, 146

Saljuq Turks, 200

Samanids of Bukhara, 198

Samarqand, 257

Saragosa, 40

Sasanids: Arab and Ibn Khaldun's respect for, 15, 210, 211, 245, 250; exception to Ibn Khaldun's model, 198

Sati, Muhammad b. Sulayman al-, 79

Scholar-official, 17, 18, 74, 106, 118, 120, 127, 128, 132

"School of Later Scholars," 93. *See also* Ghazali, Abu Hamid Muhammad b. Muhammad al-

Science (*'ilm*), 2. *See also* Philosophy

Scottish Enlightenment: John Mair, 269; John Millar, 268, 278; Joseph Black, 270; Louis XI, 268–269; Montesquieu's influence, 267–268; rationalist culture, 268, 270; role of philosophy, 268, 270, 274; Scottish bedouins, 275; speculative theology in Scotland, 269; University of Paris, Scots studying at, 268–269

Sedentary society. *See 'Umran hadari*

Sens lectures, 279

Seville: Almoravid conquest of, 65; Banu Khaldun home, 17, 33, 45; culture transferred to North Africa, 237; geography, 40–41, 246; Ibn Khaldun's visit to, 130–131; thriving Andalusian city, 132
Shah Namah, 51
Shaikh al-futya, 141
Shari'ah, and the rational state, 126, 211, 216
Shi'ah: *ghulah*, 212; Ibn Khaldun's critique, 95; idea of the *Mahdi*, 95; in Iran, 117; theology, 55, 212; Zaydi, 52. *See also* Tusi, Nasir al-Din al-; Fatimids
Shifa' al-Sa'il li tahdhib al-Masa'il (Remedy for the Questioner), 10. *See also* Ibn Khaldun; Sufis/ Sufism
*Shurtah*s, 212
Sicily, 223
Sijilmasa, 37
Simiand, François, 285. *See also* Annales School
Sinhajah Berbers, 56, 58, 59, 60, 297. *See also* Almoravids
Siyasah aqaliyah, 210
Siyasah al-fars, 210
Siyasah madaniyah, 210. *See also* Farabi, al-
Slavs, 168
Smith, Adam, 8–9, 273–278; admiring French rationalism, 174; compared to Ibn Khaldun, 2, 9, 277; dialectical method, 276; *esprit systematique*, 274, 277; Euclidian geometry, 275; explanatory power of philosophy, 274; Galen's method, 274; "The History of Astronomy," 274; human nature, 276–277; Hume and Ibn Khaldun, 271; influenced by French thought, 274; laissez-faire economics, 277; Newtonian physics, 275, 278; philosophical education, 274–275; view of human nature, 276–277; *Wealth of Nations*, 8–9, 270, 275–276. *See also* Scottish Enlightenment
Social solidarity. See *'Asabiyah*
Socrates, 23, 100
Spain. *See* Andalusia
Species/genus. *See* Philosophy
Speculative/rationalist theology, 67, 89–93. *See also* Ash'ari, Abu l-Hasan al-; Razi, Fakr al-Din al-; Ibn Khaldun; Maliki law
Stewart, Dugald, 276. *See also* Scottish Enlightenment
Sudan, 39, 126, 240
Sufis/Sufism: Baybarsiyyah *khanagah* in Cairo, 87–88; in Granada, 129; Ibn Khaldun's critique, 95; in Iranian thought, 117; theology, 99–100, 288; treatise, 10. *See also* Ghazali, Abu Hamid Muhammad b. Muhammad al-
Sultan. See *Mulk*; Sultanate

Sultanate, 11, 185, 207–227; *amir*s, 224; *'asabiyah* in warfare, 224; bureaucratic offices, 218–224; caliphate and sultanate, 212–213; coinage, 226; *diwan*s, 218, 221–222; form and matter, 184; *hakim*s, 221; *hijabah*, 218–221; inherently unjust, 240, 248, 250; irrelevance of moral ideal of, 215–216; marginal role of religion, 228; rational state, 207, 210–211; *sahib al-insha'*, 222; *tawqi'*, 222; tribal state, 184–185;*'ulama'* in, 213; *wazir*, 218–220. *See also* Economics; *Mulk*

Sultan Barquq, 142, 145, 147, 148

Syllogism. *See* Philosophy

Syria. *See* Damascus

Tabaqah, 20. *See also* Ibn Khaldun

Tabari, Muhammad b. Jarir al-, 159

Tabi'ah. *See* Dialectical model; Methodology; Nature; Philosophy

Tabriz, 82

Tagus River, 40

Tahafuut al-falasifah. *See* Ghazali, Abu Hamid Muhammad b. Muhammad al-

Tahert, 51

Tahir, 'Abdallah b., 215

Tamaddun. *See* Civilization; *'Umran hadari*

Taxation. *See* Economics

Teachers. *See* Economics

Theology. *See* Islam

Thucydides, 261

Tilimsani, Abu 'Abdallah Muhammad b. Ahmad al-Sharif al-'Alawi al-/Sharif al-Tilimsani, 121–124, 126, 127; compared to Ibn al-Khatib, 122; compared to Scottish theologians, 269; Ibn Khaldun's friendship with, 215; philosophical education, 121; quality of Maliki law, 122; religious education, 121; studies Euclid, Ibn Sina, and Ibn Rushd, 121, 290

Timur/Tamerlane/Timurid, 148–150, 298

Toledo, 40

Towns: Arabic synonyms, 28; Arabization in North Africa, 53; planning, 44; types in North Africa, 35–37; weak North African urban life, 229–230. *See also* Dialectical model; *'Umran hadari*

Toynbee, Arnold, 261

Tulunids of Egypt, 198

Tumart, Muhammad b. (Almohad), 63; bedouin, desert mentality, 64; claiming to be the *Mahdi*, 63; disciple of Ash'ari theologian, 63. *See also* Almohads

Tunis: compared with Andalusia, Iraq, and Egypt, 35, 43; Ibn Khaldun's admiration of, 70, 72; Ibn Khaldun teaching Maliki law in, 141; superior education system, 235

Tunisia merchants in Granada, 129
Turks/Turcomans: *'asabiyah* of, 150; compared to Bedouins and Berbers, 150
Turkic slaves. *See* Mamluks
Tusi, Nasir al-Din al-, 81–82

'Ulama', 67, 68, 93, 123, 124; in Cairo, 145; compared with philosophers, 104–105; deracinated class, 214; economic value, 214, 239; in Granada, 129; lacking *'asabiyah*, 214; lacking knowledge of politics, 104–105; marginalized in sultanates, 213; status in Rashidun Caliphate, 212; wealth, 241. *See also* Economics; Sultanate
Umar b. Khattab, 14, 75–76
Umar Khayyam, 115–116
Umayyad Caliphate: bureaucracy, 219; decline, 15, 214; losing control of North Africa, 46; monarchical era, 218, 226. *See also* Iberian Umayyads
Ummah, 49
'Umran, 27–28, 233
'Umran badawi: evolution to *'umran hadari*, 184; Ibn Khaldun among in North Africa 136, 142; Ibn Khaldun's analysis of, 174–179; meaning of term, 27–29, 40
'Umran hadari, 5, 8, 11, 28; *'asabiyah* in cities of Andalusia and the East, 209–210; towns dominating tribes, 183–184; traits, 5–6, 11, 27–29, 142, 170–173. *See also* Economics; *Mulk*; Sultanate
Universals. *See* Philosophy
University of Paris: Erasmus, 269; 1474 C.E. philosophical curriculum, 269; Greek philosophy at, 263; Ignatius Loyola, 269. *See also* Scottish Enlightenment

Valencia, 40
Virtuous state (*Mabadi' ara' ahl al-madinat al-fadilah*). *See* Farabi, al-
Visigoths. *See* Germanic tribes

Waqf, in Cairo, 87, 144–145
Wazir. *See* Sultanate
Wealth of Nations. *See* Smith, Adam

Yaghmurasan, 'Abd al-Wadid, 70; relations with Banu Hilal, 70
Yahya b. Khaldun, 138
Yasin, Abdullah b., 59
Yemen, 16, 45, 47
Yüan dynasty of China, 204

Zajal verse, 44
Zakariya', Husayn b. al-. *See* Fatimids
Zanatah Berbers, 68, 69, 70, 141, 163, 200, 221, 222
Zirids, 56
Zoroastrians, 166, 250